The Wild East

The Wild East

Criminal Political Economies in South Asia

Edited by Barbara Harriss-White and
Lucia Michelutti

First published in 2019 by
UCL Press
University College London
Gower Street
London WC1E 6BT

Available to download free: www.uclpress.co.uk

ISBN: 978-1-78735-325-1 (Hbk)
ISBN: 978-1-78735-324-4 (Pbk)
ISBN: 978-1-78735-323-7 (PDF)
ISBN: 978-1-78735-326-8 (epub)
ISBN: 978-1-78735-327-5 (mobi)
DOI: https://doi.org/10.14324/111.9781787353237

Contents

List of figures

List of tables

List of boxes

Notes on contributors

Barbara Harriss-White is Emeritus Professor of Development Studies, Emeritus Fellow of Wolfson College, Oxford, Professorial Research Associate at SOAS and Visiting Professor at Jawaharlal Nehru University, New Delhi. She has written, edited or co-edited and published 40 books and major reports and published over 250 scholarly papers and chapters and over 80 working papers. Her book *Rural Commercial Capital* (2007) won the Edgar Graham prize. Since 1969, through field research, she has worked on India's political economy, in particular the agricultural and informal economy, aspects of deprivation and waste.

Lucia Michelutti is Professor of Anthropology at UCL. Her major research interest is the study of popular politics, religion, law and order and violence across South Asia (North India) and Latin America (Venezuela). She is the author of *The Vernacularisation of Democracy* (2008) and co-author of *Mafia Raj* (2018), and has published scholarly articles on caste/race, leadership, muscular politics and crime and political experimentations. She is the convener of the UCL MSc in politics, violence and crime.

Nigel Singh graduated from St Antony's College, Oxford in 2009 with an MSc in contemporary India. He published on solar energy policy in India as a Research Fellow at the Institute of Defence Studies and Analyses, New Delhi. Subsequently, he was South Asia Analyst at Control Risks, advising multinationals on the region's political economy. He is a PhD candidate in creative writing at Royal Holloway, completing his first novel. Before Oxford, he produced BBC and Channel Four television programmes; he also has a BA (Hons) in English and drama from Bristol University.

Smita Gupta is an economist working on employment, rural development, land acquisition, land rights, tribal rights, displacement, mining and natural resources policy. She has prepared policy documents for the planning commission and written several research notes for parliamentary committees on employment guarantee, forest rights, mining and land acquisition. She is associated with the Adivasi Adhikar Rashtriya Manch and the Centre for Adivasi Research and Development. She has just completed two primary surveys – of tribal schools and environmental degradation due to mining – in tribal areas and is now engaged in a survey of tribal migrants from Central India to Delhi.

J. Jeyaranjan is an economist specialising in the socio-economic development of Tamil Nadu state, India. Recently, he co-edited two volumes of the *Telangana Social Development Report*, published by the Council for Social Development, Hyderabad, India. He has published several articles in leading academic journals and has contributed articles to several edited books.

Deepak K. Mishra is Professor of Economics at the Centre for the Study of Regional Development, School of Social Sciences, Jawaharlal Nehru University, New Delhi. His research interests are in the political economy of agrarian change, rural livelihoods and agrarian institutions, migration, gender and human development. He has co-authored *The Unfolding Crisis in Assam's Tea Plantations: Employment and Occupational Mobility* (2012) and has edited *Internal Migration in Contemporary India* (2016). Recently he has co-edited *Rethinking Economic Development in Northeast India: The Emerging Dynamics* (2017).

Jai Bhatia is a PhD researcher at SOAS, University of London. Her research examines the neoliberal system of accumulation in India through the lens of the telecom sector. It highlights the growing dominance of finance and the emergence of India-specific modalities of financialisation through an exploration of the political economy of regulations, the role of the state and its institutional structures, political processes, and the interrelations between state, business and public sector banks. She aims to build a portrait of progress and economic development in post-liberalised India. Prior to her PhD she worked in finance. She holds an MBA and an MSc in Contemporary Indian Studies from the University of Oxford.

David Picherit holds a PhD in anthropology and is a Research Fellow at CNRS – Laboratoire d'Ethnologie et de Sociologie Comparative (LESC), Paris. Based on long-term ethnographic fieldworks, his research explores the everyday articulations between economy and politics and the forms of violence in South India. He has conducted research on labour migration, brokerage and politicisation of low-castes in Telangana, and on criminal politicians-cum-businessmen and their henchmen in Rayala-seema (Andhra Pradesh).

Tone K. Sissener is a social anthropologist from the University of Bergen. Her major research interests include corruption, politics, law and order and land disputes, as well as violence in South Asia. Research for the chapter in this book was done as a postdoctoral Fellow at the Department of Health Promotion and Development, Faculty of Psychology, University of Bergen, and as co-researcher of the research programme 'Democratic Cultures in South Asia' at UCL. She is presently working at the Western Norway University of Applied Sciences in Bergen.

Nicolas Martin is currently an Assistant Professor in Indian/South Asian studies at the Institute of Oriental and Asian Studies of the University of Zurich. He was trained as a social anthropologist at the London School of Economics, where he produced a dissertation and a subsequent book about landed power in the rural Pakistani Punjab. Since 2012 he has shifted his attention to shifting power relations in the rural Indian Punjab, paying particular attention to new forms of dominance through control over state resources.

Arild Engelsen Ruud is Professor of South Asia studies at the University of Oslo. He writes on issues of democracy and politics in South Asia, specifically West Bengal and Bangladesh. He is author of *Poetics of Village Politics* (2003), on West Bengal's rural communism, co-editor of *Power and Influence in India* (2010, with Pamela Price) and co-author of *Mafia Raj* (2018, with Lucia Michelutti et al.).

Laurent Gayer is Senior Research Fellow at the French National Centre for Scientific Research (CNRS), currently posted at the Centre for International Research and Studies (CERI-Sciences Po), Paris. He specialises in the study of urban transformations and violent mobilisations in the Indian subcontinent (India and Pakistan). His major publications include *Karachi: Ordered Disorder and the Struggle for the City* (2014), *Muslims of Indian Cities: Trajectories of Marginalisation* (2011, co-edited with C. Jaffrelot) and *Armed Militias of South Asia: Fundamentalists, Maoists and Separatists* (2009, co-edited with C. Jaffrelot). He is currently working on a new book exploring the dialectics of law and disorder that have shaped Karachi's industrial capitalism.

Acknowledgments

This book would have not been possible without the thoughtful and critical feedback of the other members of the 'Democratic Cultures' research programme (https://www.ucl.ac.uk/democratic-cultures). Many thanks to Thomas Blom Hansen, Paul Brass, David Gellner, Sondra Hausner, Ashraf Hoque, Beatrice Jauregui, Hassan Javid, Morten Koch Andersen, Sanjay Kumar, Sanjay Kumar Pandey, Satendra Kumar, Norbert Peabody, Anastasia Piliavsky, Paul Rollier, Indrajit Roy, Andrew Sanchez and Clarinda Still. We are grateful to the participants at workshops along the way, notably Prem Shankar Jha and Avinash Kumar, and to the many others with whom we discussed ideas and findings, notably E.A. Brett, M. Rajshekhar and M. Vijaybaskar. We are especially grateful to the members of the advisory group – John Dunn, Peter Evans, David Gilmartin, Jonathan Parry, Pamela Price, John Sidel and Steven Wilkinson – for their support and advice throughout the project. Special gratitude to the project manager Pascale Searle, whose help and support has been invaluable.

We are grateful for our in loco partners: in India, the Centre for the Study of Developing Societies in New Delhi, and the University of Madras in Chennai; the Lahore University of Management Sciences in Pakistan; and the University of Dhaka in Bangladesh. We are very grateful to the European Research Council for an ERC grant ('An Anthropological Study of Muscular Politics in South Asia' – AISMA/284080) and to the UK Economic and Social Research Council for supporting the project 'Political Cultures in South Asia' (ES/I036702). They made this project possible but are not associated with its contents. Last but not least, we also wish to record our appreciation for the two anonymous reviewers at UCL Press for their penetrating and constructive comments, and to the staff at UCL Press.

Introduction

Barbara Harriss-White and Lucia Michelutti[1]

Throughout the world crime is on the increase, enforcement is being privatised and the proceeds of crime are being hidden in untaxed and unregulated jurisdictions. The distinction between the legitimate and the criminal economy is blurred. Power considered proper to the state is being decentralised and dispersed. The anthropologists of criminality, John and Jean Comaroff, go so far as to say '(l)awlessness is the presumption everywhere' (2018). The International Monetary Fund provides technical assistance on money-laundering and illegal financial activities to 120 of the world's 196 countries (Lagarde 2017).

In this book a team of political economists and anthropologists ask how this global phenomenon works in South Asia – mainly in India but also in Pakistan and Bangladesh. To get answers called for serious fieldwork, at the base of the economy. This was carried out between 2012 and 2016. Studies of natural resources, raw materials and energy, construction and the built environment, and government procurement enabled the team to trace criminal economic activity and its politics throughout the subcontinent and at a wide range of scales.

The evidence shows entangled and often collusive relations between petty crime, extensive criminal organisations, and their labour forces, on the one hand, and politicians, the police, officials, judges and law-abiding businesses on the other – relations in which it is often all but impossible to separate the legal from the illegal. Politics is systematically criminalised, and crime politicised. Italian scholars of organised crime use the term *intreccio* (intertwinement) (see for example Civico 2015) to signify that the world of crime does not exist in an alternative domain to that of the state but is deeply entangled with the actually existing state. Much of what the team found in South Asia fits this conception.[2]

This Introduction situates the research in the scholarly literature on predatory capitalism, mafia and organised crime, and the criminality of political finance. It describes the way in which political economy and anthropology have been deployed to help in integrating and analysing shards of economic evidence that are largely, but not completely, hidden from official view, and concludes by briefly summarising the 11 case studies which make up the core of the book.

But the title, 'The Wild East', was not chosen lightly. The historical experience of the North American Wild West has been an important benchmark, which needs to be described and justified at the outset.

The Wild East?

The concept of 'Wild West capitalism' has been invoked to characterise rampant, 'unfettered' capitalist expansion in both China and Russia.[3] Before launching the 'Wild East' let us briefly explain how current understandings of the Wild West might be a useful framing to grasp the nature of criminal predatory economies across India, Pakistan and Bangladesh. As Fernand Braudel wrote, history needs models, 'good or bad', 'against which events can be interpreted' (1974, xi). Lasting three centuries but culminating in the latter half of the nineteenth century, the Wild West period involved the conquest of territory in what is now North America. This territory stretched west of the Mississippi river and has only recently been identified as having been part of an immense Comanche 'empire' of bison, buffalo and decentralised settlement (Hamalainen 2009). From a rich tapestry of scholarship, two kinds of history of the Wild West can be distinguished: a bourgeois settler history and a radical history of subordination and primitive accumulation.

In the first, the 'Wild West' was conquered slowly through treaties made between competing foreign nations and native tribes, and through political compromises, military adventures and the subordination of native people and animals. Farms, ranches and towns were created, hunting trails marked and mines staked and dug. Railways and the telegraph shrank space and time, and trade shifted from a north–south axis to east–west, enticing great waves of foreign migrants. In their own narratives, the settlers of the Wild West developed ideas and values focussed on 'Jeffersonian' agrarian democracy, individualism and self-reliance. Yet, the colonisers were also spurred on by the animal spirits of markets. New technologies and the compulsions of accumulation collided with craft and independent workshop production. It was an era of unprecedented economic churning and growth (Rothbard 2017). Given that through much of this period, the state, in de jure infancy, was de facto absent; law and order, property rights and their protection were established by private agency, by 'the market', and by combinations of coercion and the spreading of ideas and practices of rule and justice. Voluntary organisations, vigilantes and collective forces protected camps and wagon trains, miners, squatters and cattlemen. Settlers made rules and determined punishments collectively before migrating; they resolved disputes through their officers on the way. In their research into property rights on the frontier, Anderson and Hill (1979) stressed that conflict was costly, that instances of crime were relatively rare, and that violent punishment was the exception rather than the rule. They characterise this period as 'anarcho-capitalism'. And they conclude that gun-battles are largely a figment of Hollywood's imagination.

The second kind of analysis points to what Marx famously called 'the extirpation, enslavement and entombment in mines of the aboriginal population' (1967, Ch. 30, 751) (together with the vast traffic in slaves from West Africa to American plantations which generated different political dynamics in the American South). Within 75 years of independence, armed settlers and militias (many consisting of expropriated British and Irish peasants and '1848er' refugees from Europe) could and did seize vast tracts of land, pillage and rape, pushing west, expropriating and violently wiping out almost all the native American people between the Appalachians and the Mississippi. It is this marginalisation and destruction of 'Indian' peoples, who were resistant to being incorporated as wage labour, that has generated the idea of the colonisation of the Wild West's being a pre-capitalist petty bourgeois imperialism rather than a process of primitive accumulation in which both the preconditions for accumulation – property ownership and 'free' wage labour (Baker 1990) – were prepared. For after the revolution, the post-independence state was structured so as to support capital and landed production. It enabled the establishment of an internal market, with countervailing power to the colonial 'mercantile drain' to Europe, in which land could be granted, sold and bought – such that the main obstacle to capitalist accumulation was the persistent lack of free wage labour. After the Civil War, the second element vital to primitive accumulation, the labour force, was to be pieced together in a 'singularly discontinuous way' (Baker 1990, 13). The newly freed black labouring under-class (most of whom remained on the land as debt-peons) was to be supplemented by waves of assetless migrants, dispossessed in their East and Southern European homelands. By 1890, the Great Plains were settled and industries and their cities were furnished with a workforce.

***

Well over a century after the Wild West was conquered, what is the relevance of these two versions of this period of American history to contemporary South Asia – how can they be used to justify the resonance of our title? Our reply is that the two approaches are useful to establish 'events to be interpreted' – and dimensions for comparison. From the first, the staking of control over resources (in South Asia below the surface as well as above); the modes of expansion of commodity economy, its scale and evolving technologies, the confrontation between craft production and capital, the roles of infrastructure and trade; contests in the development of the rule of private then public law and of democratic political control. In the second, the violent seizure of territory, transformations of forms of production and enforcement of new property rights over land and people; the roles in state and class formation of regions with radically different modes of production (in the American case, communal Indian social arrangements versus settlers versus slave plantations, long controlled by extractive merchants' capital); the mobilisation and organisation of wage labour markets given the mass extermination and enslavement of people. In both narratives: the roles of regional politics and culture, of evidence, interpretation and of myth.

All these processes are at work in the criminal economies of South Asia. Yet unlike the Wild West, the 'Wild East' reported in this book is not so much a territorial expansion as an accelerated exploitation of raw materials and energy, finance and rapid commodity production. Whereas the colonisation of the Wild West generated long-term growth, criminal exploitation in contemporary South Asia contains the potential to reduce growth rates (PricewaterhouseCoopers 2016).[4] In constituencies where politicians are charged with criminal offences, economic growth has been found to be slowed by up to 22 per cent (Prakash, Rockmore and Uppal 2016).[5] Unlike the Wild West, the Wild East is also developing after several decades of political independence, electoral democracy and functioning states. Far from shaping a process of rule of law, the Wild East has no shortage of regulatory law; instead it suffers a lack of enforcement capacities and ubiquitous enforcement failures.[6] Instead of developing state law from private or communal law, in the Wild East state law is being displaced by forms of authority vested in private property and criminal practices. While in the Wild West crime, such as it was (cattle theft, the occasional seizure of local government), is thought to have been largely parochial, in the Wild East all kinds of economic crime are reported to be rising sharply (PricewaterhouseCoopers 2016). India's corporate sector, to give just one example, has a history of grand criminal activity (capital flight, tax evasion, currency manipulation) as well as of less grand crime (procurement fraud, financial fraud, misappropriation of assets) – and by salaried labour as well as top management (Anderson and Hill 1979; Kar 2010; PricewaterhouseCoopers 2016). While the Wild West is said to have been built on individualism and self-reliance, in the Wild East, criminal violence and collusion with the state – with bureaucrats, public sector managers, the police and politicians at all levels – are crucial for furthering accumulation. Electoral democracy has to be intertwined with untraceable money. The new criminal enterprises provide both legal and black money to finance political campaigns, and thus further create or consolidate criminal political economies. When elected, criminal politicians are protected by their political immunity and their political power protects and supports returns on their political and economic investments, and on those of their cronies and clients. However, despite these structural differences, the Wild East, like the Wild West, is driven by profit and the compulsion to accumulate private property, bringing social transformations and widespread environmental devastation in its wake. In many parts of India, for example, we find that local tribal and low caste peoples are being coerced into the labour force, compelled to migrate, their resource base, life-worlds and physical and cultural environments destroyed. Like American Indians, Tribal Indians and Dalits are found to be 'ground down by growth': suffering marginalisation, starvation, contemptuously criminal exploitation and oppression (Shah et al. 2017). Among the new Wild Eastern varieties of 'gold' are air (as in spectrum), financial services, land, sand, coal, granite, stones, oil, water and other natural and biological resources such as sandalwood and meat, the construction and real estate industries, chemicals and drugs, betting and film finance. It is the connections between accumulation, the workforce, the police, the bureaucracy and party politics that incentivise the politicisation of crime and the criminalisation of politics, in which proliferate the 'mafias' and other forms of organised crime that are investigated in this book. These processes are far from linear. They are entangled processes constantly infusing each other. The 11 chapters will cumulatively piece together examples of *intreccio* that are typical of Wild East forms of economies and of local 'mafias' operating on the ground.

The concept of 'organised crime' is one that is both fuzzy (Paoli 2014) and analytically quite ambiguous (Standing 2003; Briquet and Favarel-Garrigues 2010; Vigh 2015). Criminologists and sociologists of mafias devote relatively little time to studying forms of 'organised crime' outside the Western world. In the South Asian region, historians, social anthropologists and economists have commonly focussed on 'informality' (Visvanathan and Sethi 1998; Khan and Jomo 2001; Harriss-White 2003; Srinivasan 2007), corruption (Wade 1985; Gupta 1995; Brass 1997; Parry 2000) and/or studying colonial notions of 'thuggery', 'the dacoit' and 'the criminal tribe/caste'.[7] The relation between violence (whether of gangs/vigilantes or groups/riot-machines) and politics has also generated a sophisticated body of regional literature (Brass 1997).[8] However, until recently remarkably few studies have explored the day-to-day working of the criminal economy and the specific politicisation of economic crime in South Asia (Harriss-White 2003; Gayer 2014; Kumar 2014; Sanchez 2016). In a co-authored book entitled *Mafia Raj: The Rule of Bosses in South Asia*, Michelutti et al. highlight the centrality of micro-level il/legal economies and local 'mafias' to the individual careers of gangster-politicians across South Asia.[9] These findings underline the need to move attention away from questions of criminal (political) leadership and political violence to the study also of the 'politicisation of crime' and with it the economic operations of local 'mafias'. They also suggest the need to move attention from trade in conventional illegal goods such as, for example, drugs (Jaffe 2013; Arias 2016; Civico 2015); human (or body-part) smuggling (Kleemans and Smit 2014) and/or arms trafficking (Levi 2014) to the study of the everyday criminal life of *legal* commodities. Here, we focus in particular on the illegal exploitation of natural resources, raw materials for India, Pakistan and Bangladesh's exploding towns and cities. Such 'green crimes' are often considered 'soft crimes', less harmful and affecting fewer victims than 'real' predatory crime does (Van Solinge 2014, 500). But is this true? What sort of 'mafia' does the Wild East's forms of predatory capitalism produce? How do these set of questions help us to further theorise criminal political economies and 'mafias' as an object of study?

***

The term and concept of 'mafia' has long been debated in the literature. One influential approach is to study mafia-like phenomena purely as an economic activity: mafia as an 'enterprise syndicate' (Blok 1974); 'mafia enterprise' (Arlacci 1993); and a 'protection industry' (Gambetta 1988, 1993; Varese 2001). By contrast Tilly (1985) has highlighted the relation between mafia and political sovereignty by introducing the fascinating proposition that organised crime can be compared to both war-making and state-making (see also Volkov 2002 and Varese 2011). Building on these insights Armao (2000) pointed out that what distinguishes mafia from other types of organised crime is that the former essentially uses politics and the judicial system to make a profit. According to Armao (2015, 3), when a structured and permanent group of individuals that uses violence to make profit through criminal activities 'meets politics', it gives rise to a third system called 'mafia'. It is this open and *non-legalistic* definition that we refer to when we use the term 'mafia' in this book. In the Wild East's political environment, 'mafias' did not develop in contexts in which local government authorities were unable to guarantee a minimum of security (as has been said to have happened, for example, in the cases of Cosa Nostra in Sicily or 'Ndrangheta in Calabria); instead, South Asian mafia groups tend not to pose as proto-states but rather fuse with the state and democratic electoral politics. And while Paoli (2003; 2014) describes mafias as political communities that are not fully institutionalised, the Wild East's mafias are, in many instances, deeply politically institutionalised and socially embedded. These complex multi-dimensional realities make it extremely difficult socially and legally to separate mafiosi from businessmen and politicians who connive with mafiosi. This entanglement is in reality a recurrent feature of 'mafias' across the world but it is still surprisingly little studied and theorised. Recently, for example Schneider (2018) and Ben-Yehoyada (2018) have shown how legal definitions of the Sicilian Cosa Nostra define the organisation as an internally cohesive, hierarchical and brotherhood-based system. Such views, they argue, not only hamper the prosecution of 'non-Mafiosi' collaborators but also contribute to shaping the public conception of the *mafia–political nexus* as two separate worlds (ibid.: 360). Distinctions between 'inner circles' and 'external' agents are indeed analytically problematic because in practice these groups are intertwined and interdependent. Reflecting precisely such entanglements, the now indigenous South Asian term 'mafia' is commonly used to refer to business enterprises with *political protection* that seek to monopolise particular trades, sectors and localities through extra-legal and violent means (as in the 'alcohol mafia', 'water mafia', 'oil mafia', 'coal mafia' or a variety of 'land grabbing' practices by the 'land mafia'). Such syndicates protect clients and cronies and work both against and in tandem with local politicians, the justice system and the bureaucracy (Michelutti et al. 2018, 5; Martin and Michelutti 2017).

South Asian 'mafias' operate at a range of scales. As the following chapters will show, people talk about 'small mafia' and 'big mafia'. Local expressions such as 'company', 'lobby', 'firm' or 'racket/cartel' (in Hindi English), *parivar* (family), syndicates, 'groups' or 'rings' can locally describe anything from a protection racket to a violent lobby/interest group or a handful of ambitious criminals working as part of a team. In contrast to the Italian Sicilian 'mafia' (which often embodies the archetype of a criminal hierarchical and structured organisation in the media, in the public imagination as also in sociological and anthropological discourse), the so-called 'mafias' we encountered when doing the field research for this book, while developing strong dynastic dynamics, are neither hierarchically institutionalised nor endowed with long histories. They are often new entities which make strategic use of caste and community kinship connections and cultural idioms but are not necessarily structured by them. 'Companies' and 'groups' are not appendices to coherent and centralised criminal organisations; rather they are part of broader systems of il/legal political economies. Crucially, there is a continuum between informal enterprises, criminal profit-making activities and what locals refer to as 'criminal organisations'. The art of 'getting by' often involves brushes with 'organised crime' (Pine 2012; see also Hoque and Michelutti, 2018). In seminal research Van Schendel and Abraham (2005) discussed the junctures between large-scale organised crime, micro-level organised crime and the informal economy in non-Western settings. They offer detailed case studies of arms smuggling, illegal transnational migration, the diamond trade, borderland practices and the transnational consumption of drugs in Asia, Africa, Latin America, Europe and North America. This ethnographic *tour de force* shows how distinctions between the 'illegal' (meaning prohibited by law) and the 'illicit' (meaning socially perceived as unacceptable) are historically changeable and contested. Importantly it shows how states, borders and the language of law enforcement produce criminality, and how people and goods that are labelled 'illegal' move across regulatory spaces. Building on these insights, the 11 case studies presented in this book further problematise relations between illegal and illicit by showing how 'mafias' and many captains of industry are at the apex of much more extensive criminal economic systems embedded in formal, registered and regulated institutions and, crucially, the political sphere and its bureaucracy. In the next section, before delving into the details of the particularities and nature of Wild East 'mafias', we will outline some of

the mechanisms and logics behind the development of symbiotic relations among politics, businesses and crime across South Asia over the last
four decades.

Business–politics nexus: testing a macro-economic model

Scholars across the social sciences rarely focus on the study of the
relation between business, crime and (organised) political violence,
'despite the intimate link between politics and economics' (Hazen and
Rodgers 2014, 7). A remarkable exception is provided by the political
economist P.S. Jha, who has developed a macro-level economic account
of the criminalisation of politics and the politicisation of crime in India
(Jha 2013), the country that is the main focus of this book. The two
chapters on Pakistan and Bangladesh and secondary material available
on the topic will enable us to identify contrasts and similarities across
the three countries' experiences when compared to Jha's account. In
Jha's descriptive model, the origins of the criminalisation of politics
in India are traced back first to the constitutional flaw of omitting the
means to meet the costs of running a democracy (not only the high cost
of election campaigns in demographically and territorially vast constituencies but also the ongoing 'fixed costs' of democratic politics), and
second to the 1969 decision by Indira Gandhi to ban company donations (to hobble her rivals). Funding for political parties went underground, with devastating effects on both politics and the economy.
First, intra-party democracy was stymied by the paramount need for
regional fundraising 'bureaucracies', which generated path-dependent
relations of clientelism and high economic entry barriers. These eventually solidified into dynasties across generations. Regional and local
clientelist controllers of black cash and votes emerged to take power.
Crime and physical intimidation then faced few obstacles to their development as major political forces able to perpetuate path-dependent
dynastic criminal organisations (see also Vaishnav 2017). Parties based
on identity, aspiration or region emerged not only as a result of national
parties neglecting the factors new parties used to mobilise voters (such
as caste, ethnicity, regional neglect and under-development) but also
as a reaction to the political spaces created by criminalisation. Jha
argues, however, that the newer parties must suffer similar pressures
and negotiate – and embody – political forces contradictory to their
social aspirations.

Meanwhile, criminal economic organisation networks thriving in the black economy needed protection by criminal protection rackets. In turn, the expense and inadequate protection afforded by these rackets led to old-style criminal political clients and new-style members and leaders of criminal organisations directly participating in party politics. Politics gives immunity to criminals who are elected legislators in central and state governments. Since this immunity is incomplete, criminal protection forces (parallel monopolies of force) are needed at every level (including political protection for economic protection forces). India has not only succeeded in criminalising politics but also in politicising crime.

Although two kinds of clientelism can be distinguished: first, the fundraising clientelist networks that generate political princelings and second, criminal networks which 'mobilise criminal funds and protect criminal enterprises like smuggling, bootlegging, timber theft and poaching', the two are on track to converge (Jha 2013).[10] The economic effects of the development of political fundraising are then the side-effects of struggles to control cash flows within and among parties at various scales and in different regions. They have moved through three moments, which Jha models as follows. First a *pre-emergency* period, when political funds were levied in cash (instead of tax-deductible cheques) from corporate company funders. Meeting with resistance, parties turned to small and medium local business and trade associations (see Harriss-White 1993). So, political funding in return for special economic exemptions and the protection of local capital dispersed throughout the economy and became the scaffolding that buttresses the distinctively enormous scope of India's informal economy.

Second came *post-emergency*: in a battle for control over funds between regions and centre, the latter retaliated by exacting tribute from both foreign companies and state enterprises – a practice most easily applied to the defence and energy sectors. This funding route resulted in serious, path-dependent inefficiencies from suboptimal technological choices. These include the inflation of capital costs, inflated-cost benchmarks for future projects, the 'gold-plating' of future investments with necessary subsidies to ensure competitiveness, and the institutionalising of extremely costly delays and forfeited benefits. Projects were chopped up into components in the name of competition so as to multiply kickbacks, while shoddy work, inefficiencies and irrationalities result from the politically driven shattering of megaprojects, thereby 'putting the state up for sale'. According to Jha (2013), *Outlook* reported in 2009 that, between 1990 and 2008, 33 scams cost the public exchequer US$100 billion per year. In this process, the economic space for redistributivist development activity that might have benefitted the welfare of the mass of the population and India's workforce was reduced both by lack of resources and by its irrelevance to criminal politics. Their neglect makes a mockery of much development discourse.

Third, during the reform period of market-led growth, company donations to parties have been rehabilitated – but such donations are unable to meet more than 10 per cent of election costs, so it is rational to finance individual powerful candidates. This is a cover for the crony capitalism that dominates Congress and the Bharatiya Janata Party (BJP) (Mazumdar 2008).

Small regional parties form coalitions to gain power and access to what appears to them to be a 'bloated central state'. Control over central bureaucracies and those of state corporations enables posts holding discretionary power in the regions to be allocated. Where competence yields to political connections, inefficiencies are hard-wired into the 'formal' economy. And what of resistance?[11] For Jha, India's bureaucracy is effectively immune from prosecution and has the capacity to blackmail. The police have formal powers of enforcement but are widely alleged to be co-opted and complicit. Individual politicians, officials and police may be neither corrupt nor criminals but 'resisters' face punishment ranging from career demotion to assassination.[12] The mature clientelist state, Jha concludes, is where power is exercised by a congeries of relations among business, career politicians, gangland mafiosi and the police.

While all breaches of economic law are crimes, not all crimes have a direct impact on the economy.[13] In the UPA-2 parliament,[14] nearly one-third of Lok Sabha politicians had been charged with crimes – 13 per cent with serious crimes.[15] Of the winning candidates in the 2014 elections, 34 per cent had been charged with crimes and 21 per cent with serious crimes (a 50 per cent increase over the previous parliament). Some 30 per cent of the ministers in the 2014–19 Modi cabinet faced charges; this rose to 39 per cent in 2019.[16] While robbery and forgery are directly related to economic exchanges, the accumulation of assets is also associated with murder, armed robbery, kidnapping, rape and the illegal possession of arms. If MPs are classified according to the political parties they represent, the relation between wealth and criminal charges cannot be substantiated.[17] However, from UPA-1 to UPA-2, the proportion of *crorepati* MPs doubled to 48 per cent; MPs with direct business investments must make up a much increased proportion.[18] By 2014, 82 per cent of MPs were *crorepatis* with average assets of INR 15 *crore* (nearly US$ 28 million; Association for Democratic Reform 2014); by 2019 the figure was 88 per cent.

Nevertheless, Jha's stylised economy consists of corporations and small firms (the latter of which he had earlier analysed as an intermediate regime (Jha 1980)). But India has developed what is arguably the largest and most extensive informal economy in the world, representing about 60 per cent of GDP and over 90 per cent of livelihoods.[19] India's is, in large measure, an economy of tiny businesses. From 1990 to 2011, the average number of employees in a registered business fell from three to two; 95 per cent of all businesses now employ fewer than five workers.[20] India's informal economy is also not (only) the result of poor quality law, institutional scarcity or incompetence but evolved as a deliberate creation, long before the concept of informality was invented. Regulatory law and rules were sabotaged at their inception soon after independence, to restrict their coverage to a small minority of (larger) companies, activities and labour relations (Das Gupta 2016; Dietrich Wielenga 2019). Regulatory law is also disregarded through pre-emptive development (such as when large companies register as a number of small businesses under the regulatory threshold (Harriss 1982)). And when regulatory law is flouted and evaded (as in the unreported profits, wages or rent that make up the black economy; Kumar 1999) the criminal economy develops. It involves illegal business in legal goods and services together with illegal activity in illegal goods and services (Sinha and Harriss-White 2007; Kumar 1999).[21] Estimates of this black economy vary widely – from 25–75 per cent of GDP.[22]

Yet the criminal economy is not necessarily judged by society as illegitimate, because it has its own forms of regulation and social order. When non-compliance is widely accepted, it is the compliant person who is the social deviant. The criminal economy is not only the nutrient base of mafia dynasties, it is also the economy of segmented class fractions: petty production and more or less disguised labour (Harriss-White 2012, 2014), intermediate classes and petty capital, and great state corporations. It also forms part of more or less ethnicised regional capitalisms. These show great diversity. It is only recently that regional variations in the social character of the recorded economy have been discovered and then mapped (Dasgupta 2017; Pani 2017; Harriss-White, Stokke and Törnquist 2014; Harriss-White 2017b). At present however, regional relationships between the recorded and the criminal economies are a matter of speculation in which official data face case material.

In Pakistan and Bangladesh, the mapping of the social character of regional economies is in its infancy (Chowdhury 2013; Gayer 2014; Mallick 2014). If in India many have argued that the replication on the provincial level of Indira Gandhi's authoritarian rule led to the proliferation of parochial politics, which became the bedrock of 'criminal' political elements (Bardhan 1984; 1988; Kohli 1991; Corbridge and Harriss 2000), analysts of Pakistani politics have similarly claimed that authoritarian military regimes in Pakistan have promoted the growth of factionalism, political violence and illegal forms of capitalism (Rais 1985; Waseem 1994; Jalal 1995), exacerbated in the 1980s by the rise in the heroin and weapon trades (Jalal 1995; Gayer 2014; see also Gayer in Chapter 11). In particular, over the past decade Pakistan's military has become a key player in these illegal forms of capital accumulation. The disproportionate size of the military in the country's economy is now well documented. A considerable proportion of these profit-making activities are carried out by the armed forces' 'welfare foundations', which are some of the largest conglomerates in the country. Their activities include insurance, banking, educational institutions, gas extraction, cement production and agro-industries (see Blom 2011, 31–2; Siddiqa 2007, 198–9). By the same token, decreasing industrial returns over the past few years have led to massive investments in real estate. This has been accompanied by a stark increase in land-grabbing operations (*qabza*), a lucrative activity that often sees the collusion of criminal bosses, bureaucrats and elected politicians in the form of '*qabza* groups' (Rollier 2016; see also Michelutti et al. 2018).

In Bangladesh, the Awami League lost power in 1975 to a military coup, ushering in an era of military dictatorships that lasted until 1990 when democracy was 'restored'. This unstable, violent period helped create the foundations of the era of 'confrontational' politics between the two major political parties and their bonded clients vying for resources and patronage (Lewis 2011; Gardner 1995, 2012). This process happened at the same time as a devastating combination of natural and man-made disasters, which together created conditions that helped further an unholy alliance of political violence, capitalism and crime (Ruud 2014). Autocracy gave way to democracy in 1990 but the deadly rivalry between the two main political parties is breeding a shadowy space where enforcers and their political/business bosses thrive (Lewis 2011; Jahan 2005, 2015). The question of political party funding is an extremely sensitive and very under-researched topic in Bangladesh. The political parties never disclose their funding sources. Hardly any party discloses financial information even internally. Political party funds are usually collected directly from businessmen and industrialists. Such funds are often donated voluntarily out of vested interest, but in many cases they are extorted.[23] During the democratic era, neoliberal economic policies have been accelerated compared to the previous martial period, when the policies were initially put in place (by General Ziaur Rahman, founder of the BNP). From the mid-2000s onwards GNP grew at an average annual rate of 6 per cent. The extent to which the criminal economy slows or underpins this relatively high growth rate has not been established. As in India, depending on the chosen method of calculation, Bangladesh's underground economy contributes between 45 and 80 per cent to GDP.[24] Similarly, in Pakistan there is no consensus among economists and estimates of the contribution range between 30 and 90 per cent (Zaidi 2014, 112). Definitions of formal, informal and black economies vary and overlap, further complicating estimates.[25] Regulations and definitions delimit the boundaries of such economies and are exploited and manipulated to make profits in the Wild East. Collusion with the state and the violent enforcement of economic interests are both crucial for furthering capitalist accumulation trajectories across South Asia. Enterprises providing both black and legal money to finance political campaigns create and consolidate criminal political formations.[26]

The case studies

A multidisciplinary method and analysis: political economy and the anthropology of crime

Collecting data on criminal economies and 'mafias' requires an innovative, flexible methodology. In an attempt to fuse ethnographic micro-studies of communities/villages/neighbourhoods and local industrial sectors, in the following chapters we employ a plurality of approaches derived from the theories and methods of anthropology, political economy and the economics of institutions. So, while the knowledge base we are building is unusually resilient, we cannot escape the fact that similar phenomena are described in different terms and interpreted using a variety of analytical concepts: for example, political corruption, irregular capitalism and networks of connivance, criminal corruption, criminal enterprise, mafia assemblage, syndicate, 'mafia raj', 'mastan raj' and even hydro-criminality. The richness of this collection lies precisely in approaching a common task from different starting points, both in the real economy and analytically within a multidisciplinary approach. Five chapters are contributed by six political economists who are seasoned in what the great economic anthropologist Polly Hill called 'field economics'. Six chapters employ ethnographic methodologies extensively and are the work of five experienced anthropologists and a political sociologist. We now turn to broad differences in disciplinary approaches before discussing field methods and summarising substantive results.

Political economy case studies

Jha's macro-model has informed the research design of the first five chapters and shaped i) the identification of a 'starter set' of microeconomic agents from which the field investigation is developed, ii) the initial hypotheses driving fieldwork (the local-level feedback relation between crime and electoral democracy), and thus iii) the field methods to be used for comparable micro-level research. The cases presented in Chapters 1 to 5, on the four elements – earth (illegal coal (in Jharkhand) and riverbed sand (in Tamil Nadu)); fire (the century-old subterranean fire in Jharkhand); water (hydro-crime in Arunachal Pradesh); and air (spectrum illegalities sited in metropolitan megacities) – have been approached as natural resource extraction–distribution systems. Experience recommends that a differentiated approach to businesses and their workforces is needed to capture capital–labour class relations and reflect the inter-penetration of legal and illegal practices (Harriss-White 1999). Each system is made up of elements: technologies (which make the natural resource useful, even in the case of destructive fire); social/'organisational' institutions, firms and state agencies; and their labour. These elements are dynamised by (market-mediated) economic relationships (work, money, the operating of machinery/technology/energy and the control of property) which enable commodity production and distribution to take place. A structure of secondary markets (e.g. transport, brokerage, valuation) is also essential to such systems. And through them run distributions of profit, rent and wages, allocations that are *ordered* and *controlled*, if not registered or state-regulated. The informal economy is said to be 'unorganised' but it is not *dis*organised. Exactly the same applies to the criminal economy. Control is exercised and negotiated within and between businesses, between businesses and labour, other organisations (protection) and their labour, between businesses and the state bureaucracies and agencies (including the systems of finance and justice) and between the agencies of the state. The institutional alternatives to the state through which economic order is contested and maintained are awkward to characterise since some are entirely criminal (informal syndicates, contractors' fiefdoms, criminal organisations), some operate inside legally registered entities (business associations, labour unions, even some mafia), some express authority derived from social identity (caste, gender, ethnicity, religion) and some penetrate the state itself (parallel checkpoints, collusive allocation of public resources). These are not closed systems but open ones whose flexible boundaries are shaped and dynamised by law, custom, contingency – and by the understandings and resources of researchers themselves.

While the formal political parameters of the system involve the laws that are flouted, the remit and roles of state vigilance forces and the police, the judicial and penal systems, the focus of the first five case studies has been on party politics. Before linking the two realms – economic and party political – we sought wherever possible to understand the recent development of major and minor political parties in their own terms, by questioning the social composition of parties and voters, factions and contentions within parties, and the relations of key individuals to their – and other – parties. Through guesstimates and shadowy indications, the links of party funders, cash managers and major political agents and players to the criminal economy (not always the sectors we have chosen as case material) before, during and after elections can be outlined. Political investments and achievements may be juxtaposed with the significance, if any, of immunity. This is scoping research; types of recursive links between the black economy of natural resource extraction and party politics emerged through the experience of fieldwork.

Field methods and problems of political economy

Each case study involved: i) previous experience of the sector, area and working language; ii) a period of background work; and iii) between two and four months in the field, alone or in a small team. Collecting economic data and mapping the patterns of legal-illegal enterprise and their relations to politics are not easy tasks. The mafia often buys silence, especially to do with these topics, and we tried to break this silence. The orthodox approach to economic fieldwork, involving censuses, stratified randomised samples and systematic interviews was clearly unfeasible. A systems approach to the economy and politics could be developed from stakeholder snowball techniques. The safety of researchers being a paramount consideration, basic principles of fieldwork involved not seeking out or talking to individuals who are directly involved in criminal activity about that activity – unless they volunteered. The paradox of stakeholder research on crime involving no criminal 'stakeholders' was resolved through triangulation. Data were collected through participant observation, conversations and interviews with key informants with triangulable knowledge: (often retired) journalists, local academics, lawyers, civil servants, police personnel, bank managers, NGO workers, trade unionists and transport operators, and minor politicians, party officials and members who have had in-depth experience of the sector. The objective was to construct an analytical narrative from shards of information from knowledgeable informants about the operation of the sector, i.e. how others – 'third parties' – behave. Accepting that there may be more than one narrative, the concurrence of two to three informants was taken as an approximation to a truth claim. Where, as in the case of illegal coal, one reputed official source estimates that 5 per cent of coal is diverted into the illegal economy while another reckons it varies between 25 and 50 per cent, the two stories have to be told.

This method yielded a wealth of evidence and each team member wrote field reports of 20–25,000 words. These are the sources of the first five chapters. In three respects confidentiality has been assured in the field – and observed here: confidence pertaining to place, to the source itself and sometimes to the detail of the substance divulged. These detailed sources are embedded in the unpublished field reports, which were read and discussed critically by the wider project team. Much of the evidence in the five political economy chapters in this book has, therefore, to be taken on trust.

Even with this method, which has sought to maximise the comparability of the case studies, the idiosyncrasies of place, the quiddity of sectors and the capacities of individual researchers inevitably generate original and unique analyses which constrain direct comparisons. Major problems also result from developing this 'second best' approach to economic fieldwork on illegality (for example, data, usually considered as 'basic', on costs and returns, wealth, detailed contracts, credit and the livelihoods of the labour force prove generally impossible to obtain). This book on India's criminal economy has very little economic evidence. The alternative involves the fine granularity of the ethnographic projects described in the following section; however, the latter are idiosyncratic and have issues of replicability.

The anthropological perspective and ethnography

The political-anthropological perspective – with its focus on the everyday conceptions and practices of legislature, legality, democracy, and the state at large – offers a particularly useful point of departure for understanding the relationship between the illegal and formal political and economic spheres whose everyday dimension is often left out of view in more 'top-down' institutional analyses.[27] Participant observation was the main research method employed by the authors of the six ethnographic chapters. This method is inductive and has the potential for uncovering unexpected links between different domains of social life. Hanging around, chatting, participating in daily activities and trying to understand criminal cultures and the grey zones of complicity and collusion require relationships of trust to be developed. Many of us had done fieldwork in the selected localities for a number of years before starting this project. As a matter of fact, the research sites for this project were chosen not only keeping the regional balance in mind but crucially by considering the expertise of the researchers, their personal contacts and networks and their language skills. Such skills are essential to tackle a difficult anthropological research topic such as the criminal economy.[28] Long-term anthropological fieldwork (from 6–15 months) in the everyday domains of life provided us with important insights into local cultures of leadership, criminality and politics, as well as into the workings of 'mafia methods'. These insights suggest that the study of criminal, political and economic configurations cannot be adequately captured only through the prism of the state, capitalism and the law. One must also pay attention to the way those involved in or affected by these formations make sense of them through more varied and locally relevant notions of 'the political' and 'wealth'. This includes vernacular understandings of kinship and religion, honour and masculinity, charisma and trust, and patronage relations based on community-, caste- and/or tribal-based ties. In short, one must consider the diverse socio-cultural imaginaries of power and money that undergird actors' involvement in such criminal-cum-political formations.

This immersion and the shadowing of a number of bosses with different levels of power allowed the researchers to identify a number of recurrent businesses that contribute to shape the Wild East (Michelutti et al. 2018, Chapter 1). Across the sites we studied, the real estate sector was recognised as the 'business' that provided the most profitable economic opportunities for violent political entrepreneurs over the past decade. Land and property transactions opened up new career paths that required the capacity to handle coercion, manage extra-legal activities and, most importantly, play 'the game of politics'. Besides real estate development, other violent extractive industries in which bosses were usually involved included mining (e.g. sand, granite, limestone for cement); the transport business; hotels and restaurants; the commercialisation of drugs; loan sharking, fraud, financial crimes and extortion (e.g. the collection of protection money – *goonda tax/hafta/chandabaazi* – and kidnapping); and other means of violent regulation of labour markets. The six ethnographic case studies explore a number of these sectors and related Wild East predatory forms of capitalism across North and South India, Bangladesh and Pakistan, and show how they intersect with local politics, electoral democracy, party funding and/or the formal and informal judiciary system.

Anthropological studies of economic illegality and violence often tend to focus on 'losers', 'victims' and 'bottom-barrel thieves and hustlers' (see, for example, Jeffrey, Jeffery and Jeffery 2008; Goffman 2014). Our research and analysis go empirically and analytically beyond 'informality', 'survival questions' and a focus on the poor and marginalised by also investigating multiple 'winners' and their trajectories in Wild East forms of capital accumulation. While studying local criminal business sectors we interacted with businessmen, henchmen, bosses, lawyers and politicians, as well as day labourers. This required shadowing and interviewing members of the local business/criminal families, gang members, enemies, rivals, businessmen, criminal lawyers, crime reporters, accountants, doctors, police investigators, astrologists, priests and the residents of the territories where the criminal economies we studied operate. The interviews were generally conducted in Bangla, Hindi, Punjabi, Telugu or Urdu, and less frequently in 'pure' English. Our long-term engagement with our field sites allowed us to collect granular bottom-up data that shed light on a number of questions at the heart of this book: *How do il/legal economies work de facto? Who controls and regulates them? Who is dependent on whom? And why?* Essentially, the six ethnographic case studies shed light on the complex Polanyian combination of reciprocity, exchange and redistribution (Ben-Yehoyada 2018) within South Asian mafias' systems and highlight how complicities, cooperation and opportunistic partnerships are at the heart of local and regional criminal political economies.

During our fieldwork, we were able to check our data against the preliminary results of the political economy cases studies discussed above. We attended six workshops together to discuss findings during the collection of data and the writing-up phases.[29] Importantly, such dialogue, exposure and regular triangulations allowed us to pay attention to problems of internal validity within our studies. Patterns and outliers could be observed as findings were collected across the sites. The material collected by the political economy case studies reminded the anthropologists that criminal economies and their 'mafias' were seldom only localised affairs. They showed us that it was impossible to limit the analysis of the businesses and industrial sectors to a village or a neighbourhood as they were often linked – legally and illegally – with district, regional, national and global economies. So wherever it was relevant and possible we connected our micro-level ethnographic data with information on district/state/national/international networks, economic sectors and scales of political activity derived from print media, other media and archival, research and statistical resources.

Field methods and problems in the anthropology of criminal economies
While bosses and their violent appropriations were often extremely public and visible (Michelutti et al. 2018), it was not easy to collect economic evidence and map local criminal economies. While our interlocutors were often ready to talk openly about murders they had allegedly committed or commissioned and show off their prowess by recounting unsavoury episodes of their careers, the topic of money remained an extremely sensitive one. What remained obscure and untraceable (and also risky to explore) in our field sites was the organisation of local bosses' economic activities. Businesses and related properties were often registered under 'borrowed names', namely the names of relatives, drivers or bodyguards. Thus, on the one hand, violent entrepreneurs (*dabang, mastan, badmash*) seemed to invest a great deal of energy in enacting a violent reputation, and sometimes a Robin Hood and saintly boss image. Yet on the other they took great care to conceal the existence of the organisational structure of their mafia-like enterprises and the names of their associates.

We minimised risks by exploring the criminal economy indirectly as much as possible. For example, some of us explored activities such as protection/extortion not only by studying the terrain of money and organised criminal systems of protection but also by looking into local indigenous statecraft models of virtuous kingly/caste protection, or into idioms related to protecting women and honour and/or caste. We were able to gather data safely by exploring the social embeddedness of economic crime. To elaborate, local 'mafias' present both 'highly structured and well-established organised groups based on enduring memberships and more fluid and amorphous groups, with members coming in and out according to their particular needs and opportunities' (see Rege and Lavorgna 2017, 173). At some levels, there is no controlling family, no boundaries separating members from non-members. And it is at these lower levels that we were able to gather insights on the more 'secretive' upper levels of the local mafias and their organisations. This holistic ethnographic approach and long-term fieldwork was combined with analyses of disputes, court cases and complaints to the police. Exploring court cases and police documentation helped us to enrich our ethnographic material and, at the same time, to explore how the police and the local judiciary were heavily implicated in sustaining and gaining from local criminal economies. Without police protection none of the criminal economies this book illustrates would have been able to operate.

Overview of the chapters

The case studies cumulatively reveal the micro-politics at work on different scales in economic crime ranging from theft and fraud, the flouting of laws and rules concerning planning, economic and environmental regulation as well as the control of labour, tax evasion, the flight of capital and the enforcement of political protection. Their political ramifications all challenge the previous characterisation of the politics of the states concerned. In the first chapter, on the criminal economy of coal in Jharkhand, Barbara Harriss-White and Nigel Singh explore illegal coal economies and party politics. The formal, legal, informal and criminal elements of the supply chains or assemblages of 'black' coal are found to involve a range of public sector agencies, corporations, government ministries and departments; private mining companies, public and private sector labour forces and labour unions; four scales of illegal coal – cycle wallahs, syndicates, coal traders and the mafia dynasties – and a multiplicity of other agents in derived markets for transport, forged documents, bribes, etc. Outlawed Maoist revolutionaries also receive 'revenue' from 'taxing' the transport of black coal. A totalising system of transactions that are interlocked both politically and economically binds formal, informal and criminal together. It operates at scales ranging from the local, extending through Bihar to the major informal coal market of Chandasi in UP (Rajshekhar 2014), and spreads throughout Northern India where it satisfies demand for coal for heating, brick kilns, yarn dyeing, small-scale textiles and many more workshop industries, trades and services, which are prevented from qualifying for legal access to coal and coke. In the region of Dhanbad, hundreds of thousands of exiguous and precarious unregistered and rightless livelihoods depend on illegal coal and further countless livelihoods nationwide depend on its multipliers. Spreading not just territorially but also through the political and bureaucratic systems, the local-level criminal economy is linked to New Delhi. Vast, partially registered, partially criminal conglomerate capital has been accumulated. The factoring in of this economy to the narratives of Jharkhand's democratic politics explains them in terms that transcend a characterisation as the politics of a tribal homeland, the instability of which has been attributed to heterogeneous ethnic rivalries (alluded to in Jewitt 2008). All parties have stakes in illegal coal. Political pressure points are pervaded by criminal interests that have guaranteed the party-political instability on which their criminal power flourishes.

Chapter 2 pursues the analysis of one consequence of the coal economy. In her analysis of fire and the 'mafia', Smita Gupta investigates the workings and effects of open-cast coal mining in the region of Jharia. Triggered by over a century of uncontrolled fires in India's finest (and highly inflammable) coking coal deposits, emergency powers permit surface mining technology to be used to extract and maximise the value of the remaining coal. But open-cast mines spread the fires, further threatening infrastructure and settlements, sparking accidents and now endangering the health and homes of 500,000 to 1,000,000 people around Jharia. Subterranean fire is the result not just of accidents, lightning or geological pressures but of a range of deliberate economic crimes, in flagrant disregard for laws, policies and plans by state and central government, fuelled by a self-sustaining criminalised nexus. 'Legitimate' functionaries – government servants, public sector enterprise employees, elected politicians, trade unions, corporate interests, police and other law-enforcement agencies – are linked through economic transactions with criminal gangs and their 'pocket' trade unions. The relations between trade unions, labour politics, party politics and the mafia that profit from uncontrolled fire and diverted stowage are mapped in this chapter. So too are additional crimes in which the law and rules of eligibility for rehabilitation and resettlement in regions threatened by subsidence have been increasingly restricted and then flouted with complete impunity by the agencies responsible. Reasons for such behaviour may be found in the economic and political marginalisation of eligible but low-status victims. Each day, impoverished workers successfully banished to distant, inadequate housing gulags have no alternative but to make their way back to the burning surfaces to scavenge coal.

Chapter 3 turns to the 'sand mafia' of Tamil Nadu. Here J. Jeyaranjan suggests pork-barrel politics as a conceptual lens to understand recent developments in the criminal economy of sand and its entanglement with electoral politics. He has researched the evolution of a supply system of ever-increasing economic scale, territorial reach and party politicisation. Tamil Nadu's riverbed 'sand mafia' has developed so as to satisfy the rapidly escalating demand for sand in local construction and communications infrastructure, to counter regular waves of regulatory law and legal challenges, and to negotiate constantly changing official institutions. Legal and illegal revenue from sand mining fuels party funds, enabling the rapid recent diffusion of pork-barrel politics. A new interpretation follows: of Dravidian politics moving from populism towards predation, an interpretation not fundamentally disturbed by the 2017 turmoil in the political leadership of Tamil Nadu following the death of Chief Minister J. Jayalalithaa.

In the fourth chapter grounded in political economy, Deepak Mishra researches hydro-criminality in Arunachal Pradesh through the lens of 'political corruption' and 'accumulation by corruption'. Dams in the Himalayan region of North East India have not only been projected as a solution to India's growing hunger for energy but also as the cornerstone of the 'Look East' neoliberal development strategy for the region. Apart from the questions of the ecological, economic and social desirability of such dams, Mishra reveals a new scale of hydro-criminal corruption and theft from both the state and collectively-owned tribal resources – involving several levels of politicians, bureaucrats and corporate houses interested in profit from these dams. The already nuanced and distinctive politics of this sparsely populated but culturally diverse border state (involving the politics of multi-layered citizenship, the politics of ethnicity, the politics of militarisation and the party politics of fraudulent and corrupt financial transfers from the centre to the state) is being enhanced and made even more complicated by the party-politicised politics of hydro-business.

In Chapter 5, on crime and politics in spectrum 'markets', Jai Bhatia charts the spectacularly large, rapid and corrupt expansion of telecom. As well as being socially transformative, telecom services are now a significant part of GDP and of the Indian state's non-tax revenue. While spectrum is a publicly owned natural resource, the telecom sector it energises is increasingly dominated by a corporate oligopoly at the commanding heights of the economy. Bhatia shows how the state enables the consolidation of capital in spectrum through a menu of preferential policies: pro-business licensing, state-directed credit to telecoms and consumers, tax breaks, subsidies, incentives for mergers and acquisitions, regular bailouts when telecoms are over-leveraged and loopholes for inflationary business valuations. She examines the embedded conflicts of interest leading to regulatory capture and extensive criminal behaviour. The latter includes insider information, queue jumping and discretionary allocations, retrospective/ad hoc policy changes and unpunished violations, neglect of enforcement, endemic corruption and in-kind favours. Both major parties and their coalitions have benefitted from this criminal structure, as does a proliferating system of intermediaries who aid the negotiation of post-election allegiances. Despite occasional individual scapegoats, a systemic complicity underlies large-scale and expanding capital accumulation by business and the political elite: campaign finance in return for regulatory and financial privileges, the movement into politics of corporate barons – with egregious conflicts of interest – and the graduation from politics to politics-plus-business of the political/bureaucratic families involved.

Bhatia's analysis shows how neoliberal market ideology and infrastructure is manipulated to legitimise the systemic plunder of bands of airwaves by a nexus fusing capital with political and bureaucratic elites. Vast losses to the exchequer result. Resistance comes from a variety of state institutions of regulation and enforcement – plus certain critical media outlets – but prosecution and sentencing are unusual and bail is often deployed to avoid hard punishment.

***

The six case studies grounded in anthropological analysis and/or ethnographic material further reveal how criminal economies are embedded in everyday life, how they are legitimised or de-legitimised, how they are deeply connected with caste/community and kinship networks and how political bosses, the police and the manipulation of the law create and shape 'Wild East' capitalist forms of venture. They show on the one hand how part of the criminal economy spills into economies of favour and patronage at the very local level, and on the other how they merge with 'organised crime'. To this end, in Chapter 6 Michelutti puts forward the concept of 'mafia assemblage' to encompass and analyse the fluid and yet not disorganised il/legal configurations that we all encountered in the field. As a composite concept, 'mafia assemblage' implies heterogeneous, contingent, unstable, partial and situated patterns as well as hierarchies and rules. This conceptualisation allows us to offer nuanced analyses that make sharp contrasts between 'old mafia' as discrete bounded entities and 'new mafias' as multi-network, faceless and fluid businesses.[30] The six case studies also reveal the principal role of intimidation and blackmail rather than explicit raw violence to sustain local criminal political configurations. Bribes and intimidation are central to co-opting the police and the judiciary. The law is used to cover crimes, to intimidate, to abuse power and to facilitate extra-legal forms of accumulation. The manipulation of the law further challenges dichotomisation such as informal versus formal governance and the view that 'mafias' are organisations that control social and economic flows outside the realm of the state. In addition, the criminal economies presented in the case studies reflect predatory, parochial and self-interested forms of accumulation that mirror social and cultural changes and aspirations in contemporary South Asia. Extra-legal forms of accumulation are deeply embedded in society, but 'being part of society' does not mean that they should be viewed as part of an 'anti-economic moral economy' à la Thompson (1993) or Scott (1976). On the contrary, 'immoralities', violent appropriations and the manipulation of the law are integral to social relations. Mafia 'democratic' forms of governance are based on relational modes of power and economic accumulation. Such collusions are illustrated throughout the six anthropological chapters.

More specifically, Chapter 6 explores the linkages between sand and oil mafias, caste and politics in Western Uttar Pradesh and bordering areas. Ethnographically, Michelutti scrutinises the criminal markets and the regimes of mafia governance that sand and oil help generate locally and regionally; analytically – as mentioned above – she puts forward the concept of 'mafia assemblage'. She shows how such il/legal arrangements criss-cross internal state boundaries and political constituencies across Uttar Pradesh, Rajasthan, Haryana, Madhya Pradesh and Delhi. There is a great deal of literature that looks at transnational illegal economies, at the globalisation of crime and ultimately at border areas as places where the state fails to rule efficiently (Van Schendel and Abraham 2005). Yet, this chapter shows how 'the rule of gangsters' is not only a prerogative of marginal and unconquered 'border areas'. It highlights how inter-state border areas are profitable business hubs and centres of criminal capital accumulation, as well as safe havens of impunity for the politicians involved in the businesses.

In Chapter 7, David Picherit develops these dynamics by looking at the criminal economy of 'red sanders' timber; its linkages and fusion with Telangana politics, caste factionalism and global networks that spill into the Middle East, Mauritius and China. Picherit maps out how local criminal economies shift and adapt to the changes informed by electoral democracy. Today the management and running of the red sanders timber business is in the hands of the locally elected MLA. In short, electoral democracy determines who the red sanders mafia 'boss' is. Such leadership then follows the temporalities and contingencies of elections. Picherit illustrates these cycles through the creation of the new Telangana state – carved out from Andhra Pradesh in 2014. Having traced the continuum between informal, legal and criminal economies, he describes how red sanders smuggling relies on recruiting cheap seasonal inter-state labour migrants, is organised through various layers of middlemen and subcontractors, requires political support, muscle and money, and above all depends on political power to control both labour and the actual implementation of legislation. The chapter further reflects the importance of the socio-cultural context in the red sanders trade by discussing the mobilisation of the regional heroic Robin Hood figures like the now mythical Veerappan. Finally, Picherit stresses (as do many chapter authors in this volume) the huge uncertainties and competitiveness that fuel the making and unmaking of fortunes and careers in the Wild East.

In Chapter 8, Tone Sissener explores the exploitation of another natural resource: land. Sissener shows that the justice system is deeply bounded in the politics, crime and business nexus. More specifically she investigates Kolkata's real estate 'mafias' and discusses the relation between organised crime and local municipal authorities on the one hand and the manipulation of the laws surrounding title and tenure on the other. Legal battles, with near endless appeal processes, can easily drag on for decades, making room for illegal enterprises ('the syndicates') to offer quick and favourable extra-legal or criminal settlements. The micro-politics of such 'syndicates' are studied against the backdrop of West Bengal's 'Mastan (enforcer/thug) raj'. The chapter highlights the networks of business, crime and politics that land acquisition entails and uses the concept of 'blurred boundaries' to tease out the overlap between formal/informal and legal/illegal.

This discussion is further developed by Nicolas Martin in the following chapter (Chapter 9), where he describes land grabbing in the context of urban and rural Punjab. Over the last decade, both academics and journalists have noted the growing link between politics, business and crime in this northern state. Martin focusses on the relation between the 'land mafias' and party politics and uses the concept of 'political society' to tease out his ethnography. The chapter casts a critical eye over the routinised and small-scale encroachment of village communal land in a rural Punjab district. While most literature on land grabs focusses on large-scale state-led land grabs and mass displacement, Martin shows that the latter are not the only forms of land appropriation leading to accumulation. Further, the dynamics around land grabbing described by Martin bear the imprint of political meddling. This feeds the needs for electoral mobilisation as well as the compulsions of capital accumulation. Martin's case studies reveal how politicians often help farmers to continue occupying village common lands illegally, doing so for electoral gains not necessarily consistent with the logic of 'the market' and of capital. So, what Martin describes is a 'political crime', as the perpetrators seem to be motivated by political motives rather than financial ones, though in the long run such arrangements indirectly tend to benefit relatively well-off Jat farmers at the expense of Dalits. They benefit the most well-off farmers disproportionately. Importantly, Martin's granular ethnography shows how the land grabbers are the local president of the Youth Akali Dal (the ruling party at the time of the study) and a village *Sarpanch*.[31] Thus, two figures of public authority are the main runners of the micro-level land racket.

Chapter 10 moves the analysis of the criminal economy to Bangladesh. Arild Ruud explores the legal and illegal relations between business and politics and their entanglement in the provincial town of Barisal. This chapter maps ethnographically how il/legal economies, money and politics run hand in hand in this town and how in recent years such arrangements have allowed a non-violent 'political-criminal life' to develop. But the drop in violence should not be taken as a sign of the state's strength – as is often understood in the policy world – but on the contrary as an illustration of how criminal economic and political configurations produce security and 'order' alongside violence (Gayer 2014; Arias 2016). Ruud's chapter also restates the complexity of legal and formal procedures that surround local Wild East forms of criminal political economies. Without law, crime does not pay. The complex contract and tender system he describes is marked by rules and counter-rules whose manipulation helps to cover, hide and camouflage illegal activity.

Finally Chapter 11, set in Karachi, shows again how connivance with the justice system is at the heart of criminal economies. Gayer further explores the role of the law and the issues of order and disorder in this part of Pakistan. The chapter maps out a set of systematic and brutal violations against industrial labour in the local textile industry and its intersections with the local 'real-estate mafia' and related protection rackets. Through judicial sources and the ethnography of a trial, he unravels Karachi's 'irregular' industrial capitalism as a system resorting intensively to a range of illegal practices without fully evading legal norms and the regulatory action of the courts. Rather than by its outwardly criminal nature, this mode of organisation of the economy is thus characterised by its uneven relationship with the law.

* * *

From the varied analyses in political economy and anthropology reported in the 11 chapters, from different regions, sectors of the economy and theoretical/conceptual perspectives, Wild East criminal economies and their 'mafias' emerge as 'a normal facet of capitalism, no more outside its political economy than the other capitalisms to which we add such qualifiers as "merchant," "industrial," "finance," "proto," or "crony"' (Schneider and Schneider 2011). Scholarly debate distinguishes primary accumulation from capitalist accumulation (Perelman 2001); the first entails a dual process involving on the one hand the seizure of resources prior to their productive investment, and on the other the dispossession of labour. The second is marked by the productive creation and appropriation of value by capital from labour alongside its productive re-investment. The first is associated with transition and the second with mature capitalism; however, in the 'Wild East' they co-exist in a system. This system is deeply intertwined with the state and often is the state itself. For example, in the criminal economy of coal, land and the minerals under it have been seized by state-corporates, depriving owners of anything but coal scavenging or wage-work, while at the same time the occasional court case reveals vast and diversified capitalist portfolios accumulated in the criminal economy (Chapter 1). In the Epilogue, Harriss-White examines the interconnectedness of the case studies and engages with the implications of the Wild East's normalised predatory 'system' for the economy, 'the rule of law', democracy and governance at large.

Notes

1. The authors share equal responsibility for the chapter and are listed in alphabetical order.
2. Recent ethnographies of *intreccio* and other variegated forms of sovereignty as in 'criminal governance' and the 'hybrid state' – in Latin America (Rodgers 2006, Jaffe 2013), the 'sistema' in Russia (Volkov 2002; Ledeneva 2013), and comparable situations in East Asia (Wilson 2015) and Africa (Lund 2006) – show how criminal (and violent) political configurations are often not simple entanglements of 'criminalised nexuses' or 'networks' or 'parallel states'. Rather, they are systems of political economic governance in their own right where criminals, business officials and politicians work together to create an environment that fits their needs.
3. As in Carothers 1998.
4. At the macro level, the economy suffers losses through the removal and/or unintended uses of financial and material resources. At the micro level, enterprises that are victims of economic crime see their business disrupted, and incur additional costs relating to monitoring, detection, preventative measures, fines, fees and reputational damage (PricewaterhouseCoopers 2016).
5. This has been measured innovatively with satellite photographs of light pollution, to avoid problems with existing data and inappropriate spatial classifications.
6. This does not mean that activity does not take place 'as if' laws were enforceable (Olsen and Morgan 2010).
7. For a recent overview of this literature, see the volume edited by Rao and Dube (2013).
8. For explorations of the growing nexus between crime and politics in India see also Sanchez (2016); Vaishnav (2017); Jeffrey (2010); Witsoe (2009); Jaffrelot (2002).
9. See also Brass (1997); Hansen (2001); Berenschot (2011); Gayer (2014).

10. Jha (2013) identifies a third route to fundraising consolidating predatory politics, the 'Antulay' route, involving the creation of private 'trusts' irrigated by fees for allocations of state resources of various kinds. Discovered and noted, punished but then rehabilitated in the form of the discretionary quota of development funds for elected politicians, unmonitored, and intended for distributive objectives, this official patronage resource is actually a base for private wealth appropriation by politicians.
11. On the AAP party and movement see Wyatt (2015).
12. For a summary of recent cases of murder by 'resisters' see Sharan (2012).
13. The repertoire of such crime involves practices of primitive accumulation alongside capitalist accumulation (Adnan 2013). The former requires resource seizure (not only land, but water, energy sources and minerals) together with labour displacement and eviction. The latter includes the elimination of competition (between market and state, sectors, scales, regions, castes, etc.), the protection of monopoly rents, preferential allocations of resources (through subsidies, physical infrastructure, learning rents, etc.), under-pricing of resources (especially of wage labour), the use of force and threat, tax evasion and capital flight, the sabotage, capture and distortion of policy, and the evasion of (enforcement of) regulations (for commodity and financial transactions, for environmental and labour protection, for the control of licences). It also includes control over means of redistribution. Practices include relations of clientelism, direct entry to politics, politicised organisation of election logistics, bribery, fraud, coercion and physical violence.
14. UPA-2, the second term in the twenty-first century of the United Progressive Alliance, dominated by the Congress party, was in power in central government from 2009 to 2014.
15. According to Singh (2009), while there were 128 MPs with criminal charges against them in the Lok Sabha in 2004 (24 per cent of the total), after the following election in 2009, the number had increased by 17 per cent to 150 MPs (30 per cent of the total) for which there were 429 cases pending – indicating cases involving *multiple crimes*. After the 2014 election, the proportion rose to 34 per cent (186 MPs). The trend for MPs facing serious criminal charges is starker, moving from 55 MPs charged with 302 serious cases in 2004 to 72 charged with 412 cases in 2009 (a 31 per cent increase) and to 112 in 2014 (a further 50 per cent increase) – indicating an increased concentration of multiple criminal cases (*First Post* 2014). In 2014, a total of 1,581 legislators in central and state governments faced prosecution in 13,500 cases.
16. See http://adrindia.org/content/lok-sabha-elections-2014 (accessed on 26 April 2019). Of course it is countered that accusations of crime-committing is part of the regular political to and fro, so such crimes are fabricated but with immunity extending during and often 'informally' after the period of office and with a minuscule proportion being successfully pursued (for example three in 2014, and one in 2017 (https://en.wikipedia.org/wiki/Disqualification_of_convicted_representatives_in_India (accessed 26 April 2019))), it is difficult to accept this argument.
17. See 'Criminals in Politics: India'. http://indpaedia.com/ind/index.php/Criminals_in_politics:_India (accessed 26 April 2019).
18. One *crore* is 10 million. As of 2018, INR 1 *crore* (cr) = US$ 154,000/£110,000.
19. In India informality accounts for about 60 per cent of GDP, and 84 per cent of non-agricultural employment; in Europe 20 per cent and 11–30 per cent respectively; in China approximately 40 per cent and 50 per cent, and in South Africa 25 per cent and 30 per cent (Medina, Jonelis and Cangul 2017; ILO 2018).
20. According to data from the Economic Censuses of 1990, 1998 and 2005 (see Harriss-White 2012).
21. The black and criminal economy also generates large-scale capital flight and money laundering worldwide (Global Financial Integrity 2017), compromising the capacity of the complicit political and economic elites to counter these practices (Srinivasan 2007, 2015).
22. See Harriss-White (2017a) for details.
23. See Chowdhury (2013); see also Jahan (2014).
24. In 2016, these figures were also used by the finance minister A.M.A. Muhith in one of his speeches. See BDNews Staff Correspondent (2014).
25. For discussion on the overlaps between different 'economies' see Roy (1996); Kanbur (2009).
26. For the relation between black money and election campaigns see Vaishnav (2017); on democracy and bossism see Sidel (1999).

27. Comaroff and Comaroff (2006; 2016); Heyman (1999); Roitman (2004) and Van Schendel and Abraham (2005); Auyero, Bourgois and Scheper-Hughes (2015).
28. Michelutti, Picherit, Ruud and Gayer build on a body of data collected over the course of several years. Martin and Sissener conducted fieldwork respectively in Punjab and West Bengal for 15 months and built on their previous research in Pakistan and Bangladesh.
29. Workshops were held in Zurich, 25 July 2014; Cambridge, 4–6 September 2014; Oxford, 10–12 December 2014; Arundel, June 2015; Oxford, July 2016 and Paris, December 2016.
30. For a discussion see Paoli (2014).
31. A *Sarpanch* is a village *panchayat* head.

References

Adnan, S. 2013. 'Land Grabs and Primitive Accumulation in Deltaic Bangladesh: Interactions between Neoliberal Globalization, State Interventions, Power Relations and Peasant Resistance', *Journal of Peasant Studies*, 40(1): 87–128.

Anderson, T. and P. Hill. 1979. 'The American Experiment in Anarcho-Capitalism: The *Not* So Wild, Wild West', *Journal of Libertarian Studies* 3(1): 9–29.

Arias, E.D. 2016. *Criminal Enterprises and Governance in Latin America and the Caribbean*. Cambridge: Cambridge University Press.

Arlacci, P. 1993. *Men of Dishonor. Inside the Sicilian Mafia*. New York: William Morrow.

Armao, F. 2000. *Il sistema Mafia. Dall'economia-mondo al dominio locale*. Torino: Bollati Boringhieri.

Armao, F. 2015. 'Mafia-owned-democracies. Italy and Mexico as Patterns of Criminal Neoliberalism', *Revista de Historia Actual*, 1: 4–21.

Association for Democratic Reform. 2014. *Analysis of Criminal Background, Financial, Education, Gender and Other Details of Winners*. New Delhi. http://adrindia.org/sites/default/files/Odisha_Winners_Analysis_of_Criminal_and_Financial_background_details_winners_in_Assembly_Elections_2014.pdf (accessed 17 April 2019).

Auyero, J., P. Bourgois and N. Scheper-Hughes, eds. 2015. *Violence at the Urban Margins*. New York: Oxford University Press.

Baker, E. 1990. 'The Primitive Accumulation of Capital in the United States', *Iskra*, 1(1): 1–14.

Bardhan, P. 1984. *Political Economy of Development in India*. Delhi: Oxford University Press.

Bardhan, P. 1988. 'The Dominant Proprietary Classes and India's Democracy', in *India's Democracy: An Analysis of Changing State Society Relations*, edited by A. Kohli. Princeton, NJ: Princeton University Press.

BDNews Staff Correspondent. 2014. 'Black Money on the Rise: Muhith', *BDNEWS 24*, 8 April. http://bdnews24.com/economy/2014/04/08/black-money-on-the-rise-muhith (accessed 8 November 2015).

Ben-Yehoyada, N. 2018. 'Where Do We Go When We Follow the Money? The Political-economic Construction of Antimafia Investigators in Western Sicily', *History and Anthropology* 29(3): 359–75.

Berenschot, W. 2011. 'On the Usefulness of Goondas in Indian Politics: "Moneypower" and "Musclepower" in a Gujarati Locality', *South Asia: Journal of South Asian Studies*, 34(2): 255–75.

Blok, A. 1974. *The Mafia of a Sicilian Village, 1860–1960: A Study of Violent Peasant Entrepreneurs*. New York: Harper & Row.

Blom, A. 2011. 'Pakistan: Coercion and capital in an insecurity state', *Paris Papers*. Paris: Institut de Recherche Stratégique de l'Ecole Militaire.

Brass, P. 1997. *Theft of an Idol: Text and Context in the Representation of Collective Violence*. Princeton, NJ: Princeton University Press.

Braudel, F. 1974. *Capitalism and Material Life, 1400–1800*. London: Harper and Row.

Briquet, J. and G. Favarel-Garrigues. 2010. *Organized Crime and States*. New York: Palgrave Macmillan.

Carothers, T. 1998. 'The Rule of Law Revival', *Foreign Affairs*, March–April 1998.

Chowdhury, F.A. 2013. 'Funding of Political Parties', *Daily Star* 13 October. http://www.thedailystar.net/news/funding-of-political-parties (accessed 22 January 2018).

Civico, A. 2015. *The Para-State: An Ethnography of Colombia's Death Squads*. Los Angeles, CA: University of California Press.

Comaroff, J. and J.L. Comaroff. 2006. *Law and Disorder in the Postcolony*. Chicago, IL: University of Chicago Press.

Comaroff, J. and J.L. Comaroff. 2016. *The Truth about Crime: Sovereignty, Knowledge and Social Order*. Chicago, IL: University of Chicago Press.

Comaroff, J. and J. Comaroff. 2018. 'Crime, Sovereignty and the State', St Antony's College, Oxford, 31 May.

Corbridge, S. and J. Harriss. 2000. *Reinventing India: Liberalization, Hindu Nationalism and Popular Democracy*. London: Polity Press/Blackwell.

Das Gupta, C. 2016. *State and Capital in Independent India: Institutions and Accumulation*. New Delhi: Cambridge University Press.

Dasgupta, R. 2014. *Capital: The Eruption of Delhi*. Delhi, London: Penguin Press.

Dasgupta, R. 2017. 'Delhi's "Regional" Capitalism', *Economic and Political Weekly* 52(46): 64–6.

Dietrich Wielenga, K. 2019. 'The Emergence of the Informal Sector: Labour Legislation and Politics in South India 1940–1960', *Modern Asian Studies*, forthcoming.

First Post. 2014. 'Elections 2014: 34% of Newly-elected MPs Have Criminal Cases Against Them', *First Post* 18 May, https://www.firstpost.com/politics/elections-2014-34-of-newly-elected-mps-have-criminal-cases-against-them-1531233.html (accessed 8 April 2019).

Gambetta, D. 1988. 'Mafia: The Price of Distrust', in *Trust: Making and Breaking Cooperative Relations*, edited by D. Gambetta, 158–75. Oxford: Basil Blackwell.

Gambetta, D. 1993. *The Sicilian Mafia: The Business of Private Protection*. Cambridge, MA: Harvard University Press.

Gardner, K. 1995. *Global Migrants, Local Lives: Travel and Transformation in Rural Bangladesh*. Oxford: Clarendon Press, Oxford Studies in Social and Cultural Anthropology.

Gardner, K. 2012. *Discordant Development: Global Capitalism and the Struggle for Connection in Bangladesh*. London: Pluto Press.

Gayer, L. 2014. *Karachi. Ordered Disorder and the Struggle for the City*. London, Delhi, New York, Karachi: Hurst, HarperCollins, Oxford University Press.

Global Financial Integrity. 2017. *Illicit Financial Flows to and from Developing Countries: 2005–2014*. Washington, DC: Global Financial Integrity.

Goffman, A. 2014. *On the Run: Fugitive Life in an American City*. Chicago, IL: University of Chicago Press.

Gupta, A. 1995. 'Blurred Boundaries: The Discourse of Corruption, the Culture of Politics, and the Imagined State', *American Ethnologist* 22(2): 375–402.

Hamalainen, P. 2009. *The Comanche Empire*. New Haven, CT: Yale University Press.

Hansen, T.B. 2001. *Wages of Violence: Naming and Identity in Postcolonial Bombay*. Princeton, NJ: Princeton University Press.

Harriss, J. 1982. 'Character of an Urban Economy: "Small-Scale" Production and Labour Markets in Coimbatore', *Economic and Political Weekly* 17(24): 993–1002.

Harriss-White, B. 1993. 'Collective Politics of Foodgrains Markets in South Asia', *Bulletin of the Institute of Development Studies* 24(3): 54–63.

Harriss-White, B., ed. 1999. *Agricultural Markets from Theory to Practice*. Basingstoke: Macmillan.

Harriss-White, B. 2003. *India Working: Essays on Society and Economy*. Cambridge: Cambridge University Press.

Harriss-White, B. 2012. 'Capitalism and the Common Man', *Agrarian South: Journal of Political Economy* 1(2): 109–60.

Harriss-White, B. 2014. 'Labour and Petty Production', *Development and Change* 45(5): 981–1000.

Harriss-White, B., ed. 2015. *Middle India and Urban-Rural Development: Four Decades of Change*. New Delhi: Springer.

Harriss-White, B. 2017a. 'On Demonetisation', *MACROSCAN*, January. http://www.macroscan.org/dem/jan17/dem16012017Barbara_Harriss_White.htm (accessed 8 April 2019).

Harriss-White, B. 2017b. 'Constructing Regions Inside the Nation: The Economic and Social Structure of Space in Agrarian and Cultural Regions', *Economic and Political Weekly* 18 52 (46, 18 November): 44–55.

Harriss-White, B., E. Basile, A. Dixit, P. Joddar, A. Prakash and K. Vidyarthee. 2014. *Dalits and Adivasis in India's Business Economy: Three Essays and an Atlas*. New Delhi: Three Essays Press.

Hazen, J. and D. Rodgers, eds. 2014. *Global Gangs: Street Violence Across the World*. Minneapolis, MN: University of Minnesota Press.

Heyman, J. 1999. *States and Illegal Practices*. Oxford: Berg.

Hoque, A. and L. Michelutti. 2018. 'Brushing with Organized Crime and Democracy: The Art of Making Do in South Asia', *Journal of Asian Studies* 77(4): 991–1011. doi:10.1017/S0021911818000955.

International Labour Office (ILO). 2018. 'Women and Men in the Informal Economy: A Statistical Picture'. 3rd edition. Geneva: ILO Web PDF.

Jaffe, R. 2013. 'The Hybrid State: Crime and Citizenship in Urban Jamaica', *American Ethnologist* 40(4): 734–48.

Jaffrelot, C. 2002. 'Indian Democracy: The Rule of Law on Trial', *India Review* 1(1): 77–121.

Jahan, R. 2005. *Bangladesh Politics: Problems and Issues*. Dhaka: University Press Limited.

Jahan, R. 2014. 'Political Parties in Bangladesh', CPD-CMI Working Paper series WP 2014:8. Dhaka: Centre for Policy Dialogue (CPD) and Chr. Michelsen Institute (CMI). https://www.cmi.no/publications/5229-political-parties-in-bangladesh (accessed 22 January 2018).

Jahan, R. 2015. 'The Parliament of Bangladesh: Representation and Accountability', *Journal of Legislative Studies* 21(2): 250–69.

Jalal, A. 1995. *Democracy and Authoritarianism in South Asia: A Comparative and Historical Perspective*. Cambridge: Cambridge University Press.

Jeffrey, C. 2010. *Timepass: Youth, Class, and the Politics of Waiting in India*. Stanford, CA: Stanford University Press.

Jeffrey, C., P. Jeffery and R. Jeffery, eds. 2008. *Degrees Without Freedom? Education, Masculinities and Unemployment in North India*. Stanford, CA: Stanford University Press.

Jewitt, S. 2008. 'Political Ecology of Jharkhand Conflicts', *Asia Pacific Viewpoint* 49(1): 68–82.

Jha, P.S. 1980. *India: A Political Economy of Stagnation*. New Delhi: Oxford University Press.

Jha, P.S. 2013. *How did India Become a Predatory State?* Unpublished manuscript available via authors.

Kanbur, R. 2009. 'Conceptualizing Informality: Regulation and Enforcement', *Indian Journal of Labour Economics* 52(1): 33–42.

Kar, D. 2010. *The Drivers and Dynamics of Illicit Financial Flows from India: 1948–2008*. Washington, DC: Global Financial Integrity.

Khan, M.H. and K.S. Jomo, eds. 2001. *Rents, Rent-seeking and Economic Development: Theory and Evidence in Asia*. Cambridge: Cambridge University Press.

Kleemans, E.R. and M. Smit. 2014. 'Human Smuggling, Human Trafficking and Exploitation in the Sex Industry', in *The Oxford Handbook of Organized Crime*, edited by P. Paoli, 383–96. Oxford: Oxford University Press.

Kohli, A. 1991. *Democracy and Discontent. India's Growing Crisis of Governability*. Cambridge: Cambridge University Press.

Kumar, A. 1999. *The Black Economy in India*. Delhi: Penguin.

Kumar, A. 2014. *Criminalisation of Politics: Caste, Land and the State*. Delhi: Rawat Publications.

Lagarde, C. 2017. 'Stepping up the Fight against Money-Laundering and Terrorist Finance' IMF-Blog. Available at https://blogs.imf.org/2017/07/26/stepping-up-the-fight-against-money-laundering-and-terrorist-financing/.

Ledeneva, A. 2013. *Can Russia Modernise? Sistema, Power Networks and Informal Governance*. Cambridge: Cambridge University Press.

Levi, M. 2014. 'Organized Fraud', in *The Oxford Handbook of Organized Crime*, edited by P. Paoli, 464–72. Oxford: Oxford University Press.

Lewis, D. 2011. *Bangladesh: Politics, Economy, and Civil Society*. Cambridge: Cambridge University Press.

Lund, C. 2006. 'Twilight Institutions: An Introduction', *Development and Change* 37(4): 673–84.

Mallick, A. 2014. 'Class Politics in the Era of Neoliberalism: The Case of Karachi, Pakistan'. Master's thesis, York University.

Martin, N. and L. Michelutti. 2017. 'Protection Rackets and Party Machines. "Mafia Raj" Across Western Uttar Pradesh and Punjab', *Asian Journal of Social Science*, 45(6). Doi: https://doi.org/10.1163/15685314-04506005.

Marx, K. 1967. *Capital, Volume One*. New York: International Publishers Co.

Mazumdar, S. 2008. 'Crony Capitalism and India: Before and After Liberalization. Munich Personal RePec Archive'. *MPRA Paper 19627* http://mpra.ub.uni-muenchen.de/19627/

Medina, L., A. Jonelis and M. Cangul. 2017. 'The Informal Economy in Sub Saharan Africa: Sizes and Determinants'. IMF Working Paper 17/156. Washington: International Monetary Fund.

Michelutti, L., A. Hoque, N. Martin, D. Picherit, P. Rollier, A. Ruud and C. Still. 2018. *Mafia Raj: The Rule of Bosses in South Asia*. Stanford, CA: Stanford University Press.

Olsen, W. and J. Morgan. 2010. 'Institutional Change from within the Informal Sector in Indian Rural Labour Relations', *International Review of Sociology* 20(3): 533–53.

Pani, N. 2017. 'Experiential Regionalism and Political Processes in South India', *India Review* 16(3): 304–23.

Paoli, P. 2003. *Mafia Brotherhoods: Organized Crime, Italian Style*. Oxford: Oxford University Press.

Paoli, P. 2014. *The Oxford Handbook of Organized Crime*. Oxford: Oxford University Press.

Parry, J.P. 2000. 'The "Crisis of Corruption" and "the Idea of India": A Worm's Eye View', in *The Morals of Legitimacy*, edited by I. Pardo, 27–55. Oxford: Berghahn Books.

Perelman, M. 2001. *The Invention of Capitalism: Classical Political Economy and the Secret History of Primitive Accumulation*. Durham, NC: Duke University Press.

Pine, J. 2012. *The Art of Making Do in Naples*. Minneapolis, MN: University of Minnesota Press.

Prakash, N., M. Rockmore and Y. Uppal. 2016. 'Do Criminally Accused Politicians Affect Economic Outcomes? Evidence from India, Connecticut'. http://web2.uconn.edu/economics/working/2018-08.pdf (accessed 28 April 2019).

PricewaterhouseCoopers. 2016. *Global Economic Crime Survey*. https://www.pwc.com/gx/en/economic-crime-survey/pdf/GlobalEconomicCrimeSurvey2016.pdf (accessed 20 April 2019).

Rais, R. 1985. 'Elections in Pakistan', *Asian Affairs: An American Review* 12(3): 43–61.

Rajshekhar, M. 2014. 'Chandasi: Close to Narendra Modi's Varanasi Constituency Thrives Illegal Coal Market', *Economic Times*, 15 October. http://economictimes.indiatimes.com/news/politics-and-nation/chandasi-close-to-pm-narendra-modis-varanasis-constituency-thrives-illegal-coal-market/articleshow/44818649.cms (accessed 20 April 2019).

Rao, A. and S. Dube, eds. 2013. *Crime Through Time*. Delhi: Oxford University Press.

Rege, A. and A. Lavorgna. 2017. 'Organization, Operations, and Success of Environmental Organized Crime in Italy and India: A Comparative Analysis', *European Journal of Criminology* 14(2): 160–8.

Rodgers, D. 2006. 'Living in the Shadow of Death: Gangs, Violence and Social Order in Urban Nicaragua, 1996–2002', *Journal of Latin American Studies* 38(02): 267–89.

Roitman, J. 2004. *Fiscal Disobedience: An Anthropology of Economic Regulation in Central Africa*. Princeton, NJ: Princeton University Press.

Rollier, P. 2016. 'Vies de caïds et justice informelle à Lahore (Pakistan)', *L'Homme* 3: 219–20.

Rothbard, M. 2017. *The Progressive Era*. Auburn, AL: Mises Institute.

Roy, R. 1996. 'State Failure: Political-Fiscal Implications of the Black Economy', *Bulletin, Institute of Development Studies* 27(2): 22–31.

Ruud, A.E. 2014. 'The Political Bully in Bangladesh', in *Patronage as Politics in South Asia*, edited by A. Piliavsky, 303–25. Cambridge: Cambridge University Press.

Sanchez, A. 2016. *Criminal Capital: Violence, Corruption and Class in Industrial India*. Delhi: Routledge.

Schneider, J. 2018. 'Fifty Years of Mafia Corruption and Anti-mafia Reform', *Current Anthropology* 59(S18): S16–S27.

Schneider, J. and P. Schneider. 2011. 'The Mafia and Capitalism: An Emerging Paradigm', *Sociologica* 2: 1–22.

Scott, J.C. 1976. *The Moral Economy of the Peasant: Rebellion and Subsistence in Southeast Asia*. New Haven, CT: Yale University Press.

Shah, A., J. Lerche, R. Axelby, D. Benbabaali, B. Donegan, J. Raj and V. Thakur. 2017. *Ground Down by Growth: Tribe, Caste, Class and Inequality in 21st Century India*. London: Pluto Press.

Sharan, P. 2012. 'The New Mafia Raj', *Deccan Herald*, 17 March. http://www.deccanherald.com/content/235260/mafia-raj.html (accessed 22 January 2018).

Siddiqa, A. 2007. *Military Inc.: Inside Pakistan's Military Economy*. Karachi: Oxford University Press.

Sidel, J. 1999. *Capital, Coercion, and Crime: Bossism in the Philippines*. Stanford, CA: University of California Press.

Singh, S. 2009. *The Criminalisation of Politics in India: A Study of Politicians with Criminal records in the 15th Lok Sabha*. Bhopal: National Law Institute University.

Sinha, A. and B. Harriss-White, eds. 2007. *Trade Liberalisation and India's Informal Economy*. New Delhi: Oxford University Press.

Srinivasan, K. 2007. 'Money Laundering and Security', in *Controlling Arms and Terror in the Asia Pacific*, edited by M. Vicziany, 21–44. Northampton: Edward Elgar Publishing.

Srinivasan, K. 2015. 'Money Laundering and Capital Flight', in *Indian Capitalism in Development*, edited by B. Harriss-White and J. Heyer, 190–207. Abingdon: Routledge.

Standing, A. 2003. 'The Social Contradictions of Organised Crime on the Cape Flats'. ISS Paper 74, Pretoria: Institute for Security Studies.

Thompson, E.P. 1993. *Customs in Common: Studies in Traditional Popular Culture*. New York: The New Press.

Tilly, C. 1985. 'War Making and State Making as Organised Crime', in *Bringing the State Back*, edited by P. Evans, D. Rueschemeyer and T. Skocpol, 169–91. Cambridge: Cambridge University Press.

Vaishnav, M. 2013. *Quid Pro Quo: Builders, Politicians, and Election Finance in India*. Center for Global Development Working Paper 276. http://www.cgdev.org/publication/quid-pro-quo-builders-politicians-and-election-finance-india-working-paper-276-updated (accessed 18 March 2016).

Vaishnav, M. 2017. *When Crime Pays: Money and Muscle in Indian Politics*. New Haven, CT: Yale University Press.

Van Schendel, W. and I. Abraham, eds. 2005. *Illicit Flows and Criminal Things. States, Borders, and the other Side of Criminal Things*. Bloomington, IN: Indiana University Press.

Van Solinge, T.B. 2014. 'The Illegal Exploitation of Natural Resources', in *The Oxford Handbook of Organized Crime*, edited by P. Paoli, 501–12. Oxford: Oxford University Press.

Varese, F. 2001. *The Russian Mafia: Private Protection in a New Market Economy*. Oxford: Oxford University Press.

Varese, F. 2011. *Organized Crime. Critical Concepts in Criminology*. Vol. 1. London: Routledge.

Vigh, H. 2015. 'Mobile Misfortune', *Culture Unbound: Journal of Current Cultural Research* 7: 233–53.

Visvanathan, S. and H. Sethi, eds. 1998. *Foul Play: Chronicles of Corruption 1947–97*. New Delhi: Banyan Books.

Volkov, V. 2002. *Violent Entrepreneurs: The Use of Force in the Making of Russian Capitalism*. Ithaca, NY: Cornell University Press.

Wade, R. 1985. 'The Market for Public Office: Why the Indian State is not Better at Development', *World Development* 13(4): 467–97.

Waseem, M. 1994. *The 1993 Elections in Pakistan*. Lahore: Vanguard Press.

Wilson, I.D. 2015. *The Politics of Protection Rackets in Post–New Order Indonesia: Coercive Capital, Authority and Street Politics*. London: Routledge.

Witsoe, J. 2009. 'Territorial Democracy: Caste, Dominance and Electoral Practice in Postcolonial India', *Political and Legal Anthropology Review* 32(1): 64–83.

Wyatt, A. 2015. 'Arvind Kejriwal's leadership of the Aam Aadmi Party', *Contemporary South Asia* 23(2): 67–180.

Zaidi, S.A. 2014. 'Different Governments, Same Problems: Pakistan's Economy 1999–2013', in *South Asia in Transition: Democracy, Political Economy and Security*, edited by B. Chakma, 109–26. London: Palgrave Macmillan.

1

The criminal economics and politics of black coal in Jharkhand, 2014

Nigel Singh and Barbara Harriss-White

In this chapter, an analysis of the implications of the criminal political economy for criminalised politics is developed. Probing the formally registered system for coal extraction and distribution alongside the differentiated, partially registered, segmented supply chains that have developed in response to widespread unlicensed demand and the need for coal for cooking, workshop energy and winter heating over much of North India, criminality is found to pervade the entire system. Throughout the length and breadth of this criminal assemblage, interlocked political and economic transactions entwine legal and illegal activity and accumulation assumes a great range of forms and scales. Dominated by a notorious coal mafia which has evolved atypically from a stranglehold over trade unions and mine labour, vast investment portfolios at the apex co-exist with extensive petty crime, generating returns barely covering subsistence. In a classic case of intreccio, *the economic power of the mafia, its caste-embedded battles for supremacy and its need for state and party-political power suggest that Jharkhand's distinctive politics of ethnic aspiration is very likely dwarfed by the tensions between the compulsions to unsettle and undermine countervailing politics to mafia supremacy and the compulsion to dominate local ruling and opposition parties.*

Introduction

The estimates are rough and vary widely but it seems that in the central Indian state of Jharkhand perhaps a quarter of the coal is mined, scavenged and traded illegally. Illegal coal has been framed by scholars either as a repository of poverty or as a generator of dangerous and unhealthy livelihoods in regions where there are few alternative work opportunities (Lahiri-Dutt 2007, 2014). The research reported in this chapter shows however how Jharkhand's highly differentiated il/legal coal economy is the source of immense criminal wealth dominated by a coal mafia which acts as a durable force destabilising and undermining the mainstream pro-tribal party politics of Jharkhand – a state where Scheduled Tribes form 27 per cent of the 2011 census population of 33 million.[1]

Field methods for black coal

Our research on illegal coal used the political economy field methods described in the Introduction to this book and covered conditions in 2013–14 in eight coal districts in Jharkhand, around Dhanbad, Ranchi and Hazaribagh (Singh 2014, 41), silence about which has been widely purchased by the coal mafia (Singh 2014, 30). Here this silence has been broken by gathering oblique but triangulated and positioned third-party narratives (evaluated on principles described in the book's Introduction) and by interviewing people well placed in certain businesses. The set of 45 informants that provided the field evidence used here was selected from among political party officials, labour politicians, officials in Coal India Ltd. and its subsidiaries, and representatives of the police, the law, journalism, academic research, landownership, and illegal and informal trade itself. They are listed in Appendix 1.1 on page 62. Despite this multi-sited, multi-level approach to fieldwork, major problems result from applying this method to economic intelligence. While information about relations and processes may be gathered and cross-checked, systematic evidence about assets, income, costs and returns is impossible to come by.

The social organisation of Jharkhand's illegal coal economy

To build a political analysis of Jharkhand's coal economy, first a model of its social organisation must be created. This is an exploratory exercise that suggests greater clarity on paper than the messy, unstable and unclear relations on the ground – which Michelutti and Harriss-White term an 'assemblage' in the book's Introduction. Three sets of extractive supply chain relations can be distinguished according to their regulatory status and forms of control: first, formal (state owned and/or regulated) activity; second, illegal supply (which breaks the laws by which the economy is governed); third, activity that is distinct from illegal activity due to its being informal, i.e. work either that the state does not require to be regulated or that is below a threshold for regulation or (more controversially) where state regulation exists but is not enforced (Kanbur, Lahiri and Svejnar 2012). However, much of the time, informal and illegal activities are sufficiently enmeshed as to be practically indistinguishable.

The formal organisation of coal (FC)

Even in an era recognised as neoliberal (Chatterjee and McCartney 2019), much of the FC structure consists of a large and complex set of very powerful state corporations operating under several ministries (Singh 2014, 30). First and foremost, Coal India Ltd. (CIL) dominates the local economy but is in turn regulated and formally dominated by the Ministry of Coal. Second comes Indian Railways under the Ministry of Rail, which freights vast quantities of coal throughout the country. Third is a set of state corporate subsidiaries of CIL, notably Bharat Coking Coal Ltd. (BCCL), Eastern Coal Ltd. (ECL) and Central Coalfields Ltd. (CCL). Central government public corporations are supplemented by agencies of the Jharkhand state: the Jharkhand Mining Authority (JMA) and the State Highways Department (responsible for monitoring volumes and quality through the system of check-posts). Then, major private sector entities are also formally registered and regulated: first, private coal companies (e.g. Tata) subcontracted to public corporations. Subcontracting is thought to account for an estimated 70 to 80 per cent of CIL's production. Then come heavy industrial companies with captive coal mines (e.g. Jindal). In both types of private enterprise, tight security discourages illegal scavenging.

In principle, the labour forces of these public and private entities are also formally registered and regulated. In practice, as the *Sanhati* (2011) report describes:

> In the mining areas re-composition of the working class through migration, "uneven development" and technological attacks is a constant process. We can see in a very concentrated local space and time struggles "within a proletariat" which represent the main lines of segmentation of the global working class today. The proletariat in Dhanbad has many faces: the pauperised Adivasi ("indigenous") and "rural poor" population at the fringes of the mining areas – the main base for the Maoist armed insurrection; the village workers in the "illegal mines"; the casualised workers in the main mines earning 10 per cent of their permanent workmates; the unemployed sons and daughters of local peasants and permanent workers organised in an "unemployed movement". As a whole the local workforce is under-layered by various waves of migration since the nineteenth century.

Labour unions – national and local – operate in both public and private mines. They also bridge the formal and the illegal subsystems. In some private mines, the labour force is reported to be much more complicit with management than those in CIL-operated mines because leaders are privately rewarded to deter the coal mafia control that characterises the public sector labour process. In other private mines, unions are reported to be privately complicit with management over shared returns to leaked IC while publicly antagonistic to management. This results not only from class contradictions but because management is casualising the labour force, subcontracting the operation of mines and attacking the rights of labour. In practice, throughout FC, the economic security of and the returns to labour are being eroded.

The social organisation of illegal coal (IC)

The illegal economy is 'very substantial', accounting for an estimated 300,000 livelihoods in the eight IC districts (Singh 2014, 5), of which up to 100,000 are minors (Cantera 2015). Other estimates of the material size of the IC economy vary according to the interests involved. While 'officially' in the eyes of the state corporate sector IC accounts for about 5 per cent of CIL's production – i.e. 23 million tonnes of an annual national total of 450 million tonnes (*Firstpost* 2014),[2] a local police estimate for Jharkhand alone is 20–50 per cent. This, when Jharkhand's production is 60 million tonnes, will be anywhere between 12 and 30 million tonnes, and illegal coal will be much more if scaled to the national level. The IC sub-sector is both stratified and segmented between supply chain assemblages in which there is an inverse relation between the strata and aggregate gross output (high at the top) and the number of firms (few at the top). Four distinctive scales of operation forge specific kinds of assemblages.

First, coal cycle wallahs (CCW), an estimated 48,000 in Jharkhand (Singh n.d.), are drawn mainly from the foot of the pyramid of social status: Scheduled Castes and Tribes (SCs and STs) and Other Backward Castes (OBCs). The skills of illegal coal require 'learning by doing'. Individuals or informal village-based groups of up to 10 people scavenge or steal from abandoned or active mines, from washeries, lorries and 'rakes'/'racks' – lines of railway wagons. They thrive on public sector mines and avoid privately owned or subcontracted and managed ones, repelled by their security forces (Singh 2014, 59–60). They may dump, wash and/or coke their coal and then transport it to local destinations. Demand for their commodities comes from small local workshop industries (e.g. brick kilns, sponge iron plants, yarn dye-ing), which cannot obtain coal for power through an official supply chain, and from domestic users. Though very small in scale, this is ille-gal rather than informal because supply is unlawfully scavenged from abandoned mines or stolen from public sector units, mostly with the complicity of unions.

Own-account enterprise is a deceptively simple form of produc-tion masking a range of work relations. Commonly operating on a logic of survival, in which income rather than profit is maximised, CCW are independent workers: for the most part, even in groups, they are non-accumulating petty producers. However, while more or less economically independent, some are politically regulated by being members of syndi-cates. There, working on money advances, they may be wage-labour in a 'formal' disguise; and when paid by syndicates they are outright, 'real' wage workers (Banaji 1977).

Second, syndicates themselves are groups of 10–20 'goons' (Singh 2014, 9) who bulk stolen coal from the CCW workforce and also organ-ise larger-scale transport. A colour-coded chit system denoting the status of bribes is monitored by check-post guards en route.[3] In the twenty-first century they have become increasingly more numerous and well organised and may occasionally have visible fixed assets, e.g. motorcycles to pull the heavily laden bikes of 'client' CCWs uphill, or JCBs and trucks to rent out. Most of their business is also local, but increasingly the syndicates' illegal coal – as with coal trade and mafia coal – makes its way from Jharkhand through Bihar to the largest (infor-mal) coal market in Asia at Chandasi, outside Varanasi in Uttar Pradesh (UP) (Rajshekhar 2014).

Third, coal traders (CT) engage in larger-scale theft, often deliber-ately to supplement the profits of their legitimate businesses. Sometimes known as the 'small mafia', they also use the chits described above to divert trucks and coordinate with check-post guards. Supplying small industries that are either unable to access FC due to the priority given to power stations and/or evading rationing, and are therefore forced to purchase unrationed coal, these illegal markets are the creatures of the state's incomplete management of coal distribution.

At the apex, the coal mafia numbers 24 households, the most important being long-settled Rajput 'Singh' migrants from UP and Bihar (see Chapter 6 for the Rajput-dominated mafia in UP). While using the Indian term 'mafia', the coal mafia differ from many other kinds of Indian mafia through their investments in productive activ-ity, their dealing illegally in a legal commodity and their origins in the control of the labour force (discussed below). Their knowledge and skills are transmitted tacitly within the family – combining a profit-maximising logic with that of political power. Illegal coal is sometimes a supplement to legitimate business, such as labour contracting, union control, transport for large development projects or regulated coal trading. Illegal coal can also supplement other illegitimate business: sand, for example, which should be stored in mines to protect it from fire and subsidence but in fact is often traded (see Gupta 2013 and Chapter 2), or drinking water carried from Bihar. The largest 'mafia' are substantial criminal organisations under patriarchal management with labour forces numbering thousands and with a highly developed division of tasks, including specialised protection and internal surveil-lance (Singh 2014, 18 and 42–43).[4] Their activities include extortion through threats of labour unrest, forgery of documents with fake ori-gins and destinations for commodity transactions, and the manipula-tion of auctions. The large mafia houses have visible fixed assets and a monopoly of violence over their territories, along with more or less stable truces over spatial territory, rail rakes, road transport and the control of smaller CT and syndicates, punctuated by battles for power with occasional assassinations.[5]

A great coal mafia family, if not specialising in labour politics, will have a branch devoted to union leadership – perhaps even leadership of several labour unions. Whether or not from the mafia, union leaders liaise with CIL, politicians and officials to trade IC. Coal labour union leaders can also be found as directly elected MPs. A 'handful' of private mines are reliably reported as using funds from profits that are dedicated to 'com-munity development' or 'corporate social responsibility' to pay off union mafia from challenging their security system, interfering in the labour process and diverting or stealing coal (Singh 2014, 66). This union route to mafia power is one of the outcomes of politicians' need for votes. CCWs and syndicates break section 414 of the IPC when transporting coal by bike; they break the Coal Mines Act when stealing from a mine and the Indian Forest Act when exporting illegal coal from forests. Many more regulatory acts, including all the labour laws, are flouted by CTs and the coal mafia which scale up crime involving large-scale theft, tax fraud, assault and murder (see Gupta, Chapter 2).

The IC economy also includes sectors which exist only on paper, as fake companies/mines and factories, or exist as other derived mar-kets and productive sectors that would have no raison d'être otherwise. Bribes, for instance, in which there is a market especially in state-owned companies, relate the size of regular 'commissions' to the scale of illegal operations. Markets exist for equipment (for cycles and their fortification), document forgers, the supply of diggers and trucks (sometimes moonlighting from CIL), illegal processing (washing and coking), the adulteration of coal, and for brokerage and intermediation for retail demand on whatever scale. Transactions between the syndicates and CT and between police and politicians generate livelihoods through brokerage. Money-lending agents mediate between the Chief Minister (CM) and CCWs; political touts and money carriers earn their living by arranging political deals, and organisers of immunity mediate protection services and their labour forces. In addition, other elements of the state are drawn into the making and distribution of rents from IC. These are alleged to include officials in regulating departments, revenue and commercial taxes departments, check-post/weighbridge operators, the police hierarchy – from Inspectors General and their deputies and superintendents downwards – ultimately reporting to the Jharkhand State Home Affairs Ministry. A given station may have officers in the pay of several mafias, CTs or syndicates: mafia-money power is reported to override formal rank and status inside the police force (Singh 2014, 47). The judicial and political apparatuses at local, state and national level are not above taking rents from IC. Nor are interests inside the apparatus of public corporations: for example, managers in CIL and state corporations, Indian Railways officials and union leaders – the leadership of unions 'recognised' by CIL as having common interests with management. Last but not least, the parallel, formally outlawed political structures of the Maoist Communist Party, classified as terrorists in 2009, profit from both 'providing legitimate protection' and the policing of illegal compliance (Thakur 2009).

Comments

We can see from this summary of the social organisation of IC, first, that the illegality and the social reach of IC are both extensive. FC and IC are knitted together in a nexus of 'interlocked transactions'. These are not necessarily the classical interlocked contracts in which a single contract binds conditions on two or more markets, e.g. money, labour and the marketed surplus (Subramanian 1992); rather they are a set of linked political obligations, contracts, payments and cooperative/complicit behaviour without which the IC sector would not work, yet which structure highly differentiated returns (Singh 2014, 10–12). For an example of large-scale theft, this system of interlocked transactions may be stylised (inexhaustively) as in Box 1.1

Box 1.1 The system of interlocked transactions in black coal

- The federal Ministry of Coal receives payments for postings and for delaying the implementation of regulations.
- Revenue Department/commercial tax officials organise falsification of supply chain transactions and arrange for delaying the implementation of regulations.
- Other officials silence the media, distribute cuts to junior officials.
- Police/home affairs officials are bribed for (non)enforcement and to silence the media.
- Union leaders organise the theft of raw material from mines.
- CIL managers exercise oversight of (false) permits and (false) accounts, quality, loading (false weights at weighbridges) and dispatch.
- Railway officials oversee the logistics of the illegal renting-out of individual wagons or wholesale diversion of rakes ('racks').
- State Highways Officials manage governance of 'discos' (colour-coded chits to indicate bribe status).
- Maoist cadres exact tax for protection en route.
- Forgers create documents ensuring the appearance of legal compliance.
- Politicians supervise protection, physical and bureaucratic access, patronage and evasion.
- Mafia control contracts, logistics, finance/rent allocation and protection.
- Unions manage contracts, logistics, finance/rent allocation and protection and demand extra fees from coal buyers for loading/transporting; union leaders in mafia (reported to be 9) organise labour.
- Mine labour organise cuts paid to union/mafia bosses to join union and access jobs.

Source: Singh 2014 fieldwork

While Khan (2012) has modelled such arrangements as manifestations of patronage, clientelage and faction, in fact they are more complex than these principal-agent categories would imply. Formal occupational status, social status, kinship alliances, economic assets, more or less armed capacity for physical threat against the vigilant state and criminal competitors, capacities for sharing and collective action, the capacity to protect visible fixed assets (from motorcycles for uphill stretches for groups of laden CCWs to loading equipment and transport fleets) are all at play in this system of transactions.

This summary of IC social organisation also shows how the economic and political domination over IC of a cartel of mafia families has developed from roots in labour rather than in capital. Prior to nationalisation, private mines paid protection forces to secure the owners' physical safety, prevent theft and monitor work shifts. Nationalisation required the reorganisation of the workforce: labour contractors and managers of labour camps for migrant workers emerged from among the organisers of protection. Some of the new class of labour contractors became leaders of unions, stimulated illegal trade and protected it. Then, in the Janata Dal era in 1970s Bihar, after the murder of a Congress union leader, they entered politics directly (Singh 2014, 51). Now leaders and management of national unions (such as INTUC and BMS) are widely alleged to have hidden interests in IC (see Appendix 1.2 and Gupta in Chapter 2). Public sector institutions have long been under pressure to privatise, yet FC is not only hollowed out through private subcontracting: even the 30 per cent of production it controls directly is also suffused with, and plundered by, illegal private arrangements. The resistance caused by these interests is just as serious a barrier to the formal process of privatisation as it is to any attempt to crush IC.

The politics of the economic regulation of illegal coal

Neither the informal nor the criminal economy is disordered, so one element of local politics concerns how order is achieved in the absence of formal state enforcement. Several kinds of overlapping politics are involved. We can approach the question of regulatory order first through the four strata of the IC assemblage, although it is the labour unions that have paramount regulatory authority. Second and later, we examine how elected and unelected party politicians regulate IC and prevent enforcement of the law; we then investigate the political roles played by social institutions. CCW are not collectively organised as gangs or associations. The groups of about 10 needed to coke coal are less structured than are the syndicates. Even when supplying syndicates, CCW coal and coke is sold by individuals through individual transactions (Singh 2014, 24). Sales routes and sales are established 'by local custom' through family and friends, with very loose coordination through 'ad hoc village committees'. These divide territory, protect diggers, establish routes, counter police vigilance and suppress information (Singh 2014, 35).

Syndicates regulate the use of equipment (motorcycles) collectively but, despite their name, are not noted for other regulatory capabilities. Where they employ CCWs as labour, contracts are defined verbally, specifying quantities and periods. Syndicates may reinforce bikes to carry great weights of coal (up to 2.5 tonnes a year; Lahiri-Dutt and Williams 2005).

Where syndicates' motorbikes are used to tow bikes on uphill stretches and to oversee cycle convoys some 400 metres long, the syndicate organises and rotates the CCW routes and group membership, liaises with the police and protects its CCWs at dump sites. Under these conditions, it is estimated that the productivity of CCWs doubles and penalties to CCWs for non-compliance with syndicates are fierce. Syndicates are self-organising, as are CT and the mafia – the latter through their system of family- and kin-based honour and discipline and their control over unionised labour. Three 'Singh' mafia families, originally from UP and Bihar, extort funds from the labour they lead, pay a 'randari' (informal) tax and share rents with CIL management so that labour and small private intermediaries can take coal. In this way they expand the illegal coal trade, lead unions, threaten unrest and price and bid for work (which may not be completed) (Singh 2014, 51). They also control violent caste-based youth gangs, liaise between other mafia and CIL and are pro- or anti- the casualisation of labour depending on the political party in power.

The coal mafia have territorial agreements such that their monopolies enable greater rent extraction than competition between mafia houses would. Through threats to the physical security of their workforces, certain mafia families also control sets of local unions. They are also able to manipulate auctions through intimidation and underbidding and can even manipulate CIL's e-auctions this way, so that purchase prices are cheaper than the official floors. Mining labour, both legally organised and illegally regulated, has a paramount role in IC. In the twenty-first century, two opposing political forces have agitated the labour force. One is geared towards labour casualisation and the stripping of rights – via subcontracting the extraction of coal. The second, by contrast, involves the competitive coercing of labour into unions, not simply to empower labour but also to empower the mafia to control labour in IC. Individual labourers may now belong to multiple unions. Payday credit and debt have recently been introduced as a bonding mechanism by both private companies and competing mafia moneylenders. Unions such as the Indian National Trade Union Congress (INTUC, belonging to the Congress party), the Rashtriya Colliery Mazdoor Sangh (RCMS), the CPI's United Coal Workers' Union (CWU) and the Anusuchit Jati-Janjati Chhatra Sangathan (AJCS) – all aligned with Congress – then help CIL and its subsidiaries by their complicity in fixing and stabilising wages at relatively low levels. In return labour unions regulate the supply of illegal coal through diversion and theft, refusal to comply with CIL directives, overloading of trucks, collection of rent (sometimes shared with managers) and conniving with tax fraud. When ordered, union members provide the manpower for kidnap, assault and murder. Unions are reported by many informants to have more operational power than the state corporations' apparatus. Some unions are capable of managing IC without other alliances but most take protection from union-mafia combines. Apex union-mafia families also regulate territory and control the large-scale transport of IC in railway rakes. See Appendix 1.2 for coal union leaders' business interests.

The politics of money flows to and from illegal coal: the circuit of profit

Financing IC requires amounts ranging from little more than zero (in the case of dependent CCWs) to massive amounts of capital (for the mafia). None of this is traceable – even finance for the large-scale railway-rake transport business comes from illegal/black sources – including, it is alleged, investments in working capital from black economy sources outside Jharkhand, and even outside India. Granted that elsewhere, in less criminalised sectors and regions of India's informal economy, businessmen have persistently expressed preferences for financial autonomy and against indebtedness (especially to official and traceable sources like banks), it is likely that mafia families themselves act as banks for the IC system. Indeed it was reported that of late they have hired agents to manage lending to CCWs and union labour (Singh 2014, 45). For reasons of political hedging alone, flows of money made *from* IC will differ from allegiances and political interest. In the eight coal districts, syndicates, CTs and mafia all pay politicians and their aides, officials, CIL management and the police on a sliding scale, in which mafiosi pay the most and gain the most political leverage (Daniel and Williams 2013). Mafia families are thought to be associated in quite a stable manner with given political parties despite the fact that rival wings of the largest mafia family fund them all (Singh 2014, 54 and 60) – and not just in Jharkhand but also in Bihar and Uttar Pradesh, in order to ease the route to the Chandasi coal trading hub. Large mafia families will fund individual politicians as well as political party activity in the territories they dominate: they invest the most and gain the most in return. Within the mafia there is a hierarchy, some families having to pay leading mafia families (such as the 'Singh Mansion' (*The Sunday Indian* 2013)) while others make direct political investments. And lately the volatility of party coalitions in Jharkhand has required mafia families with a single-party allegiance to diversify their funding opportunistically and fund candidates from a range of parties.

Criminal accumulation

Accumulation from IC is highly differentiated. At their most independent, CCWs are petty producers and traders, expanding through multiplication rather than accumulation but completely meshed in markets based on raw materials to which they have no property rights. Other elements in the assemblages for coal invest profit and accumulate. Syndicates invest in motorcycles and start to hire out JCBs; coal traders get hold of diggers and trucks. Mafia families route investments both privately and publicly. Privately, they are known to have invested in expanding IC and diversified into real estate and transport fleets, leisure resorts and pleasure parks in Jharkhand, hotels in Mumbai (and across other Asian countries), in sand, water and heavy equipment for development projects. Black money may be laundered through such investments, and mafia dons become 'gentlemen-traders'. For instance, the upwardly mobile OBC mafioso Dhulu Mahato, leader of the union sponsored by the local Jharkhand Vikas Morcha (JVM) party, has assets from IC estimated in 2013 at INR 200 *crore* (US$28 million), together with a fleet of 100,000 trucks (Singh 2014, 70).

Through public investments, the coal mafia are major funders of elections. Although local campaign requirements vary from INR 5 *lakh* to 50 *lakh* per candidate (Singh 2014, 70) funding often dribbles in through many small consignments of cash under INR 20,000 – the threshold for registered declarations. Funding denotes 'purchase' and the biggest mafia families are able to purchase any local politician. This generates a politics of investment, debt and dependence which will play assertively and reactively within and between parties according to their electoral success. Political and economic losses are embedded in the state: CIL's profits and revenues on royalties go to the Jharkhand state government. Industries where costs rise through the use of adulterated or low-quality, apparently 'cheap' coal also lose. Political resistance 'loses'. Political resistance so far has been countered successfully in Jharkhand by means ranging from transfers of posts to physical assault, including murder. Punishment through the legal system is rare. But when, uniquely, an ex-CM, Madhu Koda, was arrested in 2009 and successfully prosecuted, the CBI uncovered illegal trade revenues totalling around INR 4,000 *crore*. The case also revealed investments in 700 shell companies, in mines, in an off-shore island, in real estate, sponge iron, private colleges in his constituency, transport and trucking as far away as Punjab and Haryana, hotels in New Delhi and Puri, a theme park, distilleries and print media and TV channels (for strategic silence) (Singh 2014, 64). To the extent that this diversified portfolio emerged from violent seizures of natural resources and the displacement of labour, its accumulation was 'primitive'. But the productive investment in which resources have been sunk obeys the logic of advanced capitalist accumulation, with Indian characteristics.

Party politics in Jharkhand

Jharkhand nationalist parties are widely described as having used the idioms and rhetoric of aboriginal empowerment and the interests of Scheduled Castes and Scheduled Tribes to plunder natural resources (Karat 2012). In this way Jharkhand is no different from other elements of the new political wave that has conceded and created non-linguistic states.[6] The Jharkhand nationalist case involves demands for social justice and restitution from developmental marginalisation and comparative poverty, through which capital has been accumulated by outsiders to the detriment of low-caste and tribal local citizens. Inside its new borders and crammed with – to date under-extracted – subterranean industrial raw materials, Jharkhand does not lack resources for development. According to Tillin (2008), Congress has not encouraged these movements for independence – succeeding in co-opting 'less radical elements' (which, in Jharkhand, include the coal mafia) – so the political drivers have been an alliance of the BJP-in-opposition, local parties in which low castes and tribes compete, and new social movements. Together, these have generated a politics of claim – to education, reservations, jobs and better social status – but based on unstable alliances grounded in identity.

Among the elements of identity it is ironic that language is prominent. While for New Delhi and in the All-India optic, the local languages of the new states are dialects of Hindi, this is disputed by their speakers, whose case is that new states are language-based too; in Jharkhand's case, multi-lingually (Pattanayak 2013).

Jharkhand's most important local parties are the Jharkhand Mukti Morcha (JMM), the All-Jharkhand Students' Union (AJSU) and the Jharkhand Vikas Morcha (JVM). Campaigning for a tribal homeland and greater regional independence, the JMM developed with a politics unrelated to natural resources and as early as 1972 had a Marxist coordination committee led by Shibu Soren. Support was mobilised by focussing on the grievances of labourers and Scheduled Castes and Tribes. Later Soren was elected to the Government of India as an MP and forged links with Congress. While a student revolt against this arrangement created the AJSU in 1986, other splinter groups cohered to JMM in the 1990s, and Jharkhand became a state in 2000. After the 2014 election, the JMM held only 2 of 14 Parliamentary seats from Jharkhand (the remainder going to the BJP). The AJSU's originally militant regionalism has become increasingly pragmatic and AJSU is now allied with the BJP. Their president has been Home Minister in the Jharkhand legislative assembly. Meanwhile, the JMM was consolidated in 2006 from a BJP splinter. Its MP, Dr Ajay Kumar, is an IPS officer, medical doctor, holder of an MBA and industrialist who developed an anti-mafia campaign in Jamshedpur.

Political parties in Jharkhand are funded by IC, the iron ore extractive industry, as well as bauxite, steel and construction industries. The AJSU is thought to rely on the aluminium industry. JVM has maximum financial support from the very coal areas where it attempts to challenge the mafia. Congress and BJP have mafia notables but are less dependent on their funds since they are able to supplement them with national corporate donations (Singh 2014, 36). Local cash collectors are employed to bulk the donations to all parties (Singh 2014, 63) helped by coercive pressures brought to bear by mafia families on other companies. Contemporary local politics in the state are widely characterised as grounded in ethnic divisions, local problems, and short-term and small-scale mobilisations. The rising political party instability of Jharkhand weakens the chance that the state government has of crushing IC. Its relatively small number of MLA seats (81) combined with an increasing political fragility act to benefit IC and its mafia. The Legislative Assembly is too small to prevent coalitions being held to ransom by the threat of withdrawal (Singh 2014, 72). This fragility obstructs attempts to amass political opposition to IC.

Illegal coal and politics: *intreccio*

The entanglements between the il/legal economy, the state and party politics, for which Michelutti and Harriss-White invoke the concept of *intreccio* in the Introduction to this book, can be approached in two ways: the roles in party politics of those controlling illegal coal; and the reverse – the role of party politics in illegal coal.

Coal interests in party politics

Even before the 2014 election, the political interests of IC were tensely differentiated. Some CCWs have formed a political constituency of Bandhu Tirkey's Jharkhand Janadikhar Manch (JJM) – supporting the agenda of political independence. As Tillin has explained (2013) the JJM demands the independence from 'migrant' Rajput capital of local OBCs, SCs and STs, along with local tribal control over natural resources and livelihoods creation. Other CCWs support Shibu Soren's Jharkhand Mukti Morcha (JMM) on the grounds that Soren has declared their 'right' to take coal. Coal syndicates also pay JMM for the physical protection of the CCWs who provide their supplies.

In contrast with this paternalism in return for electoral support, the union leaders and other coal trade and mafia families position kin directly in politics. While all unions are vote banks for parties and family power prevails over party policy, the political allegiances of coal traders and the mafia are bound to labour union politics, which in turn are inextricable from the forms of ownership of mines. It is more efficient and less costly and risky to manage the politics of IC directly as an MLA than to leverage activity indirectly from outside the legislature through paying and patronising other politicians. As a lawmaker, the MLA is also immune from prosecution, a vital legal protection (Singh 2014, 71). Immunity is an important reason for active political engagement. Within the mafia elite of Rajput Singhs, active participation in both Congress and BJP politics is pervasive. For instance, within the Congress party union, INTUC, there is a three-way rivalry between the local MP and two MLAs not only for control of unionised labour but also for control of the illegal labour force of CCW paupers who scavenge and process illegal coal from mines. Within private subcontracted mines, unionised labour forces are bribed by local union-mafia into complying with management and resisting the mobilisation of casual labour. While inside CIL, a single (national) union may dominate a single mine or set of mines, and four unions have such 'monopolies' in mines run by BCCL, there tends to be competition between local labour unions and their local CT and mafia families. In privately subcontracted mines there is a battle to unionise their temporary casual labour because the stakes from rents and profits from IC are high and depend on the power and the roles of organised labour. In turn unions are well known to be affiliated with political parties, though some unions are diversifying their party portfolios (see Gupta, Chapter 2).

The mafia have interests in political instability because it prevents the mobilisation of sufficient political power to challenge IC. CCWs and syndicates, bound through their social identities to political parties seeking to empower them, are also bound by their livelihoods to parties protecting IC. They are unstable political resources switching according to interests and driving a politics of 'permanent crisis management'. And the unpredictability of local election timings and alliances creates demand both for mafia funds and the vote banks controlled by the mafia, so that compromising links between the mafia and parties that have campaigned against IC are growing. All of this serves to strengthen the political clout of the mafia.

Meanwhile there are strong political relationships between the Government of Jharkhand and CIL officials. Where a state government minister or official also has trade union interests, this link is direct. Thus, Finance and Energy Ministers belonging to Congress in Jharkhand are alleged to have shared CIL subsidies, diverted coal to parallel trade, organised the labour for illegal transport by 'rack' and liaised between the mafia and CIL (Singh 2014, 68). When local party politics is increasingly unstable then the nexus of mafia and CT, union leaders, police, officials in public agencies and politicians is tangled and powerful enough not just to protect IC but also to prevent the privatisation of CIL – on which this edifice rests.

Party politics in the illegal coal economy

> There are no clean politicians in Jharkhand. (Senior journalist)
> Jharkhand is already a failed state. (Central government minister)

Our evidence here is drawn from before the 2014 election in the pre-BJP era, when the state legislative assembly was a series of unstable coalitions under shifting control, but also when Jharkhand MPs from two local parties were aligned with the United Progressive Alliance government in New Delhi. Elected politicians have immunity at national and state level. But below the legislative assembly their less effective immunity is not de jure but secured de facto through the local political threats, bribes and allegiances described earlier in this chapter. So it is that in Jharkhand all major and minor parties – Congress, the BJP, JMM, AJSU, JVM, JJM plus the CPM (Maoist)[7] – have stakes in IC. These work in various ways – direct, indirect and oppositional – and in both governing and opposition parties, inside and outside Jharkhand. The most powerful MLAs in each of the five significant parties are linked to IC, while some are also contractors to the state (in mining, water, transport and labour). As of 2013, nine MPs and MLAs, including Jharkhand cabinet ministers, ran branches of national unions and control labour (threatening 'trouble at pit' for non-criminal businesses); they control dumps for CCWs, divert trucks from washeries, fix timing, transport and transactions, allocate routes and, more recently, manage loans to syndicates and other groups. MLAs sit on CIL governing bodies, control police postings within their

jurisdictions and can delay police charges, reopen closed mines for syndicates, marshal the CCW vote banks, own and finance ancillary activities
for IC such as transport, extort cuts from the profits of other companies
and use profits to invest in loyalty and votes. Mafia families themselves
engage as MPs, MLAs and mayors, not only in Jharkhand but also in Bihar
and UP, controlling politicians lower down the ranks who can deliver
vote banks, stabilising their own economic empires in the state arena and
protecting them against threat and blackmail up the political greasy pole
to New Delhi (Singh 2014, 44). In Jharkhand, INTUC leaders were Congress MLAs: alleged both to manage illegal transport and protect it politically at the Central level. A former speaker of the Jharkhand Legislative
Assembly is alleged to have invested in land sites for CCW scavenging
(registered in his wife's name), and to have used his caste contacts to
manipulate the police and to manage permits, loading, routes and protection from obstruction for syndicates. His relations with local party
officials, government officials (from district and block administrations,
Revenue and Forest Departments), with unelected cadres and members
of the JMM, JVM and AJSU are said to grease IC in return for fees, immunity and silence (Singh 2014, 49). As Jharkhand's politics is increasingly
negotiated through coalitions, the coal mafia MLAs have been all the
more vital since they have the political and economic resources necessary to hold the balance of power.

While collusion among the coal mafia, the bureaucracy, police
and politicians is thought to have been increasing since Jharkhand was
formed, outright violence against people appears to have been losing
relevance. The increasingly close four-way relationship benefits from
proximity to the site of the seat of power, Ranchi, adjoining the coal belt.
While the political analyst P.S. Jha characterises the mature clientelist
state as a congeries of relations between business, career politicians,
gangland mafiosi and police (Jha 2013), the fledgling state of Jharkhand
is proving to be no different. Yet IC may not always require the direct
involvement of local politicians. Positions in CIL, whose complicity is
vital for coal theft and truck diversion, cannot be delivered at the level
of the Jharkhand state: appointments are routed through the ministry in
New Delhi. Businesses needing preferential access to coal can lobby the
central government's Coal Ministry bureaucracy, which formulates policy on matters such as weighbridges, CCTV surveillance and electronic
stamping. Political arrangements lubricated by black money enable the
ministry to command CIL to allocate and divert coal, just as it can delay
or even stop the implementation of locally obstructive policies (Singh
2014, 24).

Apart from direct operational involvement, it is also widely reported that about half of the 81 MLAs and 14 MPs receive payment from IC. They take fees, divvy up cuts among themselves, the police and the Highways Inspectorate at state borders, manage the approval of bids to the Jharkhand Mining Authority and liaise – but do not directly operate in the sector. This kind of activity is resistant to shifting electoral outcomes (Singh 2014, 26). Meanwhile JVM MLAs formally express a politics of resistance – to 'fight the mafia'. But at the time of our research, many were reported as busy skimming syndicates and controlling CCWs for both party and individual benefit (Singh 2014, 35). Mafia funding supports, and is in turn supported by, elected governments and elected oppositions. But the majority of electoral candidates do not win. Losers are indebted to their funders. Mafia financiers are thought not to require the repayment of such debt (either in cash or kind), regarding it as a political cost (a 'loss leader'), and suggestive of Jharkhand's political fragility and of the subversion of its aspirational politics. The mafia dominates coal politics through the constitutive politics of capital/business and the control of all relevant markets for money and material goods, of labour, parties and movements, protection and force, and state penetration. Meanwhile, syndicates and less powerful CTs have similar links lower in the system but face much higher risk, may make losses, lose elections (and the funds invested in them) and enjoy spells in jail (Singh 2014, 2–14, 26). The increasing volatility of Jharkhand politics means politicians are not secure, and relinquishing immunity through electoral losses leaves IC politicians vulnerable to punishment. Once out of office, one union mafioso, Dhulu Mahato, formerly immune from prosecution for the violent release of a client from the police, was jailed (Press Trust of India 2016). To sum up in the words of local experts: the 'top power structure and state coal mafia are linked conceptually'.[8] The coal mafia has achieved 'paramountcy – instead of delegating power, they get into politics to directly control and have real power'.[9] More coal families have sought election since Jharkhand's formation:

> They have legal authority ... Jharkhand has become privatised to the local mafia. They sought the direct election to direct the resources. Now they are decision makers at the MLA and Police level and have a legal basis for being mafia ... The mafia then elect their own to allow criminal exploitation. (Professor, Indian School of Mines)

The identity politics of coal

India's extensive, socially regulated informal economy is one in which – alongside local business associations, and sometimes permeating them – so-called 'soft' institutions of identity, such as gender, ethnicity, religion, place, language and caste have proved more compatible with the capitalist economy than theorists of development have been inclined to acknowledge (Harriss-White 2003; Arora 2017). They are at one and the same time being dissolved by the needs of market exchange for acquired competences rather than ascribed character, and also being reworked to become not 'soft' but hard regulators of economic opportunity, entry and practice. While identity reflects trust, which reduces the costs of transactions, it is simultaneously used to defend sectors against a competitive free-for-all and thus protect rents and profits. Social institutions which regulate market behaviour are powerful structural elements in India's political economy. Though there is no scholarly consensus on what the dominant or prominent institutions are,[10] gender, religion, caste and ethnicity are widely accepted as expressing important forms of authority that structure India's economy.[11] The same lens needs applying to illegal coal and the question asked – which social institutions are indispensable to the criminal economic order of IC? From the research reported here the answers can only be suggestive and need further development. Extrapolated from the narratives of informants, they are those institutions and forms of political authority that were said to make sense of IC.[12] Each is summarised and then mapped onto other politics laid out earlier.

Dynasty

Modern India is suffused with political dynasties: after 2014, 20 per cent of MPs were from political dynasties, rising from 15 per cent in the BJP to half of the rump Congress. Non-watertight explanations for this range from 'family culture' and voter preference to party political encouragement for loyalty (Chandra 2016). To these, Jha would add the reduced costs when transmitted through dynasties of the knowledge, contacts and practices of mobilising untraceable party funds (Jha 2013). The mafia is not just a set of criminal organisations, it is a set of political dynasties competing against one another for 'paramount power' (Singh 2014, 34). Alongside the cross-generational accumulation of political power, mafia dynasties are also developing economic authority not only in IC but in related industries, the local bureaucracy and in labour control. Their private protection forces are drawn from the coal labour they also seek to control at work in the mines.

Caste and ethnicity

Mafia dynastic competition is also construed through caste and ethnicity. The elite Rajputs from Bihar who have settled in Jharkhand were initially challenged by local high-caste Bhumihar families (one of whose leaders was assassinated in 1977). Rajput mafia families may diversify funding to several parties – wherever they can fortify their castes as well as position their private interests strategically. These prominent business families also ensure that members are placed in the state bureaucracy and in the management of local CIL subsidiaries. Rajput networks are then consolidated in politics, the state and the economy.

But Jharkhand is a state where OBCs, SCs and STs are the largest elements in the population. The rise and fall of Dhulu Mahato should be seen in this context. Mahato, who is OBC, combines caste politics with being a union mafioso controlling the UCW (now linked with AITUC and MCC) and a party politician (in the AJSU-JVM). Two factors may account for his different party-political engagement from those of the Singhs: first, his local, 'insider' role as champion of Scheduled Castes and Tribes against the immigrant outsiders – despite the latter's several generations of residence in Jharkhand. Second, the possibility of developing a defence of the coal mafia through local politics at a stage when mafia representation in the legislative assembly had not yet been consolidated (Singh 2014, 27–30).

Summing up: there is little evidence that the politics of dynasty, caste and ethnicity does anything but strengthen the grip over IC of the Rajput mafia.

Consequences

To complete the integration of illegal coal into the account of Jharkhand's development, the final task is to suggest its implications for the economy and politics.

Economic consequences

The economic impact of illegal coal is ambivalent. On the one hand, in a so-called neoliberal era widely criticised for its jobless growth (Kannan and Raveendran 2010), IC provides hundreds of thousands of livelihoods in Jharkhand alone. IC is then supplied cheaply to satisfy a highly segmented demand for energy that lacks official entitlement to coal. These take the form of income supplements to a wide range of public sector employees, wage labour throughout the coal economy and enterprises ranging from petty production/self-employment to large criminal organisations. The unplanned investment in IC and use of its profits may have a range of legal statuses but is productive as well as unproductive.

On the other hand, the diversion of coal has a negative impact on formal industrial capacity utilisation, output and productivity – revealed at its worst in the historically unprecedented North Indian blackouts of 2012. Shortages increased demand for coal imports (estimated at 168 million tonnes and $17 billion in 2014–15 before the shock to demand resulting from demonetisation; Cornot-Gandolphe 2016). Illegal coal invites both capital flight and unplanned illegitimate overseas investment, the opportunity cost of which is the reduction of productive investment in India and local opportunities for money laundering. The diversion of revenue starves the state of public sector resources and constrains and denies the development of a redistributivist development project, which the decades-old aspirational politics of Jharkhand has had as its objective. It has set in carbon a solid structure of economic and political interests against the destruction of illegal coal.

Consequences for politics

As a result of IC, far from being ethnically aspirational, Jharkhand's politics is mired in instability and predation. The powers that might challenge IC and enforce its regulation are deactivated by the penetration throughout local politics of the interests of illegal coal.

In other Indian case studies in this book, the politics of illegal resource extraction has been concluded to be a destructive politics of mafia criminality (fire in Jharkhand, Chapter 2), predatory, pork barrel politics (sand in Tamil Nadu, Chapter 3), a politics of accumulation by corruption (hydro-crimes in Arunachal, Chapter 4), systemic plunder (airwaves for telecom, Chapter 5), a 'competitive mafia raj' and 'goonda raj' (fuel and sand in UP, Chapter 6), that of internationalised criminal capitalism (red sanders timber in AP, Chapter 7), of a mafia state (real estate in West Bengal, Chapter 8), and of politicised predation (land and property titles in Punjab, Chapter 9).

Far from developing a shadow state whose existence is dependent on formal state institutions (as theorised by Harriss-White in *India Working*, 2003), or being a failed state (as Bihar's Chief Minister characterised it in 2008; Kumar 2008), in 2014 the Jharkhand state was a highly successful mafia state. In its coal economy, legal and illegal, economic assemblages and political transactions are systemically interlocked in tangled relations of *intreccio*. While the mafia are often characterised as autonomous from the state,[13] here they are an integral part of it, capable of mediating access to it and ruling large territories – both physical and political. While CIL is the nutrient base of its largest operations, abandoned public sector mines provide the resources for the smallest livelihoods. Meanwhile the politics of identity overlay those of political parties and in complex relations of collaboration, evasion and the power of assets they bring an order to the class-based criminal economy which prevails over that of the state.

Resistance

The powerful hierarchical assemblage of IC must not be accepted as undynamic and uncontested. Although resistance was not the central focus of field research, the latter can now be used to identify interests conflicting with those of IC. These include conflict within the coal mafia itself, as well as resistance against the mafia by syndicates, CCW, mining labour, civil society organisations and movements, national political parties, the Indian government and its public sector agencies, and by the outlawed, officially terrorist Maoist party. Deserving more space than is available here, our discussion of conflict in IC can be no more than brief, selective and suggestive. First, within the mafia itself there is persistent party-politicised family feuding 'over business': property ownership (e.g. Singh Mansion) and union control. This congeries of enmity is thought to have motivated the killing with three others in March 2017 of Neeraj Singh, former Congress deputy mayor of Dhanbad and unsuccessful contestant of the Jharia legislative seat. His cousin, successful BJP MLA for Jharia and coal transporter Sanjiv Singh, has been arrested, along with Sanjiv's brother. All are from the Suraj Deo Singh, a leading Rajput mafia, dynasty (Mishra 2014; Pandey 2017).

In civil society, the alliance of peoples' movements ranges from the National Forum of Forest Peoples and Forest Workers, the local Rajmahal Pahar Bachao Andolan and the People's Union for Democratic Rights to religious orders. It is the illegal activities of FC rather than IC that tend to mobilise civil society. The case of Sister Valsa, a Catholic nun, economist and teacher, murdered in 2011 after years of death threats by forces suspected to be either mafia goons in cahoots with mine operators or alternatively Maoists, shows the lengths to which opposition will go to silence protest. Land encroachment by mining companies, delays in compensation and awards of contracts to tribal people reduced by displacement to scavenging coal illegally from company convoys have provoked outrage

(*India Today* 2011; Pohkarel and Beckett 2012; *India Today* 2017). How have these tight and yet seething and contested arrangements fared under an authoritative/authoritarian BJP regime in the state and central government? Ever since 2014, if it had wished to crush IC, the BJP has had the necessary precondition of authority. But even when political authority dominates legal due process, it is evidently insufficient to do more than reinforce local links between the governing party and the mafia.

Last, the guerrilla Maoists have aligned their political interests with those of 'rural tribals' and see the exploitation of coal as the economic power base of class enemies. This extends to the paramilitary forces protecting FC and even to the segment of organised wage labour that works on permanent contracts. In practice the Maoists' need for revenue blunts their hostility to IC. Their reputed 7 per cent tax on small mines subcontracted to CIL, on abandoned mines operated by syndicates, and the levies on both CIL's transport and that of IC have caused West Bengal's journal of dissent, *Sanhati* (2011), to evoke the 'mafianisation of the Maoists'.

Conclusions: discussion and implications

Discussion

By outlining the assemblages of formal and illegal coal, their interlinkages and implications, and revisiting the politics of Jharkhand from the perspectives, on the one hand, of the economic interests embodied in illegal coal and, on the other, of political parties penetrated by them, the wide-reaching social ramifications of natural resource crimes have been exposed. Formal-informal-illegal politics and economies are tightly intertwined and feed into each other in relations of *intreccio* which cross class, span labour- and party-politics, and penetrate public corporations and the range of agencies of enforcement. Here, let us draw together some observations from this case that are relevant to wider debates.

First, the coal mafia and violence. As a category, the mafia is used for (fictive) kin-based organisations developed for the protection of persons and violence against enemies; in being so used it challenges the state's monopoly of violence. By contrast, Jharkhand's coal mafia exercises direct violence against natural resources, and against the state's regulation of them and violations of the property rights which protect them. The extortion of natural resources is not always violent to people: its threat alone is enough for most labour to comply with criminal bosses. The pervasive 'culture of silence' constrains that of physical violence. Coal traders, syndicates and CCWs do not carry weapons. The routinely armed mafia, if attacking people, are mostly engaged in family feuding, mainly about territory.

A second distinctive characteristic of Jharkhand's coal mafia that is relevant to general debates concerns the mafia and labour. The origins of apex mafia organisations are heterogeneous, some arising through their control over mining labour through trade unions. Indeed the labour force in criminal production and distribution of coal also doubles as the mafia's protection force. A third conclusion involves the mafia and registered business; specifically the extent to which illegal business supplements – and is meshed in – legitimate activity, with the latter being used to mask the former. Yet another characteristic is the mafia's dependence on extracting resources from public corporations rather than private companies.

We can make further observations concerning the role of local political parties. In Jharkhand, parties of social and regional identity or developmental aspiration have emerged not only as responses to the past neglect of factors used for their mobilisation (caste, ethnicity, regional neglect and underdevelopment) but also as a reaction to the political spaces created by the rampant criminalisation of natural resource extraction. Here we see that they are pressured to embody political forces contradictory to their social aims: illegal accumulation diverts taxable resources from a social development agenda.

Diversity and variation are built into IC assemblages. The balance of the social components described earlier and of their powers and roles varies according to the political competence of the regional state-corporate subsidiaries of CIL; the heft of local versus national party politicians and their positioning in the IC structure; the site and the economic positioning of mafia households; the degree of competition or capture of mines by national and local labour unions; and the weight of legal business.

Implications

In this case study, the resources needed to cover the periodically convulsive and the routine day-to-day costs of Indian electoral democracy have been seen to be met (in part) through illegal coal. Coal is but one of many illegal nutrient bases for democratic politics. In Jharkhand alone bauxite, iron ore, steel and construction also supply political funds. In the different case of Tamil Nadu (Jeyaranjan, Chapter 3) the vast sums of daily tribute centralised from riverbed sand are supplemented by those from beach sand, granite, liquor and construction. The scale of these criminal flows is significant and brings corresponding political influence.

In actively abetting or ignoring this malfeasance, the state's own developmental and distributive projects are captured. The case of coal thus leads to a rebalancing of the orthodox political analysis of Jharkhand away from redistributive social justice and towards the politics of mafia accumulation through extortion and exploitation. The political space for redistributivist development activity that might have benefitted the social reproduction of the workforce is crushed by lack of resources or of relevance to criminal politics. The workforce has come increasingly under criminal control at work and its conditions of reproduction outside work are being privatised. The kind of accumulation manifested in IC is the subject of wider debate over the balance between the creation of predatory capitalism through primitive accumulation versus expanding the production of capital through the axiom of accumulation: 'Accumulate, accumulate! That is Moses and the Prophets' (Marx 1887; see also Adnan 2013 for contemporary debates). The case of IC shows that both forms of accumulation, primitive and capitalist, are at work in meshed forms and in parallel, contradictory and specific ways.

Primitive accumulation will end only when two conditions are met. First, sufficient capital will have to have been accumulated to reduce the capitalist class's need for criminal rents; and second, conditions must be such that viable states and independent political parties are needed by capital itself to control criminal rents. But this analysis of illegal coal and the other case studies of natural resource crime in this book show that there is no guarantee that processes of predatory rent, of criminal accumulation, of the undermining of legal-ethical obligations and of the sabotage and displacement of formal state organisational capacity will yield to those from legitimate profit-seeking capitalism in the foreseeable future.

Notes

1. Based on a 22,000-word field report by Nigel Singh in 2014, 'The Political Economy of the Informal and Illegal Coal Trade in Jharkhand', carried out in the pre-election spring of 2014 and building on Singh's earlier fieldwork in 2012–3, as reported in the *Guardian* newspaper; see Singh 2013. Page references refer to the unpublished 2014 document, where Singh's detailed sources are identified and the quality of evidence is carefully evaluated.
2. An alternative estimate is INR 1,800 *crore* ($4bn at 2011 rates) (Press Trust of India 2013).
3. Singh (2014, 38) provides details of routes where payment is needed.
4. Family members are said to be shadowed by non-family members so as to evaluate performance.
5. V.P. Sinha in 1977, Suresh Singh in 2013 (Singh 2014, 31 and 34) and Neeraj Singh in 2017.
6. Uttarakhand, Chhattisgarh and Jharkhand in 2000 and Telangana in 2013.

7. Maoists, internally split between faction and caste, exact 'tax' to ignore mining.
8. Senior journalist.
9. Major landowner.
10. Dominant institutions buttressing capital can be distinguished from prominent institutions (which may be the same ones) pervading workforce relationships (Hodgson 2001).
11. See Upadhya 2009, for instance, for capital and Harriss-White et al. 2013, for self-employment.
12. Gender which persists as a fundamental structure in the economy undoubtedly plays a role in IC but was not the subject of interviews in this research. See Lahiri Dutt 2014, 229–56.
13. See Michelutti's review in Chapter 6 of this volume.

References

Adnan, S. 2013. 'Land Grabs and Primitive Accumulation: Interactions between Neoliberal Globalization, State Interventions, Power Relations and Peasant Resistance', *Journal of Peasant Studies* 40 (1): 87–128.

Arora, N. 2017. *The Lottery of Birth: On Inherited Social Inequalities*. New Delhi: Three Essays Press.

Banaji, J. 1977. 'Modes of Production in a Materialist Conception of History', *Capital and Class* 1 (3): 1–44.

Cantera, A. 2015. 'The 100,000 Children Working in the Illegal Mines of India's Coal State', *Vice-News* 3 February. https://news.vice.com/article/the-100000-children-working-in-the-illegal-mines-of-indias-coal-state?preview&cb=v1422975406305 (accessed 29 April 2019).

Chandra, K., ed. 2016. *Democratic Dynasties: State, Party and Family in Contemporary Indian Politics*. Cambridge: Cambridge University Press.

Chatterjee, E. and M. McCartney, eds. 2019. *Class and Conflict: Revisiting Pranab Bardhan's Political Economy of India*. New Delhi: Oxford University Press.

Cornot-Gandolphe, S. 2016. 'Indian Steam Coal Imports: The Great Equation', *Paper OIES CL3*. Oxford: Oxford Institute of Energy Studies. https://www.oxfordenergy.org/wpcms/wp-content/uploads/2016/03/Indian-Steam-Coal-Imports-The-Great-Equation-CL-3.pdf (accessed 29 April 2019).

Daniel, F. and M. Williams. 2013. 'Special Report: "Coal Mafia" stokes India's power crisis', *Reuters* 14 May. http://in.reuters.com/article/2013/05/14/india-coal-jharkhand-dhanbad-coalindia-idINDEE94D00B20130514$36m (accessed 29 April 2019).

Firstpost (comment). 2014. 'Corruption and Crime: How Coal Mafias Fuel India's Power Crisis', 14 December. http://firstbiz.firstpost.com/economy/corruption-and-crime-how-coal-mafias-fuel-indias-power-crisis-40635.html (accessed 29 April 2019).

Gupta, S. 2013. 'Fanning A Fire In Jharia: Reap Windfall Profits And Loot The Coal'. Fact-Finding Report. Jharkhand: Communist Party of India (Marxist).

Harriss-White, B. 2003. *India Working*. Cambridge: Cambridge University Press.

Harriss-White, B., E. Basile, A. Dixit, P. Joddar, A. Prakash and K. Vidyarthee. 2013. *Dalits and Adivasis in India's Business Economy: Three Essays and an Atlas*. New Delhi: Three Essays Press.

Hodgson, G. 2001. *How Economics Forgot History*. London: Routledge.

India Today (editorial). 2011. 'Jharkhand: Family Blames Mining Mafia for Nun Valsa John's Murder', 17 November. http://indiatoday.intoday.in/story/kerala-mining-protest-nun-killed-jharkhand/1/160363.html (accessed 29 April 2019).

India Today (editorial). 2017. 'Jharkhand BJP MLA Sanjiv Singh, 3 Aides Arrested for Mayor's Murder', 12 April. http://indiatoday.intoday.in/story/bjp-mla-sanjiv-singh-aides-arrested-mayor-murder-jharkhand-dhanbad/1/926818.html (accessed 29 April 2019).

Jha, P.S. 2013. 'How did India become a Predatory State?' Unpublished, on file with author. See http://www.sunday-guardian.com/artbeat/where-did-indian-democracy-go-wrong for an abridged version.

Kanbur, R., S. Lahiri and J. Svejnar. 2012. 'Informality, Illegality and Enforcement', *Review of Development Economics* 16(4): 511.

Kannan, K.P. and G. Raveendran. 2010. 'Growth Sans Employment: A Quarter Century of Jobless Growth in Indian Manufacturing', *Economic and Political Weekly* 44(10): 80–91.

Karat, B. 2012. 'Of Mines, Minerals and Tribal Rights', *The Hindu*, 15 May. http://www.thehindu.com/opinion/lead/of-mines-minerals-and-tribal-rights/article3419034.ece (accessed 29 April 2019).

Khan, M. 2012. 'Political Settlements and the Governance of Growth-Enhancing Institutions', *SOAS Research Online*. http://eprints.soas.ac.uk/9968/ (accessed 29 April 2019).

Kumar, N. 2008, 'Jharkhand is a Failed State', *IndVikalp* 10 July. http://indiavikalp.blogspot.co.uk/2008/07/jharkhand-is-failed-state-nitish-kumar.html (accessed 29 April 2019).

Lahiri-Dutt, K. 2007. 'Illegal Coal Mining in Eastern India: Rethinking Legitimacy and Limits of Justice', *Economic and Political Weekly*, 8 December: 57–68.

Lahiri-Dutt, K., ed. 2014. *The Coal Nation: Histories, Ecologies and Politics of Coal in India*. Farnham: Ashgate.

Lahiri-Dutt, K. and D. Williams. 2005. 'The Coal Cycle: Small-scale Illegal Coal Supply in Eastern India', *Journal of Resource, Environment and Development* 2 (2, September 2005): 93–105.

Marx, K. 1887/1977. *Capital, Volume 1*, Ch. 24, p. 558. London: Lawrence and Wishart.

Mishra, S. 2014. 'Singhs Fight to Become Coal King in Dhanbad', *Times of India* 13 December. http://timesofindia.indiatimes.com/home/specials/2014-assembly-elections/jharkhand-news/Singhs-fight-to-become-Coal-King-in-Dhanbad/articleshow/45498163.cms (accessed 29 April 2019).

Pandey, P. 2017. 'Dhanbad Former Deputy Mayor's Murder: BJP Jharia MLA held for cousin's murder', *Indian Express* 12 April. http://indianexpress.com/article/india/dhanbad-former-deputy-mayors-murder-bjp-jharia-mla-held-for-cousins-murder-4609677/ (accessed 29 April 2019).

Pattanayak, B. 2013. *Language Diversity in Jharkhand*. Ranchi: Jharkhand Tribal Welfare Research Institute. https://www.academia.edu/4227936/Language_Diversity_in_Jharkhand (accessed 29 April 2019).

People's Union for Democratic Rights. 2011. 'The Real Truth Behind The Murder of Sr. Valsa John', Countercurrents.org 27 November. https://www.countercurrents.org/cc301111.htm (accessed 29 April 2019).

Pohkarel, K. and P. Beckett. 2012. 'The Murder of Sister Valsa: the Complete Story', *Wall Street Journal* 5 February. https://blogs.wsj.com/indiarealtime/2012/02/05/the-murder-of-sister-valsa-the-complete-story/ (accessed 29 April 2019).

Press Trust of India. 2013. 'Government Loses Rs 1,800 crore Annually to Coal Mafia', *Business Standard* 21 January. http://www.business-standard.com/article/economy-policy/government-loses-rs-1-800-crore-annually-to-coal-mafia-110070500025_1.html (accessed 29 April 2019).

Press Trust of India. 2016. 'Court Upholds Jail Term of BJP MLA', *Business Standard*, Dhanbad, 17 February. http://www.business-standard.com/article/pti-stories/court-upholds-jail-term-of-bjp-mla-116021701090_1.html (accessed 29 April 2019).

Rajshekhar, M. 2014. 'Chandasi: Close to Narendra Modi's Varanasi Constituency Thrives Illegal Coal Market', *Economic Times*, 15 October. http://economictimes.indiatimes.com/news/politics-and-nation/chandasi-close-to-pm-narendra-modis-varanasi-constituency-thrives-illegal-coal-market/articleshow/44818649.cms (accessed 29 April 2019).

Sanhati (editorial). 2011. 'Overview of Coal Mining in India: Investigative Report from Dhanbad Coal Fields', *Sanhati*, 21 June. http://sanhati.com/excerpted/3798/ (accessed 29 April 2019).

Singh, N. n.d. Blog: No Title. https://nigelanilsingh.wordpress.com/ (accessed 29 April 2019).

Singh, N. 2013. 'India's Coal Cycle Wallahs: "People Have No Alternative but to Steal from Mines"', *The Guardian* 6 September. https://www.theguardian.com/global-development/2013/sep/06/india-coal-cycle-wallahs (accessed 8 April 2019).

Singh, N. 2014. *The Political Economy of the Informal and Illegal Coal Trade in Jharkhand*. Unpublished field report available from the author.

Subramanian, S., ed. 1992. *Themes in Development Economics*. Delhi: Oxford University Press.

Thakur, P. 2009. 'Maoists got 30% cut in Koda's Jharkhand plunder', *Times of India* 14 November. http://timesofindia.indiatimes.com/india/Maoists-got-30-cut-in-Kodas-Jharkhand-plunder/articleshow/5230928.cms (accessed 29 April 2019).

The Sunday Indian (editorial commentary). 2013. 'The Original Don: Surajdeo Singh Became the Byword for Mafia in the 1970s and 80s', 12 May. http://www.thesundayindian.com/en/story/the-original-don/7/47532/ (accessed 29 April 2019).

Tillin, L. 2008. 'Politics in a New State: Chhattisgarh', *Seminar*, https://www.india-seminar.com/2008/591/591_louise_tillin.htm (accessed 29 April 2019).

Tillin, L. 2013. *Remapping India: New States and their Political Origins*. New Delhi: Oxford University Press.

Upadhya, C. 2009. 'The Emergence of New Business Classes', *Economic and Political Weekly* 2 May.

Appendix 1.1: Interviewees

Names have not been disclosed, in order to maintain confidentiality of sources with inside knowledge of IC and access to mafia.

Journalists: Senior editors and journalists in Ranchi and Dhanbhad of *Prabhat Khabar*; *Hindustan Times*; *Dainik Jagran*; *Times of India*; *The Pioneer*; a local Hindi newspaper stringer, Ramgarh; *The Hindu*; Reuters Bureau Chief, New Delhi.

Academics: Professors at the Indian School of Mines' Department of Management Studies; Centre for Mining and the Environment; and Dr Ramesh Sharan, economist, Ranchi University.

Political officials: A BJP Dhanbad senior official with contacts in the 'Singh Mansion' coal mafia; a senior BJP official for the ECL region; an ex-Chief Minister of Jharkhand.

Traders: an established coal trader family; individual coal cycle wallahs at an abandoned mine in Ramgarh; a private sector mining contractor, operating in CIL mines; a smaller coal trader, Ranchi.

Coal India: an ex-CIL official in the Dhanbad region; a head of security for Central Coal Fields Limited (CCL); a former member of the apex Planning Department of CIL; a local trade union official in Ramgarh.

Police: an assistant director general of the Jharkhand police force; Deputy Inspector General of Police (DIG)e, Hazaribagh, formerly Dhanbad, transferred for trying to prosecute coal mafia crime.

Lawyers: Chair of Dhanbad's Bar Association.

Union leaders, politicians: MLA for Bokaro (JVM), senior leader of Dhanbad Coal Karamchari Sangh; potential JVM MLA candidate; senior leader (now deceased), a wing of Janata Mazdoor Sangh (JMS), former deputy mayor of Dhanbad; senior leader, Bihar Janta Khan Mazdoor Sangh, Congress district Secretary; local BMS union representative, Ramgarh.

Others: Bulu Imam, major landowner.

Appendix 1.2 Jharkhand coal union factions influential in illegal coal (May 2014)

Faction	INTUC Rashtriya Colliery Mazdoor Sangh (RCMS) – Rajendra Prasad (R.P.) Singh faction
Party affiliation	Congress party
Leader's official position	Joint General Secretary (INTUC); Congress MLA for Bermo; Jharkhand Finance Minister, Energy Minister (also Welfare)

(Continued)

Alleged 'parallel' business	Transportation – road; activity 'behind the curtains' – a euphemism for illegal activity conducted within a legitimate business; cut of union funds. R.P. Singh's son Anup Singh (an aspiring politician, but not yet with an MLA seat) is actively involved in this business.
Coal India Ltd. subsidiaries	CCL, BCCL, ECL
Notes	R.P. and Anup Singh are reported to work closely with Ajay and Amit Singh (sons of Suresh Singh; confirmed by others). However, INTUC leaders are careful not to have businesses owned in their name. INTUC (the national parent organisation) claims 1.16 *lakh* members.
Faction	INTUC/RCMS – Chandrashekhar 'Dadai' Dubey faction (General Secretary)
Party affiliation	Congress party
Leader's official position	Congress MLA Bishrampur; former Congress MP for Dhanbad; MP candidate, Dhanbad 2014 (Trinamool Congress); former Jharkhand Minister of Rural Development, Panchayati Raj and Minister of Labour
Alleged 'parallel' business	Road transportation; 'behind the curtains' activity; cut of union funds
Coal India Ltd. subsidiaries	CCL, BCCL, ECL
Notes	Leader of a rival RCMS wing – both Singh and Dubey claim union leadership. Dubey stood as Trinamool Congress MP candidate 2014. Expelled from Congress in April 2014, after he criticised party leadership when he was not offered Congress's MP candidacy in Dhanbad. In March 2014, Dubey accused Chief Minister Hemand Soren (JMM) (Congress is their coalition partner) of being engaged in illegal mining and the most corrupt Chief Minister.
Faction	INTUC/RCMS – Mannan Malik wing
Party affiliation	Congress party
Leader's official position	Dhanbad MLA (Congress); President, Congress committee (Dhanbad)

(Continued)

Alleged 'parallel' business	Transportation – road; activity 'behind the curtains' – a euphemism for illegal activity conducted within a legitimate business; cut of union funds.
Coal India Ltd. subsidiaries	CCL, BCCL, ECL
Notes	He does not have explicit links to coal mafia families. However, his son Hubban Malik is linked to Ranvijay Singh (below) who funds Congress.
Faction	INTUC/RCMS – Ajay and Amit Singh wing
Party affiliation	Congress party
Leaders' official position	No official position in INTUC or RCMS; however, likely 'unofficial' funders of Congress.
Alleged 'parallel' business	Transportation; believed to work closely with R.P. Singh and Anup Singh (see INTUC/RCMS above). But they do not have their own union.
Coal India Ltd. subsidiaries	Ajay and Amit Singh's business is focussed on BCCL; but RCMS is also active in CCL, ECL.
Notes	Ajay and Amit Singh are sons of Suresh Singh, a major coal mafia don murdered in 2011.
	Suresh Singh was Congress Treasurer (with close links to INTUC) and stood as a Congress MLA candidate in Dhanbad twice, losing to Kunti Singh (BJP) from the rival Singh Mansion family (below).
Faction	Janata Mazdoor Sangh (JMS) (Jharkhand) – affiliate of the national Hind Mazdoor Sangh (HMS) – Sanjeev Singh faction
Party affiliation	BJP
Leaders' official position	Joint General Secretary of this wing recognised by the Ministry of Coal. Kunti Singh, Jharia MLA, is his mother (and widow of Surya Deo (S.D.) Singh, former Dhanbad MLA (who established the JMS and family transportation business; died 1991).
	Indu Singh (Kunti's sister) is mayor of Dhanbad (Chair of Dhanbad Municipal Corporation). S.D.'s other younger brother Ramadhir Singh is President/Chair of Ballia *zila parishad* (Uttar Pradesh). The family originate from Ballia.
Alleged 'parallel' business	Transportation; apparently road only not rail; extortion – *randari* tax.
Coal India Ltd. subsidiaries	BCCL

(*Continued*)

Notes	Sanjeev Singh (a.k.a. 'Singh Mansion') leads this wing in rivalry with his uncle Bachcha (see below).
	Sanjeev and Ramadhir are accused in the murder of Suresh Singh (below).
	Neeraj Singh is in his 30s; he has been speaking to various parties to find an MLA seat to contest. Neeraj had sought a Congress candidacy but was blocked by Congress leader R.P. Singh (above, of INTUC).
	The Surya Deo/Sanjeev/Bachcha Singh families are rivals to the Suresh Singh family; they fund opposing parties.
Faction	JMS – Bachcha Singh faction
Party affiliation	BJP
Leaders' official position	Ex JDU, RJD; former Jharkhand Minister of Urban Development in Babulal Marandi's government in 2002/3.
Alleged 'parallel' business	Transportation; apparently road only not rail; extortion – *randari* tax.
Coal India Ltd. subsidiaries	
Notes	Bachcha Singh – younger brother of S.D. Singh – leads this wing together with nephew Neeraj Singh, deputy mayor of Dhanbad (Independent). This faction is not officially recognised by the Ministry of Coal.
Faction	Bihar Janta Khan Mazdoor Sangh (BJKMS) (Jharkhand) – led by Ranvijay Singh
Party affiliation	Congress party
Leader's official position	General Secretary, BJKMS; District (Dhanbad) Secretary, Congress
Alleged 'parallel' business	Transportation – road and rail; extortion – *randari* tax.
Coal India Ltd. subsidiaries	Mainly BCCL.
Notes	Leader Ranvijay Singh is the son of Sukuldev Singh (deceased), a cousin of Suresh (see Ajay and Amit Singh above), with whom he was once linked but with whose family this faction is now in dispute over road and rail transporation. Sukuldev was also a rival of the Singh Mansion family and was attacked by S.D. Singh in the 1980s for setting up the BJKMS (and also INTUC leader S.K. Roy).

(*Continued*)

Faction	United Coal Workers Union (UCWU) (AITUC affiliated) (Jharkhand)
Party affiliation	JVM (de facto)
Leader's official position	Dhulu Mahato, Bhagmara MLA (JVM), is effectively leader (with no official title). UCWU is Dhulu Mahato's personal power base. But General Secretary is Lakhanlal Mahato. Dhulu Mahato is the biggest funder of the JVM (led by ex-Chief Minister Babulal Marandi). Dhulu claims to fight against established mafia interests on behalf of workers. As UCWU is AITUC affiliated, Dhulu will also have links to CPI(M) leaders and AITUC General Secretary Gurudas Dasgupta. But AITUC has minimal influence in Jharkhand.
Alleged 'parallel' business	Transportation (major scale). Road. Not clear yet if he is in rail; extortion – *randari* tax
Coal India Ltd. subsidiaries	BCCL: Dhulu Mahato is believed to control a third of BCCL mines. Powerful in Bhagmara and Katras pockets.
Notes	Dhulu Mahato was originally in AJSU (before joining JVM). He also worked in Samresh Singh's union DCKS where he set up Tiger Force (an organised youth gang used to intimidate management, used in workers' protests). At this time, Dhulu was in AJSU. He then left DCKS and AJSU and joined JVM. He is also believed to have originally been employed by Suresh Singh to help run his rail business smoothly (as Dhulu has good relations with OBC and ST groups; dubbed 'localites').
Faction	Dhanbad Coal Karamchari Sangh (DCKS) – led by Samresh Singh
Party affiliation	JVM
Leader's official position	Bokaro MLA (JVM); former minister in Babulal Marandi's government, 2002/3. Contested Dhanbad constituency Lok Sabha election 2014 (JVM). Long-standing trade union leader who has been in the BJP, AJSU and now JVM.
Alleged 'parallel' business	Transportation (but on a much smaller scale). Road not rail.
Coal India Ltd. subsidiaries	BCCL

(Continued)

Notes	DCKS is a small union which set up Tiger Force with Dhulu Mahato. Dhulu broke away to organise the United Coal Workers Union (he is also JVM affiliated).
Faction	**Central Industrial Trade Union (CITU)** – led by S.K. Bakshi
Party affiliation	CPM
Leader's official position	
Alleged 'parallel' business	No major 'parallel' business – but leaders may make small profits on the side.
Coal India Ltd. subsidiaries	
Notes	Little power in Jharkhand.
Faction	**Bihar Colliery Kamgarh Union (BCKU)** – CITU affiliated, led by Nitai or Yogendra Mahato.
Party affiliation	
Leader's official position	Founder, veteran Left union leader A.K. Roy, was Dhanbad MP for 3 terms
Alleged 'parallel' business	No major 'parallel' business. Roy had a reputation for being upright (though ISM's union specialist Pramod Patak says he too may have made profits).
Coal India Ltd. subsidiaries	BCCL; some parts of ECL (that are nearer Dhanbad/Jharia)
Notes	Roy fought the three Singh families (above) and had good links to OBC and local Scheduled Tribe and Caste communities.

2

Jharia's century-old fire kept ablaze by crime and politics

Smita Gupta[1]

In a sequel to Chapter 1 on coal, this chapter addresses the 'negative externality' of fire, showing how fire has become an essential input to the expansion of il/legal coal mining. It focusses on the damaging consequences of a century of unplanned, illegally negligent and dangerous mining, of sand for stowage stolen and black-marketed by the coal mafia in collusion with public corporations, of criminal pollution and lately of the surfacing of subterranean fire laying siege to Jharia town and its region. While three separate planning organisations are responsible for rehabilitation and resettlement, victims of the fiery threat to habitats and livelihoods are progressively and illegally disenfranchised by procrastinating state agencies. Some have been forcibly evicted. The irony that many disenfranchised workers are forced by lack of alternatives to scavenge coal illegally is not lost. The assemblage of fire includes complicitous trade unions, all political parties which benefit through illegal funds, officials in public corporations and government departments, the coal-fire mafia, criminal protection forces and illegal workforces. The fluidity of the fire assemblage stems in part from egregious conflicts of interest: between the coal-fire mafia, which accumulates through the destruction of coal; between labour contractors for public sector fire-fighting and sand-stowing who are also coal mafia; between compromised leaders of labour unions and exploitive interests of the coal-fire mafia; between national interests in eviction for capital-intensive opencast mining and local mafia interests in corralling a desperate labour force atop the fire for hazardous coal extraction and pilferage. The politicisation of criminal organisations and of labour and the criminal entwining of labour politics with party politics combine to make fire-crimes an exemplary case of intreccio.

Introduction: a town sitting atop a burning inferno

In the twenty-first century, the 100-year-old smouldering underground mine fire in the Dhanbad-Jharia coalfield started to erupt at the surface in the settlements of coal miners. Several single-storey houses around the colliery developed cracks. The main roads and highways developed fissures, as did the railway lines. The Director General of Mines Safety (DGMS) in the state corporation, Bharat Coking Coal Ltd. (BCCL), the Jharkhand state government and the private mining companies have all failed to undertake protective and remedial measures, and now the fire has spread under the old town. This chapter explores the nexus of economic criminal interests and politics that perpetuates the fires, shapes their 'deregulation' and subverts the state's responses to their victims.

Jharia (in Dhanbad district, Jharkhand) lies in the mineral-rich Damodar river valley covering a total area of 435 km², and is the repository of most of India's coal, copper, iron ore and uranium reserves. Industrial underground coal mining started here in the second half of the nineteenth century, after which both steel manufacturing and power generation became important economic activities. The town has a population of one million people; almost half live on top of the century-old fire and around three-quarters are affected by it. In the Jharia coalfields, there are about 110 official coal mines and reportedly a similar number of unofficial or illegal mines. They are India's chief source of coking coal, essential for steel production (see Chapter 1).

Coal India Ltd. (CIL) increasingly outsources entire opencast mines to multinational companies and companies previously only engaged in transport and logistics. Opencast production conditions have allowed the intensive exploitation of both coal and labour: and most private investment is in dynamite-blasting, heavy earth-moving machinery (HEMM), mechanical diggers and dumpers and trucks – most of which are discrete parts of the production process and easily outsourced. As a result of opencast mining, coal production by Coal India Ltd. doubled between 1991 and 2010, even as underground production fell. Companies that have leased mines from BCCL have vested interests: first, in ever-faster extraction of coal, ostensibly to 'dig out the fire and save the coal'; and second, in the fire spreading beyond officially allocated seams/areas so that they can expand opencast mining operations under the guise of emergency fire-fighting. Profit lies in more fires, not fewer.

The Jharia coalfield has over 40 workable coal seams. Unlike elsewhere in the world, here the upper seams have far superior quality coal, and the seams below the eighth level contain medium to non-coking coal. This natural bounty has proved to be Jharia's ecological undoing since it has meant cheap and quick extraction of quality coal from a spread-out area, converting the entire landscape into a large scarred coal mine, and displacing and impoverishing local people. The shaft and gallery underground mines are raided illegally. Very few are run legally by the Tatas and BCCL, and BCCL runs at a loss. The diversity of coal deposits means that mining can be undertaken and coal transported at widely differing scales, under property regimes and labour relations ranging from primitive tools to large-scale, industrial mechanised mining technology and relentless labour exploitation – and including a range of illegal activity ranging from petty theft from tailings to the grand theft of full rail wagons (Chapter 1).

In this chapter we will explain how the nexus between politics and economic crime violates policies for both fire-fighting and fire prevention on the one hand and policies for resettlement and rehabilitation on the other. Collaborator trade unions enforce this criminal economy of fire and generate a new impetus for political parties to control these trade unions. This account results from a stakeholder approach to field research over a period of several months in 2015–16 following up a nine-member fact-finding political and legal study of the fire and the processes of rehab and resettlement carried out in 2013 (Communist Party of India (Marxist) 2013). The second phase of field research focussed on the distinctive politics of fire. As in the first report, evidence was provided by residents, coal corporation and local government officials, community leaders and union members, scientists and experts. Sources have not been identified for security reasons unless permission was given or the comment is in the public domain.

The history and anatomy of coal fires

'Jharia district has been an epitome of unplanned, unscientific mining since the first mine opened in 1894, and we have been paying the price ever since' (T.N. Singh, former director of the Central Mining Research Institute, Dhanbad). Mining in Jharia started in 1894 and the first coal mine fire was reported in 1916. By 1972, there were about 70 active fires spread over 17 km^2, affecting half of Jharia's 90 mines/collieries. Landslides and subsidence are common, covering about 35 km^2 in this coalfield alone. BCCL's preference for opencast and slaughter mining methods meant that pits were dug near the abandoned underground mines,[2] which are a labyrinth of open corridors previously occupied by coal seams standing on coal pillars. When oxygen enters from the air above, it causes spontaneous combustion in deserted mines. Such fires have high ecological and economic costs, burning away a non-renewable and vital energy resource.

The fires contain highly poisonous gases such as carbon monoxide and carbon dioxide, methane, nitrogen oxides and sulphur, and other particulate matter. Not only do these cause underground explosions and land subsidence, they also contribute to cancers and respiratory diseases (Finkelman 2004). Atmospheric effects include local temperature increases and, through methane, CO_2 and radiative forcing, contribute to global warming (Chikkalur, Sagar and Sankar 2009). Groundwater levels are falling continually as, due to mining, the aquifers are disturbed and their yield is significantly reduced. Water is contaminated and acidifies due to the leaching by sulphur present in coal. Land degradation from the open pits, the overburden and the fires combine to inhibit plant life. The fire surrounds Jharia town on three sides and has entered the city in several places. In 1979, a committee chaired by Mr S.P. Gugnani, Joint Secretary in the Department of Coal, observed that:

> the gigantic and multifarious subsidence problems in Jharia Coalfield was caused due to existence of old workings with full height extraction and wide galleries, multi-seam and multi-section development under shallow depths, existence of developed seams under extracted lower seam with stowing, etc. There are many towns, villages, rivers, roads, railway line etc., in Jharia Coalfield which are standing over small pillars/stooks reported to be water logged. If, by any chance, this water drains away it may cause subsidence. In addition, fire is also active in some areas, causing danger to the surface structure. In many mines, size of pillars, which were left below the surface structures as a protective measure, is not known because of non-availability of off-set plans of abandoned workings. (Bharat Coking Coal Limited 2008)

The prevention and proliferation of fire

However, while BCCL attributes responsibility for fires to old workings or mining prior to nationalisation, it is no small irony that many of the well-known measures for preventing and controlling fires in coal mines have been developed by, and established in, India. These include hydraulic sand-stowing of hollow mines; blind-flushing with fly ash and grout; injecting inert gases, such as nitrogen, into cavities; isolating affected areas by trenching, grout barriers and back filling; surface sealing and blanking, etc. And yet their implementation is extremely lax, with only 10 fires controlled since 2008 according to available data (Raju et al. 2016). Meanwhile, the central government corporation, the largest coal company in the world, Coal India, and its subsidiaries and subcontractors are pursuing the task of extracting the coal faster than the fire spreads, which officials admit off the record is not possible. By 2002, on paper, BCCL had apparently filled the burning mines with 50 million tonnes of sand. Most experts (including BCCL officials themselves) agree that less than 20 per cent of this sand was actually brought to the affected mines and put in the pits. This is because the contracts for sand stowing were given to the same criminal organisations, known as the mafia (see Chapter 1), which controlled coal transport, trade unions, etc. False invoicing, fraudulent certification by DGMS and continued production by BCCL meant that about 80 per cent of the sand was shown on paper and paid for, but never used. This 'sand scam' earned millions for the coal mafia and was widely reported by newspapers and journalists (see Daniel and Williams 2013). Thus, the coal mafia and the BCCL officials worked openly and collaboratively: the mafia was even referred to as another BCCL 'department' since it not only regulated fire and sand but was also mobilised to break workers' movements and to lock the workforce working for state corporations into the debt and penury to be discussed below.

By the early 1990s, these fires had burnt an estimated 42 million tonnes of coking coal. Still, about 7,000 million tonnes of coal reserves are under different surface properties and around another 1,800 million are jammed under fires. Opencast mining is offered as the solution to control and 'dig out the fire' and the coal but, paradoxically, this fire-fighting measure sets previously unaffected areas on fire. Another solution that had been found feasible in certain circumstances was the rapid digging of trenches that were non-combustible. In 2009, this practice was subcontracted to two agencies that were engaged in illegal mining and, according to a journalist, 'had a vested interest in the fire jumping the trench'. The trench-digging was so deliberately slow and erratic that once again the solution became the problem and the fire jumped the barrier as oxygen spread to hitherto unexposed seams.

Non-enforcement and violations by state agencies

The coal mines regulations and the systematic support rules require that the cavities formed after the extraction of coal be immediately filled with a mixture of sand, water and fire-retardant chemicals to avoid damage to the surface area and prevent subsidence; however, these rules and regulations have never been enforced by the Director General of Mine Safety (DGMS). Even at the time of nationalisation, certificates of the mines' 'good health' were alleged to have been issued without verification, via political pressure and monetary 'gifts'. In the past two decades, since the spread of fire has assumed catastrophic proportions, the DGMS has served several 'show cause' notices to BCCL for non-compliance with fire regulations. In the mid-2000s, it even recommended a total ban on mining, pending compliance. This was not accepted. Clearly, '(t)he stumbling block in controlling fire is not lack of technology, but the incompetence of BCCL itself'.[3]

As per the law, no mining can take place at or below the surface within 50 metres of a highway or railway track; therefore, the underground mining by BCCL under and close to the highways and railway lines is a blatant violation. A letter from the chair of the railway board to the Secretary of the Ministry of Coal, dated 5 April 2002, charges BCCL with undercutting the safety and stability of railway lines in the area by 'indiscriminate mining without following safety provisions stipulated by the Directorate-General of Mine Safety' (quoted in Sethi 2006). In response, BCCL asked the railways to hand over the Dhanbad–Pathardih railway line on lease, wanting the 182.27 acres below the rail-line in order to dig out the fire, mine the coal and expand hydraulic sand stowing. To quote a BCCL manager in the field: 'of course it is a violation, but the coal below the railway line was of high quality'. The railway board fell in line and leased the land to BCCL for 15 years.

Regulative shift: from stabilising fires to mass displacement of selected victims

In 1979, a committee headed by Mr S.P. Gugnani in India's Department of Coal examined the safety of people living over underground workings. It determined the policy formally implemented until 2005. This comprised three inter-related but distinct strategies: i) fire-fighting measures to douse and cut off the fires; ii) stabilisation of old workings to repair and halt fires and subsidence in controllable areas; and iii) evacuation and rehabilitation of inhabitants in uncontrollable ones. BCCL's 2005 *Master Plan for Dealing with Fire, Subsidence and Rehabilitation in the Leasehold of BCCL* (updated in March 2008) changed the Gugnani approach. 'The final and permanent solution is evacuation of the affected area and rehabilitation' (BCCL 2008, 17), it specified, doing away with the distinction between controllable and uncontrollable areas in inhabited subsidence-prone unstable areas; people would henceforth be evacuated irrespective of the degree of control. This reversed the government's stand in the supreme court. The supreme court order dated 16 January 2008 stated:

> (a)s regards fires and subsidence of earth in the mining areas, two reports have been filed by the Committee appointed by this Court ... It is pointed out by the learned Amicus Curiae *that no serious steps have been taken either for rehabilitation of the residents of the affected area or for controlling the fires in these areas ... many a time the remedial measures are not taken and whatever action is taken so far, are not sufficient.* (Jharkhand High Court 2011, emphasis added)

According to a field interview with Ashok Aggarwal of Jharia Bachao Samiti:

> Very little was actually done by way of mitigation and redress. The fires are purposely not being put out by BCCL. They want the fire to spread. All political parties are united on this, because the illegal mining that is facilitated and even accelerated by the fire funds parties in their elections and in feeding their foot soldiers, not to mention in affording luxurious lifestyles. It is no surprise that the entire political class wants the fires to spread. The situation was deliberately allowed to escalate and then it was very easy for the authorities to throw up their hands and declare that the situation is now out of control!

G.K. Bakshi of CITU too is of the view that BCCL did this because their interests (plus those of the private companies to which the mining is outsourced) lie in letting the fires burn. Opencast mining is BCCL's preferred mining technique, but laws relating to forests, land acquisition and public infrastructure have to be complied with in order to move into new coal-bearing territories. An array of squatters, occupiers, tenants, owners, workers, residents, *panchayats*, etc., has several types of rights on these lands, whose claims have to be addressed through due process. Only in an emergency and life-threatening situation can the state exercise extraordinary powers, on 'humanitarian' grounds, to bypass due process and forcibly evict people without proper resettlement and rehabilitation. One of the 'humanitarian' procedures is even more aggressive coal mining. The fire is the perfect *fait accompli* and coal mining is both the cause and effect in this pursuit of profit. Where a fire does not create a sufficiently hazardous situation or the inhabitants prove to be more stubborn, and when all else fails, the police have been used to forcibly remove the residents – a measure justified as combining their immediate survival interests with the national interest (Gupta 2013). The BCCL chief managing director has declared that 'the fire is being dealt through engaging hired Heavy Earth Moving Machinery and coal thus released is being mined and sold'.[4]

Contractors are recruited from coal mafia families, other private companies and family members of politicians from all the mainstream political parties, and BCCL has regularly outsourced several operations, including fire-fighting, to them. Of course, the central governing party (which controlled the Coal Ministry and BCCL) also captures contracts but it has been tactically important not to alienate the opposition excessively and to distribute some contracts to them in order to ensure their complicity. As the mining technology shifted towards highly mechanised HEMM-based opencast mining, which required far less investment, the fire provided the golden opportunity to hand out 'fire-fighting' excavation contracts that were nothing but an excuse to bypass all procedures and rules and award de facto coal mining rights. This becomes clear from an analysis of some of the recent contracts that have been awarded for 'excavating the fire'.

The Dhanbad coal-fire mafia has developed a nexus of interests with politicians, officials, owners of industries and leaders of trade unions which is the stuff of Indian legends: Bollywood cinema publicly depicts the blurring of lines between law, law enforcement and crime – to which the public at large acquiesce.[5] Relationships have developed complexity and the 'politicisation of criminals' is perhaps now as relevant a concept as the 'criminalisation of politics' (National Commission to Review the Working of the Constitution 2001).

The coal-fire mafia: a product of 'nationalisation'

After the mines were nationalised, the mine owners were replaced by a criminal class complicit with BCCL. It is this mafia that is responsible for perpetuating the fires. Some pre-existing private mines, escaping takeover through bribes and influence, continued as illegal entities. The coal mafia took over as contractors and managers of these illegal mines, and acted as a combination of jobber-labour-overseer-foreman-trade union leader in the legal BCCL mines (*Sanhati* 2011). The mafia took over contracts in three areas – labour, transport and sand stowing – with transport contracts serving as a facilitator both for illegal coal mining and for the fudging of sand transport records, overstating the volume of sand actually carried to the mines. The impact of this on the fire was disastrous: fire-proofing happened only on paper. In many instances, the top strata of this mafia came from a section of the coal industry's trade union leadership, operating through regional allegiances and caste dominance to preserve its authority. Local Bhumihar and Rajput dons set up armed gangs and trade unions of people from their areas and castes. Trade unionists say that it is extremely difficult – near impossible – in many parts of Dhanbad for authentic trade union work to break through these caste and regional ties cemented by loans, employment and other forms of patronage. In turn, the mafia helped corrupt BCCL officials to amass huge illegal wealth in return for ignoring the non-execution of fire-prevention/fighting measures, says S.K. Bakshi, a prominent CITU leader, in an interview with the author: 'Huge contracts were given by BCCL to companies set up by Suraj Deo Singh and his family to fill up abandoned mines with sand. The fire spread because management turned a blind eye.' The theft, diversion and trade of coal on the black market, overstated and fabricated fire-preventive/fire-fighting operations and transport costs, and fraudulent labour contracts and muster rolls all occurred through what has been called the 'usurpation of the state' (Bharti 1989).

Labour politics then fed party politics. One retired bureaucrat reported facing great political pressure in the 1990s when he tried to push the Dhanbad administration to inspect trucks operating late at night or before dawn to check if they were laden with sand to fill the mines or instead with stolen coal. He said, 'Party leaders are nothing but gang leaders. They ensured that men of their ilk were elected to local bodies, the state legislature and Parliament.' He explained that the secret annexures to the still-classified Vohra Committee Report, set up by the Ministry of Home Affairs in 1993 to examine the functioning of criminal syndicates/mafia organisations and their links with government officials and political leaders, contained incontrovertible evidence against several Dhanbad politicians and bureaucrats on how they 'set the city on fire'. He reported that secret logs maintained by two corrupt railway employees showed that about twice the amount of coal accounted for left Dhanbad daily, only to vanish en route at an unscheduled stop in the forest. 'All this coal was being dug up in the name of digging out the fire, no records are being kept of quantities in the name of urgency. The fire is a Godsend for these vultures.' The spread and intensity of hazardous mining expanded and with it, inevitably, the fire spread – as did indiscriminate opencast mining, ostensibly to dig out the fire.

Fire and safety: the coal-fire mafia and trade union interventions

History bears witness to the severe brutality of class struggle against the labour movements in mining areas (Simeon 1996). For this very reason, trade unions have tended to be caught in a political paradox; both are vehicles of the class struggle as well as its biggest antagonists. In the case of Dhanbad, a powerful section has been co-opted, developing into the foundation and organising principle of the mafia. This has meant the loss of an important institution for democratic rights mobilisation and struggle. The undermining of workplace safety through the crushing of genuine trade unions and the complicity of the mafia-unions have also fanned the fires. The All India Trade Union Confederation (AITUC) and its later offshoot Confederation of Indian Trade Unions (CITU) represent the communist trade unions active in the area since the onset of mining. By the late 1960s, the ultra-left Maoist-Leninist trade unions also became active with the ascendancy of Bihar Colliery Kamgar Union (BCKU) led by A.K. Roy. On the other side of the party political spectrum, the All India Trade Union Congress (INTUC), the Bhartiya Mazdoor Sangh (BMS), affiliated respectively to the centrist Congress and right-wing Bharatiya Janata Party (BJP), and the Janata Mazdoor Sangh (JMS) union, affiliated to the self-acclaimed 'socialist' (not communist)[6] mafia, viewed their members as tools in this economic and political fight to accumulate money and power, through collaboration with mine management. Mafia dons like V.P. Sinha, Suraj Deo Singh and Suresh Singh combined party politics, trade union and mafia activities. As class collaborators, they became the natural enemies of the leftist trade unions, killing many of their leaders. The most crucial linkage between the mafia and coal mining was through the labour contractors. In the classic pattern of jobbers, credit played an important role in contracts linking the money-lender, the labour contractor and the trade union leader. At the mine offices when wages were disbursed, the mafiosi ensured compulsory monetary extractions from the workers. Members of the mafia also ran gambling and liquor dens, further skimming workers' wages. The mafia controlled trade unions and used agitational tools such as the *gherao*, lightning strikes and demonstrations as real or potential threats to extort protection money from illegal mine owners and the public sector undertakings (PSU). Besides being victims of such extortion, managers of BCCL also used these selfsame trade union leaders to discipline troublemakers.

Thus, workers had to face hostilities from the growing coal mafia. A.K. Roy then provided the workers with an organisation to defend themselves.[7] Vehemently opposed by the mining management and the collaborator trade unions, his was one of the few trade unions that raised the issue of industrial safety and hazardous mining. After the Emergency in the mid-1970s,[8] the 'mafia dons' decided to become politicians – initiating the process of 'politicisation of criminals' in this region. The mafia realised that bribery alone was not enough to influence state policies in their favour; elected representatives also often failed to protect them adequately. Therefore, they needed to enter legislative institutions directly; this also legitimised and reinforced their power through immunity. For example, while being a mafia don, Suraj Deo Singh (from 1977 to his death in 1991) and after him his widow Kunthi Singh (from 2004 to 2014) were legislators. His strong links with socialist politicians like Jaiprakash Narain and Chandrashekhar, the former Prime Minister of India (also from Balia district in UP), helped (Iqbal 2012; Kalbag 2013). The infiltration of the socialist parties by criminals and local strongmen accelerated as the fortunes of the Indian National Congress faded after the Emergency, a phenomenon that continues to this day.

A.K. Roy then had to respond and first successfully defeated these hostile forces in the Bihar assembly elections in 1967. The BCKU entered electoral politics as the Marxist Coordination Committee (MCC) and such was Roy's appeal that he was elected MLA while being incarcerated during the Emergency. He represented Dhanbad three times, each in the Lok Sabha and the Vidhan Sabha, and started losing only after liberalisation, in 1991. After Suraj Deo Singh died, many of his clan occupied public offices, in recent times mostly contesting on BJP tickets. The mayor and deputy mayor of the city are presently drawn from feuding factions of the family, as are the MLAs from Dhanbad and the adjoining Bokaro region. Two family members contested the Jharia assembly seat in the 2014 elections, one on a BJP ticket and the other from the Congress. Such extensive party-political penetration affects both the extent of the fires and the safety of mining conditions.

The politics of fires and mine accidents

A senior serving officer in the safety watchdog the Directorate General of Mines Safety (DGMS) told me in January 2016 that 'safety was not at all a concern for BCCL and CIL and there have been too many accidents in the coalfields'. The same factors that led to the unmitigated spread of the fire also generate a large number of mining accidents in Jharia: unscientific mining compounded by institutional and political collusion to compromise safety. The undermining of trade unions destroyed this important watchdog role. The DGMS official commented:

> (A)fter nationalisation and under the mafia regime, DGMS completely surrendered and abdicated from its watchdog and regulatory role. Even though CIL and its subsidiary gave orders worth *crores* of rupees for safety equipment, gear and interventions, these were through contractors and sub-contractors, which were mostly controlled by the mafia. Little or nothing was done.

The other reason why safety is undermined is economic – not only the desire for increased private income streams but also concerns for production 'efficiency'. Meeting production targets has meant initiating cost-cutting measures, the increasingly hazardous mining of previous workings or mines adjacent to abandoned workings, and reckless opencast or slaughter mining. Safety norms such as the mandatory thickness of barriers between water bodies are then ignored. Abandoned waterlogged mines are not maintained, air pockets are not tested and seepage is neglected. The Bagdigi colliery disaster in February 2001, which killed 29 people, was caused during the pursuit of a 60,000-tonne shortfall in the 1.8 *lakh*-tonne annual target. The compulsory 60-metre barrier that separated Bagdigi from the waterlogged abandoned Jairampur mine had been breached. Workers' lives are given the lowest priority: most workers are not recorded, nor are most accidental deaths. However, the trade unions cannot escape some of the responsibility for lack of safe working conditions since there is a mandatory tripartite safety committee made up of representatives from trade unions, the BCCL management and central government. Yet this does not meet regularly; often no meetings are held for years.

Charred by underground fires: the Bagdigi, Bhatdih and Sugamdih explosions revisited

If the failure to prevent mining accidents is investigated further, criminal reasons why fires continue unabated are revealed. After flooding, the second most pervasive cause of accidents and loss of life is explosions. Fires cause underground roofs to collapse due to the accumulation of methane and coal dust – as happened in the New Kendra colliery where 55 miners were killed in January 1994. 'The important reasons for explosions include the absence of fire stoppings; the absence of mechanical ventilators in fire-affected seams; the use of open lamps rather than safety lamps; overly thin and un-maintained strata between the seams... Methane accumulation can be controlled through three measures – ventilation, safety lamps and methano-metres and, most importantly, hydraulic sand-stowing of used mining channels. Further, the coal-air suspension, which makes the methane even more lethal, needs constantly to be settled with water spraying', according to a geologist at the Indian School of Mines, Dhanbad (interviewed in December 2015). There is abysmal managerial and regulatory failure in this regard. 'It is a real scam. The management basically manufactures a roof collapse at the opening of the channel and seals it with sand, for show. The tunnels are in fact empty spaces which collect methane. I am convinced that this inadequate stowing and sealing is the cause of the Bhatdih and many other explosions,' said a CITU leader, speaking in 2016 about the 50 miners killed in a September 2006 accident in Bhatdih. He said

> The actual trigger was probably an electric spark caused by old wiring which had remained unattended for three decades... The Bhatdih colliery management was using a dangerous explosive in an inadequately ventilated, un-stowed, third-degree gassy mine with poorly-maintained electric cables and full of the highly volatile and combustible methane and coal dust. Is there any doubt that this accident is man-made, like the fire in the Jharia coalfields?

Brinda Karat, a former member of parliament who repeatedly raised the issue at the central and state government levels, observed:

> All agencies – BCCL, CCL as the mine owners, DGMS as the regulatory authority and the central government (which is entrusted with mine safety under the constitutional division of responsibilities) – have abdicated their responsibility. The mafia and its collaborator unions not only terrorised the city for profit and power, but also enforced the management's lackadaisical culture and cost-saving practices threatening workplace safety and workers' lives. The same factors that cause accidents also spread the fire.

Fire and the illegal coal economy

Quite apart from the fact that illegal coal accounts for about 20 per cent of the total annual output (by the government's own admission) (India Environment Portal, n.d.) and feeds the accumulation trajectories and political might of a few people, it is, as explained in Chapter 1, a very important source of livelihood for thousands of working-class families. Coal is used as energy by thousands of small informal businesses that do not qualify for coal from official sources. Although those on the lowest rung of the pyramid earn a pittance, it is nonetheless an important alternative to the retrenchments and lost jobs after neoliberal labour reforms and mechanisation.

Chapter 1 describes the four major forms taken by the illegal coal sector in Jharia.[9] Two further aspects shape the nature of the criminality of fire: first, the underlying labour relations – distinguishing hired labour-based employment from family labour-based self-employment; and second, the stage dominated by illegal activity – production or distribution.

To consider the first of these, labour relations, an estimated 100 mines are sites of unauthorised or unregulated mining managed by powerful politicians-businessmen using hired labour. Unscientifically and unsafely exploited, these mines accelerate the spread of fire. In such sites the poorest self-employed workers and their unpaid family labour also scavenge for coal, bribing law enforcement officers and, at the same time, being victimised by them. Their collection grounds include the hazardous abandoned underground shafts, fire-affected subsidence holes, parked lorries, railway sidings and wagons and open-cast mines. A huge number, they are victims of the fire as oustees and are subject to hazardous labour processes. Many retrenched workers displaced from the fire-affected areas have taken up scavenging to subsist. At abandoned burning mines in Jharia, men, women and even children scavenge daily to sell their pickings on the local market. Since coal scavenging is their main source of income, any relocation which does not afford alternative livelihoods will be met with resistance. In Boka Pahari and many other similar settlements, thousands of people live over blazing coal fires and earn a fraction of the minimum wage. Not only is this activity physically dangerous – constant exposure to the threat of accidents, inhaling poisonous gases – it is also regarded by law enforcement agencies as trespassing. Facing disciplinary measures from mine companies and enforcement agencies, scavengers and coal cycle wallahs are forced to pay a share of their labour as bribes to police officers and other mining officials.

In the second aspect, whether it is production or distribution in which illegality predominates, we can locate cases where coal is diverted by the legal owner or leaseholder, with the help of transporters and hired labour, from its specified purpose to other uses, such as brick kilns. BCCL managers responsible for monitoring are mostly complicit but plead helplessness given the political clout of the mine owners and other coal traders and mafia involved. The theft of coal in transit – from trucks and railway wagons, by organised gangs hiring groups of foot soldiers (with the collusion of railway and other government functionaries) – supplies illegal coal for traders and for the dominant mafia.

Fire provides the justification and the smokescreen behind which these illegal activities occur. Fire creates hazardous workplaces and is, in turn, created by unscientific and unsafe techniques. Illegal mines contribute further to the spread of fire to new areas since no precautions are taken and explosions are common. Such mines include a whole range of enterprises – from small-scale village mining with primitive equipment to highly organised, large-scale and semi-mechanised mines employing hundreds of workers, in connivance with CIL. We found instances where the same mine was operated illegally and legally, such as in Basra where 25 local brick kilns purchase the illegal coal mined from the 10-foot upper seam, while the lower layer is mined by CIL. Often, mines which are considered unremunerative for working by CIL at its regulated wage and safety standards are informally transferred to the highly unsafe, labour-intensive and low-paid but more profitable illegal realm, through the labour mafia. The hallmark of these mines is their low safety standards, which cause deaths and fires – both unrecorded. So, a large part of the local workforce, especially in rural areas, is absorbed into these hazardous and underpaid illegal activities. 'No political party that is interested in winning elections will ever suggest the closure of these illegal mines', said a senior journalist in January 2016.

Eviction, resettlement and rehabilitation (R&R)

Despite the long history of the fire and the several committees and enquiries that have been set up to address it, and despite their recommendations (which embodied more or less the same approach of combining fire control and stabilisation, with recourse to human resettlement only where land stabilisation was impossible), very little has been done by way of mitigation and redress. As with fire, so with rehabilitation: the law is frequently broken. Once the situation had been deliberately allowed to develop uncontrolled, the authorities evaded responsibility for its outcome. Both the central government and CIL/BCCL have evaded liability for R&R as conceived in the law and policy.

The evasion of liability for R&R by CIL and the Indian government

In India, the legal right to resettlement and rehabilitation for project-affected persons was not recognised by law until 2013, and was guided mostly by policies from different ministries: railways, highways, etc. To a large extent, access to the process of rehabilitation was the outcome of political or popular mass movements against displacement. As an outcome of such political resistance, Coal India Ltd. also introduced a policy to address the R&R of people affected by mining. However, over time, coverage and entitlements narrowed.

R&R entitlements of workers

Even though they may have been working the mines for years, and sometimes decades, BCCL employees find their rights constantly violated since they are designated by BCCL as 'contract workers' bound to contractors engaged in 'work of a temporary and peripheral nature'. Several courts have ruled this to be a 'sham and bogus' practice, and have decreed that long-term workers should be treated as direct employees of the company since the work is evidently of a perennial and permanent nature.[10] Under the Mines Act 1952 (periodically amended), all these unorganised sector contract workers would be designated as 'employed in a mine' with full liability borne by the 'mine owner'. This early definition of eligibility included all forms of labour, employment and management, with little scope for mischievous interpretation and misuse. In fact, the Mines (Amendment) Bill, 2011 (Government of India 2011) expands the definition of 'owner' to any person having 'ultimate control' over the affairs of the mine. The moment contract workers are recognised as bona fide mine workers and BCCL is recognised as the 'owner' or 'principal employer' irrespective of intermediation by contractors and subcontractors, they hold all the statutory and non-statutory rights conferred upon BCCL workers, including to full R&R.

The entitlements of 'affected persons'

The scope of the law is inclusive. Section 13 (2) (j) of the Mines and Minerals (Development and Regulation) Act of 1957 empowers central government to make rules about the rights of third parties in cases where 'any such party may be prejudicially affected for reason of any prospecting or mining operations'. Even the Mines and Minerals (Development and Regulation) Act of 2015 (Government of India 2015) makes provisions that benefits should accrue to 'the family affected by mining related operations of the company', including livelihoods essential to mine workers such as refuse sweeping and retail trading. There appears to be no ambiguity in the legislative intent of these formulations: it is to ensure that R&R reaches *any and every family* adversely affected by *any and every mining-related* activity. However, the executive – through the Ministry of Coal and CIL – have deliberately and substantively undermined this legislative intent in successive policy documents (CIL's R&R policy or the Jharia Action Plan) by excluding many groups of formally eligible victims. Below we discuss two examples of the repercussions of this progressive and extra-legal exclusion from eligibility. In one, the definition of 'affected persons' in the R&R policy of CIL is fairly inclusive and covers most categories – encroachers, owners and livelihood-dependents. By adding the phrase 'involuntary displacement for any other reason' it also makes CIL responsible when their mining has adverse effects on 'residence or other property or source of livelihood' or 'involuntary displacement' by any activity (not only a project) of CIL including – but not restricted to – land acquisition. This clearly includes the fire and subsidence-affected victims too. But such persons have progressively been denied coverage, with eligibility being restricted to land losers or bona fide land owners to the exclusion of squatters and encroachers. Similarly, in the second example, even though the Jharia Master Plan is designed for CIL areas, it excludes the provision of a job to families affected by fire and subsidence, even though this is required by CIL's own R&R policy (Coal India Limited 2008). In 2012, CIL diluted its own 2008 policy by inserting the additional condition that entitlements would only accrue to those losing at least two acres of land. DGMS is the enforcement agency responsible for declaring areas as fire-affected and endangered or unsafe for human settlement. Unless DGMS process is followed and the area is declared dangerous, the provisions of the Master Plan do not kick in. In 12 years, DGMS has surveyed only 30 per cent of the area.

There are three legal frameworks within which R&R takes place in the leasehold lands of BCCL.

1. The comprehensive Master Plan (approved by the Ministry of Coal and the government of Jharkhand) deals with fire, subsidence and rehabilitation, with R&R for non-BCCL persons ('encroachers' and owners) in the areas declared endangered by BCCL/DGMS, financed by the Ministry of Coal and implemented by the government of Jharkhand.

2. In the non-endangered areas within the leasehold, Coal India's 2012 R&R policy kicks in only when land acquisition proceedings have started. It restricts entitlements to only those 'displaced persons' who are what it calls 'entitled project affected persons': persons who lose more than two acres of land. Displaced people appreciate the entitlements under this policy because it offers jobs as economic rehabilitation. But very few people are eligible.

3. A recent BCCL intervention has resulted from a BCCL Board decision to enforce so-called 'local settlements' and provide 'temporary' R&R to 'encroacher' families residing in the coal-bearing areas where opencast mining is underway (e.g. 292 families from the Ghanoodih opencast mine can squat on BCCL land with no rights whatsoever and receive meagre financial assistance from BCCL of INR 10,000 per family). As discussed below, these are completely illegal evictions and violate the Master Plan as well as Coal India's own policies.

Illegal eviction as 'temporary' resettlement by BCCL

In several localities, people live in small settlements on the upper terraces of opencast mines. Many of these hamlets are also home to the unorganised contract workforces of these same mines, whose employment is as insecure as are their lives. As the fire expands into these areas and fire-fighting excavation is contracted out, BCCL in connivance with the contractors and local police – and in a shocking illegality – dynamite out 'encroachers', who should be considered 'affected persons' under CIL's own R&R policy. BCCL gives a one-time lump sum settlement of INR 10,000 and a temporary plot on a reclaimed and refilled mined site to construct houses (at victims' own cost!). This is both a dishonest and undemocratic ploy to deprive the oustees of their R&R rights.

The practical role of the Coal Ministry's Master Plan

The Master Plan package has one serious flaw: its complete disregard for employment and sustainable livelihoods. While it formally caters for residence and basic needs, it does not provide for any economic rehabilitation. Furthermore, relocation has been planned to locations where employment is not available. This has made the process extremely unpopular among the oustees. This unacceptable R&R is admitted on record by even the most senior BCCL and state government officials, two of its three main architects.[11] The Belgoria township built under the Master Plan bears eloquent testimony to the indifference and inaction of the various actors – BCCL and the state government's Jharia Rehabilitation and Development Authority (JRDA) – over the last 17 years. No public consultation process was initiated by the agencies before planning the resettlement site nor was consent sought. Sustainable livelihoods and access to public programmes and development schemes were not ensured, resulting in no access to basic needs for food and social security, or to social infrastructure. Even burial sites were not made available; nor was transport available in the remote site, 8 km from Dhanbad. 'New Jharia township' in Belgoria is a complete misnomer for this rather sorry apology for resettlement, consisting of an already dilapidated and crumbling cluster of ugly housing with blocks of cement falling off and large cracks, mould and seepage spots marking almost the entire set of flats.

The location of Belgoria is a problem, given the distance and its poor and costly connectivity to Dhanbad and Jharia where health and educational facilities are sited. Several oustees (women in particular) quit their employment because of prohibitive travel costs. There is, in fact, no health centre, hospital or medical care except for a token mobile health van which BCCL sends in a couple of times a month for a few hours. People have to travel to Dhanbad or return to Jharia for healthcare, which is private and costly. We were told that, after hiring a private vehicle in the absence of ambulances, a woman died in labour on her way to hospital in Dhanbad. While there is a ration shop for PDS supplies, less than a fifth of the households have ration cards. A few shops have sprung up but there is no marketplace. The importance of various identity cards like the voter ID, ration card, MGNREGS job card, etc., cannot be overemphasised, as these not only establish identity but are also a necessary

condition for access to various citizenship rights. These include development programmes and schemes such as the employment guarantee, subsidised food, pensions, scholarships, health care, disability allowances,
anganwadis (nurseries) and crèches, etc. Lack of ID is therefore a violation of the Master Plan itself.

Slow R&R: a conflict between local and central politicians?

Most officials on record either blame 'the people' themselves for not
shifting or sometimes admit to problems in how the R&R strategy is
implemented. The official nodal agency for shifting non-BCCL families
from endangered zones, the JRDA, claims that the main bottleneck in
the implementation of the Master Plan is the unavailability of land.
To resettle the 55,000 families from 595 sites, the estimated requirement of land for JRDA is 2,700 acres and the arrangement is that BCCL
will provide this. BCCL argues that this is impossible because it has
no vacant safe areas. An alternative hypothesis regarding the mystery
behind why the endangered people have not been resettled would
invoke the relationship between crime, politics and policy in reaping
coal profits. Put simply, the R&R has not happened because the business nexus between local politicians and illegal mining interests wants
the workforce to stay where it is, atop or near the illegal mines and
sites of theft and scavenging. A strong incentive and vested interest
among the local and regional politician-industrialists to maintain the
status quo would explain on the one hand the persistence of illegal coal
mining profits and on the other the ineffective R&R. The entire edifice
of illegal profits rests on the easy and cheap availability of a destitute
workforce which has no alternative to the precarious and hazardous
theft, mining and scavenging of coal.

In early 2016, several communist trade union leaders and a
right-to-information activist reported an emerging conflict between local
political leaders and the central leadership over R&R. While the local politicians, who are also in the coal business, are keen to maintain the status
quo and have this army of scavengers and labourers live on burning land
close to the sites of illegal mining, theft and diversion, the national-level
political leadership wants to evict all residents and allocate the entire
fire-affected area for opencast mining to large national and multinational
private companies. In the short run, the relocation of the workforce to
distant areas would create a labour shortage for the illegal operators and
a crisis of livelihoods for those resettled. According to a retired BCCL senior manager, the BCCL management is divided – with those among the

local functionaries that accumulate rents from corruption worried that they will soon suffer reduced political status in the hierarchy of illegal coal when the big mining companies with direct reach to the central government of India come to Jharia. Meanwhile, the middle class and its institutions are quiescent. One would think that if the very bowels of a town were on fire, it would cause immense outrage and disquiet, and so the absence of rage outside the shanties around mines is surprising. But the caste and ethnic composition of the oustees is distinct from that of the local middle classes...

Conclusion: crime, mining, fire and politics

When coal was nationalised in 1971, the PSU Bharat Coking Coal Ltd. (BCCL) became the main coke-producing company in the Jharia region. The non-enforcement of legally mandated and compulsory precautionary and remedial measures generated unscientific and unregulated coal mining, causing unconstrained underground fires. These fires are fanned in a premeditated and cynical fashion through the criminal economic practices described in this chapter. The increasingly intensified extraction of coal – through opencast mining without any regard for the safety requirements of the land and the workers – is driven by outsourcing to private mafia-owned companies. Paradoxically, extraction through opencast mining is presented as the solution to the fire whereas, in fact, it is a cause. Ironically, corruption in the purchase and transport of sand for stowing in mines to combat fire was the incentive for the growth of the coal mafia in the first place. BCCL works through contracts to powerful coal-fire mafia organisations, exploiting a pauperised workforce. It earns profits through fabricated fire-fighting work, illegal mining, large-scale theft of coal and sand, extortion and protection and real estate development, intertwined with legitimate mining, transport and other auxiliary contracts.

The mafia has penetrated all of the mainstream parties in Jharkhand, and its ability to change policies in its favour through bribery or through nepotism – appointing sons and relatives of politicians and bureaucrats in its companies – has given it political legitimacy and clout. The coal-fire mafia has not shied from eliminating trade unionists from left-wing parties and has run its own collaborator unions. This means that the central and historically crucial role of labour in workplace safety has been seriously compromised. This mafia feeds on the fire. Fire helps bypass legal procedures for the application and regulation of prospecting licences or mining leases. Fire increases illegality and illegality spreads the fire – a vicious cycle of crime and destruction that undermines hundreds of workers' health and livelihoods while devastating the environment. The central government now favours mass eviction but lacks a coherent and legal plan for rehabilitation and resettlement. A clamour to evict all the residents threatened by fire and subsidence has grown, now supported by the mainstream national political parties who have developed interests in large mining contracts. A contradiction is developing, however, between local illegal mining interests and the Master Plan, because of the fear of losing the cheap workforce willing to labour in the hazardous fire. It is indeed ironic that a town whose very existence is based on coal mining, to which labour has migrated from different parts of the country, is likely to be physically obliterated by this very activity.

Notes

1. Co-ordinator, Centre for Adivasi Research and Development, New Delhi. Engagement with policy research on *adivasi* (indigenous people, literally forest-dwellers) issues has taken me to Jharkhand, Chhattisgarh and other parts of Central and Eastern India, and the North East. I am extremely indebted to activists and researchers for their solidarity and deep insights into these issues. In particular, I will mention Adivasi Adhikar Rashtriya Manch, Chhattisgarh Bachao Andolan and the Campaign for Survival and Dignity. For the people living on the fire, I hope this paper becomes a small contribution to raising awareness of the disaster.

   Professor Barbara Harriss-White, on one of her several impressive and gruelling field visits to India, read a fact-finding report I had previously written on fire and displacement in Jharia and suggested I collaborate on the research programme that resulted in this book. She provided the framework and research outline and greatly enhanced the report with her comments and suggestions, for which I remain deeply indebted to her. She helped me 'walk the extra mile' in relating the fire to economic crime and policy.

   I also thank the University of Oxford for providing the resources for a survey and field visits, in a very smooth and stress-free manner.

2. Slaughter mining methods involve the extraction of coal from upper subterranean seams alone, while opencast mining extracts from the surface.

3. D.D. Mishra, Director, Central Mining Research Institute (CMRI) and expert on Jharia fires, quoted in an interview by R. Mahapatra (2015).

4. Minutes of the Expert Appraisal Committee (Thermal and Coal Mining) 17–18 December 2012, Ministry of Coal, New Delhi.

5. Gangs of Wasseypur, Gundey, Koyla, to name a few.

6. This is a strange paradox in India where several ruling-class regional parties describe themselves as socialists and followers of Lohia largely on account of their anti-Congress stance in the 1970s and 1980s.

7. Expelled by the CPI(M) in the late 1960s allegedly for left deviation and Naxalite sympathies, he organised most of the contract workers in private mines and formed the militant and formidable Bihar Colliery Kamgar Union.

8. A period of 21 months beginning in June 1975 during which Indira Gandhi ruled India under a state of emergency, overriding democratic process.

9. We have conducted a detailed study on illegalities in coal mining and its role in spreading fire in Jharia: see Gupta 2017. This section is a summary of the paper.

10. There are several citations for this, e.g. Ahmedabad Electricity Company Ltd. vs. Electricity Mazdoor Sabha 2000 84 FLR 5 Gujarat HC.

11. The third being the union government. See Report of the Standing Committee on Coal and Steel (2012–13) 15th Lok Sabha (Government of India Standing Committee on Coal and Steel 2012–13).

References

Bharat Coking Coal Limited (BCCL). 2008. *Master Plan for Dealing with Fire, Subsidence and Reha-bilitation in the Leasehold of BCCL*. Central Mine Planning and Design Ltd. http://www.bccl-web.in/PDFs/MPLANBCCL-2008.pdf (accessed 29 April 2019).

Bharti, I. 1989. 'Usurpation of the State: Coal Mafia in Bihar', *Economic and Political Weekly* 24(42, 21 October): 2353.

Chikkalur, A., A. Sagar and T. Sankar. 2009. 'Sustainable Development of the Indian Coal Sector', *Energy* 34(8): 942–53.

Coal India Ltd. 2008. *Resettlement and Rehabilitation Policy of Coal India Ltd*. http://www.centralcoalfields.in/indsk/pdf/employ_land/land_rules/r&r_policy%202008.pdf (accessed 29 April 2019).

Coal India Ltd. 2012. *Resettlement and Rehabilitation Policy of Coal India Ltd*. https://www.coalindia.in/DesktopModules/DocumentList/documents/CIL_RR_2012_100412.pdf (accessed 29 April 2019).

Communist Party of India (Marxist). 2013. 'Fanning a Fire in Jharia: Reap Windfall Profits and Loot the Coal'. Jharkand: CPI(M).

Daniel, F.J. and M. Williams. 2013. 'Special Report: "Coal Mafia" Stokes India's Power Crisis', *Reuters*, 14 May. https://in.reuters.com/article/india-coal-jharkhand-dhanbad-coalindia/special-report-coal-mafia-stokes-indias-power-crisis-idINDEE94D00B20130514 (accessed 8 April 2019).

Finkelman, R.F. 2004. 'Potential Health Impacts of Burning Coal Beds and Waste Banks', *International Journal of Coal Geology* 59(1–2): 19–24.

Government of India. 2011. *Mines (Amendment) Bill. Bill No. X of 2011*. http://www.prsindia.org/uploads/media/minesamendment.pdf (accessed 29 April 2019).

Government of India. 2015. *The Coal Mines (Special Provisions) Act, 2015*. https://indiacode.nic.in/handle/123456789/2146?view_type=browse&sam_handle=123456789/1362 (accessed 29 April 2019).

Government of India Standing Committee on Coal and Steel. 2012–13. *The Coal Mines (Conservation & Development) Amendment Bill, 2012*. Fifteenth Lok Sabha, New Delhi. http://www.prsindia.org/uploads/media/Coal%20Mines/SC%20Report-%20Coal%20Mines%20Bill.pdf (accessed 29 April 2019).

Gupta, S. 2013. 'Fanning A Fire In Jharia: Reap Windfall Profits And Loot The Coal.' Fact-Finding Report. Jharkand: Communist Party of India (Marxist).

Gupta, S. 2017. 'Contribution of Illegal Mining to Jharia's Mine Fire: Case Studies from Dhanbad', working paper, Centre for Adivasi Research and Development.

India Environment Portal. n.d. *Report on the Prevention of Illegal Coal Mining and Theft: Introduction*. http://www.indiaenvironmentportal.org.in/files/Report-Prevention%20of%20%20illegal%20coal%20mining%20and%20theft.pdf (accessed 29 April 2019).

Iqbal, J. 1999. 'The Real Gangs of Wasseypur who live life on their own terms', *India Today*, 30 November. https://www.indiatoday.in/magazine/society-the-arts/story/20120903-gangs-of-wasseypur-anurag-kashyap-brutal-mafia-vengeful-families-759560-1999-11-30 (accessed 29 April 2019).

Iqbal, J. 2012. 'The unreality of Wasseypur', Kafila.org, 17 September. https://kafila.org/2012/09/17/the-unreality-of-wasseypur-javed-iqbal/ (accessed 29 April 2019).

Jharkhand High Court. 2011. 'Court On Its Own Motion vs State Of Jharkhand & Ors'. https://indiankanoon.org/doc/781214 (accessed 29 April 2019).

Kalbag, C. 2013. 'Mafia gang leader Suraj Deo Singh calls the shots in Dhanbad', *India Today*, 1 August. http://indiatoday.intoday.in/story/%60mafia-gang-leader-suraj-deo-singh-calls-the-shots-in-dhanbad/1/392150.html (accessed 29 April 2019).

Mahapatra, R. 2015. 'Consigned to Flames', *Down to Earth*, 7 June. https://www.downtoearth.org.in/coverage/consigned-to-flames-15497 (accessed 29 April 2019).

National Commission to Review the Working of the Constitution. 2001. 'Review on the Working of Political Parties Especially in Relation to the Elections and Reform Options'. http://lawmin.nic.in/ncrwc/finalreport/v2b1-8.htm (accessed 29 April 2019).

Raju, A., A. Singh, S. Kumarand and P. Pati 2016. 'Temporal Monitoring of Coal Fires in Jharia Coalfield, India', *Environment and Earth Science* 75: 989.

Sanhati. 2011. 'Overview of Coal Mining in India: Investigative Report from Dhanbad Coal Fields'. http://sanhati.com/excerpted/3798/ (accessed 29 April 2019).

Sethi, A. 2006. 'Burning Issue', *Frontline*, 18 November. http://www.frontline.in/static/html/fl2323/stories/20061201001304900.htm (accessed 29 April 2019).

Simeon, D. 1996. 'Coal and Colonialism: Production Relations in an Indian Coalfield, c. 1895–1947', *International Review of Social History* 41(S4): 83–108.

3

Sand and the politics of plunder in Tamil Nadu, India

J. Jeyaranjan

The chapter shows the working of Wild East forms of criminal economies by exploring the evolution of pork-barrel politics and organised looting in Tamil Nadu. It shows a shift from populist to predatory forms of politics by unravelling the local il/legal economy of sand mining. In contemporary Tamil Nadu, profits from the criminal extraction of sand are directly and indirectly injected into the electoral process and are employed to fund vote buying – a tactic of electoral fraud widespread in this part of India. Criminals fund political parties, shaping vote outcomes through vote buying as well as through the allocation of preferential policies and state resources after the elections. Expert commissions of enquiry have exposed law-breaking by the sand mafia assemblage in the state. The criminal economy of sand is resisted by social and political activists, students, exceptional journalists and public interest lawyers.

Introduction: Tamil Nadu and criminal populist politics

When the criminal politics of riverbed sand is factored into the politics of the southern state of Tamil Nadu, far from being populist, what emerges is pork-barrel politics with Tamilian characteristics. In this chapter we make a first attempt to map the hidden connections between electoral politics and cash amassed and distributed illegally from the 1980s to the present. Our focus on the political and economic logistics of criminality in riverbed sand mining represents a case where a known criminal source of cash is deployed in politics, one among many (granite, beach sand, liquor and real estate). For the past 50 years, the state of Tamil Nadu has been under the rule of either the DMK (Dravida Munnetra

Kazhagam; Dravidian Progressive Party) or the AIADMK (All India Anna Dravida Munnetra Kazhagam). While in government, both parties introduced many important welfare programmes, some universal, some targetted. For instance, the food security programme in the state is one of India's best, with universal coverage and every household entitled to 20 kg of rice every month at no cost. Similarly, a midday-meal programme provides free lunches for all schoolchildren in the state. A health sector programme ensures the availability of vital medicines in all state hospitals. And, as well as drawing resources from the federal pool, the state has used its own resources to expand the number, scope and coverage of such schemes and programmes. To boost its public distribution system, for example, Tamil Nadu has managed to draw food stocks from the central pool in excess of its allocated quota – as the federal pool is always left with surplus in its annual outlay due to poor and very low levels of uptake by less-developed states. As a second example, the Integrated Child Development Services (ICDS) programme was expanded in parallel with assistance from the World Bank in Tamil Nadu beyond the provisions of the Indian government funding (Vivek 2015, 7). Another notable scheme that doubled cash assistance to beneficiaries is the support given to pregnant women. While the centre gives INR 6,000 as assistance to each pregnant woman, the state matches with an equal sum and, as of 2016, provides total assistance of INR 12,000.

It is therefore unsurprising that the academic discourse for politics in Tamil Nadu is broadly located within a narrative of 'populism', with a specific scholarly meaning that puts people's welfare at the core (Swamy 1998; Subramanian 1999; Harriss 2000). Many labels have been developed to describe this focus. Wyatt (2013a), for example, attributes the new kind of policies enunciated by the AIADMK since 2011 to 'protection populism'. By contrast, the policies adopted by the DMK in its earlier avatar were termed 'empowerment populism' (Swamy 1998, 110). Subramanian (1999) distinguished the policies of the DMK as 'assertive populism' and those of the AIADMK as 'paternalist populism'. The DMK too has since moved towards 'paternalist populism' (Swamy 1998). The recent framework adopted by AIADMK, since it came back to power in 2011, is identified as 'technocratic populism' as 'it best expresses the combination of "people-centred" politics and the enthusiasm for more effective delivery of governance outcomes' (Wyatt 2013a, 373; 2013b). Most recently, Walton and Crabtree (2018) have invoked Tamil Nadu as an exemplary case of 'crony populism'.

The argument that the politics of these two parties is 'populist' is premised on a direct link between the policies of mass welfare and the electoral outcome (exemplified by Swamy 1998 and Subramanian 1999). Welfare programmes broaden the party base and win elections. But is there such a direct, one-to-one, linear relation between the welfare policies of the ruling party and electoral outcomes? Is electoral politics so simple and uncomplicated to comprehend? On the contrary, a perusal of the Tamil Nadu legislative assembly results since 1984 indicates that there is no direct link between the policies of the party and electoral outcomes. Electioneering has not been a simple process in which welfare schemes implemented by a given political party have won them votes.

The supremacy of people's political agency in elections can be best understood through an analysis of the electoral outcomes of recent assembly elections. The 2006 assembly election brought the DMK to power and the electoral victory was widely attributed to a very promising manifesto. The DMK government kept its promises and introduced an INR 2/kg rice programme along with a complete waiver of farm loans. It launched the free distribution of colour television sets, LPG stoves, health insurance and a social security scheme for agricultural labourers and farmers. It also introduced a massive free housing programme that converted thatched huts into concrete houses. With this array of welfare schemes, the party faced the assembly elections in 2011 only to lose very badly. While this electoral defeat is attributed to a whole host of reasons (Jeyaranjan and Vijayabaskar 2011) it is clear that 'populism' alone does not fetch votes.[1] Local field experience of elections suggests a very different narrative – that of pork-barrel politics, starting locally but spreading to the entire state during the previous parliament and assembly elections.

'Money for votes' politics

Apart from fast-tracking the implementation of welfare and government programmes in a by-election, the most important evidence is the distribution of cash to voters.[2] The well-known 'Thirumangalam formula' of distributing money to most of the voters in a constituency gained notoriety during the 2009 by-election in that constituency during the DMK regime. Each voter was paid INR 3–5,000 by the ruling DMK, which then won massively, as documented in news sources including Raju 2015; Krishna 2014; and Hiddleston 2011. During by-elections, each cabinet minister is put in charge of an assigned electoral area and has to engage about 10,000 voters. Payments of INR 5,000 to each voter cost about INR 50 million per constituency. There may be 20 ministers deputed to the constituency to do such 'election work', and by distributing this kind of cash to about 10,000 voters in their respective areas the entire constituency is saturated with cash. The outcome of such a concentrated effort by the entire state cabinet and ruling party (both AIADMK and DMK) has been that they have not lost a by-election from 2001 to now. Through the development of pork-barrel politics with Tamilian characteristics, the DMK won all the by-elections during its regime and the AIADMK has repeated this feat during its own terms.

During the 2014 parliament elections and in the 2016 assembly elections, Chief Minister Jayalalithaa adopted the Thirumangalam by-election formula to distribute money to voters. The scale of this strategy is mind-boggling. On average each parliamentary seat is six times larger than an assembly seat. Never before in the history of either parliamentary or assembly elections in Tamil Nadu has money been distributed on such a grand scale. In each assembly constituency, AIADMK cadres identified 50–75,000 non-DMK, and non-AIADMK voters and each of these non-Dravidian party voters was given INR 1,000 to vote for the AIADMK. The DMK and other candidates could not generally match the ruling AIADMK's scale of money-distribution. Even opposition candidates commanding that scale of private money realised that they lacked the AIADMK's efficient distribution machinery for elections. Consequently, the AIADMK used the power of money to win most of the seats it contested. Tamil Nadu politics therefore needs to be understood in a way that transcends the boundaries set by mainstream 'populist' discourse. In turn the complex interconnections of massive amounts of money disbursed to voters during elections and the source of such vast amounts of cash need to be probed.

Urbanisation and construction, welfarism and riverbed sand

Tamil Nadu and neighbouring states in South India are not only developing through welfare expenditure but have also been witnessing steady economic growth with a corresponding increase in per capita income (alongside gross inequality).[3] Rapid urbanisation has led to nearly half of the total population living in towns and cities (Sivakumar 2011). Demand for housing is also rising due to the consumption linkages when agricultural incomes are supplemented by non-farm livelihoods. Through social sector policies and the public distribution system for rice, the state subsidises the everyday requirements of the population, thereby releasing money for other expenditure, including housing. An efficient public transport system encourages daily commuting to work. Remittances from migrant workers outside the country are also on the rise. All of these developments combine and lead to an increase in demand for housing. The state has its own construction and housing programmes and the real estate and private, labour-intensive construction sector together set the conditions for a booming demand for materials. Cement and concrete production relies on sand as an important ingredient. Although there is an alternative in the form of fly ash and 'M-sand' (granite crushed into minute granules with machines), these materials cannot satisfy demand. M-sand is costlier than river sand, and river sand is available as a natural resource in the state (see Chapter 6 for UP).

The supply of riverbed sand prior to the 1980s

During the 1980s, the growth rate of the state was some 25 per cent lower than in the twenty-first century;[4,5] the level of urbanisation too was lower, as was demand for building materials, with sand for construction drawn from local sources. Sand was manually loaded onto bullock carts from the nearest riverbed. A paltry fee was collected for the sand by the local *panchayats*. Effectively, sand was available as a free good that could be appropriated for an insignificant fee by cart owners. Sand was transported whenever the carts that were habitually rented out remained idle, meaning that the capacity utilisation of the carts was enhanced. Most of the cost of sand covered labour and transport. Sand mining provided a small-scale livelihood for poor owners of a cart and a pair of bullocks who lived in, or close to, a town. There were no regulations governing the local extraction of sand from riverbeds. In cities like Chennai, small lorries (known as half-body lorries) were hired to bring sand from nearby sources. Sand mining was undertaken using manual labour; few engaged in the activity and it fell beneath the politicians' radar.

The entry of politicians

During the late 1980s, when the real estate boom started, demand for sand increased. Small-time mining using carts and manual labour was unable to meet this demand. Apart from covering transport and labour, a significant component of the price was for sand *per se*. For the first time, sand developed value as a commodity. Since sand was a common property resource, it came up on the politicians' radar. Money started to play a very important role in everyday political life; apart from becoming involved in real estate, arrack shops and bars, politicians also entered sand mining. Disputes over sand mining among small-time local politicians attracted the attention of higher-level politicians, who gauged the potential for money in sand from the intensity of such disputes. Investing their own resources, they co-opted local politicians as junior partners in sand ventures. Political power shielded them from regulatory rules that could be enforced by local revenue officials and the police. In turn the revenue officials and police also sensed the profit from sand mining and started to test it by demanding regular (and increasing levels of) bribes.

In the 1980s, the regulation of sand shifted from the jurisdiction of the local *panchayat* to the Public Works Department (PWD). The PWD identified areas of excess sand deposits in riverbeds and permitted their removal so that river water could flow unhindered. The removal of excess sand deposits was auctioned by the PWD. District-level politicians from the AIADMK and the strong men from the opposition party, the DMK, colluded across party lines to form cartels, bid low and yet win contracts to remove sand. Profits were shared among the cartel members with advance payments sometimes replacing a share in profits. Thus, at the district level, sand became an important source of cash for the two Dravidian parties. Through the control of sand contracts and sales, the district secretaries and ministers from the districts also benefitted from sand mining. As the demand for sand increased, so the cashflow swelled and competition intensified. So too did physical violence. Sand auctions grew to be arenas for ever greater displays of muscle power, political power and money, by means of which competition was elbowed out.

Scale and impact

Increases in demand, prices and cash flows led to the indiscriminate mining of sand. The small-time operators owning bullock carts were barred from working on the riverbeds. Machines were introduced to expand the scale of excavation. The regulatory conditions stipulated for quarrying were ignored. For several years, no one realised what the danger of unplanned mining would be, during which time violations had severe consequences:

(1) The area where sand was to be removed was not marked.
(2) The sand was scooped from depths of 15 feet, whereas approval was never given for removal deeper than 3 feet.
(3) Machines were used for loading when by law they were banned.
(4) Each load was limited to 2 units (200 cubic feet), but this was routinely exceeded.

(5) Very few loads were recorded and routine unpermitted loads cheated the treasury.

(6) Lease periods were extended by false claims that miners had not completed the removal of the contracted quantum of sand and, based on the affidavit, the miners obtained court orders extending their contract period.

(7) There was no practical monitoring by the officials formally responsible.

Mining as organised looting: the early 1990s and the entry of Fort St George

The AIADMK took power in the 1991 legislative assembly elections. J. Jayalalithaa became Chief Minister (CM) and many consequential decisions were taken during her first tenure. The disproportionate assets case that landed her in prison in 2014 is a product of that time. Chennai city was booming and the Palar river was the main source of sand for the city's construction industry. 'M.', a Dalit from Chengalpattu town on the banks of the Palar, which in that stretch is a wide sandy riverbed, dry for most of the year, was a fleet owner, a supplier of sand to Chennai and part of a cartel paying the district administration regularly for Palar sand. A district collector gave him the blueprint for a new system whereby he could have a monopoly right over Palar sand provided he struck a deal with the CM's friend, Ms Sasikala. He was also assured by the collector that the latter would negotiate the deal.

The deal came through in 1993. M. had to pay INR 1 *crore* every week to Ms Sasikala, the friend and confidante of the CM, and in turn he had the monopoly of Palar sand in the Chengalpattu stretch. The monopoly was formally conferred on M. by invoking the power under Rule 39 of the Tamil Nadu Minor Mineral Concession Rules through which the government can invoke its ownership right over the state's mineral deposits. It can avoid open auction and issue a government order based on an application from the contractor to quarry in a particular plot of land over a specified period in return for a payment. This extraordinary power was intended to preserve and develop the mineral wealth of the state and to be invoked in the 'public interest'.

Using this loophole in the interpretation of the law, M. was appointed as contractor. This initiated a looting of monumental proportions that continues to this day. Given that M. paid promptly and the deal proved mutually effective, the same model was extended to other river basins in the state and the same rule was invoked for awarding similar contractual monopolies during that time. From among these contractors, 'O.A.' captured contracts for several sand quarries in the state's riverbeds. Meanwhile, M., enjoying the monopoly bestowed by the government machinery, prospered for three years until the 1996 elections. Since the deals were transacted directly with the political apex, the district-level administration was under his complete control, money poured in and he promptly paid the agreed sums to all concerned, including the personal aide of the CM. Sand mining reached a new 'height' in the Palar basin, with the district administration reduced to silent spectators, shorn of all regulatory oversight powers. Since M. complied promptly with contractual obligations, he retained the contract until the following elections.

His success and the wealth he managed to accumulate in a short span of time indicated the potential of sand mining: he was able to purchase the largest bungalow in Chengalpattu, previously owned by a big landlord (who was the symbol of feudal wealth and stereotyped as such in many Dravidian movement plays scripted by DMK leader Annadurai). It was indeed a more than symbolic moment, one whose significance was publicly appreciated when 'sand money' purchased the long-standing manifestation of local 'feudal wealth'.

During the following decade, this set of political arrangements and pay-offs became the model for sand mining. Control of, and returns to, sand mining shifted permanently to the CM's office in Fort St George. This was also the period when the state government machinery experienced a role reversal, from being an employer resourced from legal revenue to being an employee paid from illegal loot to regulate and secure this stream of politically legitimised criminal money against capture or sabotage by others. The government's principal duty was thus to check the 'illicit' sand mining while protecting the contractor's 'legal' mining.

Regime change in 1996 and the continuation of the system

The anti-Jayalalithaa wave that swept Tamil Nadu during the 1996 general elections brought the DMK back into power. Jayalalithaa was defeated in her constituency, where voters were angered by her widespread corruption, reputed arrogance and ugly display of wealth. Seamlessly, the DMK assumed control of sand. The contract system for sand continued, with a few DMK notables forming a cartel and seizing the Palar contract from M. Without experience or infrastructure, they brought in O.A. as their partner in Palar dealings. In the process O.A. was outsmarted and ousted from the Trichi and Thanjavur district quarries, which are located in the Cauvery river systems and have the largest deposits of sand in the state. 'M.D.', the Trichirapally strongman of the DMK, developed rent-sharing formalities with Fort St George, found suitable local partners and controlled all the sand mines in these two districts. Mining intensified further with blatant violations of contractual conditions:

1. Although the contract was only for a particular plot of land specified in the lease deed, the contractor treated the entire riverbed as their leasehold.
2. Contractors dug down to any depth until the sand was exhausted.
3. The use of machinery became more common.
4. Mining continued brazenly throughout daylight hours.
5. The movement of sand to neighbouring states increased.
6. Permit laws were extended through legal orders.
7. Lease periods were extended by the same means.
8. Protests from the local community were crushed.
9. Officials were given their due share and they, in turn, faithfully served the interests of the contractors.
10. The nexus between the politicians, contractors and officials grew so much stronger that the regime change from AIADMK to DMK did not alter any elements or relations in this system other than the replacement of politicians.

During these eight years, from 1993 to 2001, sand emerged as a perennial source of cash for the ruling party (irrespective of whether it was the DMK or AIADMK). The sand contractors organised the work, collected the money and gave a major share to the ruling party chief. The law was blatantly violated and a massive revenue stream was appropriated and diverted from the state exchequer to the ruling political elite.

However, the extension of a contract was not entirely within the domain of the state government. Contractors could go to court and apply for an extension with the connivance of the ruling party. Yet since many players were competing for more *benami* contracts,[6] rivalries among the contractors intensified and inevitably some were marginalised while others emerged victorious under both AIADMK and DMK regimes. Fort St George came to feel the marketing system needed fine-tuning and tightening to confer absolute control over the sand sector. With the firm hold of the top political boss, a single-window system for cash flows would increase the efficiency with which money was extracted from the contractors.

Exposure of blatant misuse of special power by the state

In invoking the special power of Rule 39 of the Tamil Nadu Minor Minerals Concession rules, the state administration hardly bothered with its duties vested in the law as the custodian of public property. In awarding such leases to the sand contractors, it had systematically flouted all the regulatory law. This was amply demonstrated in the judgment on a set of writ petitions filed in the High Court of Madras in 1997, judgment on which was delivered in 2001. The petition by Mr Kuppusami, a leading lawyer and social activist from Karur, challenged the granting of a contract by the PWD to Mr K. Ramaswamy and questioned the very basis of invoking Rule 39. The court, while conducting the trial on these writ petitions, summoned files and records. After perusing the material filed before the court, it found that there was no reason for the contracts to be awarded on the basis of Rule 39 because, since no grounds were mentioned as to how the contractor would develop the mineral wealth of the state, no public interest was involved. The contractor had not been selected based on tender or auction. The state had arbitrarily used its powers to bestow this special privilege on the contractor in an act said by the judge to be 'whimsical'. The government had decided on the lease apparently based on the recommendation of a high-level committee. But while the committee had recommended a lease for 10 hectares, a lease of 25 hectares was proposed in the government order. And later, the recommendation of the committee had been altered retrospectively to 25 hectares of land. When the land was leased out, no plan of the leased area was either attached or approved. This strategic omission was to enable the contractor to mine in the survey area mentioned in the government order to a total extent of 334,140 hectares of riverbed. Using this loophole, the contractor had obtained several orders from the court for the change of plots during all of which the original plot was never surrendered. The 'consideration' or rent for the lease was INR 1 *lakh* in the first year, with a 20 per cent enhancement over the next four years. However, from the one quarry alone, the weekly earnings from sand were estimated by the court to be INR 1 *crore*, thus fetching an annual income of INR 50 *crore* for an investment of INR 1 *lakh*. Even more blatant was the non-registration of the lease deed.

The judgment clearly indicated the corrupt motives behind the process of granting the original lease under Rule 39 of the Tamil Nadu Minor Minerals Concession Rules. The judgment observed that:

> (b)esides, the materials available on the file disclose that the exercise of power is not *bona fide* but it had been resorted to for *a priori* considerations. It could even be suggested as born out of corrupt motive, and corrupt obligation had advanced the cause of individual to the detriment of the state exchequer. (W.P. No.16010/97 and 6712, 6713 of 1998 p 50 of the Judgment dated 30.4.2001 in the High Court Judicature at Madras.)

The judgment quashed the lease and also ordered the quashing of 35 other grants that had been made invoking Rule 39. It further commented that 'the State government should have ordered investigation by the CBI … if it had not been done so far'. Obviously, the state government bureaucracy refrained from ordering any investigation by any agency as they were aware of the involvement of the Chief Minister and her friend.

The state as a camouflage for looting: the direct entry of the state as a fair player in sand mining

In 2001 the AIADMK was returned to power. In July 2002 another judgment was pronounced by the Madras high court which paved the way for the AIADMK government to assume the moral high ground and take over sand mining as a state monopoly. Filing a contempt petition, Mr Janardhanan of Chennai contended that the state – represented by the bureaucracy – had failed to enforce the order of the high court of Madras regarding illicit mining in the Kosasthali river, located north of Chennai city. The high court had appointed an advocate commissioner, Mr Ashok Chakravarthy, to assess conditions in the riverbed during an earlier hearing and had passed a set of orders. None of the earlier orders had been honoured and another contempt petition was filed by the same petitioner. The state argued that it had complied fully with the earlier orders and that the illicit mining was under control – which was vehemently contested by the applicant. The same advocate commissioner was appointed once again to assess the situation on the ground. The latter vouched for the contentions of the petitioner and the high court ordered the government to constitute a high-level committee consisting of scientists, geologists and environmentalists to conduct a survey with reference to sand quarrying and the damage caused. The state was also ordered to follow the recommendations of the committees and to pass necessary legislation.

The judgment blamed the local political leaders who 'anchor the whole operation as the conduit for the huge bribes fuelling the well-oiled network'. It added that the 'contractors are extracting many times the permitted amount of sand, as enforcement agencies turn a blind eye … Government officials who are supposed to check illegal sand quarrying join hands with sand smugglers'.[7] Acting on the directions of the high court, the state constituted a high-level committee, which submitted its report in June 2003. The committee found that rivers and riverbeds belonging to the state had been seriously damaged. The river ecology had also suffered due to indiscriminate and unscientific mining. The committee also assessed the damage caused over time by heavy machinery to the riverbeds, banks and electrical and hydraulic structures.

The main recommendations of the high-level committee include:

1. Entrusting the mining of riverbed sand to a single agency.
2. No roads to be constructed in riverbeds.
3. No heavy machinery.
4. Quarrying time to be restricted between 6 am and 6 pm.
5. Maintaining proper accounts for the quantum of sand quarried.
6. Disseminating information about the lease.
7. Severe penalties and punishment for violations.
8. Prevention of quarrying in *patta* (legally owned) lands located within 250 m of the riverbank.

In its instructions, the high court clearly stated that the government follow the recommendations of the high-level committee. So the government accepted the recommendations of the committee and issued Government Order M.S. No 95, dated 1 October 2003, based on them. From the following day, it cancelled all the contracts and leases for sand mining in public land as well as on *patta* lands. From then on, the state became the sole miner of sand in the state. This was done 'in the public interest' to ensure:

1. The elimination of indiscriminate and unscientific sand quarrying.
2. The uninterrupted availability and supply of sand in a regular and orderly manner to the common public.
3. The availability of sand at affordable prices to common public, thereby effecting a reduction in the cost of construction.
4. The augmentation of the state government's revenue. (Government of Tamil Nadu, G.O. M.S. No 95 dated 1.10.2003, 1)

Following this government order, the Tamil Nadu Minor Mineral Concession Rules 1959 were amended with the addition of a new clause, 38A, which gave the state the monopoly right over sand. The amended rule has survived all challenges in the high court and the supreme court and, to this day, the State of Tamil Nadu is the sole agency entitled to mine sand in the state.

The questions as to why the state chose to take that recommendation of the court seriously and to appoint a high-level committee to look into the ill effects of sand mining by contractors, and – more importantly – how parties making huge amounts of illicit money through their contractors from 1993 onwards would countenance the possibility of foregoing it and diverting this flow of funds to the state exchequer deserve further discussion. Demand for sand was growing daily and money was pouring in to the Chief Minister and her friend Sasikala through the contractors. No reprimand, mild or strong, from the judiciary or press reports could make the ruling party relinquish the use of income from sand for political purposes. Until then, even in court affidavits, the AIADMK government repeatedly swore that sand was mined as per the guidelines. It is a puzzle why the government took the advice of the high-level committee and went in for a state monopoly system controlling huge cash flows hitherto the domain of the party and private coffers.[8]

It is certain that civil society activists and the media considered the decision of the state to take over sand mining as a victory against the illegal sand industry. 'The state had assumed the role of guardian angel. The fragile ecology of the entire river system in the State, we believed, would be restored and rejuvenated and would remain there safe in its hands,' said Mugilan, an environmentalist (Rajasekaran 2015). 'While hailing the government's action, Ossie Fernandez, one of the conveners of the Campaign for the Protection of Water Resources – Tamil Nadu, described the government's action as a "step forward" in protecting water resources' (Viswanathan 2003). This euphoria was short-lived. The Public Works Department was selected to be the sole agency for sand mining in Tamil Nadu. It started mining operations and managed them for about three months. The state's own sand mining operation led to chaos. The PWD managed to load fewer than 200 lorryloads of sand from each quarry against requirements for over 10 times more. Consequently, sand was in short supply and its price skyrocketed throughout the state. Whether this was caused by the inability of the department to manage the logistics of sand, or whether the shortage was deliberately designed at the behest of the erstwhile contractors to dislodge the department from sand mining was, at first, anybody's guess. Be that as it may, the PWD had to bring back the contractors to handle the logistics of sand.

The re-entry of the contractors and restoration of cash flow to Fort St George

Subsequent events clearly indicated that the chaos was engineered to enable the re-entry of contractors into sand mining. Loading operations were contracted out through the tendering process – all falling into the hands of 'O.A.', the large sand contractor of the earlier system, chosen by Jayalalithaa to be the sole contractor. While in the paper records, many 'lifting contractors' were named as working in different quarries in the state, all were O.A. *benamis* and O.A. became the de facto owner of all the state's sand. Department officials did not even supervise sand mining. They received monthly cash packets directly from O.A. The new rate for the state-level bribe was INR 25 *crore* a month and to be paid in cash directly to Jayalalithaa through named *benami* contracts for all O.A.-controlled quarries. Although PWD constantly claimed that as an arm of the state it has been judicious in exploiting sand, it neither undertook sand mining nor had any control over mining operations. Unlike in the past, a smokescreen had now been created that withstood any paper scrutiny. The department claimed in all affidavits filed before the court that it mined scientifically and thus did not harm the ecology and environment. But underneath this facade, a brilliant scheme of perennial looting has been established with an efficient system of single-window negotiation, where only one contractor remits the agreed sum at the designated location and is responsible for all other costs, payments and cuts.[9]

The economics of sand mining by the lifting contractor (LC)

While PWD is the formal operator of sand mines in Tamil Nadu, the entire operation is actually controlled by the lifting contractor (LC), who chooses the appropriate sites for the sand pits or quarries and notifies the PWD. The district collector then permits the quarry to be developed. The LC mobilises machinery and labour. Poclains[10] scoop the sand and the lorry fleets transport it to roadside yards. The LC paves motorable roads in the riverbed for the smooth and quick extraction of sand. Every day the LC produces about 100 demand drafts (a negotiable instrument issued by a bank directing another bank or branch to pay a certain sum to the payee) drawn in favour of the PWD and the PWD officials issue permits to quarry 100 loads of sand. One load of sand is 2 units (1 unit is 100 cubic feet). Although the permit is restricted to 100 loads every day, the LC continuously scoops and transports to the yard as many loads as required, using its own vehicles. Whoever wants to buy sand has to go to the yard and pay for it in cash. As of 2015–16, sand transactions were measured using the unit of the bucket. The machine that loads the vehicle scoops the sand into a bucket. Each bucket costs INR 500. Sand lorries range from ordinary trucks to large 'up-to-date modern' dumpers. A normal lorry can take seven buckets of sand. Thus, a lorry-load of sand is worth INR 3,500. Larger lorries can take 10 buckets with a total value of INR 5,000. The number of lorry-loads of sand sold per day varies from yard to yard – between 1,000 and 5,000 loads each. Estimates of the number of loads sold daily vary enormously. If there are 50 quarries and if 3,000 loads are packed from each quarry, 150,000 loads of sand could be loaded every day throughout the state. If INR 3,500 is paid for each load, the total amount collected per day could be INR 525 million. Extrapolating, the annual amount collected would be INR 19,162.50 *crore*.[11] The annual proceeds from the sale of sand that are remitted into the government's treasury account total just around INR 200 *crore*, as per the demand for grants on PWD presented in the assembly (Rajasekaran 2015). All the rest (in the region of INR 19 *lakh crores*) is shared between the contractors, the politicians, the bureaucracy and others. The main contractor bears the costs of operation.

In an investigation by *Frontline,* the current affairs magazine, into sand mining (Rajasekaran 2015) the notional loss to public finances due to the unofficial lifting of sand per annum was estimated at INR 2,300 *crore*. This calculation is premised on the fact that quite a substantial amount of sand sold in the yard is not reported, and the estimate of loss to the exchequer is based on the actual number of loads of sand sold. So the actual prices at which sand is sold at the yards are as crucial as the quantities involved. Sand prices at the yard are four to five times higher than the price fixed by the state. Thus, there is gross under-reporting both of sand sold and of the price at which sand is sold. If the calculation is reworked based on the actual price of sand in the yard, it would also come to our estimate. Three thousand loads of sand per quarry from 50 quarries amounts to 150,000 loads and each load at the rate of INR 3,500 per load works out to INR 525 million. The annual accrual could be estimated at INR 19,162.5 *crore*. The DMK treasurer (by 2017, also executive leader) M.K. Stalin has also estimated the magnitude of the loot in sand at INR 19,000 *crore*, which corroborates our estimate.[12] Stalin's estimates are grounded in his experience as the deputy Chief Minister from 2006–11, when the same arrangement was functioning during the previous DMK regime as well!

The current system is reported to involve the lifting contractor 'S.R.' paying INR 10 *crore* in cash every day to the Chief Minister. This contractor controls the operation of all the sand and soil quarries in the state. The state and district administration cooperates with S.R.'s agents and employees. His business partners include the Finance Minister ('O.P.S.') and another cabinet minister who both share the collection – unlike earlier when they received a fixed monthly payment. The sand quarries functioned under this same arrangement during the previous DMK regime as well, but O.A. had to confine himself to the northern region leaving the Cauvery segment to K.C.P., a prominent DMK industrialist from the Cauvery region. When the AIADMK returned to power, O.A. regained complete control and lost it to S.R. only in 2015. Then S.R. outbid O.A. and got the deal in his favour mainly due to his proximity to O.P.S., who was the Chief Minister in 2015 when Jayalalithaa was out of power and imprisoned.

Democratic politics and illegal money from sand

In Tamil Nadu, electoral-democratic party politics involves armies of local party functionaries or cadres. The lifting contractor (LC) uses money systematically to co-opt each one of them.

While the chief of the ruling party receives about INR 300 *crore* every month (a daily stream of INR 10 *crore* (US$ 1.5m)) from the sand LCs, other lower level representatives of the people also receive sand contractors' money every month. Every village *panchayat* president in whose territory a quarry is located is reported to be paid INR 100,000 ($1,500) by LC every month; village councillors receive INR 10,000 ($150) monthly. The local member of the legislative assembly is reportedly paid INR 500,000 ($7,500) per month for every sand quarry located in his constituency. The union secretaries of the ruling party and the main opposition party are also paid monthly by quarry managers. High-level payments to other political functionaries are handled by the representatives of the LC. It is not only the elected representatives of the people who are on the LC payrolls. Officials of all the departments concerned are paid on a monthly basis depending on their status and power: the highest paid at the district level are district collectors and the police superintendents. All relevant officers further down in the hierarchy are on the LC payrolls. There are a few exceptions that refuse to accept money and are shunted out at the earliest opportune moment. Local representatives of the press are also paid every month. The media coverage of sand mining by the local representatives of the state and national media is minimal and uncritical compared with other stories they cover.

Sand money and the response of the state

From various reports submitted by the court-appointed advocate commissioners, it is evident that when the relevant officials are paid generously by the LC on a regular basis, the official machinery works entirely in the interests of the LC rather than fulfilling its mandated role. The advocate commissioner documented the indiscriminate mining in Kosasthalai river in 2000 and 2002. Indiscriminate and unscientific mining was also extensively documented by the expert committee appointed by the high court to examine the Tamiraparani river.[13] All other subsequent findings have indicated the perpetuation of unscientific and indiscriminate sand mining. The claims of the PWD in all the above cases were found to be blatant lies. Its officers claim with impunity that the mining was scientific despite the findings of the experts and advocate commissioners. Important violations that are recorded as evidence in these cases and that continue unabated include:

1. The mining area is not specified.
2. The mining area is not demarcated and identified.
3. A mining plan is not prepared.
4. The quantum of sand to be mined is not specified.
5. The quantum of sand mined so far is not specified, recorded or disclosed.
6. The sand loaded is hugely under-reported (100 loads reported versus 3,000 loads unreported per quarry).
7. Money collected for sand is seriously diverted.
8. Sand is enormously over-charged.
9. Cash is collected for all the sand sold. All transactions thus happen outside the formal system and generate huge flows of black money.
10. Sand is scooped from the entire depth of the deposit (whereas the permitted depth is only 1 metre).
11. Far more machines than permitted to scoop are used.
12. Unauthorised roads are built in the riverbed.
13. Permanent structures are built in the riverbed.
14. Water courses are diverted.
15. Unauthorised quarrying takes place near the water supply works, bridges and irrigation heads.

16. Bunds are broken.
17. Scant regard is paid to the boundaries of villages where a quarry is permitted.
18. Sand is moved to the yard and sold from there though the court has banned the operation of yards in the past.
19. Sand is quarried round the clock while as per the court order mining can be done only from 9 am to 6 pm.

The monitoring committee meetings at the *taluk* (district sub-division) and district levels are routinely passing identical minutes verbatim, meeting after meeting, indicating the level of their seriousness. Environmental assessments are done by non-experts and are sometimes granted without evidence from field conditions. All these violations are reported in various advocate commissioners' reports and in the expert-committee reports submitted to the courts.

Thus the enforcement systems that have been established have all been corrupted by the sand contract system. Enforcement is on paper alone. The relevant officials collude with the LC. The servants of the people are now the slaves of the contractor.

Democratic protests and the sand contractor

Flouting all rules and norms, the entire state machinery works for the smooth functioning of sand mining and transport. However, indiscriminate sand quarrying and transport leads to enormous ecological and social problems in the vicinities of the riverbed quarries. Water tables are depleted. Irrigation is affected as wells run dry; profits decline as crops dry up. Drinking water becomes scarce. With the stagnation in agriculture, crop-production and employment are both in jeopardy. Roads and pathways are destroyed. Fatal accidents on paths and roads are on the rise with the continuous movement of heavy vehicles laden with sand. This ecological destruction and social danger is not taken passively. People resort to *dharnas* (strikes), hunger strikes, road blocks, representations, petitions, exhibitions and so on. In response, the sand contractor deploys multiple methods to negotiate such protests, including:

1. In extreme cases, assassinating the person protesting.
2. Maiming and injuring individuals to terrorise them.
3. Physical assault by private armies hired by the contractor.
4. Using the police to fabricate false cases, arrest and harass the protestors.

5. Entangling protestors in prolonged litigation.
6. Manipulating caste identities to divide protestors.
7. Directly bribing protestors with money.
8. Offering work to compliant villagers on a regular basis.
9. Employing small-time local leaders as supervisors.
10. Funding temple festivals, sports events and annual village festivals.
11. Funding the construction of temples.
12. Organising medical camps.
13. Offering cash loans to buy assets.
14. Hiring local vehicles to move the sand from the riverbed to the yard.
15. Prioritising local vehicles to transport sand from the riverbeds.
16. Issuing parking and access tokens to local leaders who can cash them by selling them to lorry drivers from outside the region, thereby helping the latter to jump the queues.
17. Making regular payments to local leaders.
18. Awarding scholarships to students from the villages where quarries are located.
19. Bribing litigants who go to court to drop their cases.
20. Buying the lawyers who appear for the litigant.

There are few exceptions where the community has defied this barrage of 'carrot and stick' tactics and with the help of the courts has stopped the contractor. To illustrate, through a court order, Nallakannu, the veteran CPI leader, succeeded in stopping sand mining in the Thamiraparani river for five years. Kuppusamy of Karur managed to get the court to quash the lease granted under Rule 39 of the Mines Act. Shanmugam of Anbil won a court order to close certain quarries in Cauvery and Kollidam that had been functioning illegally for more than five years. Raju, a lawyer, managed to have mining suspended in the Vellar riverbed in Vriddachalam (for details, see Ilangovan Rajasekaran 2015). In these exceptional cases people were mobilised to struggle against the designs of the LC and the state machinery. But in a large number of other instances, with the active connivance of the state government machinery, the contractor has successfully neutralised the democratic protests of the victims.

Judicial interventions and sand mining in Tamil Nadu

The Tamil Nadu judiciary has intervened in important ways to address the disastrous effects of sand mining activity. It put an end to the private contracting system and led to direct mining by the government department.

It banned sand mining in certain quarries for a specified period of time whenever it took note of indiscriminate mining. However, the judiciary has turned a blind eye to the massive corruption in sand. While it had provided patchy relief to certain villages, it failed to ask, or shied away from addressing, the basic question as to how a government department could flout all norms and continue functioning since 2001, while claiming to the contrary. Who is behind this audacity? In a democratic system how can such massive corruption continue so blatantly? The victims have knocked at the doors of the court on several occasions for verdicts and the court has, on some occasions, appointed its own fact-finding commissions. All the commissions have reported that there is no account of the quantity of sand mined but confirmed its blatant and indiscriminate extraction. The courts have suggested new methods of monitoring but the government has never implemented any of them. Instead of scrutinising the failure of the state machinery and the bogus affidavits, the court keeps suggesting even more regulation. Committees appointed by the courts have repeatedly shown the falsity of claims in affidavits submitted by the departments to the courts. Despite this, the courts continue to have faith in the departments of the state and assign more and more responsibilities to the very departments that are the principal violators of the law. No court has ever demanded evidence of the beneficiaries of this malfunctioning system.

Conclusion

The case of sand clearly indicates the close link between democratic politics, elections and crime in exploiting natural resources. The existing scholarly consensus about Tamil Nadu's politics overwhelmingly ignores the complex web of welfarism, corruption and clientelism at its core. Our case study of criminal enterprises in sand reveals the 'money-for-votes' politics that has spread through the election process and is now firmly entrenched not only in electoral democracy but also is an indispensable part of the democratic polity of the state. Black money is generated in sand mining by siphoning substantial sums to the ruling party's private coffers, thus diverting potential tax revenue from the state exchequer. A part of this money is deployed during elections to pay voters for their votes. Thus money that should have found its way from state investments into development schemes is used for cash payments for votes.

Corruption used to be understood as a by-product of Dravidian politics. The elected party used the state exchequer to expand its populist schemes so as to retain an electoral base. However, a new politics has developed in which money is disbursed during election campaigns to voters throughout the state, resourced through the crime of extracting natural resources, like sand. In the new arrangement, populist disbursements from the state exchequer are spliced during elections with pork-barrel transfers of cash to most of the voters throughout the state – practices that now define the democratic process. Our examination of natural resource crimes has resulted in a radically different and new interpretation of politics in Tamil Nadu. It also warrants more case studies (such as on criminality in granite, liquor and beach sand) to establish the entrenchment and institutionalisation of other 'convection systems' of criminal accumulation, bound to the democratic process.

Notes

1. Arm-twisting by the Congress party for more seats, the 2G scam, a formidable opposition alliance, the acute electricity shortage, food inflation, land grabbing and brazen corruption by lower-level DMK functionaries and the extraconstitutional power wielded by the first family (that of Karunandidhi, the then Chief Minister) are some of the reasons for the DMK's defeat in those assembly elections.
2. We interviewed politicians, officers, contractors, journalists, law officers and middle-men. All of them shared with us details about sand mining and politics on the condition of anonymity. Hence, the evidence in this chapter is not attributed and has to be taken at face value alone.
3. The mining of beach sand is outside the scope of the research reported here; see Suresh 2015.
4. Based on information collected through interviews with persons associated with this process and whose identity cannot be revealed.
5. At 8.5 per cent per annum in real terms from 2004–14 and at 6.5 per cent in the 1980s and 90s; see Government of India 2015; Kohli 2006.
6. Contracts disguising the identities of transacting parties.
7. Paras 22, 23 and 25 of the Judgment of Madras High Court dated 26.7.2001 in Contempt Petition Number 561/2001.
8. These cash flows were not spent entirely on elections. Massive properties were acquired over time and because of such accumulation both Jayalalithaa and Sasikala were sentenced to four years of imprisonment by the supreme court of India. Sasikala is serving her prison sentence; Jayalalithaa died in 2016. See Ravishankar 2017 and Subramanian 2017 for an attempt to unravel the wealth accumulated by Jayalalithaa and Sasikala.
9. This brilliant plan introduced by Jayalalithaa was not a new concept to emerge after the PWD takeover of sand mining. The system had been conceived and implemented earlier, during her previous regime between 1991 and 1996. TAMIN is a state-owned corporation involved in mineral mining, including granites. During the early 1990s, granite exports boomed; an engineer-turned-civil service official (I.A.S.) was directing TAMIN. In collaboration with a small-time contractor in Madurai, he conceived the idea of lifting contracts and showed the private profit matrix that makes it possible for the ruling party to use public wealth. The small-time contractor who began as a lifting contractor for TAMIN in Madurai eventually grew into a multi-billionaire who came to control all of TAMIN's granite mines. He is the king-pin behind the granite scandal of present day Tamil Nadu (for more details, see Rajasekaran 2015).
10. A poclain is a mechanised digger with buckets and grabs to move rocks, rubble, earth and sand.
11. This estimate is based on interviews with former sand yard managers and employees in Tirichirapalli district. For an all-India estimate, see Rege 2016.

12. *Dinakaran, Tamil*, 3 September 2015, Trichy edition p. 5.
13. Order of the High Court of Madras in WP.NO.11562/2010. The court found that most of the rules of the Mining Act were flouted in the Kollidam riverbed (order dated 3 August 2012 in WP(MD) NO.4699 of 2012). Indiscriminate and unscientific mining was reported by the advocate commissioner in the Cauvery riverbed (WP(MD) NO.9336 of 2015) in Trichy district.

References

Government of India. 2015. 'Indian States by GDP Per Capita Growth'. Ministry of Statistics and Programme Implementation. http://statisticstimes.com/economy/gdp-capita-growth-of-indian-states.php (accessed 29 April 2019).

Government of Tamil Nadu. G.O. M.S. No. 95, dated 1 October 2003.

Harriss, J. 2000. 'Populism, Tamil Style: Is it Really a Success?' *Review of Development and Change* 5(2): 332–46.

Hiddleston, S. 2011. 'The India Cables: Cash for Votes a Way of Political Life in South India', *The Hindu*, 16 March. https://www.thehindu.com/news/the-india-cables/lsquoCash-for-votes-a-way-of-political-life-in-South-Indiarsquo/article14949621.ece (accessed 29 April 2019).

Jeyaranjan, J. and M. Vijayabaskar. 2011. 'Not by Patronage Alone: Understanding Tamil Nadu's Vote for Change', *Economic and Political Weekly* 46(22): 13–5.

Kohli, A. 2006. 'Politics of Economic Growth in India, 1980-2005 Part II: The 1990s and Beyond'. http://www.princeton.edu/~kohli/docs/PEGI_PartII.pdf (accessed 29 April 2019).

Krishna, S. 2014. 'AIADMK Functionary Held for "Distributing Money"', *The Hindu*, 19 April. https://www.thehindu.com/todays-paper/tp-national/tp-tamilnadu/aiadmk-functionary-held-for-distributing-money/article5927592.ece (accessed 29 April 2019).

Rajasekaran, I. 2015. 'The Mother of All Loot', *Frontline* 32(14). https://frontline.thehindu.com/cover-story/the-mother-of-all-loot/article7391496.ece (accessed 29 April 2019).

Raju, K. 2015. 'Dravidian Parties Trying "Thirumangalam formula"', *The Hindu*, 25 January. https://www.thehindu.com/todays-paper/tp-national/tp-tamilnadu/dravidian-parties-trying-thirumangalam-formula/article6819908.ece (accessed 29 April 2019).

Ravishankar, S. 2017. 'Sasikala DA Case Verdict: What You Need to Know About Original High Court Ruling', *The Wire*, 14 February. https://thewire.in/law/flawed-jayalalithaa-verdict-finally-heads-to-supreme-court (accessed 29 April 2019).

Rege, A. 2016. 'Not Biting the Dust: Using a Tripartite Model of Organized Crime to Examine India's Sand Mafia', *International Journal of Comparative and Applied Criminal Justice* 40(2): 101–21.

Sivakumar, B. 2011. 'Census 2011: Tamil Nadu 3rd most urbanised state', *Times of India*, 20 July. http://timesofindia.indiatimes.com/city/chennai/Census-2011-Tamil-Nadu-3rd-most-urbanised-state/articleshow/9292380.cms (accessed 29 April 2019).

Subramanian, L. 2017. 'The Hunt for Amma's Assets', *The Week*, 4 June. https://www.theweek.in/theweek/cover/properties-that-are-part-of-jayalalithaas-legacy.html (accessed 29 April 2019).

Subramanian, N. 1999. *Ethnicity and Populist Mobilisation: Political Parties, Citizens and Democracy in South India*. New Delhi: Oxford University Press.

Sukhtankar, S. and M. Vaishnav. 2014. 'Corruption in India: Bridging Academic Evidence and Policy Options'. New Delhi: India Policy Forum and National Council of Applied Economic Research.

Suresh, V. 2015. *Amicus Curiae Status Report of the Madras High Court Seeking Interim Directions* WP 1592, Chennai. https://www.scribd.com/document/337647051/Amicus-Curiae-Status-Report-in-the-Madras-High-Court (accessed 29 April 2019).

Swamy, A. 1998. 'Parties, Political Identities and the Absence of Mass Political Violence in South India', in *Community Conflicts and the State in India*, edited by A. Kholi and A. Basu, 108–48. New Delhi: Oxford University Press.

Viswanathan, S. 2003. 'Taking on the Sand Lobby', *Frontline* 20(22). https://frontline.thehindu.com/static/html/fl2022/stories/20031107003503800.htm (accessed 29 April 2019).

Vivek, S. 2015. *Delivering Public Services Effectively: Tamil Nadu and Beyond*. New Delhi: Oxford University Press.

Walton, M. and J. Crabtree. 2018. 'Crony Populism'. Talk at the Centre for Policy Research & Trivedi Centre for Political Data, Ashoka University, streamed online at http://www.cprindia.org/events/7099 (accessed 29 April 2019).

Wyatt, A. 2013a. 'Populism and Politics in Contemporary Tamil Nadu', *Contemporary South Asia* 21(4): 365–81.

Wyatt, A. 2013b. 'Combining Clientelist and Programmatic Politics in Tamil Nadu, South India', *Commonwealth and Comparative Politics* 51(2): 27–55.

4

Himalayan 'hydro-criminality'? Dams, development and politics in Arunachal Pradesh, India

Deepak K. Mishra

Grounded in political economy, this chapter explores the il/legal economies of dams by exploring the crime-governance nexus produced by dam construction. It considers the politics of hydro-development, of political parties, of corporate houses and of local ethnic competition. Processes are traced to show the criminalisation of politics as well as rampant accumulation from crime and corruption in and around dams and infrastructure for hydro-electricity. This evidence not only shows extensive inefficiencies in the management of water but also how 'hydro-criminality' requires the violation of customary 'norms of violation' in access to watercourses, forests and land, the breaking of state law and the manipulation of loopholes and environmental laws.

Introduction

In the Himalayan region of North East India, dams have been projected not only as a solution to India's growing hunger for energy but also as the cornerstone of the neoliberal development strategy for the region. In Arunachal Pradesh alone, a state of 1.3 million people spread out over 83,743 km² of mountainous land cut by mighty rivers, nearly 160 memoranda of understanding (MoU) for hydro-electricity projects,[1] hardly noticed at the national level, have been signed. A group of activists, with support from students and directly affected locals, oppose the construction of these dams for two broad reasons: first, the ecological, economic and social desirability of such dams; second, the question of criminal corruption regarding these dams, involving politicians, bureaucrats and corporate houses. This chapter focusses on the second course of resistance: the linkages between dams, development and political corruption in the Himalayan state of Arunachal Pradesh.[2]

Dams in the context of neoliberal development

In Sunil Khilnani's evocative expression, 'India in the 1950s fell in love with the idea of concrete' (Khilnani 1999). Nehru himself called large dams the 'temples of modern India', part of the strategy of rapid industrialisation through hydro-electricity, flood control, navigation and fisheries, lean-season river flows, improved roads and irrigation for agricultural transformation. Yet dams also led to the enclosure and flooding of land, deskilling and displacing large numbers of people, disproportionately from Scheduled Castes and Tribes which were already poor and marginalised. They generated environmental problems, ranging from loss of biodiversity to soil salinity (D'Souza 2008). In the post-reform phase (since the early 1990s), as the Indian economy started to grow at historically unprecedented rates, 'energy security' has been among the key concerns of the state.[3] And the 'securitisation of water' has delegitimised alternative perspectives on water and livelihoods. As Hill observes:

> Accelerating the construction of hydro-power in the Himalayas becomes portrayed as something akin to a geostrategic imperative, with the effect that some commentators demand the silencing of dissent and the scrapping of due process around the social, environmental and economic impacts of planned projects within their borders. Discussion over the appropriate courses of action to counter the perceived "illegal" or "unjust" construction taking place on the other side of the international border (China) tends to have a singular focus on technocratic supply-side solutions of building more large-scale dams and empowers those with expertise in that domain at the expense of other visions of what development could or should entail. (Hill 2015, 733)

Hydro-power is being propagated as a 'clean' source of energy and mega dams are being projected as an indispensable component of India's development strategy. Unlike the multi-purpose dams of the past, they are increasingly being justified on the grounds of power generation *alone*; and the state's role as the primary agency for energy infrastructure has been replaced by the idea of the state as coordinating the participation of the private power sector (Schneider 2015). Both the Shukla Commission Report and the Vision 2020 document prepared by the DONER (Ministry of Development of the North Eastern Region, Government of India) emphasised the national demand for energy and the infrastructure deficit of the region as a key hindrance to its response. And these ideas were given great significance in India's Look East policy, which aspires to integrate North East India with East and South East Asia (Haokip 2015; Das and Thomas 2016). Other factors reinforced the case for developing hydro-power in North East India. The persistent and heavy fiscal dependence of the North Eastern states on central government grants contradicted the assumptions of the neoliberal federal order, operationalised through provisions like the Fiscal Responsibility Act.[4] Meanwhile the 'success' of two hilly states, Himachal Pradesh and Sikkim, in generating their own fiscal resources through hydro-power strengthened the argument that hydro-power potential could be leveraged to end the fiscal dependence on the central government of the mountainous, 'special category' frontier states (Mishra and Upadhyay 2017). So, policy has been changed to incentivise hydro-power and encourage private sector investment. These include tax exemptions, a provision for up to 40 per cent of saleable energy to be privately traded, and special access to benefits of the Mega Power Projects policy (for circumstances when electricity is generated for more than one state). Inter-ministerial groups, special task forces, single-window clearance procedures and monitoring by the central government add to the institutional complexity of hydro-power development. These initiatives ride roughshod over local customary law. Land in Arunachal is owned by tribal communities governed by customary law, and private ownership of land has been forbidden (Harriss-White, Mishra and Upadhyay 2009; Mishra 2015).[5] People other than Arunachal Pradesh Scheduled Tribes (APST) cannot legally hold land occupancy certificates. And in the absence of a legal land market, the valuation of commonly held land for collective compensation purposes is an arbitrary exercise where undervaluation is hard to prove in a court. In the rest of this chapter we explore the relation between legal crimes in hydro-development, the flouting of customary norms and party politics.

Dams in Arunachal Pradesh: contestations over development

Although discussions about the hydro-power potential of Arunachal Pradesh are long-standing, it is only since 2000 that a serious effort to exploit this potential has started (Ete 2014). Central and state government politicians have mastered and propagated a new discourse expressing the centrality of dam-construction for Arunachal's future development. The state's hydro-power policy proclaims that the state could be 'floating' on 'hydro-dollars', as Middle Eastern oil states do on 'petro-dollars' (cited in Baruah 2012). In March 2015, the then Chief Minister Nabam Tuki, who also held the finance portfolio, claimed after the commissioning of just three ongoing hydro-power projects in the state that it would earn INR 445 *crore* (INR 4.4 billion ($66 million)) annually as revenue from 12 per cent power supplied by the projects free for the state to sell.[6] At the completion of all ongoing projects, Arunachal Pradesh would meet 40 per cent of India's power demand and graduate from severe dependence to financial self-sufficiency. The political elite has recognised two road-blocks to completion: first, environmental clearances – the state's own procedures protecting the Himalayan ecosystem and societies immediately engaged with it – and second, civil society demands for compensation and political mobilisation against dam construction in Assam and in Arunachal Pradesh.

The interests in 'hydro-criminality'

The politics around the signing of MoUs to build dams is shrouded in a great deal of stealth and secrecy. MoUs are decided not through open competition but at the apex level, formally that of the Chief Secretary but in practice at the level of the Chief Minister. It is the Chief Minister and a few of that minister's coterie who make the decisions to award contracts. Other politicians down to local MLAs representing regions to be affected by dams profess ignorance of details (Ete 2014).[7] While Arunachal has a special nodal Department of Hydro-power Development to monitor and implement MoUs, in practice, after signing, another kind of bureaucratic politics comes into play. While the initial signing of MoUs is implemented through the state-level bureaucracy, ground-level processes of surveys, impact assessments and clearances involve a large number of central government agencies, particularly the Indian government's central cabinet (if special concessions to regulations are required) and the Ministry of Environment and Forests, which operates with compartmentalised responsibilities and tasks. Then, when construction begins, a further range of local players enter hydro-development.

Capital

Many companies work in the increasingly complex economic structure of the hydro-power sector in Arunachal, prominent among which are public sector companies, such as the North Eastern Electric Power Corporation Limited (NEEPCO), constructing large dams in three districts and also taking over projects allotted to other developers or through joint ventures.

From DONER data, the private-sector share of power generated is likely to be around 57 per cent while, of the total MoUs signed, 86 per cent are with private sector companies. In a series of reports in the *Economic Times*, the investigative environmental journalist M. Rajshekhar pointed out that three different kinds of companies 'flocked to Arunachal' to develop hydro-power. The first were large private sector power companies, like that of Naveen Jindal, a prominent industrialist and then Congress party MP. These companies aimed 'to expand and diversify capacity'. Jindal Power Ltd. (JPL), a subsidiary of Jindal Steel & Power Ltd., is involved in several hydro-power projects, three of which operate through subsidiaries in collaboration with the Arunachal Pradesh Hydro-Corporation. Meanwhile Reliance Power is operating in 11 locations inside the state. The second were EPC (engineering, procurement and construction) firms, which saw a chance to move up the value chain. Mostly from Andhra Pradesh, they had experience in building dams and other large construction projects, but not of financing and operating them.[8] The third were companies which had neither experience in building dams nor the desire to build hydro-projects; they simply wanted to sell their contract speculatively to the next buyer for quick profits.[9] Playing smaller roles were 'companies in the business of, among other things, seeds, travel, highways and real estate' (Rajshekhar 2013). The *Economic Times* report points out:

> The company with the maximum number of licences, 12 in all, to build and operate hydro-power projects in Arunachal Pradesh is Energy Development Company (EDC). Amar Singh, the former Samajwadi Party leader, is its chairman, and actor Amitabh Bachchan was on its board till July 2011. Around the time it bagged 10 of those Arunachal projects, adding up to 500 MW, EDC was operating 16 MW of hydel capacity. This is one kind of mismatch in the efforts of Arunachal to become a hydel powerhouse overnight. (Rajshekhar 2013)

The very fact that so many of the companies were from Andhra Pradesh should not be taken as entirely accidental. However, although middlemen who acted as go-betweens between Arunachal politicians and the Andhra owners of these companies were mentioned in interviews, no further details were forthcoming other than that such middlemen have careers brokering transactions in a range of projects such as roads, buildings and bridges.

The bureaucracy

Members of the next class of actor, bureaucrats and technocrats, mainly work as 'junior partners in fixing the deals'.[10] Yet the junior partner is of great significance at the stage after deal-making when basic procedural formalities have to be addressed. Alongside the processes of survey and construction, bureaucrats at different levels protect the interests of private companies. Land acquisition has proved to be an extremely difficult process and support from the district administration and local politicians was crucial for the construction process. The safety and security of personnel and materials, the transport of machines and building materials, the negotiation of local demands and minor accidents all needed brokerage by the local administration. Even when public sector companies like NEEPCO are building infrastructure and dams, this local bureaucratic support to private business is essential since work is constantly being subcontracted to private companies. Government officials rarely voice their experiences in public. A small proportion oppose hydro-power development programmes per se, while others view hydro-power generation as a necessary step towards the development of Arunachal Pradesh, and yet others distinguish the likely benefits of dams for future development from the pervasive and systemic corruption that characterises their execution.

Local politics

As construction work is launched, local politicians – the local Arunachal Minister, MLA and their followers – come to control the work.[11] It is they who negotiate with local *gaon burhas* (headmen) and villagers, prepare and broker the deals on formal and informal compensation packages, act as arbitrators in cases of conflict and provide informal sources of security for the staff, machines and materials.[12] It is hard to imagine that all these micro-political and economic services would be provided without any quid pro quo. Two different classes of operator support the activities of the companies at the local level – although some individuals combine both roles. One is the politicians, who make deals with company officials; they also help set the terms and conditions for the various kinds of deals, rents and bribes (in cash and kind) offered to others. The second group is the contractors, who are provided with work orders and supply orders as part of these deals. Often linked to the politicians through family and local ethnicity, contractors have been very vocal in organising support for the dams. The village-level leaders, such as the *gaon burha* and the *panchayat* members, also play significant roles in dam construction. Land and forests are legally under community (tribal) control; hence community support is a precondition to dam projects. Some village leaders are simply clients of local MLA patrons and act as their representatives on the ground. However, since they have to face their villagers on a day-to-day basis, they do not necessarily agree with the project managers – many are sceptical about the benefits of dams. From the perspective of their interests, these dams and dam construction companies are a threat to their livelihoods and resources. Some of them even actively supported and organised the anti-dam movement. Many, however, are unable to resist. While their tribal people expected them to protect their land and forests from encroachments, the local leaders lacked the financial power or social prestige and influence to confront their MLAs and other powerful politicians intent on forcing this transformation through.

Civil society

Local intellectuals (school, college and university students and teachers; government officials, a small number of journalists, NGO workers and independent researchers) do not constitute a coherent interest group. Until recently, civil society in Arunachal Pradesh had a relatively narrow base. However, the politics of dams has created a new space for political mobilisation through a range of organisations. The resistance to dams has been strongest in the Siang valley, where a large number of organisations such as Forum for Siang Dialogue, Siang People's Forum, Sirit Siyom Banggo Dam Affected Peoples' Forum, Siang Bachao Andolan and the Nyiko Bachao Forum have been active in resisting the dams on various grounds. Other prominent groups include the Save Mon Region Federation from the Kameng-Tawang region. Anticipating the likely adverse impacts of these dams on the lower riparian areas of Assam, a strong people's movement has also taken root in Assam. Prominent among these groups is Krishak Mukti Sangram Samiti, Assam led by Akhil Gagoi, a leader who was also part of the Anna Hazare-led movement for a Jan

Lokpal Act. Several NGO groups, such as Barefoot College, Tilonia, South Asia Network of Rivers, Dams and People (SARDP) and Kalpabriksha are also involved in various ways, particularly in advocacy against the dams. Among all these actors, probably the most affected and yet least heard are rural people living near proposed dams and their infrastructure. Despite hearing rumours that their lives are going to be greatly affected by the dams, they have never been formally consulted. When interviewed for this research, their dominant narrative was that dams might be necessary but the way they were being executed prioritises the interests of the 'rich and powerful' over those of 'ordinary local people'. Many were also cynical about the anti-dam groups because agitators seemed to pursue their own self-interest, by bargaining with the ruling party or with the construction companies for a share in contract work or compensation money, rather than fighting for justice, the environment or for the wider interests of local society.

The contours of contestation

In this section, we examine one of the cases of local resistance and conflict that dam construction has triggered concerning the flouting of tribal norms for the extraction and management of natural resources as well as about political decisions. This case study enables us to draw some conclusions about the relations between customary crime, legal crime and politics, which will be developed in the next section.

Among the proposed dams in Arunachal Pradesh, it is opposition to the Siang river dam projects and the mega hydel (hydroelectric power) project over the Subansiri that is the most developed. The Siang river dams are being proposed in areas dominated by the Adi tribe, one of the two largest tribal groups in the state. The Adis' apex collective political institutions, called Kebang, are well organised (Danggen 2003). Adis are relatively well educated[13] and well represented among the Arunachali elite, which consists of politicians, bureaucrats and the professionally skilled. Adi opposition to the dam project, which was to be constructed by the JayPee group, a private consortium, was grounded in ways suggestive of the pervasive criminality of dam-building. Inadequate information at the early stages and doubts about its environmental impacts and socio-economic benefits were at the core of opposition to the project. The legal requirement for public hearings based on adequate information-sharing has been rampantly violated. According to a recent press release by the Siang Indigenous Farmers' Forum and Siang People's

Forum, their opposition to the project is on the following grounds of negligence:

> [S]uch insensitive and indiscriminate allocation of all the river valleys of the state in general and Siang belt in particular may lead to tribal holocaust due to multiple impact of environment hazards, demographic changes due to migrant labour, loss of social habitat of the tribal people, change in socio economic policy of the state due involvement of corporate politics in the state against the tribal interest. There is no adequate Govt (sic) policy to redress the grievances of project affected people and there is no clear cut Govt policy on relief, rehabilitation, settlement and compensation for land loss in case of installation of mega dams in the Siang valley either from union Govt or state Govt... Arunachal Pradesh have 80 per cent forest cover, but all the forest are private forest owned by private individual or community and the same is duly recognized under the customary practices. But despite recognition of land rights under the customary practices, the Govt is yet to come out with clear cut policy for recognition of the same. (*Arunachal Times*, 3 March 2015)

In a policy no-man's-land, such questions of ownership and compensation were common to almost all the projects in the state. What was unique to the Siang dams was the higher levels of political awareness, the multiple centres of power within the local community and the political competition they generated. The value of fertile plains-land collectively owned by the Adi was also another reason why submergence of such land was locally unacceptable; it flouted customary norms. At an early stage of this project, the then Chief Minister of the State, Dorjee Khandu, strongly favoured the construction of the dam and attempted to mobilise opinion in its support. A newspaper report summarises the unambiguous support that the dam construction got from the political leadership:

> Chief Minister Dorjee Khandu reiterated his stand over the need of improving the economic background of the state to make it self-sufficient and self-reliant... The Chief Minister was addressing a consultative meeting of the project affected people of East Siang with the government and Jay Pee group at the Banquet hall today... Even for a small project we need to plead the Centre for fund, the chief minister lamented. Hydro Power is only such resource which could sail Arunachal Pradesh towards sustainable and resourceful

development, he assertively said... Taking part in the discussion, MP Ninong Ering, MLAs Tamiyo Taga, Ralom Borang and Passang Dorjee Sona strongly advocated for construction of the project. (*Arunachal Times*, 9 September 2010)

The student organisations in the area, particularly the Adi Students Union (AdiSu), were opposed to the project on the grounds that it countered local peoples' rights over land and forests. The AdiSu alleged that:

the [outcome of the] meeting was pre-decided as the meeting was held with the sole motive to take pro dam decision... [A]ll the delegates of the meeting were pro-dam people with vested interests who have been brought to Itanagar by the government and Jaypee Associates. It's a blot on democracy and indigenous people's rights by the Government and the Jaypee Associates whose only motive is profit.[14] (*Arunachal Times*, 9 September 2010)

The protestors, organised under various names, not only mobilised at the grassroots level but also attempted to collaborate with NGOs and movements in various other parts of the country, notably Assam. In a meeting held in Guwahati, RTI activist and General Secretary of Siang Indigenous Farmers' Forum, Tashik Pangkam, alleged that 'nine MoUs were recently signed clandestinely without any public hearing... All norms concerning big dams – be it land acquisition, rehabilitation of displaced people, downstream impact assessment, forest clearance, etc, – are being violated with impunity.' Anti-big dam activist Neeraj Vagholikar, while questioning the rationale behind the centre's hurry in clearing mega dams in Arunachal Pradesh, said that it had not learned any lessons from the Lower Subansiri hydro-electric project stalemate.[15]

Opposition has also grown in Assam to dams in Arunachal Pradesh. Often the issue is framed as an Arunachal-versus-Assam problem, echoing the conflicts around the still-unresolved land boundaries that have been used in the past by political parties in both states to create rifts. The political confrontation picked up momentum in mid-2011. 'East Siang district administration on May 23 had warned the people that strong action would be taken against anti-dam protestors if they take law into their hands' (*Arunachal Times*, 27 May 2011). As tensions escalated, the Central Reserve Police Force (CRPF) resorted to force: lathi charges and blank firing to disperse agitators.

Since that turning point, the politics of the Adi belt has centred on the question of hydel projects. The Bane Kebang, the Adi's apex body, has been confronted with an existential crisis as it has become very difficult for them to take a stand on hydel. According to a relatively younger member of the Kebang in an interview,

> The top leadership consists of influential members of the community, which means they are either former and serving bureaucrats or businessmen. While there have been repeated demands from the public for taking a stand on the issue, it has been very difficult for the leadership to take a stand that would go against the government and the politicians of the ruling party.

Reports on the 36th Annual Conference of the Adi Bane Kebang sum up the dilemma of the organisation. Tayi Taggu, chair of the Hydro Power and Surface Communication Committee (HPSCC), elaborated on the hydro-power potentialities of the state, especially the Siang river, and explained why dams were the need of the hour:

> Mega dams in Arunachal might not be fully viable, but we can certainly opt for smaller dams. We have already submitted a memorandum to the government in this regard… The Siang is an international river, and since China which controls its headwaters has already started building dams on it, we must not relegate ourselves to the weaker side. (*Echo of Arunachal*, 12 November 2015)[16]

International prestige is at stake.

If they took positions on the question of desirability of dams, tribal government institutions such as the Kebangs were attacked from within. An opinion published in the *Arunachal Times* under the provocative title of 'Kebang versus Development' even accused one such Kebang of creating the grounds for future conflicts between APSTs and the emergence of 'anti-national activities':

> The kebang was organized just to oppose the Lower Siang HE Project (2700 MW) to be executed by Jaypee Arunachal Power Ltd.… there were no such valid points of discussion about the refusal of this project. We all know that Arunachal Pradesh can excel in Hydro Power. It will provide employment facilities both directly and indirectly to our young generation. Almost all big developers of India like Reliance, Jaypee, L&T, DS Group are in Arunachal Pradesh only because of Hydro Power… The members of Bogum Bokang Kebang expressed that they are ready to take extreme action against those

who are in favour of hydro-electric project. That is a clear indication of communal conflict and inter Adi society clash in the near future. I *request all forums of Adi Communities not to invite non Adi person in our Adi kebang*. (*Arunachal Times*, 18 October 2011, emphasis added)

Several general patterns of political engagement emerge from the contestations that characterise the construction of dams in Arunachal. First, it has led locally to deep *socio-political polarisation*. Tribal community institutions have a long history of consensus-building through negotiations and bargaining, which has expressed itself through electoral politics in Arunachal. Despite the fact that regional parties have been in power only for very brief periods of time and that national level political parties – Congress and in recent years the BJP – dominate state politics, local politics in the state is anchored to inter- and intra-community solidarity as well as competition (Ghosh and Mishra 2013). The new dam-based modes of delivering development will have significant effects including rising inequality, the concentration of political power and erosion of the local social trust through which tribal society governs itself. The killing of two people by police gunfire, during protests against the arrest of a prominent anti-dam activist, is a rare incident of political unrest and violence in Arunachal.[17]

The second kind of political engagement reinforces the private interests and power of state-level legislators. The signing of MoUs and MoAs at the apex level is followed by a series of negotiations with local interests, in which the MLA and his or her associates and the district administration are key players. Managing and suppressing dissent, these figures also act as local guarantors for the project. This local authoritarian politics around dams builds and consolidates disregard for law.

Third, and in contrast, by opposing the criminality of the dam projects, local activists have tried to create solidarity networks within and outside the North East, which, again is a relatively new phenomenon in a state where nativist politics has strong roots.

Fourth, as Ete (2014) comments, the politics of these

contestations are, [however], more layered than merely a "resistance against destructive development". There is a range of local conflicts being played out: conflict between communities and the state, between communities and private companies, as well as intra-community contestations. These conflicts demonstrate the complexity of the local politics of hydro-power development. (Ete 2014)

Linking dams and the political process

It is now possible to explore the links between the institutional context in which dam construction has been undertaken in Arunachal Pradesh and the political processes in the state. Earlier we exposed the implications of the corruption and violation of customary norms associated with dam construction and party politics in Arunachal. Within the limitations of the evidence collected, in this section we reflect first on how the politics of dam construction is embedded in the state's complex politics, and second on how the politics of dam construction and the corruption around it has also influenced politics in the state.

Corruption and election cycles

Political corruption has a different connotation in popular experience in Arunachal Pradesh from that identified in the constitutional framework – which refers to deviations from the rule and/or from established legal parameters. Corruption is often seen in relational terms, embedded in the informal economies and tribal norms of reciprocities and patronage. However, there are increasing indications that this local relational concept of corruption is being violated and contested.

It is now fairly common for politicians to bribe voters – in cash and in kind – during the elections. There are obvious links between the calculative philanthropy of politicians at election time and the massive corruption that has effectively been normalised in the electoral politics of the state. This involves the siphoning-off of public money for private benefit, thereby breaking many procedural norms and laws of the land. In the few cases that have been discussed in public, the typical modus operandi was to divert public money to private accounts by awarding supply orders to close relatives.[18] This corruption cascades in cycles of reciprocity and 'retail' corruption that is ever more decentralised, but which is linked to high-level multi-*crore* scams.

The links between scams and state politics came to the forefront when Kalikho Pul (who was Chief Minister of Arunachal for a brief period, after the legislators of the ruling Congress party broke away and formed a government under his leadership with the help of the BJP) lost power following a ruling by the supreme court and committed suicide in his official residence. His long suicide note gives details of many alleged illegal deals involving politicians and judges.[19] These include private commissions from the auctioning of rivers, the systematic private embezzlement of official development funds, of financial transfers for the power sector and the public distribution system, for SGSY logistics,[20] flood relief, other funds for central government's sponsored schemes, and non-Plan expenditure and bribes for transfers and promotions. While criminal malpractices and corruption are widely regarded as wrong outside the election cycle, when they underpin electoral politics then they are morally normalised.

Political parties and corruption

The relationship between the looting of state resources and electoral democracy is very strong. Other chapters in this book confirm that it is by no means confined to the contemporary era, to Arunachal Pradesh or North East India. In the case of Arunachal Pradesh, as elsewhere, political corruption needs to be embedded in the political economy of development itself to be understood.

While corruption has been theorised as an outcome of excessive state intervention and the resulting rent-seeking behaviour of bureaucrats, liberalisation has led to an increase in corruption rather than eliminating it (Harriss-White and White 1996). Key to understanding the centrality of, and increase in, corruption in Arunachal's politics is the role of central assistance to the state government. The fiscal dependence of the state on central government has been one of the significant undercurrents of centre–state politics in the region (Ghosh and Mishra 2013). The use of ethnic politics by local elites for state power and 'rents' has been a persistent feature of India's development (Adduci 2012). But while in other contexts, access to state power becomes a means to extract a rent from various sources, including capitalists, in Arunachal and other hilly states 'given the overwhelming significance of the government sector in the economy, the state itself becomes the primary site of rent extraction and conflicts over it' (Ghosh and Mishra 2013, 306, emphasis added). The social and economic mobility of tribal elites and individual accumulation trajectories within tribes is rooted in access to state resources through both lawful and unlawful means:

> Occupationally this group consists of politicians, businessmen and traders, and bureaucrats. The expansion of the state bureaucracy, of construction and infrastructural activities undertaken by the military and the civil administration, the timber trade and general trading and business opportunities in consumption goods created by the emergence of the urban, service class have nurtured these elites. But the key to their economic base is their access to

the resources of the state, which has depended in turn upon their capacity to exploit an ethnicised polity and society. (Harriss-White, Mishra and Upadhyay 2009)

The opening-up of the hydro-power sector to private capital is probably the first major break in these relations of criminal accumulation, and in this sense the scaled-up pattern of Indian corruption is being mainstreamed in Arunachal. As yet, the significance of local state resources persists. The routine instability and frequent switching of loyalty to the party in power at the centre is rooted in this political economy of rent seeking and the competition around it.

Ethnic networks are key to this persistence, structuring political competition. Reciprocities are transacted through the distribution of favours – such as work orders, supply orders, bureaucratic positions – in cash and also in kind (TV sets, motorbikes, cars and medical expenses). This criminal predation is sanctioned by tribal communities, precisely because the loot is shared. In turn, when corrupt politicians are attacked by rivals, ethnic networks are mobilised. Politicians, for example, have protected bureaucrats and contractors who have grabbed government land (often the gardens of government buildings) in a quid pro quo for their support. In the absence of a strong capitalist class, this system of political and economic crime has given rise to a regime of accumulation by corruption.

Property rights over water

Hydro-power development cannot take place without establishing a set of transferable property rights over water. In Arunachal, political corruption involving water dates to the era before the 'MoU virus', as the then Minister of State for Power Jairam Ramesh described the AP situation in 2008 (Chakravartty 2015). From time to time, the post-colonial state has asserted its rights over rivers and streams,[21] whereas, in local contexts, many community leaders still describe all bodies of water as the collectively owned property of the local tribe. Recently however, through promoting schemes like fish ponds, the state has helped create private property rights over water bodies. The destruction and private commercialisation of common property rights has done nothing but accelerate under hydro-power development. It is difficult, however, to pin legal concepts of corruption and crime on these relationships. Given the property rights structures and the fact that rules governing the transfer of property are either absent or ambiguous, it is local collective moral norms that supply the basis for judgments, punishments and movements of political resistance.

Hydro-power projects as a new site of accumulation by corruption

Building dams creates opportunities and costs, which are unequally distributed across society. Local politicians, private tribal contractors and bureaucrats obtain new fields of power and rents. The Inner Line Permit, which restricts entry to outsiders and prevents their purchasing land or immovable property or obtaining trading licences, has created rents for those tribal people able to rent out land, apartments for offices and domestic use, business licences and rent from the state (Harriss-White, Mishra and Upadhyay 2009). This ethnically segmented business class is tightly networked to politicians, either through family or clan linkages or patronage relations. Their access to government supply orders is negotiated through ethnic competition and political brokerage. Shares in contract work and supply orders are often an index of a tribal community's bargaining strength (Harriss-White, Mishra and Prakash 2017). Dams and the associated investment in roads have opened up further scope for rent collection for this class. Allotting work orders to firms owned by close family members of prominent ruling-party politicians is routine. Frequent allegations against prominent politicians involve them siphoning public money through a combination of fraud and nepotism. However, such is the dense thicket of secrecy among the political elite that it is only through Public Interest Litigation and court investigations that these cases are brought into the public domain.

The mechanisms of 'hydro-criminality'

It is therefore difficult to unearth the exact ways corruption and crime take place. However, by collating fragments of information with insights provided by informants, we have mapped their workings. Some of these processes are specific to dam construction, while others are part of the general political landscape of Arunachal. Given the lumpy capital investment, prolonged gestation period and flow of profits over time, the redefinition of property rights over water is crucial for profits from hydro-power (Baruah 2012). There are two key implications for corruption. First, property rights over water and the terms and conditions under which they are transferred to the hydro-power developer are crucial to the project's profitability. Second, given the risky nature and magnitude of the initial investment that is required and the long gestation period that follows, the developer is dependent on those who (formally or informally) safeguard and guarantee these rights during the lengthy construction phase. The stream of returns likely to be generated after the dam is operational and the capacity of the developer to mobilise large initial sums of money are crucial indicators of the capacity to bribe. Our research has identified a set of modes of corruption reported to have taken place in the construction of dams.

1. The state's power to allocate rights over flowing water for commercial use in itself has triggered corrupt bargaining for property rights. As Rajshekhar (2013) points out, there was no regulatory control over the state government's rationing permission for such transfer of property rights. This has resulted in a much higher number of projects that can be justified on grounds of demand or feasibility. Furthermore, permission to construct dams was granted to parties without any transparent competitive bidding, allowing the emergence of a clandestine secondary market for signed MoUs.

2. Because of the ways the contracts to build dams were awarded, many companies were granted permission without any prior experience of dam construction. Insider information suggests that the two key parameters that governed such access were proximity to ruling party politicians and the ability to mobilise bribes. This then incentivised the illegal market in MoUs.

3. Public sector banks financed the private companies. MoUs guaranteed the mobilisation of such loans but they were also contingent on political patronage. The manipulation of the 'joint venture' arrangement between private companies and state agencies, when the projects awarded to some private companies were re-designated as joint venture companies with state-owned corporations, was another source of fraud.

4. The flouting of existing legal provisions, the deliberate manipulation of information and evidence during the preparation of feasibility studies and fraudulent clearance procedures, environmental impact assessments, detailed project reports and cost–benefit analysis have led to substantial profits for private firms. Companies were unlikely to be able to manipulate the early data-intensive phases without backing from politicians and bureaucrats, in both the state and the central government.

5. Apart from property rights over water, the construction of dams involves acquiring a substantial amount of land for reservoirs, construction sites and other installations. In Arunachal Pradesh, compensation for such land involves additional complications because, while land is formally owned by the village communities

or the government, informal private property rights over land have developed in practice. Often, as soon as the land acquisition process starts, powerful elites encroach upon this land and then demand compensation as private owners. In fact, this has been one of the ways through which local elites are pacified by private companies. In some other cases, a nominal amount is given to the village funds as compensation for the collectively owned land while a substantial amount is given to influential people and local leaders.

6. Payments to the state exchequer as royalties from the sale of power have not yet started to flow in, but by 2015 some INR 14,000 *crore* of advance payments had already been made by several Public Sector Units.[22] After taking over as Chief Minister on 9 April 2007, Dorjee Khandu promised to reopen the state-owned APEX Cooperative bank whose 32 branches had lain defunct for two years after a loan scam of over INR 200 *crore* had been unearthed. Within a few weeks, the CM secured a loan of INR 225 *crore* from the PSU power major – the North-eastern Hydropower Corporation – and poured liquidity into the bank, enabling it to reopen, much to the relief of hundreds of thousands of depositors who were mostly poor locals (*The Hindu*, 4 May 2011). According to critics, among the major defaulters of the cooperative bank, causing its closure, had been politicians and their associates.

7. Probably the biggest source of corruption is through the award of work and supply orders to the individuals nominated by politicians. These range from work orders related to infrastructure building, to supply orders and resettlement sites. Huge stone-crushers have appeared near the dam sites. The stones and sand are collected from the village commons, but individual informal suppliers gain substantially in the process. Thus, the corrupt patronage network facilitates primitive accumulation.

8. There are provisions for the employment of local people in the dam projects but recruitment is finally decided by the local leaders and company officials, rather than through transparent, formal processes of recruitment.

9. Payments of bribes in kind by the construction companies to local politicians and influential persons are prevalent. They take several forms – from truckloads of cement, iron rods, sand and other construction materials to occasional help through the use of company vehicles.

10. Employees of dam construction companies and local businessmen have also created novel ventures with rapid illegal profits.

For example, the diversion of truckloads of cement and other dam construction materials and the off-loading of some of it for clandestine sale on the black market generates fraud in so-called joint ventures.

During the frequent periods of political crisis in Arunachal, the ability to generate sufficient cash to buy support from MLAs is alleged to be crucial to their resolution. The financial support from dam construction companies is likely to play an important role.

What are not being documented here are the *secondary* or *derivative cycles of corruption*, because these do not necessarily result from dam construction alone. However, lower-order corrupt practices by local officials, traders and others are incentivised through the demonstration effects of politicians and senior bureaucrats.

The implications of 'hydro-criminality' for party politics

The signing of large numbers of MoUs prior to hydro-development has proved a major departure from business as usual. From the politics of clientelage – demanding ever greater resources from the central government, underpinned by the threat of Arunachal's being a militarily sensitive border-state – a new politics of local resources has emerged. 'From beggars for jobs, our youth could be providers of jobs', said a politician in the Arunachal state assembly. Has the new politics of dams altered state politics in fundamental ways, or is it simply yet another manifestation of well-established corrupt and criminal practices?

Our field research has implications for answering this question.

1. While transparency was never the hallmark of policy-making in the state, there is a new intensity of secrecy regarding the signing of MoUs. Informed public discussion or debates (even within the political classes) regarding the desirability of the projects or about the commitments that are being agreed to in these MoUs are conspicuous by their absence.
2. After the top-level signing of MoUs (usually in the CM's office), local MLAs and ruling-party politicians are mobilised to operationalise the plans, which cement longstanding patronage networks.[23]
3. In the recent past, there has been opposition to the construction of dams, mostly by villagers likely to be directly affected by dam construction and subsequent operation, which has added a new

dimension to politics in the state. Politics of resistance, and the attempts to quash resistance, are opening up a new idiom of politics in the state.

4. Company representatives have intensified coercive efforts to get written consent from local leaders and *panchayat* representatives; often the text of such agreements (prepared by the company) is deliberately vague about promised benefits.

5. Apart from politicians, local contractors act as intermediaries between the construction companies and the local people, adding complexity to the class fractions competing to accumulate capital.

According to Rajshekhar, who explored what he called 'Hydelgate' in Arunachal, hydel in Arunachal has four parallels with the controversial politics of coal-block allocations in 2006–09, which he also investigated. First, Arunachal agreed both more hydel projects than planned, and at greater physical capacity and with greater financial demands on the state. Second, the state used discretionary powers to allot dam sites, thereby increasing the clout of state politicians, bureaucrats and local brokers to influence allocations. Third, besides sector heavyweights such as Reliance Power, Jindal Power and NHPC, the list of 55 companies featured speculators with experience, if at all, in unrelated businesses. Fourth, construction has barely begun. The state does not have adequate roads or transmission lines. Companies lack appropriate finance (Rajshekhar 2013). The 2016 judgment by the National Green Tribunal on the Nyam Jang Chhu Hydro-electric Project (NJC-HEP) in Tawang[24] mentions the following violations of established legal procedures: deliberate concealing of facts; improper impact evaluation; and faulty assessment of the impacts of the project on the part of the bureaucrats.

The case of 'hydro-criminality' in Arunachal may be understood as part of larger processes of accumulation in post-liberalisation India with implications for politics in the state. First, with increasing competition for money that comes through normal government channels, the enhanced rents act as key sources to finance elections, buy the support of fellow politicians and control the (ruling) party machinery. Single families or dynasties have come to dominate the political scene in an unprecedented fashion, likely owing their resources to a step-change in the social concentration of fraud and bribery. However, because the day-to-day safety of the skilled personnel employed by the companies at the dam sites cannot be guaranteed from above, many local-level negotiations have also taken place with locally influential politicians and others. These have involved their incorporation as partners in contract works, the allocation of jobs to local kinspeople and bribes in cash and kind (particularly cement and other house construction materials).[25] So, the large number of dams provides scope for local-level elites to increase their shares of bribes and fraud in kind because their support is crucial for the day-to-day protection and survival of company officials.[26] The two processes, one of concentration and the other of diffusion of fraudulent accumulation, interact.

Set against these findings is the argument that dams may not have altered the political process significantly. Power relations between the central leadership (of the party in power, whether the Congress party or the BJP) and the state leadership remain ones of abject dependence. However, during and after the state and parliamentary elections in 2014, hydro-power dams have risen up Arunachal's political agenda. Ministers and politicians of the ruling party have defended them in public, linking dams to the 'pride' of the people of Arunachal ('from being a deficit/dependent state, we can become a giver/contributor to rest of India'), to a secure and prosperous future for future generations, while only a few opposition leaders have criticised the dams.[27] The politics of hydropower, however, has not thrown up a new political leadership, in terms either of personalities or of ideological positions. Leaders of the anti-dam activists are cynically feared capable of switching sides – after claiming a share of the illegal tribute for themselves. Rural respondents regularly alleged that those who claimed to represent their interests had already struck deals with company managers or politicians.

Nevertheless, earlier rounds of field surveys and first-hand knowledge of political developments in the state lead us to suggest that anti-dam agitations are creating new political spaces the effects of which are as yet unknown. This dissent results from two factors: first the betrayal of tribal peoples' access to resources, and second, the use of force against protesters in a way that is not normal in the state. Without a pan-Arunachal body organising resistance, there are only a few instances of localised movements being coordinated and extending solidarity to various groups in Assam, Delhi and elsewhere (Gohain 2008). In a political context dominated by differences between 'indigenous' tribal people and 'outsiders', this has clearly been a political innovation. This process is developing elsewhere in North East India, as Chowdhury and Kipgen (2013: 207) observe:

'It is the crisis of alternative political and cultural imagination that has stopped the process of a "creative appropriation" of the nationalist discourse on the "North-east", to frame a counter hegemonic discourse… However,… the situation is not entirely bleak, as the recent developments of forging identity beyond the local level renders hope that in the near future a regional level identity might be conceived.' Similarly, in the context of Sikkim, it has been argued that 'hydro-power protests have widened the space for dissent against government high-handedness, not only in dam construction, but also in other realms of governance and politics' (Huber and Joshi 2015, 21).

Arunachal's party politics shows continuity in its competitive plunder of the stream of public funds transferred from New Delhi. Meanwhile, the proliferation of bargaining with private dam-building companies has created scope both for an increased centralisation of power and for a revival of older forms of corrupt local patronage for logistical and protection services.

The overall logic of neoliberalism that tends to equate the business interests of corporations with 'market-led development' in the collective interests of all has further legitimised such practices and helped to isolate those who voiced disagreements over hydro-development. Deregulation and greater private sector participation are not enough to reduce rent-seeking (Harriss-White 1996), and the structural dimensions of 'hydro-criminality' need far greater attention than have been accorded to them.

Notes

1. Activists citing various other sources claim that the actual number of MoUs signed so far is 223 (*Assam Tribune*, 8 August 2015). The exact number of MoUs that have been signed so far and their status has itself become a major political question. The Central Ministry for the Development of North Eastern Region put the number of projects to be undertaken as 86 in 2010. In March 2015, the state government, under Chief Minister Nabam Tuki, stated in the assembly that 'The State Government has allotted 160 hydro-electric projects of installed capacity of 46948.20 MW to various CPUs & IPPs. Out of 160 HEPs, Ranganadi St-I HEP (405 MW) is under operation while Kameng HEP (600 MW), Pare HEP (110 MW) & Subansiri Lower HEP (2000 MW) are under execution' (*Arunachal Times*, 10 March 2015).
2. Because of its political sensitivity, the research method involved an exploratory survey of purposively chosen key informants. Many respondents were apprehensive, speaking only under conditions of anonymity. The reliability of their information was cross-checked through triangulation. Focus-group discussions on the experience of hydro-power development were also conducted with villagers. In this research, we have extensively, but not uncritically, relied upon local newspapers, published in English, the medium of instruction in the state, to substantiate the various arguments made in this paper. Though owned mostly by politicians from the state, over the years the 'Letters to the Editors' columns of these newspapers have been used by the local population to express their opinion vociferously. So the subject matter of this chapter is not whether a specific crime or corruption has taken place or not; rather it is about how the alleged acts of corruption and criminality are perceived by various actors on the ground.

3. However, dam-building in the Himalayas is not just an Indian phenomenon. Several studies have contextualised the recent rush for construction by China, India, Nepal, Bhutan and other nation states (Dharmadhikary 2008).
4. The Fiscal Responsibility and Budget Management Act 2003 was aimed at eliminating Arunachal's revenue deficit and bringing down fiscal deficit to 3 per cent of GDP. For a critical discussion see Jha (2011).
5. On March 12, the state assembly passed the controversial Arunachal Pradesh (Land Settlement and Records) (Amendment) Bill, 2018, under which ownership of land is conferred on those Arunachali citizens possessing 'certificates of land possession/occupancy' (https://scroll.in/article/872474/arunachal-pradesh-gives-individuals-ownership-of-land-but-will-they-really-benefit-from-it). This chapter describes conditions before this Act.
6. See *Echo of Arunachal*, 11 March 2015; *Arunachal Times,* 10 March 2015.
7. During our field investigations, we found that even those 'public leaders' (three to be precise) with connections with the MLAs and ministries were not aware of the details of the signing of MoUs. Bureaucrats (four) involved in the execution of the MoUs and dealing with ramifications of such contracts seem to be aware of the shadowy deals but even they had no definite knowledge of the specifics of the deals (for example who contracted whom, what the 'percentage' is that is paid as a bribe, etc.), although all of them admitted that money must have changed hands.
8. For the full report, see http://articles.economictimes.indiatimes.com/2013-04-30/news/38930347_1_hydel-arunachal-projects-jindal-power.
9. 'Seeing the huge interest from hydel promoters, they began going to a state politician, taking a project, bringing it to a level where a company could buy it from them and start construction,' according to A.K. Mathur, the head of Synergics India, a hydelpower consultancy in Noida (quoted in the *Economic Times*, 30 April 2013).
10. A state government employee, aged about 50, claiming to have known the players.
11. This stylised description is based on interviews with several key informants, such as: (a) a manager of a private construction company who was in charge of operations; (b) a retired government servant who has developed an interest in social work; (c) an anti-dam activist; (d) a contractor, who is also, incidentally, a government servant, engaged in building houses at a rehabilitation site; and (e) local academics.
12. The following incident, reported in the newspapers, highlights the role played by politicians in case of a conflict between the companies and the people. '[Local MLA Mama Natung] was addressing a public gathering at Seba village under Pijerang circle of East Kameng district after inaugurating a Bailey bridge over Papu River constructed by Sussi Infra Pvt Ltd in presence of Deputy Commissioner Sandeep Kumar Singh and Krishna Paradeshi Project Head of Sushee Pvt Ltd. The said bridge collapsed in March 29, 2014, after subcontract company ARTHA's overloaded machinery plied over a weak bridge. The Sushee Pvt Ltd later took over the matter and entered agreement with the local MLA and youth of Seba village, agreeing to build new Bailey bridge over it' (*Arunachal Times*, 5 December 2015).
13. The first college in Arunachal Pradesh was established in Pasighat in Adi territory. For a discussion on the evolution of the town and its implications for tribal identity politics, see Prasad-Aleyamma (2014).
14. Rights of local communities over land and forests are protected in Arunachal Pradesh as per the Arunachal Pradesh Land Settlement and Records Act, 2000 and the Balipara, Tirap, Sadiya Frontier Tract Jhum Land Regulation, 1947.
15. *Assam Tribune*, 9 August 2015.
16. The two reports published in the *Arunachal Times* on the same day highlights the pressure on the local community organisations.
17. For details, see Gupta Kashyap 2016.
18. Accepting money during election campaigns is one openly acknowledged deviation from the rules, described in many of our interviews.
19. The text of the suicide letter was published in English (see *Wire* staff 2017).
20. Suvarnajayanti Gram Swarozgar Yojana (SGSY), launched in 1999, is India's anti-poverty programme through rural self-employment, focussing on self-help groups for women.
21. The Arunachal Pradesh Land Settlement and Records Act 2000 classified all water bodies as property rights of the government.
22. *Arunachal Times*, 3 March 2015.

23. This is not to imply that there are no cases of contestation, bargaining or 'disloyalty' within the patronage networks. As one villager who supports the anti-dam agitation put it: 'We told the minister. We are loyal to you and will still vote for you in the elections. But on the issue of dams, we do not support you.'

24. Copy of the judgment available at eLaw.org (n.d.). For further discussion of the case, see Alley (2017); Ghosh (2013); and Sivaramakrishnan (2015).

25. A report published in the *Indian Express* of 13 December 2016 on allegations of corruption in a hydel project, based on a report by the chief vigilance officer of a public sector unit, describes the nature of collaboration between politicians, government officials and private sector companies (Tiwary 2016).

26. Threats include the following: threat of physical violence to company personnel; forcible lifting or theft of machines or raw materials; demanding of favours or services, e.g. transport in vehicles for other purposes; disruption of work.

27. *Arunachal Times*, 8 October 2010.

References

Adduci, M. 2012. 'Neoliberalism and Class Reproduction in India: The Political Economy of Privatisation in the Mineral Sector in the Indian State of Orissa', *Forum for Social Economics* 41(1): 68–96. doi:10.1007/s12143-011-9091-z.

Alley, K.D. 2017. 'Modes of Governance in India's Hydropower Development', *Wiley Interdisciplinary Reviews: Water* 4 (2). Wiley Online Library. doi:10.1002/wat2.1198.

Baruah, S. 2012. 'Hydropower, Mega Dams, and the Politics of Risk', *Seminar* 640.

Chakravartty, A. 2015. '"MoU Virus" Hits Arunachal Pradesh', *Down to Earth*, 4 June. https://www.downtoearth.org.in/news/mou-virus-hitsarunachal-pradesh-33962 (accessed 2 May 2019).

Chowdhury, A.R. and N. Kipgen. 2013. 'Deluge Amidst Conflict: Hydropower Development and Displacement in the North-east Region of India', *Progress in Development Studies* 13 (3): 195–208. doi:10.1177/1464993413486545.

D'Souza, R. 2008. 'Framing India's Hydraulic Crisis: The Politics of the Modern Large Dam', *Monthly Review* 60(3): 112–24.

Danggen, B. 2003. *The Kebang: A Unique Indigenous Political Institution of the Adis*. Itanagar: Himalayan Publishers.

Das, G. and C. J. Thomas, eds. 2016. *Look East to Act East Policy: Implications for India's Northeast*. London: Routledge.

Dharmadhikary, S. 2008. 'Mountains of Concrete: Dam Building in the Himalayas', Berkeley, CA: International Rivers.

eLaw.org. n.d. 'Before The National Green Tribunal Principal Bench New Delhi – Appeal No. 39 Of 2012'. https://www.elaw.org/system/files/savemon.pdf (accessed 20 June 2017).

Ete, M. 2014. 'Hydropower Development in Arunachal Pradesh: A New Narrative in Natural Resource Politics'. Heinrich Böll Stiftung, India. https://in.boell.org/2014/11/10/hydropower-development-arunachal-pradesh-new-narrative-natural-resource-politics (accessed 8 April 2019).

Ghosh, P. and D.K. Mishra. 2013. 'Party Dynamics in a Border Region: Meeting the Political Challenges of India's North-Eastern Hill States', in *Party System in India: Emerging Trajectories*, edited by A.K. Mehra, 297–324. Atlanta and New Delhi: Lancer.

Ghosh, S. 2013. 'Access to Information as Ruled by the Indian Environmental Tribunal: Save Mon Region Federation v. Union of India', *Review of European, Comparative & International Environmental Law* 22(2): 202–6. doi:10.1111/reel.12028.

Gohain, H. 2008. 'Big Dams, Big Floods: On Predatory Development', *Economic and Political* Weekly 43(30): 19–21. doi:10.2307/40277761.

Gupta Kashyap, S. 2016. 'In Fact: Behind the Firing and Deaths in Tawang, Anti-dam Protests and Abbot-lama Tussle', *Indian Express*, 4 May. https://indianexpress.com/article/explained/in-fact-behind-the-firing-and-deaths-in-tawang-anti-dam-protests-and-abbot-lama-tussle-2783149/ (accessed 29 April 2019).

Haokip, T. 2015. 'India's Look East Policy: Prospects and Challenges for Northeast India', *Studies in Indian Politics* 3(2): 198–211.

Harriss-White, B. 1996. 'Liberalization and Corruption: Resolving the Paradox (A Discussion Based on South Indian Material)', *IDS Bulletin* 27(2): 31–9.

Harriss-White, B., D.K. Mishra and A. Prakash. 2017. 'Inclusive Development, Citizenship and Globalisation: The Case of Arunachal Pradesh', in *Rethinking Economic Development in Northeast India: The Emerging Dynamics*, edited by D.K. Mishra and V. Upadhyay, 136–50. London: Routledge.

Harriss-White, B., D.K. Mishra and V. Upadhyay. 2009. 'Institutional Diversity and Capitalist Transition: The Political Economy of Agrarian Change in Arunachal Pradesh, India', *Journal of Agrarian Change* 9(4): 512–47. doi:10.1111/j.1471-0366.2009.00230.x.

Harriss-White, B. and G. White. 1996. 'Corruption, Liberalization and Democracy: Editorial Introduction', *IDS Bulletin* 27(2): 1–5. doi:10.1111/j.1759-5436.1996.mp27002001.x.

Hill, D.P. 2015. 'Where Hawks Dwell on Water and Bankers Build Power Poles: Transboundary Waters, Environmental Security and the Frontiers of Neo-Liberalism', *Strategic Analysis* 39(6): 729–43. doi:10.1080/09700161.2015.1090679.

Huber, A. and D. Joshi. 2015. 'Hydropower, Anti-Politics, and the Opening of New Political Spaces in the Eastern Himalayas', *World Development* 76 (289374): 13–25. doi:10.1016/j.worlddev.2015.06.006.

Jha, P. ed. 2011. *Progressive Fiscal Policy in India*. New Delhi: SAGE Publications Pvt. Limited.

Khilnani, S. 1999. *The Idea of India*. Delhi: Penguin.

Mishra, D.K. 2015. 'Agrarian Relations and Institutional Diversity in Arunachal Pradesh', in *Indian Capitalism in Development*, edited by B. Harriss-White and J. Heyer, 66–83. Abingdon: Routledge.

Mishra, D.K. and V. Upadhyay. 2017. 'Locating North Eastern Region in a Globalising India', in *Rethinking Economic Development in Northeast India: The Emerging Dynamics*, edited by D.K. Mishra and V. Upadhyaya, 1–18. London: Routledge.

Prasad-Aleyamma, M. 2014. 'Territorial Legends: Politics of Indigeneity, Migration, and Urban Citizenship in Pasighat', *Economic and Political Weekly* 49(22): 111–20.

Rajshekhar, M. 2013. 'Hydelgate: Why Arunachal Pradesh's Hydel Boom Is Going Bust', *Economic Times*, 30 April.

Schneider, K. 2015. 'Arunachal's Unfinished Lower Subansiri Dam Could Be Tomb for India's Giant Hydropower Projects', *Scroll*, 12 June. https://scroll.in/article/718809/arunachals-unfinished-lower-subansiri-dam-could-be-tomb-for-indias-giant-hydropower-projects (accessed 8 April 2019).

Sivaramakrishnan, K. 2015. 'Ethics of Nature in Indian Environmental History: A Review', *Modern Asian Studies* 49(4): 1261–310. doi:https://doi.org/10.1017/S0026749X14000092.

Tiwary, D. 2016. 'Vigilance Probe Red-flags Fraud and Corruption in Arunachal Hydro Project', *Indian Express*, 13 December. https://indianexpress.com/article/india/vigilance-probe-red-flags-fraud-and-corruption-in-arunachal-hydro-project-kiren-rijiju-4424240/ (accessed 20 June 2017).

Wire staff. 2017. 'Full Text of Kalikho Pul's 60-page Secret Note', *The Wire*, 10 February. https://thewire.in/politics/kalikho-pul-note-full-text (accessed 29 April 2019).

5

Crime in the air: spectrum markets and the telecommunications sector in India

Jai Bhatia

This chapter explores the intertwining of crime and governance produced in the markets for spectrum. In so doing it traces the criminalised expansion of telecom. It investigates the systemic plunder of airwaves and a form of intreccio that involves capital, political and bureaucratic elites. Crimes result from privileged and discretionary control over information and resources, politicised manipulation of regulative laws and selective enforcement failures.

Evidence is suggestive of large-scale and expanding capital accumulation by business and the political elite and the exchange of regulatory and financial privileges in return for campaign finance. Alongside widespread nepotism and cronyism the chapter traces important parallel shifts into politics on the part of corporate businessmen and into business on the part of politicians and officials. It shows how regulative law is effectively manipulated and how politicians modify law retrospectively to make ad hoc exemptions benefitting political-cum-business cronies.

The capture of spectrum in the air for telephony is among India's most egregious economic and social achievements,[1] and is often cited as an example to justify the economic reforms of the 1990s. Telecom is touted as one of India's most successful sectors for its booming spectrum markets, its market-driven policy initiatives, and for how the industry has come to provide telecom services to the vast majority of the population at affordable rates. The subscriber base of wireless telephony increased from 5 million in March 1991 to 1.2 billion subscribers in March 2016 (TRAI 2017), and the cost of services fell by 87 per cent between 2001 and 2015 (*Economic Times* 2015).[2] The telecom sector has also been economically and socially transformative as it has come to contribute 6.5 per cent (US$140 billion) to India's GDP in 2016 (Government of India 2017b), compared to a global telecom sector that contributes 4.4 per cent (US$2 trillion) to worldwide GDP (KPMG 2017). Sinha (1996) and Virmani (2000) have argued that as a part of India's critical infrastructure, greater connectivity through telecommunications has led to a boom in other industries such as information technology, software and e-commerce. In addition, various studies have found that the 'mobile (phone) revolution' has benefitted and empowered various groups in Indian society, including women (Prasad and Sreedevi 2007), fishermen (Abraham 2006) and the poor (Souter et al. 2005).

Although the telecoms sector is dominated by some of India's best-reputed business houses, including Reliance Industries' Reliance Jio, the ADAG Reliance Group's Reliance Communications, Birla Group's IDEA Cellular, Tata Group's Tata Teleservices and Bharti Group's Bharti Airtel, it has been well publicised as being riddled with instances of misallocation of spectrum, financial scandals and fraud. Problems have been documented in the fragmentary and uneven implementation of policy, insider knowledge of policy changes, under-invoicing of telecom revenues, clientelism and corruption. For example, in the 2G spectrum scandal, spectrum was under-priced and allocated to specific companies favoured by the then Union Minister for Telecom, Andimuthu Raja. The Comptroller and Auditor General (CAG) calculated that the 2G allocation scandal resulted in the loss of INR 176,000 *crore* (US$26 billion) to the exchequer (Bhandari 2012; Kaushal and Thakurta 2010). Subsequently 122 licences were cancelled by the supreme court of India in 2012 and the Telecom Minister Raja and many others who were involved were jailed for their offences (Acharya 2012; Bhandari 2012). However, such punitive action did not curb corruption or stop scandals and frauds. There have been several further instances, most notably allowing Reliance Communications and Tata Teleservices to convert their 'limited mobility' licences (or CDMA) to general licences (or GSM) without participating in an auction as required by a supreme court mandate.[3] The allocation of Broadband Wireless Access (BWA) spectrum to Reliance Jio was also controversial, provoking allegations of fraud in how the spectrum was acquired from the state. The CAG estimated 'undue benefit' – i.e. the loss to, or theft from the public exchequer as a result of these two cases – to the magnitude of INR 12,626 *crore* (US$2.8 billion)[4] and INR 19,000 *crore* (US$4.1 billion)[5] respectively (CAG 2015; Thakurta and Chaudhuri 2015; Thakurta 2016).

This chapter explores two key elements of the spectrum markets in India: first how a sector modelled on market (neoliberal) principles manifested constant and recurring scandals and fraud such that it quickly became a textbook case of regulatory capture and crony capitalism. More specifically, it examines a narrowing alliance between the political and economic elites. Second, how the role of the state changed with respect to 'creating and maintaining healthy markets',[6] where market ideologies, policy processes and the regulatory infrastructure were all manipulated to legitimise the systematic plunder of a natural resource such as spectrum.[7] To this end, this chapter is organised as follows. First, the political economy of spectrum markets is outlined. Second, the role of the state in creating and maintaining spectrum markets on neoliberal principles is examined. Third, the consequences of the narrowing alliance between the state and business elites are analysed to show why the scale, frequency and magnitude of scandals has not decreased over time, despite a neoliberal policy regime which theoretically offers an assault on rent-seeking from a slimmed-down, transparent and accountable state (Harriss-White and White, 1996).

Political economy of spectrum markets

At the heart of the telecom sector is the scarce natural resource of spectrum (or bands of airwaves) which are owned by the Indian state. The state leases out spectrum to private businesses for a set period of time to provide telecom services. It auctions this spectrum and in return receives non-tax revenues (including up-front spectrum payments from auctions, spectrum instalment payments, spectrum usage charges, fines and other charges), which amounted to INR 56,034 *crore* or 22 per cent of the state's non-tax revenue for 2015–16 (Government of India 2017b). Table 5.1 provides further details of the state's revenue from the telecom sector between 2009–10 and 2015–16. For businesses, the allocation of spectrum is one of the most important transactions: it is access to spectrum that gives businesses the ability to provide and expand their telecom services. Access to greater quantities and qualities of spectrum also enhances their competitive edge in providing services. Currently, spectrum for the use of commercial wireless telephony is auctioned in bands or frequencies between 800MHz and 2400MHz. Lower frequency airwaves have a

Table 5.1 Indian government revenue receipts

Contributions to communications receipts (in *crores*)							
Particulars	*2009–10*	*2010–11*	*2011–12*	*2012–13*	*2013–14*	*2014–15*	*2015–16*
Licence fees	9,792	10,030	11,161	11,500	12,651	14,068	14,974
Spectrum usage charges	3,423	3,861	4,850	5,201	6,115	6,930	7,550
Upfront auction payments		106,262		1,108	18,269	10,808	21,607
Auction instalments							1,326
Other fees	2,664	395	1,390	1,093	3,079	-1,182	10,577
Total	**15,879**	**120,548**	**17,401**	**18,902**	**40,114**	**30,624**	**56,034**

Telecom sector's share of non-tax revenue (in *crores*)							
Particulars	*2009–10*	*2010–11*	*2011–12*	*2012–13*	*2013–14*	*2014–15*	*2015–16*
Communication receipts	15,879	120,548	17,401	18,902	40,114	30,624	56,034
Total non-tax revenue	116,276	218,603	121,671	137,355	198,870	197,857	251,260
Share of total	**14%**	**55%**	**14%**	**14%**	**20%**	**15%**	**22%**

Source: Government of India 2017a; IRCA 2016; Non-tax revenue receipt budget 2016

longer wavelength or range, and therefore can carry the telecom signal greater distances, but have a low bandwidth, which restricts the ability to carry data. In comparison, higher frequency airwaves have a shorter range but a higher bandwidth and therefore can carry greater amounts of data over shorter distances.

India's telecom market is the product of the Indian state. Spectrum markets in India came into existence in 1994 when private businesses were first allowed to enter the telecom sector and bid for spectrum. In order to understand the development of this market, the preconditions of the telecom sector prior to opening up need to be outlined. In the 1970s and 1980s, due in part to import restrictions, the licensing of manufacturing activities and a lack of infrastructure, the Indian economy was characterised by chronic shortages of goods and services. In the telecommunications industry, the average waiting time for a fixed (land) line telephone connection was between 5 and 10 years (Sridhar 2011). In 1991, there were five million telephone connections with another five million on the waiting list (Sridhar 2011). Petrazzini

(1996) claims that the Department of Telecom's (DoT) dismal performance was not entirely a failure of state policy but rather a reflection of the Indian bureaucracy's practices of petty corruption, misuse of privilege and patronage. These problems in the state's institutional structure meant that neoliberal reforms could take root without much political resistance. Indeed, market-oriented telecom reforms were welcomed as they almost immediately alleviated the problems of shortages, delays and bureaucratic control.

The decision to restructure the telecommunications industry started with the National Telecommunication Policy 1994 (NTP-94), which allowed private companies to enter the wireless telecoms market. Sinha (1996) points out that instead of licensing two or three private companies to provide telecom services nationally, the DoT created 22 'telecom circles' or licences specific to a geographical area, allowing several private companies to participate in telecom market space. The explicit goal of such a policy was to ensure the uniform development of national telecom networks in rural and urban areas alike. It also encouraged competition and reflected the state's commitment to creating a market-based economy (Virmani 2000; Gupta 2002). It helped the state to create a market for spectrum and the entry of so many private firms into the telecoms market led to an increase in demand for spectrum. In order to build spectrum markets, the Indian state created an independent regulatory institution, the Telecommunications Regulatory Authority of India (TRAI), whose sole focus was to establish a liberal (competitive) market environment. The DoT previously functioned as both policy-making body and regulator; however, these two roles could not be reconciled without a conflict of interest, as it was part of the DoT's mandate to generate non-tax revenue for the government. It was also obliged to protect the interests of state-owned MTNL and VSNL,[8] which made private and foreign businesses nervous (Sinha 1996). Sinha (1996) argues that this conflict of interest made US companies reluctant to participate in telecom tenders. International pressures also increased, as India's entry into the World Trade Organization (WTO) brought pressure to create an independent regulator that could enforce spectrum property rights.

Another crucial step in the state's development of spectrum markets was the setting up of the Telecommunications Dispute Settlement and Appellate Tribunal (TDSAT) in 2000. The judicial system was weighed down with a backlog of cases stretching back 30 years. Since any judgment took years to be handed down, the development of the Telecom

Industry was delayed (Moog 1992; Mashru 2013). By contrast, the TDSAT adjudicated disputes and disposed of appeals in a reasonable time frame. The creation of a separate tribunal dealing specifically with tele-com-related cases helped enforce and secure property rights over spec-trum for private companies, which in turn established the credibility of spectrum rights and increased market confidence. The state's method of allocation of spectrum was central to the planning and growth of spec-trum markets. Since 1994, the Indian state has trialled many methods of allocation, including: i) a 'beauty contest', where interested firms submit business plans to a government committee, which judges candidates on who best meets the criteria published; ii) 'first come first served', where firms are allocated spectrum in order of the receipt of their applications for spectrum; and iii) 'auctions', where firms have to compete with each other by bidding for spectrum. Each method was supported by eco-nomic rationales and deemed suitable for the circumstances of the time. Allegations of corruption, nepotism and patronage permeated the vari-ous methods of allocation – indicating that the problem was not in the choice of allocation method but in the way in which the methods were implemented (Kaushal and Thakurta 2010; Bhandari 2012). The next section argues that under the guise of promoting the development of markets, the state has implemented a pro-business policy regime that has narrowed the alliance between the state and telecom businesses and has legitimised repeated instances of impropriety and the brazen plunder of spectrum. Big business houses, politicians and bureaucrats work hand in glove with each other criminally to appropriate the assets of the state. They are able to evade the law and bend regulations to illicitly enrich themselves. There have also been a considerable number of cases inves-tigated by the Central Bureau of Investigations (CBI), the CAG and the Income Tax and Enforcement Directorate (ED) where the state's guardi-ans of a natural resource, be it coal, oil or spectrum, were found guilty of aiding its plunder.

Making and maintaining 'markets' and 'business'

In the 1990s, the formal ideology of the Indian state changed from a mixed economy (where, despite the extent of the informal economy, the state was the driver of much industrial development) towards a mar-ket-dominated economy where the state gradually liberalised trade, deregulated industrial policy and privatised many state-owned enter-prises outside essential commodities and defence – reasoning that a market-led economy would accelerate development. The telecommunications sector was one of the earliest reflections of this change in state ideology. Prior to opening up the telecom sector to private investments, the state was the sole provider of telecom services. With the move to the market economy, the role of the state became that of a facilitator providing the right environment in which private businesses could flourish. This often meant that, in the name of 'creating and promoting' markets, the state could undertake a series of pro-business policy changes that specifically favoured existing domestic business houses.

The discrepancy between the state's pro-market ideology and pro-business policy practices, despite being regarded by some analysts as 'spurious' (e.g. Panagariya 2008), is vital to understanding the narrowing alliance between state and business (Kohli 2012). A pro-market ideology, where the state limits its role in the economy and permits markets to decide the allocation of resources, asserts that markets will result in optimal allocations of resources. Policies such as privatising public sector companies, reducing subsidies, restricting the state's role in commodity price fixing, easing tariffs on foreign goods, devaluing the currency and encouraging private investments are preconditions to this allocative process.

However, in practice, the Indian state created and implemented policies that were pro-business rather than pro-market. It did not retreat from the forefront of the economy or cede allocation decisions to markets but instead repeatedly intervened to support the growth of private businesses. On the supply side, the state actively facilitated the availability of capital, labour, technology and even entrepreneurship (Kohli 2012). Capital was made available by providing credit from state-owned banks to big businesses, via tax cuts and direct subsidies. Labour was repressed and any activism was actively discouraged by the state as well as business (Kohli 2006). In the case of technology and entrepreneurship, the state invested in education and research and development, and negotiated with foreign firms to facilitate technology transfer. On the demand side the Indian state adopted an expansionary monetary and fiscal policy regime. On the one hand, the monetary regime made credit for consumption easier to obtain in terms of equated monthly instalments (EMIs) on consumer durables, auto-loans and credit card overdrafts, while on the other hand an expansionary fiscal policy regime reduced the taxes and tariffs on imported goods. The exchange policy was also kept favourable to trade: exports were incentivised through duty drawback schemes such as the Duty-Free Replenishment Certificate (DFRC) and Duty Entitlement Passbook (DEPB) and cheaper credit through the Export Packing Credit (EPC) scheme. The production of goods for domestic and foreign consumption was promoted through a myriad of subsidies and tax rebates. The state also indulged in activity that distorted prices, such as undervaluing the Indian rupee, subsidising exports and making wages lag behind productivity gains, in order to encourage businesses to profit and grow. The state's pro-market rhetoric masked its pro-business policy regime, which systematically ensured the profitability of private businesses. Such a pro-business policy regime was not only legal but also gained legitimacy and popularity over time as an important developmental tool. The Bharatiya Janata Party (BJP) led by Prime Minister Narendra Modi won the 2014 elections on the basis that their development model was superior to any previous government's, because they had adopted a pro-business attitude to designing the policies that governed the economy (and would provide jobs…).

In the telecoms sector, it is evident from both policy recommendations and constant public rhetoric about 'creating and maintaining healthy markets' that TRAI, the independent telecoms regulator, created pro-business institutions to regulate the sector, which accelerated capital accumulation in the private telecom businesses and put their interests above those of either the state or telecom consumers. Every time telecom companies faced a financial crunch the regulator would urge the DoT to 'revitalise the sector' by changing policies to enhance the profitability of telecom companies. For example, in 2017 the new entrant Reliance Jio started a price war and as a consequence the profitability of all the telecom companies decreased significantly, so much so that many of them found it difficult to service their debt and began defaulting on their loans. The state conveniently stepped in to reduce the spectrum usage charges (SUC) from 6 to 2 per cent and extended the spectrum instalment payment period from 10 to 15 years, which immediately lowered companies' financial obligations and reduced their cash outflow, in turn boosting their profits. All major policy changes have been unidirectional in favour of private businesses and can be traced back to moments of decline in the profitability of the private telecom companies as examined below. The field experience and methods are laid out in the Appendix to this chapter, below.

The change from National Telecom Policy 1994 to New Telecom Policy 1999

The National Telecom Policy of 1994 permitted private operators to provide telecom services through the issue of telecom licences. These licences required their holders to pay a fixed licence fee. Many companies rushed to get a licence to enter the telecom markets. Given that wireless technology was a new technology, it was difficult to predict how consumers would behave or what pricing would allow the markets to grow, and businesses quickly found themselves over-leveraged and unprofitable. Business associations such as the Cellular Operators Association of India (COAI) lobbied the TRAI and the DoT to help reduce the financial pressure on the private telecom businesses. In 1999 the sector was on the verge of collapse when the New Telecom Policy (NTP) 1999 was introduced, allowing existing licence holders to switch to a revenue-sharing model in place of the fixed licence fee. This policy change allowed telecom businesses to renege on their contractual obligations to the state, which freed them from the obligation of paying the high fixed annual licence fee that they had agreed to pay while bidding for the spectrum. It allowed them to switch to a licensing regime whereby they could pay a percentage of their earned annual gross revenue (AGR). Such a change in policy meant that the telecom companies did not have a fixed financial obligation to pay but paid licensing fees only as a percentage of the revenue they earned, which immediately had a positive impact on profitability and revived the sector. In other words, the state came to the aid of telecom companies through this policy change, which legally permitted them to convert their spectrum obligations from a fixed cost to a revenue-dependent cost, which led to telecom companies becoming profitable. Higher profits in turn boosted the future expectation of profits, which boosted the business valuations of telecom companies.

Change from New Telecom Policy 1999 to New Telecom Policy 2012

In the aftermath of the 2G scandal verdicts, where the supreme court of India cancelled 122 licences belonging to telecom companies, many had to bid again for their 2G licences and financed their re-purchase of spectrum by taking on more debt. As a result the telecom sector was once again overleveraged and in the financial doldrums. Subsequently, in 2012 a new policy was introduced to 'revitalise' the sector once again. Unlike NTP 94 and 99, where telecom companies could bid for no more than two circles (with the state's intention of promoting competition among many telecom companies), the National Telecom Policy (NTP-2012) allowed companies to switch to a Unified Access Service Licence, which permitted telecom companies to hold spectrum across all telecom circles. This policy spurred financial activities such as mergers and acquisitions, with the intention of capitalising on cost savings from financial or debt restructuring, operational and network synergies and the cost savings that would arise from economies of scale. In addition, the NTP-2012 went a step further, allowing private companies to not only pool and share their spectrum but also trade their spectrum with the stated goal of creating efficiency (Department of Communications, GOI 2012). While this move is consistent with market ideals, allowing telecom companies to trade and thus commoditise spectrum has the potential to create a secondary market for spectrum in which companies can speculate for profit. Here, there is a danger of shifting the companies' focus from providing efficient and effective telecom services to gleaning as much profit as possible from trading.

Change from New Telecom Policy of 2012 to (Expected) New Telecom Policy 2018

In 2016, the entry of Reliance Jio triggered a price war in the telecom sector, which led to a steep fall in the average revenue per user (ARPU), a key measure of profitability. To stay competitive in the market most telecom companies have to bid for every new generation of spectrum, which has led most to take on progressively more debt. Spectrum obligations and interest costs further increased the mountains of debt the telecom companies acquired. For example, the average debt-to-equity ratio in the telecom sector in 2016 is 2.53, which means for every rupee of equity there are 2.53 rupees of debt. Bharti Airtel, the market leader in terms of revenue and number of subscribers, has an even higher debt to equity ratio of 4.96 (Mulgaonkar 2016; Bhatia and Palepu 2016). Telecom companies have also been showing signs of stress, given the high levels of leverage. In early 2017, Reliance Communications, an ADAG Reliance Group company and the fourth largest telecom company, defaulted on a INR 49,000 *crore* (US$7.5 billion) loan (Reuters 2017). Once again, a new telecom policy is expected in 2018, which in the name of 'revitalising the market' will further benefit the telecom companies.

Foreign direct investment regulations

The Ministry of Finance defines foreign direct investment (FDI) limits on foreign equity investment in Indian companies sector by sector. In line with other sectors, the FDI limits for the 'Basic and Cellular Services' increased to 100 per cent in 2016 (49 per cent through the automatic route[9] and over 49 per cent with government approval), allowing Indian companies to tap foreign investors. The demand from foreign capital has led to pressure to increase business valuations of telecom companies, which has in turn allowed the Indian promoters of telecom companies to sell a part or all of their stakes in their telecom companies at a substantial profit.

Alternatively, they partner with the foreign companies on very favourable terms. Although the state's continuous pro-business policy changes
have accelerated the process of legal capital accumulation in the telecom
sector, they have also spurred a host of illegal and criminal activity within
the sector. In the next section I analyse the illegal and criminal activities
that have been investigated by state agencies and discussed widely in the
media, and argue that these illegal activities increased as a consequence
of the ever-closer alliance between the state and business. In addition, the
next section also argues that these illegal activities have led to a constant
recurrence of scandal, fraud, corruption and financial impropriety in the
telecom markets and that such activities are not a deviation from India's
neoliberal market system but rather an innate characteristic of it.

The narrowing alliance between the state and business

In fact, India's telecom sector has quickly become a textbook case of regulatory capture.[10] The size, scale and the quantum of money involved
in spectrum markets has attracted politicians and bureaucrats who see
power in their ability to allocate spectrum to private businesses. Politicians (such as ministers for telecoms, communications and finance)
and bureaucrats (such as telecom secretaries, finance secretaries, TRAI
Chairmen, TRAI secretaries, DoT and TRAI advisors, etc.) are responsible
for the entire span of the policy process from formulation, implementation and evaluation to addressing and formally enforcing contraventions.
Such responsibilities bestow upon them the formal power to direct benefits subversively to specific businesses. Such instances can be seen in
the examples mentioned below. The means by which specific businesses
benefitted illegally include (but are not limited to) providing businesses
with prior knowledge of policy changes, retrospectively changing policies, allowing ad hoc exemptions, adopting alternative interpretations of
specific policies in specific cases,[11] poor (uneven) implementation of policies, discretion in permitting businesses to exploit policy or procedural
loopholes, and systematic disregard of blatant violations of policy.[12]

With the entry of private businesses into new sectors of the economy, politicians and bureaucrats become the gatekeepers: allocating
and managing scarce resources, regulating property rights and rationing
access to state assets. Together they enrich themselves and their political
parties. Over time such relationships develop into a nexus of politicians,
bureaucrats and businessmen. Through bribes or in-kind favours, private
businesses in turn cultivate individual or partnership relationships with

them. Often such relationships are institutionalised through a parallel system of working where the big business houses already have deep connections to political parties and state institutions. Every state officer that takes charge tends to be keen to toe the political line as they enjoy the rents and windfall benefits (bribes, in-kind benefits, etc.) of being posted to that position. The relationship between business and political parties has become critical to political party finances, as a significant quantity of political contributions and electoral campaign financing comes from their business patrons.

Another trend that shows the narrowing alliance between the state and business is that many businessmen have become politicians and vice versa. For example, Dayanadhi Maran, who with his brother Kalanidhi Maran owns Sun Group, an organisation with interests in television, broadcasting and telecommunications, became the Minister of Communications and was subsequently accused of using his powers as Telecom Minister to aid Sun TV's business interests (Kaushal and Thakurta 2010; Bhatia and Palepu 2017). Similarly, Vijay Mallya, the owner of the now-defunct Kingfisher Airlines, was also a two-term MP; in 2002 his position as a member of the consultative committee for the Ministry of Civil Aviation and the standing committee on commerce gave rise to a serious conflict of interests. Mallya used his privileged position to obtain undue benefits for his business, which included large loans from public sector banks (Rajshekhar 2016). In another case of conflict of interest, Kupendra Reddy, a real estate baron from Karnataka, was made a member of the select committee on the Real Estate (Regulation and Development) Bill, 2013 and (to no surprise) was subsequently accused of using his position to aid his business interests (Rajshekhar 2016). There are other such examples.

In the telecommunications sector, the key source of crony capitalism, corruption and clientelism is the market system itself. This dates back to the opening up of the sector to private investment – and its effects are debated. On the one hand, supporters of neoliberalism argue that fraudulent behaviour is an aberration from normal market practice by unscrupulous companies – facilitated by poor regulation (Bhagwati and Panagariya 2013). On the other hand, critics see a systemic problem as inherent to a profit-seeking environment, while the regulations designed to curb this behaviour are undermined by the guardians of the system (politicians and bureaucrats) themselves. In 1996, for example, the Union Minister for Telecommunications in the PV Narasimha Rao Congress government, Sukh Ram, was investigated by the Central Bureau of Investigation (CBI) for irregularities in awarding telecom contracts to private telecom companies (Kaushal and Thakurta 2010). The first information report (FIR) noted that INR 3.62 *crore* were found in suitcases at his residences, which the CBI alleged were bribes that Sukh Ram had taken in exchange for favours he had granted as Telecom Minister. Increasingly dispensable as a member of the Congress party 'old guard', Sukh Ram was in 2009 found guilty of misusing his position as Telecom Minister when he awarded a contract to supply polythene insulated jelly filled (PIJF) cables for the Telecom Department to a private firm, Haryana Telecom Limited (HTL), for INR 30 *crore* in exchange for bribes – as per the court proceedings (PTI 2011; *India Today* 19 November 2011). Sukh Ram was sentenced by the special CBI court to three years of imprisonment for 'being part of a criminal conspiracy to defraud the exchequer' and amassing assets disproportionate to his known income (Kaushal and Thakurta 2010).[13]

Both major political parties belong to institutionalised criminal caucuses of politics and business. Bureaucrats serving outgoing politicians are vulnerable to investigations and said to keep sensitive records hidden at home, while appealing for protection to ousted ministers, themselves open to reprisals. In 1999, Pramod Mahajan (a member of the BJP) was appointed as Telecom Minister and was subsequently accused of blatantly bending rules to aid the Reliance Group (Bhupta 2015; Kaushal and Thakurta 2010). Reliance Infocomm (RIC) acquired a basic telephony licence, which had a bundled CDMA licence for last-mile coverage; these licences were popularly referred to as 'wireless local loop (WLL)' licences or limited mobility licences. The sluggish CBI investigations found that Pramod Mahajan had permitted RIC to obtain 'full mobility' and become a nationwide operator without paying the full licence fees. RIC had paid INR 533 *crore*, whereas another cellular operator had paid INR 1,633 *crore* over the same time period for the same licences (Bhupta 2015; *Times of India* 3 January 2006; Kaushal and Thakurta 2010). Subsequently, the comptroller and auditor general (CAG) also confirmed that the loss to the exchequer and undue benefit to the Reliance Group was in the region of INR 1,100 *crore* (*Times of India* 3 January 2006). In addition, the CBI investigations into Pramod Mahajan's activities revealed further details of the quid pro quo relationship between Pramod Mahajan and the Reliance Group, one involving a business-political family and not merely an individual.[14] RIC issued a total of one *crore* shares to three companies, namely Fairever Traders, Softnet Traders and Prerna Auto, for INR 1 apiece (*Times of India* 3 June 2006; *Economic Times* 9 June 2011). These three companies were associated with Ashish Deora, who was the business partner of Rahul Mahajan and Anand Rao, Pramod Mahajan's soh and son-in-law (*Economic Times* 9 June 2011; Jagannathan 2014; *Times of India* 2006). Within two months RIC issued a further 32 *crore* shares to Reliance Communications Infrastructure Ltd. at a premium of INR 52.71 (*Economic Times* 9 June 2011). The CBI alleged that Pramod Mahajan received a kickback in the form of the under-priced shares (*Economic Times* 9 June 2011; Jagannathan 2014).

In 2006, the then Telecom Minister Dayanidhi Maran was accused of accepting kickbacks for assisting the Malaysian-based Maxis Group to acquire Aircel Ltd by allegedly 'arm-twisting' Aircel's former chairman C. Sivasankaran to sell the company (Vaishnav 2017). After a subsequent decade replete with other scandals involving other telecom companies, together with snail-paced investigations, as per the charge sheet eventually filed by the CBI in 2016, it was alleged that Dayanidhi Maran's family business, Sun Group, received an investment of INR 740 *crore* in exchange for his assistance in helping Maxis Group acquire Aircel Ltd (*Firstpost* 19 December 2016; Bhatia and Palepu 2017). Sun Group was not the only telecom fraud involving political–business families. The Aircel–Maxis case also involved the former Congress party Finance Minister, Palaniappan Chidambaram, who was accused by the CBI and the enforcement directorate of misusing the power of his office in granting Foreign Investment Promotion Board (FIPB) approvals to foreign companies to invest in Indian companies. Maxis Group's aquisition of a 99.3 per cent financial stake in Aircel violated the 74 per cent upper limit on foreign direct investment in the telecom sector at that time. In investing INR 3,514.45 *crore*, Maxis Group also violated prevailing foreign investment regulations requiring any investment in excess of INR 600 *crore* to be reviewed by the FIPB and its recommendations to be forwarded to the cabinet committee on economic affairs (CCEA) for a final decision. In this case, the file was never sent to the CCEA; instead the Ministry of Finance under Palaniappan Chidambaram received the FIPB's recommendations and approved the investment (Bhatia and Palepu 2017). In May 2012, the Bharatiya Janata Party (BJP) raised a ruckus in parliament, accusing Chidambaram of corruption in the Aircel–Maxis case. The BJP MP Subramanian Swamy alleged that in exchange for providing the requisite FIPB approvals, Chidambaram's son Karti's company received a 5 per cent equity stake in Aircel Ltd. Chidambaram claims that these allegations were a political attack by the BJP on the Congress party, while the CBI and ED continue their investigation into the individuals involved (Bhatia and Palepu 2017).

The Aircel–Maxis controversy also highlighted a legal loophole that many foreign companies use to circumvent FDI norms while attempting to stay within the legal limits of FDI regulations. Lawmakers and bureaucrats are aware of this loophole but choose to adopt an alternative legal interpretation of FDI policy: although the Maxis Group owned only 74 per cent of the equity, it used non-convertible preference shares to invest in 99.3 per cent of the equity, thereby allowing them to bypass the FDI limits of the time (Bhatia and Palepu 2017). Such preference shares often receive a fixed dividend and have dividend priority over equity shareholders. Preference shares can be either irredeemable or redeemable, non-convertible or convertible into equity shares, and can have cumulative or non-cumulative dividends. As per the Foreign Exchange Management Act (FEMA) of 1999, only fully and mandatorily convertible preference shares by a foreign buyer would be counted as FDI. All other kinds of preference shares are treated as debt and open to the interpretation adopted by the bureaucrats.

As a result of the Aircel–Maxis controversy, Dayanidhi Maran was forced to step down as Telecom Minister and Andimuthu Raja was appointed in his place. In 2008, under Raja's leadership, 2G spectrum was allocated on a first-come-first-served basis. However, many private companies used their influence and closeness with politicians and bureaucrats to manipulate the system and were awarded under-priced telecom licences, many of which were then sold onward to foreign investors for a large profit (Bhandari 2012). The CAG report[15] of March 2010 highlighted how some businesses illegally received prior insider knowledge that the deadline for the first-come-first-served spectrum allocation was going to be 'preponed' at very short notice (CAG 2010). These favoured businesses had prepared their demand drafts, letters of intent and other relevant documents before the new cut-off date (Bhandari 2012; Thakurta and Gatak 2012; Kaushal and Thakurta 2010).

Three months after spectrum was allocated, the Department of Telecoms revised their guidelines for intra-circle mergers and acquisitions. The guidelines dropped any mention of the word 'acquisitions' and read 'Any permission for merger shall be accorded only after completion of three years from the effective date of the licences', which meant that only mergers would be prevented, paving a way for companies that had won spectrum licences to be acquired by foreign firms at terms very favourable to their Indian promoters (Kaushal and Thakurta 2010). For example, Swan Telecom was one of many companies to be incorporated with the intention that it would bid for 2G spectrum. Swan Telecom had capital of INR 28 *crore* (US$4.4 million) in 2007 and was awarded 22 licences in 2008 (Mankotia and Raj 2011; Bhandari 2012). Subsequently in 2008, it managed to sell 45 per cent of its stock to the UAE telecom company Etisalat for US$900 million (Kerr and Fontanella-Khan 2008).

The CAG of India estimated the loss to the exchequer from the under-pricing of 2G spectrum to be approximately INR 176,000 *crore* (US$26 billion), which subsequently led to the cancellation of 122 licences by the supreme court of India in 2012 (Bhandari 2012; Acharya 2012; Kaushal and Thakurta 2010).

Broadband Wireless Access (BWA) spectrum auctions in 2010 were also riddled with controversy, including several allegations of criminal intent by manipulation of the rules. It was alleged first that Infotel Broadband Services Private Limited (IBSPL), a private firm that won BWA spectrum at an auction, was fronting for the Reliance Group, and second that after the auction was conducted and the licences allocated the regulations were changed retrospectively to benefit the Reliance Group. IBSPL had paid-up capital of INR 2.51 *crore* with one client, from which it earned INR 14.78 *lakh* and had a bank balance of INR 18 *lakh*, yet IBSPL had managed to meet the financial requirements for the spectrum bidders and provided a bank guarantee of INR 252.5 *crore* as earnest money (which was several hundred times its capital) (Gatak and Thakurta 2016; Thakurta and Chaudhuri 2015). The DoT had, perhaps conveniently, failed to check the creditability of IBSPL. As soon as IBSPL won the BWA spectrum, its authorised share capital was raised two thousand times from INR 3 *crore* to INR 6,000 *crore*, and 75 per cent of its shares were issued to Reliance Industries Limited (Gatak and Thakurta 2016). Subsequently, IBSPL was renamed Reliance Jio Infocomm Limited. Gatak and Thakurta (2016) cite a draft report of the CAG, 'The DoT failed to recognise the tell-tale sign of rigging of the auction right from [the] beginning of the auction', which reveals that many state institutions were aware of the violations but, with fractured jurisdictions and no ex ante powers, to date little has been done to address them.

The BWA spectrum auction originally stipulated that this spectrum could be used only to provide broadband or data services. This prevented its holders from providing 'voice' services. Many telecom companies did not bid for this spectrum (or bid aggressively for higher and higher amounts) as the regulations restricted its use for voice. After IBSPL had won a majority of the BWA spectrum and had been acquired by Reliance Industries, the regulations were changed to allow voice calls over the BWA spectrum.[16] The regulator and the DoT justified the change in policy as reflecting the 'march of technology', where the next step following 'Internet Protocol (IP)' was 'Voice Over Internet Protocol' (VOIP) technology. The question still arises as to whose interests were served by the BWA spectrum's not being priced with VOIP in the first place. The CAG reported that such a retrospective policy move allowed Reliance Jio to enter the telecom markets by paying an 'entry fee' of INR 15 *crore* and a 'migration fee' of INR 1,658 *crore*, while benefitting to the tune of INR 22,842 *crore*, which they would have had to pay had they bid fairly for the BWA licence that allowed voice calls (Gatak and Thakurta 2016).

Corruption and the links to political party finances

The public discourse on corruption and crony capitalism seldom goes beyond pinpointing an individual politician or bureaucrat when he or she is caught in an illegal or criminal activity. It is the greed of the individual in question or his/her lack of ethics that attracts condemnation. The institutions, processes and relations constituting the system of which they are part are never publicly questioned. Yet it is widely accepted that corruption cannot take place without the tacit agreement of a whole chain of people working in a particular state department, and it is also very unlikely that the political party to which the individual belongs knows nothing of their activities. It is most likely that the bribes are shared up and down the chain of command.

Political parties are also likely to benefit from corruption scandals, as money obtained criminally can be used for election campaign expenses while bypassing regulations designed to make political party finances more transparent. In 2014, the Centre for Media Studies estimated the amount that political parties spent on parliamentary elections to exceed US$4.6 billion – of which only 2.2 per cent could be traced back to donors and recipients (*Economist* 2014). As per the election commission's rules, political parties are legally not allowed to spend more than INR 70 *lakh* (US$115 thousand) per parliamentary seat, but it is common knowledge that political candidates spend between 50 to 100 times that amount on their election campaigns (*Economist* 2014; Mahajan 2016). In 2012, the Observer Research Foundation think-tank reported that parliamentarians from Congress and the BJP openly discussed their spending INR 20 *crore* (US$3.3 million) on their campaigns when the official limit was INR 16 *lakh* (US$26,000) (*Economist* 2014). In 2016, the Union Minister of Finance, Arun Jaitley, also alluded to the extensive use of black money in political party finances in a *Doordarshan News* interview (Mahajan 2016).

There is only one political repercussion I want to see with this (demonetisation) and that is that politics and the process of elections will also get cleaned because of this. This will have an effect on political parties as well. So far in our country there has been a practice of invisible political funding, that will also have to be visible in a democracy. (Arun Jaitley, 10 November 2016)

Although there are several ways whereby political parties generate black money, corruption is the champion. In 2014, criminal cases were pending against more than one-third of the elected members of parliament, demonstrating the extent to which crime, corruption and politics are linked (Vaishnav 2017). If the politician is uncharged, he or she continues to run for elections while amassing wealth both personally and for the party. If caught, then a politician is scapegoated as an individual. The question then arises of the specific conditions under which a political party chooses to save its candidate. Although there is no direct answer, my fieldwork may be able to shed some light on these conditions.

Over the course of my fieldwork, many telecom bureaucrats acknowledged that they feared being investigated by the CBI and/or ED after retirement or when the government changed. Many of them believed that they would become victims of politically motivated investigations when an incoming government would want to show up the outgoing government as incompetent and corrupt. Often investigations would start by looking into the activities of low-level bureaucrats and slowly spread to the entire chain of command, giving the politicians time to make backroom deals. Pradip Baijal, a former chair of the TRAI, described his experience facing an investigation motivated by political malice in his book *A Bureaucrat Fights Back* (2016) and in an interview with me. He explained how he had had to seek the help of Arun Shourie and Yashwant Sinha (the Telecom Minister and the Finance Minister respectively at the time when he was TRAI chair) to resolve the case against him. Many bureaucrats explained that they coped with the fear of being subjected to politically motivated investigations by keeping a copy of every document they signed. In political circles, it is also well-known that criminal cases against politicians are often not resolved but kept pending for years so as to allow the government in power to bring the case to centre stage and use the threat of punishment (jail time) and bad press to limit the actions of the political party in opposition. At times, political parties have no choice but to allow their ministers to go to jail. Very often after the media frenzy calms down the minister is allowed bail and is able to continue with political and social duties.

For example, A. Raja, the Telecom Minister (and a member of the DMK), was arrested with 15 others (including Kanimozhi, the DMK patriarch M. Karunanidhi's daughter) accused in the 2G spectrum scam case in February 2011. Raja spent 15 months in jail before he was granted bail (Kattakayam 2012). In 2017, Raja and others were acquitted of any wrongdoing in the 2G spectrum case on the basis of a lack of evidence (Kumar 2017). It remains a mystery as to why in 2012 there was enough evidence in the first place to jail Raja and his associates and why that evidence was insufficient in 2017. Another mystery concerns the case's delays. It might have been providential timing: just before the 2G scandal verdict was given, there were many rumours that the BJP was considering an alliance with the DMK in Tamil Nadu. These rumours were further fuelled by Prime Minister Modi's visit to Tamil Nadu, where he met the ailing DMK leader Karunanidhi, in November 2017 (*CNN News 18* 7 November 2017; *Hindustan Times* 7 November 2017). Internal party politics may also play a role in politically motivated investigations: many media sources reported on Dayanidhi Maran's 'stepping on the toes of DMK patriarch Karunanidhi and his sons', as a result of which he was punished with continuous investigations into his actions as Telecom Minister (Ramadurai 2011).

The ways in which businesses transact with political parties have also evolved. Kochanek (1996) in his seminal study of business lobbying in India highlighted the practices of 'briefcase politics', whereby industrial capitalists would commonly illicitly buy influence with money after political contributions, legitimate or otherwise, were banned in 1969 (Mazumdar 2008; Kohli 2012; Panagariya 2008; Kochanek 1987). McDonald (1998) argued that the Reliance Group had succeeded in reversing the client–patron relationship, in which state officers competed to bring profitable opportunities to the Reliance Group in return for financial rewards. Businesses offered substantial financial rewards in the form of political contributions, election funding and bribes at the party level. Meanwhile, at the individual level they offered jobs in the private sector that might benefit a bureaucrat's family, or offers of post-retirement employment, admissions and scholarships to schools or colleges, or access to elite hospitals, housing communities, etc.

Over time, there has been a push towards formalising the purchase of political influence through the use of advocacy groups, think-tanks and policy and industry consultants who act as middlemen and often organise conferences and closed-door meetings between industry professionals and state officials to facilitate backroom deals. For example, Niira Radia, a known lobbyist, was caught on tape by an Income Tax Department wiretap, speaking to top businessmen about the shares of benefits that each would receive when Raja became Telecom Minister (*Radia Tapes* 2009). It seems that big business conglomerates (with interests in several sectors) view their relationships with the government strategically. Political contributions (legal and illegal) are thought of as a fee to yield influence or to access any government department. When a specific favour is to be granted by the government then the business pays a variable cut, to be apportioned to all involved. So business leaders cultivate individual relationships with important political party leaders in the belief that, since political parties hold power transiently, as long as the business leader has contact with each political party, he or she will be able to draw on that relationship when necessary. It seems that when a party loses power, political contributions are diverted to the winning party and the system of corruption and influence persists.

Conclusions

Spectrum markets in India represent a key example of the neoliberal nature of India's economy. The wireless telecom sector was built on forms of application of market principles that allowed private businesses to dominate telecom service provision. Spectrum rights are at the heart of the telecom markets; they are necessary for the provision of telecom services and have a value in themselves because telecom companies often engage in mergers and acquisitions to obtain these rights. Acting as market regulator, promoter and guardian, the state created a market for spectrum rights, which allowed a private oligopoly to own and control these rights for a set period of time. The state is formally responsible for overseeing the functioning of the market and stepping in when there is a risk of disruption. In the telecom sector, the state actively and legally promoted the interest of private businesses in the name of revitalising telecom markets whenever profits were threatened. Most of the companies that formed the telecom oligopoly belonged to the big domestic business houses, such as the Tatas, Birlas, Reliance, etc. The telecom companies often borrowed large sums of money from public-sector banks in order to bid in the spectrum auctions (Ghosh and Guha 2017; Press Trust of India 2017). While increasing competition among telecom companies reduced their revenues, high interest rates squeezed margins. Every time these telecom companies have found themselves over-leveraged and unprofitable, the state has stepped in and revised the telecom policies in order to reduce the financial pressure on the companies. Most of the large policy changes can be traced back to the financial difficulties facing private telecom companies; from the National Telecom Policy 1994 to the New Telecom Policy 1999 to the New Telecom Policy 2012 and once again in 2018 when a New Telecom

Policy was introduced as the National Digital Communications Policy, aiming to address the current difficulties of ballooning debt and falling revenues in the sector. The regulators' rhetoric that 'healthy companies make healthy markets' masks the extensive financial assistance that the state provides to the private telecom businesses of some of the richest conglomerates.

As the representatives of the state, which both creates and regulates spectrum, politicians and bureaucrats are in positions of power as policy makers, regulators and enforcers. Their inherent conflicts of interest are exacerbated when they then grant favours to specific businesses. The market economy has blurred the distinction between formal legal 'discretion' and criminal behaviour. Many big business houses use their extensive networks across various state departments to cultivate relationships with state officials and political parties. Corruption is endemic in the telecom sector. This sector has witnessed an unprecedented number of scandals, which have involved titans of Indian industry and major political parties, Telecom Ministers, Finance Ministers, Prime Ministers and senior bureaucrats. Crimes have included illegally providing specific businesses with prior knowledge of policy changes, retrospectively changing policies in their favour, allowing ad hoc exemptions and going slow on investigating violations of policy. Very often the judicial procedure is used to delay or completely avoid paying fines; telecom companies file a case appealing the fine levied by the DoT, and while the case goes on for many years, the telecom company in question continues operating. State–business relationships in the market-led economy have become extremely lucrative for state officials individually and for the political parties in power as well as for businesses. The scale and the magnitude of the sums of money involved have vastly increased over time, amplifying corruption, clientelism and patronage.

Notes

1. Here spectrum refers to a range of radio waves.
2. The cost of an outgoing local call fell from INR 6 per minute in 2001 to INR 0.80 per minute in 2015 (*Economic Times* 2015)
3. The DoT, in consultation with the TRAI, changed the law so as to advantage Reliance and the Tatas. The then chair of TRAI, Pradip Baijal, was investigated over allegations of providing Reliance with a 'back door' into the telecom sector. See page 157 for details. The Tatas benefitted less as their CDMA licences were mainly for the big metros. The requirement for an auction to allocate spectrum was mandated by the supreme court only in 2012, during the delivery of the verdict on the 2G scandal. In this case, the law itself was tweaked by the state to make an exception to advantage specific businesses.
4. In 2005 the exchange rate was INR 45.01 to the dollar
5. In 2010 the exchange rate was INR 46.30 to the dollar

6. This was a mantra expressed widely by informants during fieldwork, in both private and public contexts.
7. The system has become increasingly neoliberal, which over time normalises, legitimises and rationalises the actions of politicians and bureaucrats. Most of my interviewees representing state institutions were investigated for wrongful action at some point or another but they seemed to believe that their actions (of giving away spectrum cheaply) were justified by revolutionising the telecom markets. The DoT, TRAI and TDSAT (even RBI) state institutions often rationalise bad practice in the telecom sector – and the institutional framework was set up so as to bail out the sector every time the private 'telcos' got into trouble.
8. Mahanagar Telephone Nigam Limited is a state-owned telecommunications service provider. Videsh Sanchar Nigam Limited is a formerly state-owned telecom company now owned by Tata Communications.
9. The automatic route of foreign direct investment gives foreign companies permission to invest in Indian companies without prior approval from the Ministry of Finance.
10. The capture of the regulators by those regulated.
11. Adopting alternative interpretations of specific policies in specific cases refers to bureaucrats and politicians interpreting a particular law/regulation in a way that benefits a specific business but switching back to a more stringent interpretation for other businesses, giving the first business a competitive advantage. An example is found in the case of interconnection charges (IUCs); i.e. charges that telecom company A must pay telecom company B for the use of B's network when A's customers want to call B's customer. Until 2016, the IUC charge per call was fixed at 14 *paise* and on average total revenue to telecom companies from IUCs amounted to approximately INR 20,000 *crore* (Rathee 2016). In order to provide some certainty over costs incurred by telecom companies, the TRAI was committed to leaving the IUCs at 14 *paise* for the next few years. With the entry of Reliance Jio in late 2016, the TRAI began a consultative process of revising the IUCs down. As Reliance Jio was a new entrant in the market, their customer base would make proportionally more outgoing calls and receive fewer incoming calls in comparison to other networks, which would mean that Reliance Jio would end up paying other telecom companies more in IUCs than it would receive. Merrill Lynch estimated that with an approximate subscriber base of 30 million, IUCs would cost Reliance Jio INR 2,400 *crore* in its first year of operations (Parbat 2017). The TRAI chair R.S. Sharma interpreted the TRAI mandate, which was to ensure that there is high quality of services and that consumers are protected, to mean that IUCs needed to be reduced so as to reduce the number of call failures arising from the Reliance Jio network. Subsequently, IUCs were reduced to 6 *paise*, leading to a windfall gain for Reliance Jio (*Hindu Businessline* 2017). Other telecom companies lost out on revenues that they would otherwise have made.
12. The punishment for contravening policy is often just a fine, which, if it exceeds a certain amount, is disputed in court. Such court processes drag on for years while the telecom companies continue their operations normally (which includes violating other policies).
13. From media reports, it seems that Sukh Ram served the sentence. He was also convicted and sentenced by different courts in three different but related cases, which, at age 91, he is still appealing in higher courts. After a six-year wait, a hearing was tabled for May 2018. Meanwhile in 2017 he crossed from Congress to the BJP but rejoined Congress in 2018.
14. There is no public evidence that money passed from the individual to their political party, though this is widely alleged in private.
15. Many such reports are leaked in draft, after periods spent wrestling with misinformation and attempts to manipulate, and ultimately are published in a mellower form.
16. Using the cloak of transparency, consultative papers are released by the TRAI, and are open to public comment. Advocacy professionals and telecom consultants write reports supporting the change. TRAI then issues its recommendations to the DoT, which then decides and implements the changes. Both major parties are privy to this process.

References

Abraham, R. 2006. 'Mobile Phones and Economic Development: Evidence From the Fishing Industry in India', *Information Technology and International Development* 4(1). https://itidjournal.org/index.php/itid/article/view/241 (accessed 20 April 2019).

Acharya, G. 2012. 'India: Case Study on the Supreme Court Ruling on the 2G Spectrum Scam', SSRN Scholarly Paper ID 2048719. Rochester, NY: Social Science Research Network. http://papers.ssrn.com/abstract=2048719.

Baijal, P. 2016. *A Bureaucrat Fights Back: The Complete Story of Indian Reforms*. New Delhi: Harper Collins.

Bhagwati, J. and A. Panagariya. 2013. *Why Growth Matters: How Economic Growth in India Reduced Poverty and the Lessons for Other Developing Countries*. New York: PublicAffairs.

Bhandari, B. 2012. *Spectrum Grab: The Inside Story of the 2G Scam*. New Delhi: Business Standard Books. http://spectrumgrab.com/.

Bhatia, J. and A. Palepu. 2016. 'Predatory Pricing or Predatory Behaviour? Reliance Jio', *Economic and Political Weekly* 51(41). http://www.epw.in/journal/2016/41/insight/reliance-jio.html (accessed 8 April 2019).

Bhatia, J. and A. Palepu. 2017. 'Circumventing Institutions: Did Chidambaram Subvert the Foreign Investment Promotion Board?' *Economic and Political Weekly* 50(23): 7–8.

Bhupta, M. 2015. 'Reliance Feud: Pramod Mahajan Link Add Political Colour to Ambani Battle', *India Today*, 28 February. https://www.indiatoday.in/magazine/economy/story/20050228-ambani-row-pramod-mahajan-link-add-political-colour-to-battle-788144-2005-02-28 (accessed 8 April 2019).

CAG. 2010. 'Union Performance Report of Civil Allocation of 2G Spectrum', Comptroller and Auditor General of India. http://www.cag.gov.in/sites/default/files/audit_report_files/Union_Performance_Civil_Allocation_2G_Spectrum_19_2010.pdf.

CAG. 2015. 'CAG Audit Report on Communication and IT Sector Presented'. Press Release. New Delhi: Comptroller and Auditor General of India. http://cag.gov.in/sites/default/files/press_release/press_release_8_may_2015_20of2015.pdf (accessed 8 April 2019).

CNN News 18. 2017. 'Why DMK And BJP Are Cozying Up To Each Other', *News18*, 7 November. https://www.news18.com/news/politics/why-dmk-and-bjp-are-cozying-up-to-each-other-1569491.html (accessed 8 April 2019).

Department of Communications, Government of India. 2012. *National Telecom Policy 2012*. New Delhi: Author. http://www.dot.gov.in/sites/default/files/NTP-06.06.2012-final.pdf (accessed 8 April 2019).

Economic Times. 2011. 'CBI to Probe Telecom Violations under Mahajan's Term', *Economic Times*, 9 June. https://economictimes.indiatimes.com/industry/telecom/cbi-to-probe-telecom-violations-under-mahajans-term/articleshow/8783545.cms (accessed 8 April 2019).

Economic Times. 2015. 'TRAI reduces ceiling tariffs for national roaming; lower call rates effective from May', *Economic Times*, 10 April. https://economictimes.indiatimes.com/industry/telecom/trai-reduces-ceiling-tariffs-for-national-roaming-lower-call-rates-effective-from-may-1/articleshow/46863169.cms (accessed 27 June 2019).

Economist. 2014. 'Black Money Power', *The Economist*, 4 May. https://www.economist.com/blogs/banyan/2014/05/campaign-finance-india (accessed 8 April 2019).

Firstpost. 2016. 'Aircel-Maxis Case: Charges to Be Framed against Dayanadhi Maran, Others on 22 December', *Firstpost*, 19 December. http://www.firstpost.com/politics/aircel-maxis-case-charges-to-be-framed-against-dayanadhi-maran-others-on-22-december-3163282.html (accessed 8 April 2019).

Gatak, A.R. and P.G. Thakurta. 2016. 'The Immaculate Conception of Reliance Jio', *The Wire*, 4 March. https://thewire.in/23620/the-immaculate-conception-of-reliance-jio/ (accessed 8 April 2019).

Gewirtz, S. and J. Ozga. 1994. 'Interviewing the Education Policy Elite', in *Researching the Powerful in Education*, edited by G. Walford, 186–203. London: UCL Press.

Ghosh, S. and R. Guha. 2017. 'Over 10 Banks Red Flag Anil Ambani's Reliance Communications over Missed Loan Payments', *Economic Times*, 29 May. http://economictimes.indiatimes.com/industry/banking/finance/beleaguered-reliance-communications-banking-on-aircel-brookfield-deal-proceeds-to-avoid-npa-tag/articleshow/58885495.cms (accessed 8 April 2019).

Government of India. 2017a. *Union Budget 2017–18: Analysis of Tax and Non-Tax Revenue Receipts*. Annexure 2. New Delhi. http://indiabudget.nic.in/rec.asp?pageid=1 (accessed 8 April 2019).

Government of India. 2017b. Department of Telecom Annual Report 2016–17. New Delhi: Ministry of Communications. http://www.dot.gov.in/sites/default/files/Annual%20Report%202016-17.pdf (accessed 8 April 2019).

Gupta, R. 2002. 'Telecommunications Liberalisation', *Economic and Political Weekly*, April. http://www.epw.in/special-articles/telecommunications-liberalisation.html (accessed 8 April 2019).

Harriss-White, B. and G. White. 1996. 'Corruption, Liberalization and Democracy: Editorial Introduction', *IDS Bulletin* 27(2): 1–5.

Hindu Businessline. 2017. 'TRAI Decides to Slash IUC Rate to 6 Paise from 14 Paise', *Hindu Businessline.com*, September. https://www.thehindubusinessline.com/info-tech/trai-decides-to-slash-iuc-rate-to-6-paise-from-14-paise/article9865219.ece (accessed 8 April 2019).

Hindustan Times. 2017. 'DMK-BJP Alliance Is Very Much in the Realm of the Possible', *HindustanTimes.com*, 7 November. https://www.hindustantimes.com/editorials/dmk-bjp-alliance-is-very-much-in-the-realm-of-the-possible/story-qW71xlE5P8Z1Zq1oKACcQJ.html (accessed 8 April 2019).

India Today. 2011. 'Former Telecom Minister Sukhram Sentenced to 5 Years in Jail', 19 November. https://www.indiatoday.in/india/north/story/former-telecom-minister-sukhram-sentenced-to-5-years-in-jail-146260-2011-11-19 (accessed 8 April 2019).

IRCA. 2016. 'Telecom Sector – Continues to Be Healthy Contributor to the Non Tax Revenues of Government of India'. New Delhi. http://www.communicationstoday.co.in/images/reports/201607-Telecom-Sector-Update-ICRA.pdf (accessed 8 April 2019).

Jagannathan, R. 2014. 'CBI, CAG Bring Ambani's Actions into Sharp Focus', *Firstpost*, 20 December. https://www.firstpost.com/business/cbi-cag-bring-mukesh-ambanis-actions-into-sharp-focus-24408.html (accessed 8 April 2019).

Kattakayam, J. 2012. 'A. Raja Gets Bail after 15 Months in Jail in 2G Spectrum Case', *Hindu Businessline*, 15 May. https://www.thehindubusinessline.com/economy/a-raja-gets-bail-after-15-months-in-jail-in-2g-spectrum-case/article20434825.ece (accessed 8 April 2019).

Kaushal, A. and P.G. Thakurta. 2010. 'Underbelly of the Great Indian Telecom Revolution', *Economic and Political Weekly*, December. http://www.epw.in/insight/underbelly-great-indian-telecom-revolution.html (accessed 8 April 2019).

Kerr, S. and J. Fontanella-Khan. 2008. 'Etisalat Takes 45% Stake in India's Swan Telecom', *Financial Times*, 23 September. https://www.ft.com/content/f4fe0f18-898b-11dd-8371-0000779fd18c (accessed 8 April 2019).

Kochanek, S. 1987. 'Briefcase Politics in India: The Congress Party and the Business Elite', *Asian Survey* 27(12): 1278–301. https://doi.org/10.2307/2644635.

Kochanek, S. 1996. 'Liberalisation and Business Lobbying in India', *Journal of Commonwealth & Comparative Politics* 34(3): 155–73.

Kohli, A. 2006. 'Politics of Economic Growth in India, 1980–2005: Part I: The 1980s', *Economic and Political Weekly* 41(13): 1251–59.

Kohli, A. 2012. *Poverty amid Plenty in the New India*. New Delhi: Cambridge University Press.

KPMG. 2017. 'Accelerating Growth and Doing Business in India: Telecommunications'. ASSOCHAM.

Kumar, N. 2017. 'A. Raja, Kanimozhi, Others Acquitted in 2G Spectrum Allocation Case', *The Hindu*, 21 December, sec. Delhi. http://www.thehindu.com/news/cities/Delhi/a-raja-kanimozhi-others-acquitted-in-2g-spectrum-scam-case/article22121626.ece (accessed 8 April 2019).

Mahajan, K. 2016. 'Demonetisation Alone Won't Stop Black Money in Political Funding; Electoral Reform Needed', *Firstpost*, 28 December, sec. Politics. https://www.firstpost.com/politics/demonetisation-alone-wont-stop-black-money-in-political-funding-electoral-reform-needed-3177106.html (accessed 8 April 2019).

Mankotia, A. and R. Raj. 2011. 'CBI on Swan Telecom Hunt Seeks Details of Delphi', *Financial Express*, 23 February. http://www.financialexpress.com/archive/cbi-on-swan-telecom-hunt-seeks-details-of-delphi/753574/ (accessed 8 April 2019).

Mashru, R. 2013. 'Justice Delayed Is Justice Denied: India's 30 Million Case Judicial Backlog', *The Diplomat*, 25 December. http://thediplomat.com/2013/12/justice-delayed-is-justice-denied-indias-30-million-case-judicial-backlog/ (accessed 8 April 2019).

Mazumdar, S. 2008. 'Investment and Growth in India under Liberalisation: Asymmetries and Instabilities', *Economic and Political Weekly* 43(49): 68–77.

McDonald, H. 1998. *The Polyester Prince: The Rise of Dhirubhai Ambani*. St Leonard's, New South Wales: Allen & Unwin.

Moog, R. 1992. 'Delays in the Indian Courts: Why the Judges Don't Take Control', *Justice System Journal* 16(1): 19–36.

Mulgaonkar, A. 2016. 'Reliance Industries Prefers Using Debt to Cash for Capex', *Business Standard India*, August 6. http://www.business-standard.com/article/companies/reliance-industries-prefers-using-debt-to-cash-for-capex-116080501886_1.html (accessed 8 April 2019).

Ostrander, S. 1993. 'Surely, You're Not In This Just to Be Helpful. Access, Rapport, and Interviews in Three Studies of Elites', *Journal of Contemporary Ethnography* 22(1): 7–27.

Panagariya, A. 2008. *India: The Emerging Giant*. New Delhi: Oxford University Press.

Parbat, K. 2017. 'Telecom Sector Reels under Heavy Debt and Falling Revenue', *The Economic Times*, 17 June 2017. http://economictimes.indiatimes.com/news/company/corporate-trends/telecom-sector-reels-under-heavy-debt-and-falling-revenue/articleshow/59184371.cms (accessed 8 April 2019).

Petrazzini, B. 1996. 'Telecommunications Policy in India: The Political Underpinnings of Reform', *Telecommunications Policy* 20(1): 39–51. https://doi.org/10.1016/0308-5961(95)00046-1.

Prasad, P. and V. Sreedevi. 2007. 'Economic Empowerment of Women through Information Technology: A Case Study from an Indian State', *Journal of International Women's Studies* 8(4). https://vc.bridgew.edu/jiws/vol8/iss4/8/ (accessed 29 April 2019).

Press Trust of India. 2011. 'Former Telecom Minister Sukhram Sentenced to 5 Years in Jail', *India Today*, 19 November. https://www.indiatoday.in/india/north/story/former-telecom-minister-sukhram-sentenced-to-5-years-in-jail-146260-2011-11-19 (accessed 8 April 2019).

Press Trust of India. 2017. 'Supreme Court Agrees to Hear SBI, PSU Banks in Aircel-Maxis Case on Feb 3', *Business Standard*, 24 January. http://www.business-standard.com/article/current-affairs/supreme-court-agrees-to-hear-banks-in-aircel-maxis-case-117012400269_1.html (accessed 8 April 2019).

Radia Tapes. 2009. 'The Raja-Radia Tapes', *Outlook India*, 2009. http://www.outlookindia.com/website/story/the-raja-radia-tapes/268064/?next (accessed 8 April 2019).

Rajshekhar, M. 2016. 'How Do so Many Industrialists Get Into the Rajya Sabha?' *Scroll*, 21 March. https://scroll.in/article/805332/how-do-so-many-industrialists-get-into-the-rajya-sabha (accessed 8 April 2019).

Ramadurai, C. 2011. 'Madras Masala', *New York Times*, 18 October. https://india.blogs.nytimes.com/2011/10/18/madras-masala/ (accessed 8 April 2019).

Rathee, K. 2016. 'Trai Extends Date for Receiving Comments on Interconnect Charges', *Business Standard India*, 3 September. http://www.business-standard.com/article/economy-policy/trai-extends-date-for-receiving-comments-on-interconnect-charges-116090201192_1.html (accessed 8 April 2019).

Reuters. 2017. 'RCom to Sell Part of Business by September, Pay off Debts, Says Anil Ambani', *The Wire*, 2 June. https://thewire.in/143124/rcom-to-sell-part-of-business-by-september-pay-off-debts-says-anil-ambani/ (accessed 8 April 2019).

Sinha, N. 1996. 'The Political Economy of India's Telecommunication Reforms', *Telecommunications Policy* 20(1): 23–38. https://doi.org/10.1016/0308-5961(95)00045-3.

Souter, D., N. Scott, C. Garforth, R. Jain and O. Mascarenas. 2005. 'The Economic Impact of Telecommunications on Rural Livelihoods and Poverty Reduction: A Study of Rural Communities in India (Gujarat), Mozambique and Tanzania.' http://www.gamos.org.uk/images/documents/The%20Economic%20Impact%20of%20Telecommunications%20on%20Rural%20Livelihoods%20and%20Poverty%20Reduction%20-%20Summary.pdf (accessed 30 April 2019).

Sridhar, V. 2011. *The Telecom Revolution in India: Technology, Regulation, and Policy*. New Delhi: Oxford University Press India.

Thakurta, P.G. 2016. 'A Call for Review', *Economic and Political Weekly*, June. http://www.epw.in.ezproxy.soas.ac.uk/journal/2016/24/perspectives/call-review.html (accessed 8 April 2019).

Thakurta, P.G. and J. Chaudhuri. 2015. 'The Rs 19,000 Crore Mystery: How the CAG Figure for "Undue Benefit" to Mukesh Ambani's Reliance Jio Shrank', *The Caravan*, 31 May. http://www.caravanmagazine.in/vantage/4g-19000-crore-mystery-cag-figure-undue-benefit-mukesh-ambanis-reliance-jio-shrank (accessed 8 April 2019).

Thakurta, P.G. and A.R. Gatak. 2012. '2G Scam No One Talks about: Telcos Got Twice the Spectrum', *Firstpost*, 30 May. http://www.firstpost.com/business/the-2g-scam-no-one-talks-about-telcos-got-twice-the-spectrum-325596.html (accessed 8 April 2019).

Times of India. 2006. 'SC Notice to CBI over Mahajan "favouring" Reliance', *Times of India*, 3 January. https://timesofindia.indiatimes.com/india/SC-notice-to-CBI-over-Mahajan-favouring-Reliance/articleshow/1356146.cms (accessed 8 April 2019).

TRAI. 2017. 'Telecom Subscription Data (Press Release No. 34/2017)'. Press release. New Delhi: TRAI. http://www.trai.gov.in/sites/default/files/PR_No_43_Eng_13_06_2017.pdf (accessed 8 April 2019).

Vaishnav, M. 2017. *When Crime Pays: Money and Muscle in Indian Politics*. New Haven, CT and London: Yale University Press.

Virmani, A. 2000. 'A Communications Policy for the 21st Century', *Economic and Political Weekly*, May. http://www.epw.in/perspectives/communications-policy-21st-century.html (accessed 8 April 2019).

Appendix: Field methods

My research was conducted between October 2016 and December 2017 in Mumbai and Delhi. The main sources of data collection included in-depth semi-structured elite interviews with bureaucrats, politicians, industry leaders and regulators. I also attended telecommunications industry events, conducted a financial evaluation of telecommunications companies, drew on official and semi-official 'grey' literature on telecommunications policy as well as newspaper and magazine articles and books written by interviewees (or about the interviewees) on their experiences in the telecom industry. I consulted previous interviews given to the media by interviewees and any 'street' knowledge that I could get from journalists that would improve my understanding of the sector. I triangulated information through these various sources to verify information. The academic literature mentioned some of the main challenges with elite interviews which were applicable to my research: gaining trust and building a rapport with the interviewee, whether the researcher should record or not and ethical issues (Ostrander 1993; Gewirtz and Ozga 1994). I did not find any of these challenges to be difficult when conducting my research. For me trust was not an issue; I did not need my interviewees to trust me, I needed them to respect my research, which was a challenge which I discuss below. All the elite interviewees were very clear from the beginning as to whether I could record or take notes. This was not a problem; I simply had to follow the wishes of the interviewee. In terms of ethical issues, all my interviewees were adults and industry veterans and gave their informed consent to me interviewing them. In my case, none of my interviewees asked to remain anonymous.

For my elite interviews, I faced a different set of challenges from those emphasised in the literature. The first was to identify potential interviewees. In any industry, there are a number of key people that industry insiders implicitly know of and respect. It becomes critical to find out who these people are because in all my interviews I was asked, 'Who else are you going to speak to or have spoken to?' Answering this question set the tone for the interview and signalled my credibility as a researcher to the interviewee. At times I found some interviewees to be very similar, but I found that being known as a credible researcher often outweighed the costs of doing an extra interview. I also found newspaper reporters and journalists to be a very good source for identifying key people.

One of the most difficult aspects of elite interviews is the researcher's ability to tap into the existing networks of people in the area being researched. Most 'elites' in my study – bureaucrats, business leaders and policy makers – are very busy and seldom make time to speak to a student unless they get a reference or a recommendation from their friends, family or colleagues. The researcher's ability to leverage their personal and professional connections to tap into this network is critical. Once they get an opening into a network then it becomes a question of the researcher's persistence and skill to secure introductions to other people in the network. This problem is further complicated because there are several such networks of people: in my case, networks of bureaucrats, networks of telecom business managers and networks of policymakers. At times these networks overlapped, allowing the researcher access to other networks, while at times it worked as a disadvantage as some people would assume that the researcher had ulterior motives given their association with the other networks. In my case, navigating networks was one of the most challenging aspects of elite interviews.

Another challenge of conducting elite interviews is preparation. Mine included full background research: where the interviewee grew up, went to school, college; what positions they have held; their political party affiliations; whether there have been any scandals/court cases against them; their hobbies or social clubs, etc. Reading everything written by them and about them becomes important; often the first question I was asked was whether I had read their book and what I thought of it. Also, going through their previous interviews is important so as not to ask the same questions again. I was once caught off guard by an interviewee who answered a question by asking me whether I had seen the TV interview he had given a few weeks ago – he said he had answered this question there and that I should go home and listen to it. I couldn't ask a follow up question as I didn't know what his answer was. In addition, I found that many interviewees appreciated being asked about an answer that they had given in an older interview – the surprise that I had watched that interview flattered them and helped me build a rapport with them. In order to fully gain from an interview, days of preparations were needed.

After such intense preparations, it was very challenging to deal with cancellations and last-minute postponements. For example, I once spent over six weeks arranging and preparing for an appointment with a former attorney general of India and flew from Mumbai to Delhi specially for this appointment. When I arrived at the appointed time, I was made to wait outside for three hours in the summer heat of Delhi only to be told that 'Sir is busy so he can't see you'. In the moment, dealing with the frustration of wasted time, money and energy is very difficult. Another example was when I was told by an interviewee that 'perhaps we should continue this interview when you are more advanced in your research', which in other words meant that I was wasting his time. I found dealing with such criticism quite disheartening and bouncing back from an interview gone wrong was tough. Another major challenge concerns the kind of questions asked, which reflected credibility as a researcher. If my questions were too simple, the interviewee would lose interest quickly; if the question was too complicated then they wouldn't attempt to answer it. Finding the correct balance was critical. Background research and reading or listening to previous interviews was a good way to find that balance. Many guides to elite interviews suggested that to build a rapport with the interviewee the researcher should find a common connection such as shared interests, being a member of the same social clubs, or having attended the same universities, etc. In my experience, I found this advice to be quite unhelpful. Many of the policy makers I interviewed were educated at Oxford, which is where I also studied. It did not help me to have Oxford University as a common connection. Instead I found that if I asked the right questions, I gained their respect as a researcher, which allowed me to build a better rapport with them.

Finally, another important challenge that I faced was how to understand the points of view of the people who did not agree to be interviewed. In the academic literature and guides to elite interviews, I did not find any comprehensive advice on how to fill in the knowledge gaps, when persons critical to the sector refuse to be interviewed. In my case, the perspectives of Telecom Ministers were vital to building an accurate historical narrative of the telecoms sector in India. When I asked various Telecom Ministers for an interview, I received standard replies telling me that as there were court cases pending against them, the matters were *sub juris* and therefore they were not allowed to speak about them. However, one of the ministers' lawyers got in touch with me and said, 'Please watch his television interviews over the last year and you will have everything you need'. Although I was aware that this advice was given in self-interest, I found it to be quite useful for filling in gaps in my research. Not only did I listen to their interviews but I also got hold of the various supreme court judgments, which provided me with details of both sides of the argument and allowed me to build a more holistic historical picture.

6

The inter-state criminal life of sand and oil in North India

Lucia Michelutti

This chapter explores the inter-state criminal political economies of the sand and oil mafias in North India. It puts forward the concept of 'mafia assemblages' to nuance understanding of 'organised crime' and simultaneously provides insights into contemporary political formations. Mafia assemblages in the studied cases are not hyper-fluid, autonomous and amorphous illegal networks; nor are they discrete, structured, hierarchical and bounded 'mafia systems'. The criminal economies of sand and oil constantly mutate, transform and break up as they adapt to new business opportunities and political constraints. The chapter explores how the sand and oil mafia assemblages intertwine and how the very same local political bosses protect (and are part of) them. Contrary to economic analysis that emphasises different tax rates as the main engines of cross-border criminal economies, the working of sand and oil mafias suggests that it is instead the search for impunity by political bosses and the nature of caste territorial sovereignties that drive criminal economies in border areas.

This chapter investigates North Indian criminal political economies by looking at two locally intertwined il/legal commodity chains: sand (*baloo*) and oil (*tel*). It is based on fieldwork observations and on interviews with key informers – criminal bosses, syndicate members, police officers and criminal lawyers – as well as on long-term research on local cultures of caste sovereignty, kinship and territoriality.[1] The setting is a provincial town and a rural *tehsil* (sub-district) in Western Uttar Pradesh (UP) and its bordering areas in Rajasthan, Haryana, Madhya Pradesh and the National Capital Region (NCR). Sand is available and illegally mined from the Yamuna, Chambal and Banas rivers. Crude oil and fuel are pilfered from the Mathura-Jalandar pipeline. This 535 km-long pipeline, from Mathura Indian Oil Corporation via Delhi, Panipat and Ambala, transports petrol products to various consumption centres in Delhi, UP, Haryana, Uttarakhand and Punjab.

In many parts of the globe, criminal groups have emerged as prominent illegal suppliers of sand (Beiser 2015; Rege 2016; Rege and Lavorgna 2017, 160; Romig 2017). Equally, oil rackets are a source of illegal revenue for a variety of transnational mafia-like groups. In India, there is undeniably plenty of illegal money to be made from oil products and to be shared among refinery company personnel, engineers, the police, politicians and local communities and this is often reported by the press (see for example Anand 2016). It is also a well-known public secret that petrol pumps are an extremely lucrative business for which the licence is difficult to obtain and often granted to politicians or members of their families. Similarly, it is common knowledge that sand is managed by varying combinations of labourers, local contractors, mining companies, mobsters, the police, bureaucrats and politicians (Witsoe 2009). In this book we have already explored some of these dynamics in Tamil Nadu (see Chapter 3). Both the il/legal sectors under study here (the oil and sand 'businesses') are at the heart of what Michelutti et al. (2018) conceptualised as mafia raj (rule of mafia).[2] These business activities do not produce wealth but rather capture wealth through violent assertions of authority and/or through political encompassment.[3] Unfortunately, the exploitation of sand destroys riverbeds and natural resources, and the adulteration of fuels contributes to the high levels of air pollution present in Indian towns and cities today. These are the outcomes of serious environmental crimes, crimes that flout the laws protecting riverbeds and air quality. Ethnographically this chapter scrutinises the criminal markets and the regimes of mafia governance that sand and oil contribute to generating. Crucially, I will show how such arrangements criss-cross internal state boundaries and political constituencies.

There is an emerging anthropological literature that looks at transnational illegal economies (cf. Scheper-Hughes 2003; Vigh 2015), the globalisation of crime (Nordstrom 2007) and ultimately at border areas as places where the State fails to rule efficiently.[4] Yet, throughout this book we show that 'mafia raj' is not only a prerogative of marginal and unconquered 'border areas'. This chapter further confirms this point. In India, internal borders have been historically exploited in a variety of ways to gain profit and to secure impunity (Harriss 1977). Yet there is no study which looks at Indian inter-state border areas as profitable business hubs and prime centres of criminal capital accumulation, and, importantly, as safe havens of impunity by political violent entrepreneurs. By contrast the press, TV, social media and fiction and movies are full of stories about 'inter-state rackets'. In India, the term 'racket' is often used as a synonym for organised crime. Particularly in conversations, it is popularly employed to underline illegal activities that are perpetuated by gang-like groups and to contrast such 'serious (organised) crimes' with more socially embedded informal enterprises where it is not always possible to distinguish gang members from non-gang members and whose activities, despite being illegal, are often socially condoned as licit.[5] These distinctions are, however, in practice very blurred. In this chapter, I will show how exploring the nature of inter-state rackets may provide a means to map where 'organised crime', informal networks and a plethora of actors meet, co-function and produce threshold spaces in which 'order and disorder, lawful and unlawful, norm and exception, outside and inside conflate. It is in these spaces that arbitrary violence is practiced as legitimate and necessary, and where the reality of the inter-twinement [the mafia raj] takes shape' (Civico 2015, 22). In the cases of the sand and oil illegal business I conceptualise such continuums as the 'sand mafia assemblage' and the 'oil mafia assemblage'.

I find assemblage theory attractive because it provides a vocabulary to grasp both the fluidity of the studied criminal, political and economic configurations as well as their dense structuring and territorial materialisation at given times. More specifically I draw on the concept of assemblage proposed by Deleuze and Guattari (1987) to problematise the concept of 'organised crime' and simultaneously to provide insights into the nature of contemporary governance and issues of impunity in North India.[6] Mafia assemblages are not hyper-fluid, autonomous and amorphous illegal networks; nor are they discrete, structured, hierarchical and bounded 'mafia systems'. On the ground, the criminal economy constantly mutates, transforms and breaks up as it adapts to new business opportunities and political constraints (cf. Standing 2003). The 'Wild East' predatory ethos is in constant movement and there are no singular organising principles or logic behind its structuring; however, this does not mean that sand and oil 'mafias' are disorganised. On the contrary, mapping their tentative and unstable arrangements will help to single out what is fluid, what is fixed, when, where and for what reasons. Importantly, such an exercise will make tangible and visible the symbiotic assemblage of complicities and opportunistic partnerships that structure and provide contingent legitimacies to local mafia raj regimes. This chapter is divided into four parts. The first explores the economic and political backdrop against which the sand mafia and oil mafia assemblages operate. It outlines the predatory economies, the political polarisation and the uncertainty that characterises the local Wild East. The second and third parts document the itinerant economic opportunities that sand and oil offer to local violent entrepreneurs and populations. They describe the broader il/legal sand and oil commodity chains, and the strategies employed to exploit profit at different stages of the supply chain. I will illustrate the 'cultural, regulatory and policing factors' (Rege and Lavorgna 2017: 162) that support and enable the studied local mafia assemblages to operate (and govern) with relative impunity. In the process, I will also outline the various types of relationship that emerge around sand and oil and how they shape varieties of life strategies for the people and communities that exist in their midst. The concluding fourth part examines the implications of such chains of il/legality for capital accumulation and the role of 'border territories' in creating and maintaining the necessary impunity to allow such accumulations and 'mafia raj' regimes.

Western Uttar Pradesh – the 'Wild East'

Predatory economies

Western Uttar Pradesh has undergone tremendous economic and social transformations over the past two decades. Today, over 200 million people live in the state, a fifth of whom are Muslim. The rest are mostly Hindu, divided broadly between three mutually antagonistic caste groups: the upper-caste Brahmins and Thakurs (the local Rajput caste); the lower-caste Dalits; and the 'other backward classes' such as the Yadavs. This region of Uttar Pradesh has been increasingly thought of in the popular national perception as the Sicily of North India. Western Uttar Pradesh is widely known for its endemic violence, for being culturally shaped by the 'macho' ethos of its dominant castes like Jats, Yadavs, Gujars and Thakurs, and for being marred by communalism and caste-based conflicts. Available statistics and sociological studies have defined this area as the cradle of 'a subculture of violence' and the home of 'institutionalised riot systems'.[7] However, what is perhaps deeply misleading is the portrayal of this region uniquely as a poor provincial backwater. This is a land where over the past decade fortunes have been made in one generation and where upward mobility and entrepreneurship are fully entrenched in the imagination and fantasies of the younger generations. As outlined in the Introduction to this book, the economy of this region has also been changed by the commercialisation of agricultural land and changes in land use. We are witnessing skyrocketing real estate prices as a result of quicker access to Delhi, thanks to the construction of the Yamuna Expressway and its proximity to the industrial and residential hubs of Noida and Faridabad. These developments have given rise to an intense scramble for valuable economic assets and have opened up a space for violent entrepreneurs, whom I shall call *dabangs* (bosses), and for their flexible organised 'companies' to regulate and control illegal trade and production in legal commodities or services related to urban development and the expansion of infrastructure (Michelutti et al. 2018, Chapter 1). The power syndicates involved in the area are many – as the following pages will show, they are also flexible, volatile, fragmented and in constant flux. To complicate their mapping, the socio-cultural and economic area in which they operate overlaps with four states: Rajasthan, Haryana, Delhi and Madhya Pradesh. Hence, most local 'mafia' networks are inter-state criminal groups, which makes them difficult to police. Unfortunately, there is a complete lack of coordination between central and state police bodies. India does not have a national-level agency to coordinate the efforts of the state police forces; nor does it have central enforcement agencies to fight organised crime. There is no agency to collect, collate, analyse, document and act as a central exchange of information relating to national, inter-state gangs operating in the country and internationally (Sharma 1999: 112). It follows that by simply crossing the border with Rajasthan a person who commits a murder in UP can easily avoid being investigated, caught and prosecuted. So, this area enjoys an extra layer of impunity due to its inter-state geographical character. More specifically the *tehsil* under study, which I shall call Jaganpura, borders two states in the proximity of the NCR (National Capital Region). The *tehsil* has the highest rates of recorded murders and attempted murders in the district. High levels of crime exist in symbiosis with routinised forms of social and political violence and conflicts. Rajputs and Jats are the most numerous and powerful castes in the area, followed by Brahmins, Gujars, Chamars and the Muslim communities.

From competitive mafia raj to monopolistic mafia raj

Local criminal economies have been shaped not only by economic liberalisation but crucially by the opportunities created by lively multi-party competition, paired with a high level of communal and caste-based conflict in the areas where they govern.[8] It has been established that political parties select criminal candidates in those areas where social divisions are the most contested.[9] From the mid to late 1990s, Uttar Pradesh started to witness the political rise of iconic bosses.[10] The Samajwadi party governments of 2002–07 and 2012–17 have been labelled as 'Goonda Raj'/'mafia raj' due to the high proportions of elected MLAs with criminal histories; between 2012–17 in particular (when data for this chapter were collected), Western Uttar Pradesh presented what Martin and Michelutti (2017) defined as a 'competitive mafia raj'. These are highly violent forms of bossism that are triggered by the co-existence of multiple and competitive centres of power, which tend to clash. These are settings where criminal bosses can enter directly into politics. Mafia raj configurations are, however, always in flux. The victory of the BJP in the state elections in March 2017 may signal the end of a competitive cycle. In 2017, the SP was defeated by the BJP, which won in part on an 'anti-mafia raj' ticket. The newly appointed Chief Minister, Yogi Adityanath – a controversial figure himself, with a criminal record – had made his reputation by transforming his gangster-dominated constituency, Gorakhpur, into a 'safe' Hindu territory and, I would suggest, into a 'monopolistic mafia raj'.[11] Monopolistic mafia raj are regimes that present a centralised and authoritarian form of racketeering. In the case of Gorakhpur, majoritarianism has been combined with Adityanath's youth force organisation, the Hindu Yuva Vahini, its vigilante practices and 'encounter killings'.[12] While it is certainly too early to assess if and how the 'Gorakhpur model' will be replicated across UP,[13] there is certainly evidence from daily news that 'the mafia raj' is still alive and is now camouflaging itself under 'saffron scarfs' (Lal 2017, Chauhan 2017, Talukdar 2017).[14] This masquerade allows key players to keep breaking the law and maintain impunity – much in the same manner as the SP supporters did for the previous five years. In the locality under study, the key Thakur and Jat bosses have now conveniently joined the BJP (cf. Michelutti forthcoming). The result is that in Jaganpura the local criminal/political leadership has remained intact despite the change of power. If anything, under the new Thakur Chief Minister, Rajput bosses feel emboldened (Alam 2017; Sharma 2017). Since Adityanath's appointment, caste riots (and encounter killings) rather than communal riots have been rampant in Western Uttar Pradesh and reported by the press (see for example Kishore 2017). The Thakurs are out to get revenge against the Dalits and backward castes and their criminal Muslim 'companies'. It should also be noted that despite 15 years of government by lower castes, Thakurs still hold a disproportionate share of political representation across the state. Crucially, they also remain the second most affluent caste. I shall return to the nature of Western UP 'mafia raj' and the entwining between caste sovereignty, kinship and criminal political capital in the concluding section, after exploring the sand and oil mafia assemblages.

The sand (*baloo*) mafia assemblage

The main actors

The boom in the construction business in the NCR coupled with the lack of an alternative to river sand has made illegal mining a lucrative economic activity in Western Uttar Pradesh. Over the past two years, sociologists of crime have shown how India's sand mafias have developed into sophisticated organised crime groups (Rege 2016; Rege and Lavorgna 2017). In 2013, during my fieldwork, two cases brought to the limelight the spoils of mafia syndicates in the region under study. These events highlighted the brutality of this criminal sector as well as the ecological disasters that it is causing. The first case involved the famous don-turned-politician, Raghuraj Pratap Singh, alias Raja Bhaiya. In 2017, the 'Raja' was elected as an assembly representative for Kunda for the sixth consecutive time. The criminal career of this Thakur boss is mired in controversy. By 2002, he was reported to have 44 criminal cases registered against him, including serious charges such as attempt to murder, dacoity and abduction, and in March 2013 the don was accused of 'criminal conspiracy' in the killing of a police officer who was allegedly investigating the local sand mafia before he was murdered. The case was processed by the CBI. Raja Bhaiya was acquitted on the charges in August 2013.

This case brought to national and international attention the kind of violent capitalist accumulation that Uttar Pradesh riverbeds are currently generating. It also contributed to developing the spectral image of 'sand mafia' and more generally of the mafia in this region. When I started fieldwork, I was surprised by how frequently the theme of 'mafia' (and in particular 'land', 'sand', and 'oil' mafia) cropped up in the everyday conversations of my informants. Newspapers, TV and social media report on 'mafias' on an almost daily basis. These reports and their everyday discussions contribute to popularising the term along with 'mafia' power in the collective imagination. Popular fantasies about their brutality and tight organisations contributed to reify them as unitary arrangements. It follows that in the field, it was impossible to separate analytically the material fragmented reality of the sand and oil mafia assemblage from the unitary 'mafia-idea' that people often had. These are indeed two aspects of the same process and both equally important.[15]

After the Raj Bhaiya scandal, a few months later the suspension of Durga Shakti Nagpal, an IAS officer, hit the headlines and fuelled the daily conversations of my informants. Before she was dismissed, Ms

Nagpal was allegedly investigating illegal sand mining in the nearby district of Gautama Budda Nagar. Her suspension provoked a national outcry and much talk in and around Jaganpura. However, in the *tehsil* it was the killing of two young men caught transporting illegal sand on the Yamuna river that brought the materiality of sand mafia directly into my field notes. Coincidentally, at the time of these killings I was shadowing several local bosses, entrepreneurs and politicians who had become involved in the formal and informal 'regulation' of the incident. A number of these individuals are part of what locals refer to as the 'big' mafia, 'the Cartel' or 'the Lobby' or 'the Crime Mafia'.[16] To elaborate, it all started on a summer morning in 2013 when I went to observe the *darbar* of a prominent local political figure, popularly known as Thakur Dabang. When I arrived at his house I immediately realised that something was not right. TV and newspaper reporters were present in large numbers and Thakur Dabang was nowhere to be seen. His brother-in-law was doing his best to deal with the demands of journalists. I was soon told that early that morning two young men who belonged to Thakur Dabang's village in Jaganpura *tehsil* had allegedly been killed by the police for not paying 'the tax'. The two boys were transporting sand in their tractor. According to the brother-in-law, the police did not ask for the usual pre-agreed INR 200 'tax' toll to cross the bridge on the Yamuna river; instead, they asked for more money. The driver and his colleague refused, a fight broke out and the two men died. A few hours later, a mob of people from the area attacked the local police station in protest. Consequently, four more people were also injured. The police officers in charge of the local *thana* (police station) were immediately suspended on charges of administrative lapses (but not of extortion). The first two days after the murder were critical for understanding how apparently distant and unconnected individuals and groups formed an integral part of an inter-state 'sand mafia assemblage'. It should be noted that in this area sand-lords mainly engage in speculation rather than actual sand extraction. Money is made purely by moving sand around, marking up the price, and trying to eliminate competition and avoid a price increase. In the bordering districts of Rajasthan and Madhya Pradesh, these bosses and their companies, syndicates or groups are known as 'the UP mafia'. In these areas, villagers have been roped in as commission agents who collect sand, provide storage and sell it to the Jaganpura bosses. 'The UP mafia' then transports and sells the sand in Uttar Pradesh cities and in the National Capital Region.

***

A big *panchayat* meeting was called on the same day of the murder and a second one followed a few days later. This type of meeting is locally called *Bayalishi* (gathering of 42 villages) and is part of the informal structure governing the local Thakur caste. Thakurs are divided into two groups in this area: Gaurua Thakurs and Jadon Thakurs. The latter are considered higher in rank and related to the Raj of Alwar in Rajasthan while the former are often described as 'impure' Rajputs of Muslim descent and belong to different clans: Khacchwas, Jasawats and Sissodiya. The *panchayat* meeting brought together representatives of all the main clans and lineages. Such gatherings are usually used to settle disputes and arrange compensation outside the courts, but I would suggest that they are also contexts in which the social relations of 'mafia business' are cultivated and brotherhood solidarity is nurtured among potentially violent competitors.[17] 'Blood money' is often sanctioned by these caste/community *panchayats*. Local bosses often act as adjudicators. In the literature much emphasis has been placed on the role of informal adjudication processes in enforcing caste and gender-specific behaviour, such as honour killings, ordered by *khap panchayats* (extra-legal caste/community courts) in particular in cases involving the Jat community.[18] However, less attention has been devoted to investigating the adjudication of murders and violent crimes related to the local Wild East forms of capitalism. The settlement of the two boys' deaths by the Thakur *panchayat* provided a window to explore the complexity and interconnection between caste, kinship, territory and 'mafias'. Importantly, it revealed the role that Thakur and Jat caste sovereignties have in structuring and controlling local illegal economies and related inter-state rackets. Jaganpura – a backwater rural *tehsil* – has given birth to three powerful local bosses. Two belong to the Rajput community and one to the Jat community. The latter is popularly known as 'the don of dons'. The three bosses went to school together and are rivals but share common economic interests and businesses. What holds them and their businesses together is a willingness to seek control of and defend their territory and operational base for their illicit activities and, crucially, as immunity hubs. They share an interest in staying out of jail and acquiring and maintaining impunity.

Varieties of sands and sand 'businesses'

In Jaganpura, people are involved in multiple sand supply chains – each with different degrees of profitability and each requiring different levels of protection. The structure is, however, not simplistically vertical, as the concept of chains assumes; at each point of the chain there are also horizontal forms of competition. It is truly an 'assemblage' rather than a 'chain'. The inter-state sand racket that I will describe involves three types of sand and a myriad of actors and dispersed groups.

The most prestigious sand is called *banas* and is mined on the banks of the Banas river in Sawai Madhopur in Rajasthan, approximately six hours by car from Jaganpura. Sawai Madhopur is known for Ranthambore, a wildlife reserve. The southern part of the district, with its large stone quarries, is known for its nexus of crime and dacoit-contractor-politicians and bonded labour. In 2013, the market price for *banas* was INR 40 per cubic foot. The second most profitable sand was mined from the Chambal river in Morena district in Madhya Pradesh. This area lies about four hours by car from the core organisational centre of Jaganpura.[19] Morena is notorious for illegal sand and stone mining. In March 2012, the killing there of IPS officer Narendra Kumar made the national headlines. The officer was murdered while he was trying to stop the driver of a tractor carrying illegal sand (see for example Singh 2012). In 2016, another police constable was killed in a similar fashion when he tried to stop a vehicle carrying illegally mined stones. Finally, the local Yamuna river offers the cheapest sand (*baloo*). This was the type of sand being transported by the two young men murdered in Jaganpura.

In all three districts Thakurs play a pivotal role in the sand economy. Morena is well-known for the power of Thomar Rajput clans, which have historically produced famous Robin Hood-type dacoits and have for centuries been key protagonists of the 'bandit-economy' of the Chambal region. Sawai Madhopur is instead a well-known *Meena* tribal area but Thakurs, Gujars and Jats govern and dominate the local criminal political economies. It follows that a regional Thakur kinship network links Jaganpura to the neighbouring state's economies. This is not only a trans-border area ideally suited for the illegal sand market but also the territory where Thakur marriage exchanges and alliances usually take place. Thus, we have a situation in which business and profit-driven connections overlap with kinship and caste ties. The kinship structures of the Thakurs (and also Jats) have traditionally been connected with territoriality. These two castes both claim Kshatriya origins and have a lineage view of caste.[20] Paramount to this structure is a preferential hypergamous marriage system which operates at a regional level.[21] I suggest that their horizontal cluster-type organisation and marriage systems have an elective affinity with the inter-state/regional economies (legal and illegal ones) studied here. In particular the use of kinship, family and locality ties, more than caste per se, provides a fertile group for cooperation, trust, loyalty and the secrecy needed to protect and enforce illegal operations.[22]

The mining of *baloo, banas* and *chambal* sand occurs in environmentally protected areas where there is a blanket ban on sand mining. The sand 'mafia assemblage' presents both highly structured and well-established organised groups based on enduring membership together with more fluid and amorphous groups, with members joining and leaving according to their needs and opportunities.[23] At some levels, there is no controlling family, no boundaries separating members from non-members. At the time of this fieldwork, people who worked in the sand mafia sector usually singled out four sets of material arrangements that interrelate and at times overlap.

At the top, we find 'the *baraa* (big) mafia', 'the Cartel' or 'the Lobby'. This is a fluid core management group involved not only in sand mining but also in a variety of other illegal activities, for example oil pilferage and adulteration, as I will discuss in the following section of this chapter. It is run by local violent entrepreneurs, many with important political seats and mainly belonging to the Thakur and Jat communities, as explained earlier. This core group does not coordinate all the activities of the assemblage but rather it protects its most profitable and violent components. Their involvement in the sand business is motivated by the pursuit of profit and power.

The second level of the sand mafia assemblage was referred to using the term *baloo mafia* or the *baloo* 'syndicates' (see also Witsoe 2009). These are groups of 10 to 15 people (but some reach up to 45 members) that usually own their trucks and machines. The bosses of these syndicates are often in real estate and are sometimes related in kinship terms to members of 'the big mafia'. Locally, these syndicates are also mainly dominated by Thakurs and Jats.

The third level is populated by what locals call the *baloo tekhedar* (sand contractors). These are small-scale entrepreneurs. They are usually individuals who are keen to take risks and accumulate money quickly. They work independently and usually transport sand from the Chambal and Banas rivers and re-sell it in the NCR or nearby Uttar Pradesh towns. For example, Sunil (40 years old) belongs to this category. He has been doing this work for the past five years. He has three tractors and one truck. Usually, independent freelance contractors do not own their own vehicles. They often prefer to hire trucks and dumpers and sometimes also hire drivers on a daily/weekly basis. However, Sunil has his own truck. He usually employs two or three labourers – according to his needs. Sometimes he works for the *baloo mafia* but mostly he works solo. He does about three trips per month and sells his 'product' on the highway as all the other contractors do. At night, the highway transforms itself into a sand market. Alternatively, contractors can also use intermediaries. These brokers are usually the owners of *tal* (local shops that sell construction materials).

To recap, we have 'the big mafia', the syndicates and the independent contractors. The sand mafia assemblage also has a further layer composed of the villagers who traditionally engaged in sand mining. They usually employ camel trucks and extract *baloo* sand from the Yamuna and use it for personal/village consumption.

How profitable is the illegal sand business? Table 6.1 and Boxes 6.1–6.3 sum up the relative variable costs and profits to be made by extracting, transporting and selling different types of sand in winter 2014 in the cross-border *tehsil* and area under study. The range of returns (Table 6.1) was estimated by members of the syndicates and should be regarded as indicative. This is also the case for the data presented in Boxes 6.1–6.3. Thus, a dumper/truckload which can be filled with seven tonnes of *chambal* sand was selling at INR 25–30,000 in December 2014. The costs for the driver and labour amounted to INR 5,000, while the cost for 'protection' was about INR 4,000 (for the police and for RTO (Regional Transport Officers)). The total costs amounted to INR 17,500, which allowed for a net profit of INR 17,500 per truckload. It is estimated that around 300 dumpers were filled in the area daily.

The highest single cost component in this business consists of the 'protection' fees. It is this extorted money that goes to feed 'the big mafia' coffers and directly and indirectly sustains local political machines. Firstly, the police need to be paid. Every police station located on the sand commodity chain path, i.e. near a place of extraction and/or along the route of transportation from brokers to the final buyers, needs to be bribed. The syndicates usually pay the *thanas* on a monthly basis. They also need to pay 'the big mafia' to operate with impunity. This is also usually done on a monthly basis. By the same token, the police must pay 'the big mafia' in order to protect their extortive relations with the syndicates

Table 6.1 Indicative revenues from selling sand, 2014

Type of sand	Ranking (demand & profit to be made)	River	Place of mining	Profit (%)
Banas	I	Banas	Sawai Madhopur (Rajasthan)	100–50
Chambal	II	Chambal	Morena (Madhya Pradesh)	100–25
Baloo	III	Yamuna	Western UP	75–125

Box 6.1 Banas sand business (Rajasthan), 2014

BANAS

A truck of *banas* sand from Sawai Madhopur district (capacity 1,400 cubic feet).

Cost paid for mining *banas* sand (equipment, rent of equipment, maintenance): INR 6,000

Cost of fuel (from Sawai Madhopur to Jaganpura): INR 4,000

Average expenses paid for protection (RTO/police/checkpoints): INR 5,000

Labour (drivers and labour used for loading and unloading the sand): INR 5,000

Cost price (CP) = 6,000+4,000+5,000+5,000 = INR 20,000 (One trip with a capacity of 1,400 cubic feet of sand)

Selling price (SP) to the *tal* = INR 30 x 1,400 cubic feet = INR 42,000

Profit = SP−CP

Profit = 42,000-20,000 = 22,000

Profit% = Profit/CP x 100 = 22,000/20,000 x 100 = 110%

A syndicate with 4 trucks which makes 5 trips in a month can earn 22,000 x 5 x 4 = INR 440,000 per month

Earning per year = 440,000 x 12 months = INR 5,280,000 or US$88,000

Source: Fieldwork 2014/2015

and independent contractors. Unlike the syndicates, the independent contractors pay the police only when they are caught. Paying 'the tax' on a regular basis, however, is cheaper in the long run and hence more profitable. In addition, it also allows operations in broad daylight. Without regular payments, mining operations and transport need to be hidden and confined to the night. Out of all the groups and individuals involved in the sand sector, the local villagers who still mine with camel trucks are the biggest losers as they do not have protection. They must pay when they are caught by the police. Most of the time they end up in jail because they do not have the money for 'the tax'.

However, the highest protection fee cost is charged not by the police but by the Regional Transport Officers (RTO), who play a large role in the studied sand mafia assemblage as they rely mainly on cross-state

Box 6.2 Chambal sand business (Madhya Pradesh), 2014

CHAMBAL

A truck full of *chambal* sand from Morena district (capacity 1,400 cubic feet).

Cost paid for mining *chambal* sand (equipment, rent of equipment, maintenance): INR 6,000

Cost of fuel (from Morena to Jaganpura): INR 2,500

Average expenses paid for protection (RTO/police/checkpoints): INR 4,000

Labour (payments made to driver, helper and labour used for loading and unloading the sand): INR 5,000

CP = 6,000+2,500+4,000+5,000 = INR 17,500 (One trip of capacity 1400 cubic feet sand)

SP to the building material shop (*tal*) = INR 25x1,400 cubic feet = INR 35,000

Profit = SP–CP

Profit = 35,000–17,500 = INR 17,500

Profit% = Profit/ CP x 100 = 17,500/17,500 x 100 = 100%

A syndicate with 4 trucks which makes only 5 trips in a month can earn 17,500 x 5 x 4 = INR 350,000 per month

Earning per year: 350,000 x 12 months = INR 4,200,000 or US$70,000

Source: Fieldwork 2014/2015

transportation for their revenue. Like the police, RTOs are also paid by the syndicates on a monthly basis. How does it work? RTOs have developed partnerships with the owners of *dhabas* (roadside restaurants) and created a systematic way of collecting 'the tax'. Truck drivers transporting illegal sand need to purchase 'stickers' at selected *dhabas* and then place the stickers on the front of their windshields. The sticker signals that they have paid 'the toll' and that nobody should stop them while they pass through the district and various state borders. In this way, RTOs collect 'the tax' in a safe, systematic and organised fashion from the *dhabas* and manage to collect revenue across three states. The owners of the *dhabas* receive a cut.

In addition to the police and the RTOs, the musclemen (goons) who run the *chungis* (check points) also charge fees. Their fee is usually proportional to the capacity of the vehicle used to transport the sand. According to the size and load of the vehicle, it could be somewhere between INR 100–1,000. At times, local 'muscle' also needs to be paid by

Box 6.3 Yamuna river sand business (Uttar Pradesh), 2014

BALOO

Baloo sand is comparatively cheaper than *banas* and *chambal* sand.

Baloo is mined at the local level and is required for the construction of small buildings. It is mainly used for plastering house walls.

Baloo is mined using tractors, bullock carts or camel carts (not with lorries and drilling machines).

A tractor containing 120 cubic feet of *baloo* sand is sold for around INR 1,500.

Which means that the cost of 1 cubic foot of *baloo* is INR 12.50

Source: Fieldwork 2014/15

the contractors to operate on the river sand beds. Thus, there are at least four entities that need to be paid to extract criminal revenues from sand with relative impunity: the police, the RTO, the big mafia and the local musclemen at check points and in the areas where sand is extracted and loaded.

Besides protection, the other significant cost component is labour. Casual labourers are used to extract and load and/or store the sand. Workers are usually paid on a daily basis. They are at the bottom of the hierarchy of the sand mafia assemblage. The labour force is mostly composed of Dalits, often women, who are paid INR 300–500 per day. It is heavy work and in 2014 it paid relatively well compared to agricultural labour, which pays around INR 200 per day. Moving up the labour hierarchy we encounter the drivers. Drivers are usually young, otherwise unemployed men who come from middle or upper castes. They are paid about INR 10,000 per month or, if they do it on a casual basis, around INR 600 per day. The syndicates take good care of the drivers and protect them. Good and loyal drivers, and more importantly fearless drivers, are an essential part of the business. If they are caught the syndicates usually try to keep them out of jail. The same protection is not granted to the casual labour, however, who when caught are usually not helped.

A multiplicity of actors contribute to illegal sand extraction and commercialisation; however, how much they receive for their labour varies wildly. Such inequalities reflect enduring caste-hierarchical patterns. The core organisational structure of the syndicates is mainly Thakur/Jat while the casual labour is Dalit. The former are relatively well protected from law enforcement, possess authority and accumulate wealth and power. This core 'elite' group also governs other criminal economies in the area, such as the oil mafia.[24]

The oil (*tel*) mafia assemblage

The Mathura Refinery was built in 1982 to meet the demand for petroleum products in the North Western region of the country, which includes NCR. The refinery is strategically located along the Delhi–Agra National Highway about 154 km from Delhi (Indian Oil n.d.). In India, oil is heavily regulated and many petrol products are also state subsidised. Like other state-owned industries, the refinery has its township with its own colonies, schools, hospital and recreational activities on the outskirts of the city. In the available literature, refineries have often been the sites where the materiality of oil and pollution has been studied. These analyses have shown how hydrocarbon politics deeply affects local political economies.[25] Equally, metal structures such as pipelines have been used to reflect on the relations between materiality and politics (Barry 2013). Pipelines are said 'to form part of dynamic assemblages in which the expertise of engineers, metallurgists and other material scientists' come together critically (Barry 2013, 10). And it is precisely this mix of expertise that is also required for large-scale oil pilfering. As in the case of the criminal economy of sand, the oil mafia assemblage also has multiple components, each offering different degrees of profit and involving different types of crime, risks and protection. A multiplicity of actors, groups and networks populate the illegal oil market: some deal with pilfering, some with transport and smuggling, some with storage and others with adulteration and distribution via petrol-pumps. They are all connected directly or indirectly. At the top, the most profitable and risky oil business is direct pilferage from pipelines.[26] Siphoning crude oil and oil products from securely monitored pipelines requires a great deal of engineering skills. The groups with the capacity to drill and steal oil are called 'gangs'/'rackets' (English terms are used). These groups are usually composed of 5 to 10 individuals. To steal oil from pipelines, high-level technological expertise and skills are required. Gangs also need to possess a developed inter-state network to distribute and sell large quantities of oil products. They also need the cooperation of a variety of players: tankers, ration shop owners, Civil Supplies Department officials, the police, the villagers where the drilling is taking place and the protection of the 'big' mafia. As with the previously discussed case of the sand mafia, protection is one of the most important and expensive costs in the criminal oil economy. As a criminal lawyer explained:

> Without political protection the oil mafia does not exist. One can have all the skills in the world. It is mafia protection that is the integral ingredient of this criminal activity. Skills are necessary, but they are also relatively cheap to buy and even cheaper to extort. To ensure police protection is more difficult. One needs the protection of a politician. (R.K. Pandey, lawyer, 50 years old)

Brutal killings of Indian Oil corporation workers, government officers and crime reporters have made it clear to the local villagers and refinery employees alike that the oil gangs make 'offers which cannot be refused'. While documenting these dynamics locally, I bumped into the Jaganpura 'protectors' and 'the don of dons'. Many Jaganpura bosses own petrol pumps or their relatives do.

Pilferage

It is the Mathura–Jalandhar pipeline that is generally targetted by local syndicates. Indian Oil Corporation reported more than 50 instances of oil theft in 2015, 59 in 2014 and 42 in 2013 (see Kumar 2017). A criminal lawyer told me that the incidence of pilferage has increased significantly since 2005. The IOC lays its pipelines with security devices to avoid thefts. For example, it was explained that the Jamnagar–Mathura pipeline is coated with optical fibres that send out signals in case of theft or tampering with the pipelines. The oil mafia, however, have devised ways to defeat such anti-pilferage measures.

During my fieldwork, there were four major cases of pilferage in the area. These events allowed me to explore the complexity, heterogeneity and brutality of the illegal oil economy. Generally, informants did not talk so openly about the criminal life of oil as they did about sand. When comparing the two criminal activities, they all seemed to agree that the oil mafia was 'real', 'proper' and 'serious' organised crime. In popular lingo 'organised' also often means 'dangerous'. In November 2012, during my first month of fieldwork, hundreds of mini-oil refineries were discovered across the Uttar Pradesh and Rajasthan border, many of them in the Jaganpura *tehsil* itself. When I discussed the discovery with people from the area, my attention was invariably directed to a murder that had happened the previous year. A young man was killed for allegedly having informed the police about a number of 'oil safe houses' under the protection of 'the don of dons' who at the time was a state minister. The police lodged an FIR (First Information Report) against the local boss and his alleged associate Mr H.H. While collecting data on petrol adulteration H.H.'s and his protector's names came up again and again. H.H. was described as the main strategist and leader of the largest and most powerful oil syndicate in the region. H.H. openly ran his business from one of his seven petrol stations. Local criminal reporters seemed reluctant to report on his activities, as did the police. In short, H.H.'s petrol racket was a public secret. Everybody seemed to know about it. H.H. was eventually arrested in 2017 and accused of orchestrating one of the biggest oil thefts in Indian history, soon labelled as 'The great INR 100 *crore* Indian oil steal'. He is currently in jail. The racket involved petrol pump owners, political bosses and police officials from Uttar Pradesh, Rajasthan, Haryana and Delhi.

This interstate operation involved a meticulous plot, as a journalist explained in great detail:

> Investigation revealed that the gang members had started working on it about two years ago. First, they purchased a plot in the ATV Colony situated down the national highway that passes through Mathura city. The Mathura-Jalandhar pipeline from which oil was stolen passes through this colony. They constructed a room on the plot… The gang members started digging a tunnel from inside the room to connect with the pipeline which was running about 100 metres away from the room… Pipeline is running 15 feet deep under the surface and they constructed the tunnel at the same level so that it could connect to the pipeline. They had installed lights and fans to provide air and lighting inside the tunnel… About 100 tankers were pressed into service to transport the stolen oil from the pipeline to different petrol pumps… The tankers had fabricated bodies and forged chassis numbers. (Kumar 2017)

This operation had run undetected for the previous three years. But despite the spectacular and sensational titles in the press and on television, locally nobody seemed surprised. This is because, as I mentioned above, everybody seemed to know what was going on. The interesting question to ask then is: Why were the police asked to intervene only in February 2017? Why was H.H. arrested only in March 2017? The timing, I suggest, is certainly not random. He was accused during the 2017 Uttar

Pradesh state election campaign and arrested during the first month of rule by the newly appointed government. At the time newspaper headlines highlighted how the new Chief Minister Adityanath was out to punish the 'oil mafia'.

Election campaigns are unstable times for 'mafias'. It is worth being reminded that bosses' authority is always provisional (Michelutti et al. 2018). Their businesses' survival and prosperity always depend on a negotiated lack of law enforcement. Elections are arenas where impunity is often negotiated. State and national elections can trigger changes regarding who protects whom. Thus, at the time of elections, the main aim of criminal political formations is to do whatever is possible to maintain the integrity and continuity of their businesses. However, there are instances, like in the case of H.H.'s arrest, when such integrity is challenged. Informants speculate that H.H.'s protection was withdrawn. However, they also noted that by contrast his alleged business partner-cum-protector 'the don of dons' had smoothly changed party, saved his skin and gained political authority in a different party.

Smuggling and adulteration

Large-scale spectacular robberies are, however, not the only element of the local oil criminal economy. Oil is stolen not only through pilferage but also through everyday, routinised forms of smuggling by 'legal' and 'illegal' tankers: the so-called 'tanker mafia'. Drivers and owners of tanks populate this level of the oil racket and through my fieldwork I have come to know many of them. In the district, there are entire neighbourhoods that have been sustaining themselves since the early 1990s through the transport business and illegal smuggling and adulteration of refinery products. Such activities are said to have boomed over the past 15 years. In the *tehsil* under study the protagonists of this economy are the tanker drivers, the ration shop owners, the Civil Supplies Department officials and the police. The nexus that links them facilitates the adulteration of oil and the sale of subsidised kerosene and adulterated oil in the open market. The easiest way to adulterate petrol and diesel is to add kerosene. Other popular methods are the mixing of naphtha or a solvent. The factors that encourage adulteration are the following: 1) the existence of differential tax levels for the fuel and the adulterating substance; 2) differing prices of fuels and adulterants on the market; 3) lack of monitoring and consumer awareness; 4) lack of mechanisms and instruments to check fuel quality on the spot.

Adulteration is conducted in a variety of ways and places. It is done in 'safe houses' where stolen oil is stored. Usually such houses are located in rural and deserted areas and the operations are carried out at night. The *tehsil* under examination is often used. Adulteration is also conducted during transportation from IOC to the destination. This often takes place at selected *dhabas* along the highway. As with the sand mafia, *dhabas* play an important role in the oil mafia assemblage. Drivers stop to eat and while they consume their meal, oil is extracted from the tanks and adulterants added to compensate.

The tanker mafia needs kerosene and other adulterants and indirectly creates the 'kerosene mafia'. Ration shop and PDS outlet owners play a big role in hoarding state-subsidised kerosene rations. Kerosene is allotted to registered ration card holders. The ration shop owners usually fix the number of days when kerosene is distributed in the area. While people queue to get their quota, the shop owner often announces that the stock has run out. I witnessed this scene again and again. The kerosene is then sold to the 'oil mafia'. Ration shop owners usually give a cut to Civil Supplies Department officials who are supposed to check the card holders and keep a record of what they receive. Flying squads conduct regular mock raids and walk away after receiving their 'tax'. Similarly, Octroi (municipal entry tax) officers facilitate the transport of kerosene by not verifying the required documentation. They are usually paid monthly for not doing their duty.

Conclusion: inter-state rackets and the political economy of impunity

Describing cross-border illegal activities in Chad, Roitman (2006: 249) explained that 'Ultimately, while viewed by most as illegal, unregulated economic activities and violent methods of extraction are also described as legitimate; most often, these alleged exceptional practices are elaborated by local people as rational or reasonable behaviour'. Jangapura presents similar patterns and understandings. While pilfering from pipelines is considered by many 'a crime', the smuggling and adulteration by tankers is considered a normal practice and hence an illegal but licit 'way of getting by' while earning a massive profit. In the previous sections, I showed how the oil mafia assemblage is composed of the 'oil gangs', 'the tanker mafia', 'the kerosene mafia' and a variety of entrepreneurs, administrators, engineers, police officers and petrol pump owners (who are also often politicians). Similarly, the sand mafia assemblage is formed by a complex mix of syndicates, individual entrepreneurs, casual labourers and contractors.

I have illustrated how these two illegal sectors are populated by multiple actors, dispersed groups, networks and organisations that extract illegal revenues from sand and oil at different levels of the 'commodity chains'. I have attempted to untangle the relations between these different components and in the process identified the presence of what locals call 'the big mafia', 'the Cartel' or 'the Lobby', whose role is allegedly to control the supply of protection to a variety of illegal activities in the region. Looking at the intersection of the criminal life of sand and oil from a border district allowed me to observe the marked degree of flexibility and dispersion of mafia enterprises as well as the presence of a hierarchical component and a 'managing core' that accumulates capital at the top and in a particular place. Contrary to an economic (but also sociological) analysis that places emphasis on different tax rates as the main engines of cross-border criminal economies, my material suggests that it is instead the search for immunity that drives criminal economies in border areas. To elaborate, Desmond Arias (2016) recently argued that the extent to which illicit capital accrues in a place is critical to understanding micro-level muscular economic regimes of governance. Illicit entrepreneurs accumulate resources and can spend these funds on a host of activities. Some of this might involve further developing their business, but their activities are likely to cross over into legal activities as they seek to launder money and develop legitimate business interests. In the case of Jaganpura, a great deal of resources seem to be invested outside the actual *tehsil*. Bosses are known to own hotels, restaurants, transportation companies, petrol pumps and estate development agencies in nearby wealthier towns and cities in the NCR or in other parts of India and abroad. By contrast they invest locally in strengthening their political careers and/or the ones of emerging local leaders as strategies to cultivate immunity. The prerogative is to keep their residential 'territory' secure. As the sociologist of mafias Federico Varese argued: 'unlike many business executives, (mafiosi) do not migrate unless driven to do so by circumstance: police surveillance, pending prosecution, internal disputes and gang wars, or as the unintended consequence of state mandated relocation'. (Varese 2011, 190–1). As Machiavelli famously said, 'The Prince has to reside among his people'.

Remaining in place enables them to keep an eye on each other, apprehending and punishing misappropriations of capital, embezzlement, or rogue pursuits that attract police attention. They are also heavily dependent on local knowledge collecting reliable information, engaging in gossip and communication and on extensive networks of friends and accomplices, many in the political and criminal justice systems, who must be cultivated through memorable face-to face encounters. (Schneider and Schneider 2011, 13)

For the local Jaganpura bosses, it is of paramount importance to invest in an environment that they can trust and that protects them. This is explicitly executed by supporting and grooming young leaders in the local government authorities, primarily through the colonisation of the *Zila Parishad* (district council – ZP). This local layer of 'mafia raj' is extremely understudied. ZP are almost totally ignored by social scientists, which is quite remarkable since ZP office-bearers often wield more power than other elected representatives. Crucially they are more embedded in the region with other public organisations than MLAs or MPs. The importance of ZPs lies in the fact that they are a point of convergence for local politics, economic institutions and the bureaucracy or the main institution that links the state with local society.[27] It should be noted that the chair of the ZP is also the head of the district board, of which all the ZP members, MLAs, MPs, MLCs, Block Pramukhs and Gram Pradhans are members. Controlling the ZP means keeping a check on economic and political competitors on the rise. But impunity is not only achieved by putting into elected positions trusted key people who are able to transfer officers and cover investigations if in need. What these local 'mafia state' structures provide are also extra-legal forms of justice that avoid the police and the courts altogether, as the above description of the caste/community *panchayat* showed. Finally impunity is further maintained by grooming connections in the bordering states. It is achieved by securing hiding places – in case absconding becomes a necessity – in nearby Rajasthan, Haryana and Madhya Pradesh. These are worlds where in order to survive (and stay out of jail) people need to live in perfect 'symbiosis with a myriad of protectors, accomplices, debtors of all kinds, informers, and people from all strata of society, who have been paid, bribed, intimidated or blackmailed' (Falcone and Padovani 1993, 81). But it should also be emphasised that escaping police prosecution can also be an easy and simple affair. As stated in the introduction to this chapter, there is a complete lack of coordination between central and state police bodies. It follows that by simply crossing the border with Rajasthan or Madhya Pradesh or Haryana a person who commits a crime in Jaganpura can easily avoid being investigated, caught and prosecuted. Crossing the inter-state border means disappearing. Thus, for many Jaganpura residents immunity is a simple five-minute ride away. Inter-state border crossing is a well-tested and effective way of avoiding the law. The simplicity of this act is quite astonishing and, in many ways, reinstates how at the heart of the Wild East criminal economies have a state that both passively and actively allows 'mafia assemblages' to operate and thrive. In recognition of this weakness, over the past year attempts have been made to set up a new police body (the Inter-state Crime Coordination Committee) to ensure better coordination between state police forces in the National Capital Region and border areas. It remains to be seen whether the committee is ultimately implemented and how its work will shape the forms of impunity discussed by this chapter.

Notes

1. Research for this article was conducted between March 2012 and February 2017. The names of subjects whose security could be compromised by publishing their identities have been changed. All translations are mine.
2. For the purpose of this analysis I define a proto-typical 'mafia raj' as a system in which bosses/violent entrepreneurs (Blok 1974; Sidel 1999; Volkov 2002) and their entourages 'assume both the political leadership and the monopoly of the economic and financial resources of the State' (Armao 2015) (see the Introduction to this volume). These are systems of governance where '[even] the official is illegal' (Gayer 2014: 39) and where nested criminal 'official' actors replace the 'state' as the privileged partners of capitalism. For a more in-depth explanation of this conceptualisation and its variety of ethnographic manifestations see Michelutti et al. (2018).
3. See Li (2018) on 'mafia system' and oil plantation in Indonesia.
4. See for example Van Schendel and Abraham (2005); Gellner (2013).
5. On the usage of the concept of organised crime with regard to the exploitation of natural resources see Van Solinge (2014).
6. On assemblage see also Ong and Collier (2004).
7. See, for example, Dreze and Khera (2000); Oldenburg (1992); Marwar (2014); on riots and communalism see Brass (1997).
8. See Michelutti and Heath (2013; 2014) for a study of these dynamics in this area of Uttar Pradesh.
9. See for example Vaishnav (2011); Banerjee and Pande (2007).
10. For a recent documentary on the Dabang of Uttar Pradesh see https://www.youtube.com/watch?v=cr2VK8I5xOY.
11. For a detailed exploration of this process see Chaturvedi, Gellner and Pandey (2019).
12. 'Encounter killing' is a term used to describe killings by the police or the armed forces, allegedly in self-defence, when they encounter suspected gangsters or terrorists.
13. Vigilante groups like Hindu Yuva Vahini and Bajrang Dal are armed and dangerous, demonstrating ganglike and 'mafioso' behaviour, yet, as Sen has shown, their mobilisation strategies and violent actions are usually not treated as gang actions. Among these groups 'The boys use words such as "soldiers" *(sepahi)* instead of "gangs" and "war" *(ladai/yudh)* instead of "vigilantism", and they employ these categories to position themselves in (their impression of) an urban "warscape" – for them, the city is "war" *(yeh sheher ek jung hain)*' (Sen 2011). What distinguishes these squads from gangs is the ambiguity among local authorities in relation to these groups – which are not treated as delinquents but rather as 'social workers' or 'party workers'.
14. Saffron is the colour of the Hindu nationalist organisation – hence 'saffron scarfs'.
15. On the mythical and aesthetic power of mafia raj see Michelutti et al. (2018).
16. 'Crime mafia' is taken to mean syndicates/groups whose main activity is enforcement.
17. Schneider and Schneider (2011: 9) discuss the role of banquets and hunting parties for mafiosi in Sicily.
18. On *khap panchayats* in India see Kaur (2010).

19. Sand mining is banned in Morena district as it is part of the Chambal Ghariyal sanctuary. Despite the ban, mining has been rampant for the past five years. Legal mining started to be permitted from October 2016.
20. See Michelutti (2008: Chapter 4).
21. Castes related to a Rajput-like culture are said to 'share a centrality of territorially defined lineal kinship in their lives which leads them to experience caste in ways both similar and, at the same time, different from caste as we know it generally, i.e. as a set of agnatic and affinal groups dispersed over a wide territory' (Unnithan-Kumar 1997, 3). Similarly, the subdivisions of Rajput-like castes are of a different order than other caste communities. They generally have few 'endogamous' subdivisions and, on the contrary, are divided into numerous 'lines', 'branches' and 'clans', which have an exogamous character. In such a system, status is ascribed not only to endogamous groups but also to exogamous groups.
22. Similar to caste, 'ethnicity' has often been considered in the mafia literature to be an important element of organised crime: for example Nigerians rely on tribal networks, Albanians and Kurds on extended-clannish families; kinship is also a pillar of the Calabrian-based 'Ndrangheta.
23. See Rege (2016).
24. The criminalisation of politics is often explained as a by-product and an effect of the rise of the lower castes and Dalits in politics and rising political competition (Jaffrelot 2002). My findings suggest, however, that the criminal economy and with it wealth and criminal capital are still very much in the hands of the upper-castes despite 20 years of backward and Dalit rule in the state.
25. See, for example, Watts (2008); Auyero and Swistun (2009); Campbell (2005).
26. Examples of such pipelines include the Mathura–Delhi Pipeline (MDPL), a 147 km-long pipeline transporting petroleum products from the Mathura Refinery to Bijwasan in Delhi; the Mathura–Tundla Pipeline (MTPL), a 55 km-long separate pipeline which runs from Mathura to Tundla; the Bijwasan–Panipat Naphtha Pipeline, a 111 km-long pipeline from Bijwasan in Delhi to Panipat transporting naphtha from the Mathura Refinery to Jalandhar; and the Mathura–Bharatpur Spur Pipeline, an 8-inch diameter, 21 km-long product pipeline from the existing Mathura station of Mathura–Tundla Pipeline to the Indian Oil terminal at Bharatpur. There are also pipelines that carry crude, such as the Salaya–Mathura Pipeline (SMPL).
27. One of the few available studies on ZP is an unpublished Masters dissertation by Rajkamal Singh (2016).

References

Alam, M. 2017. 'Dalit vs Thakur: Who is Behind the Simmering Conflict?' *Al Jazeera*, 27 May. http://www.aljazeera.com/indepth/features/2017/05/dalit-thakur-simmering-conflict-170526124705563.html (accessed 15 July 2017).

Anand, U. 2016. 'Supreme Court Asks Government to Check Rampant Adulteration at Fuel Pumps', *The Indian Express*, 27 August. http://indianexpress.com/article/india/india-news-india/take-steps-to-check-rampant-adulteration-at-fuel-pumps-sc-to-govt-2998446/ (accessed 26 June 2017).

Arias, E.D. 2016. *Criminal Enterprises and Governance in Latin America and the Caribbean*. Cambridge: Cambridge University Press.

Armao, F. 2015. 'Mafia-owned-democracies. Italy and Mexico as Patterns of Criminal Neoliberalism', *Revista de Historia Actual* 1: 4–21.

Auyero, J. and D. Swistun. 2009. *Flammable: Environmental Suffering in an Argentine Shantytown*. New York: Oxford University Press.

Banerjee, A. and R. Pande. 2007. 'Parochial Politics: Ethnic Preferences and Politician Corruption', KSG Working Paper No. RWP07-031. http://ssrn.com/abstract=976548

Barry, A. 2013. *Material Politics: Disputes along the Pipeline*. Oxford: Wiley.

Blok, A. 1974. The Mafia of a Sicilian Village, 1860–1960: A Study of Violent Peasant Entrepreneurs. New York: Harper and Row.

Brass, P. 1997. *Theft of an Idol: Text and Context in the Representation of Collective Violence*. Princeton, NJ: Princeton University Press.

Beiser, V. 2015. 'The Deadly Global War for Sand', *Wired*, 26 March. http://www.wired.com/2015/03/illegal-sand-mining/ (accessed 4 August 2018).

Campbell, D. 2005. 'The Biopolitics of Security: Oil, Empire, and the Sports Utility Vehicle', *American Quarterly* 57(3): 943–72.

Chaturvedi, S., D. Gellner and S. Pandey. 2019. 'Politics in Gorakhpur since the 1920s: The Making of a Safe "Hindu" Constituency', *Contemporary South Asia*. https://w.tandfonline.com/doi/full/10.1080/09584935.2018.1521785?fbclid=IwAR2dr11Mp-ziBlXZSJnkXa95G39tNqvZH giqsm1OsAvrseYqc40Chq-EFg0& (accessed 11 January 2019).

Chauhan, A. 2017. 'Team Under SSP Mathura to Probe Assault on Cops in Agra', *Times of India*, 27 April. http://timesofindia.indiatimes.com/city/agra/team-under-ssp-mathura-to-probe-assault-on-cops-in-agra-by-right-wing-men-dig-agra-range/articleshow/58382278.cms (accessed 28 April 2017).

Civico, A. 2015. *The Para-State: An Ethnography of Colombia's Death Squads*. Oakland, CA: University of California Press.

Deleuze, G. and F. Guattari. 1987. *A Thousand Plateaus*. Minneapolis, MN: University of Minnesota Press.

Dreze, J. and R. Khera. 2000. 'Crime, Gender, and Society in India: Insights from Homicide', *Population and Development Review*, 26(2): 335–52.

Falcone, G. and M. Padovani. 1993. *Men of Honour: The Truth About the Mafia*. London: Warner Books.

Gayer, L. 2014. *Karachi. Ordered Disorder and the Struggle for the City*. London, Delhi, New York, Karachi: Hurst, HarperCollins, Oxford University Press.

Gellner, D. 2013. *Borderland Lives in Northern South Asia*. Durham, NC: Duke University Press.

Harriss, B. 1977. 'Besieging the Free Market: The Effects of the Paddy-Rice Levy', in *Green Revolution? Technology and Change in Rice Growing Areas of Tamil Nadu and Sri Lanka*, edited by B.H. Farmer, 268–73. Macmillan: London.

Indian Oil. n.d. 'Mathura Refinery'. https://www.iocl.com/AboutUs/MathuraRefinery.aspx (accessed 14 May 2019).

Jaffrelot, C. 2002. 'Indian Democracy: The Rule of Law on Trial', *India Review* 1(1): 77–121.

Kaur, R. 2010. 'Khap Panchayat, Sex Ratio and Female Agency', *Economic and Political Weekly*, 45(23): 14–16.

Kishore, R. 2017. 'UP Elections: Why the Rhetoric of Caste vs Development Rings Hollow', *Livemint*, 27 January. http://www.livemint.com/Home-Page/YfaZFWuenE9U4ScnusVAWK/Why-the-rhetoric-of-caste-vs-development-in-UP-polls-rings.html (accessed 15 June 2017).

Kumar, V. 2017. 'The Great Rs 100 Crore Indian Oil Steal', *Indian Express*, 26 February 2017. http://www.livemint.com/Industry/JTWXgKrigigK0AH7ORXgKK/Oil-firms-confront-theft-from-pipelines.html (accessed 6 May 2017).

Lal, R. M. 2017. 'Yadav Attacks Yogi Adityanath Govt on Law and Order: What Lies Beneath SP Leader's Sudden Anger?' *Firstpost*, 27 April. http://www.firstpost.com/politics/akhilesh-yadav-attacks-yogi-adityanath-govt-on-law-and-order-what-lies-beneath-sp-leaders-sudden-anger-3409700.html (accessed 28 April 2017).

Li, T. M. 2018. 'After the Land Grab: Infrastructural Violence and the Mafia System in Indonesia's Oil Palm Plantation Zone', *Geoforum 96* (November): 328–37.

Martin, N. and L. Michelutti. 2017. 'Protection rackets and party machines. Comparative Ethnographies of "Mafia Raj" in North India', *Asian Journal of Social Science*, 45: 6.

Marwar, S. 2014. 'Mapping Murder: Homicide Patterns and Trends in India, An Analysis from 2000–2010', *Journal of South Asian Studies*, 2(2): 145–63.

Michelutti, L. 2008. *The Vernacularisation of Democracy*. Delhi and London: Routledge.

Michelutti, L. forthcoming. 'Circuits of Protection and Extortion: Sovereignty in a Provincial North Indian Town', in *South Asian Sovereignty: The Conundrum of Worldly Power*, edited by D. Gilmartin, P. Price and A.E. Ruud. Delhi, London: Routledge.

Michelutti, L. and O. Heath. 2013. 'The Politics of Entitlement: Affirmative Action and Strategic Voting in Uttar Pradesh, India', *Focaal – Journal of Historical and Global Anthropology* 65: 56–67.

Michelutti, L. and O. Heath. 2014. 'Cooperation and Distrust: Identity Politics and Yadav-Muslim Relations in Uttar Pradesh, 1999–2009', in *Development Failure and Identity Politics in Uttar Pradesh*, edited by R. Jeffery, J. Lerche and C. Jeffrey, 128–164. New Delhi: Sage.

Michelutti, L., A. Hoque, N. Martin, D. Picherit, P. Rollier, A. Ruud and C. Still. 2018. *Mafia Raj: The Rule of Bosses in South Asia*. Stanford, CA: Stanford University Press.

Nordstrom, C. 2007. *Global Outlaws: Crime, Money, and Power in the Contemporary World*. Berkeley, CA: University of California Press.

Oldenburg, P. 1992. 'Sex Ratio, Son Preference and Violence in India: A Research Note', *Economic and Political Weekly* 27(49/50): 2657–62.

Ong, A. and S.J. Collier. 2004. *Global Assemblages: Technology, Politics, and Ethics as Anthropological Problems*. London: Blackwell.

Rege, A. 2016. 'Not Biting the Dust: Using a Tripartite Model of Organized Crime to Examine India's Sand Mafia', *International Journal of Comparative and Applied Criminal Justice* 40(2): 101–21.

Rege, A. and A. Lavorgna. 2017. 'Organization, Operations, and Success of Environmental Organized Crime in Italy and India: A Comparative Analysis', *European Journal of Criminology* 14(2): 160–82.

Roitman, J. 2006. 'The Ethics of Illegality in the Chad Basin', in *Law and Disorder*, edited by J. Comaroff and J.L. Comaroff, 247–72. Chicago IL: University of Chicago Press.

Romig, R. 2017. 'How to Steal a River', *New York Times Magazine*, 1 March. https://www.nytimes.com/2017/03/01/magazine/sand-mining-india-how-to-steal-a-river.html (accessed 21 June 2017).

Scheper-Hughes, N. 2003. 'Keeping an Eye on the Global Traffic in Human Organs', *The Lancet* 361: 1645–8.

Schneider, J. and P. Schneider. 2011. 'The Mafia and Capitalism. An Emerging Paradigm', *Sociologica* 2: 15–22.

Sen, A. 2011. 'Surviving Violence, Contesting Victimhood: Communal Politics and the Creation of Child-Men in an Urban Indian Slum', *South Asia: Journal of South Asian Studies* 34 (2): 276–97.

Sharma, L. 1999. 'The Organized Crime in India: Problems and Perspectives', *Resource Material Series* 54: 82–129. Tokyo: UNAFEI.

Sharma, S. 2017. 'No Matter Who Wins Uttar Pradesh, This Caste Group is Always Ahead', *Scroll*, 1 March. https://scroll.in/article/830346/why-the-thakurs-of-uttar-pradesh-stoop-to-conquer-at-the-time-of-elections (accessed 15 June 2017).

Sidel, J. 1999. *Capital, Coercion, and Crime: Bossism in the Philippines*. Stanford, CA: University of California Press.

Singh, M.P. 2012. 'Mining Mafia Mows Down Young IPS Officer in Morena', *The Hindu*, 8 March. http://www.thehindu.com/news/national/other-states/mining-mafia-mows-down-young-ips-officer-in-morena/article2974155.ece (accessed 15 June 2017).

Singh, R. 2016. *The Politics of Zilla Parishads: The Case Study of Saharanpur District*. MA diss., Ashoka University.

Standing, A. 2003. *The Social Contradictions of Organised Crime on the Cape Flats*. ISS Paper 74. Pretoria: Institute for Security Studies.

Talukdar, S. 2017. 'Hindutva Mixed with Lawlessness: Why Restoring Law and Order is UP CM Yogi Adityanath's Biggest Challenge', *Firstpost*, 24 April 2017. http://www.firstpost.com/politics/hindutva-mixed-with-lawlessness-why-restoring-law-and-order-is-up-cm-yogi-adityanaths-biggest-challenge-3401374.html (accessed 28 April 2017).

Unnithan-Kumar, M. 1997. *Identity, Gender and Poverty: New Perspectives on Caste and Tribe in Rajasthan*. Oxford: Berghahn Books.

Vaishnav, M. 2011. *The Market for Criminality: Money, Muscle and Elections in India*. Unpublished manuscript, Columbia University.

Van Schendel, W. and I. Abraham, eds. 2005. *Illicit Flows and Criminal Things. States, Borders, and the other Side of Criminal Things*. Bloomington: IN: Indiana University Press.

Van Solinge, T.B. 2014. 'The Illegal Exploitation of Natural Resources', in *The Oxford Handbook of Organized Crime*, edited by P. Paoli, 13–31. Oxford: Oxford University Press.

Varese, F. 2011. *Mafias on the Move. How Organized Crime Conquers New Territories*. Princeton, NJ: Princeton University Press.

Vigh, H. 2015. 'Mobile Misfortune', *Culture Unbound: Journal of Current Cultural Research* 7: 233–53.

Volkov, V. 2002. *Violent Entrepreneurs: The Use of Force in the Making of Russian Capitalism*. Ithaca, NY: Cornell University Press.

Watts, M.J. 2008. 'Blood Oil: The Anatomy of a Petro-insurgency in the Niger Delta', *Focaal* 52: 18–38.

Witsoe, J. 2009. 'Territorial Democracy: Caste, Dominance and Electoral Practice in Postcolonial India', *Political and Legal Anthropology Review* 32(1): 64–83.

7

'Red sanders mafia' in South India: violence, electoral democracy and labour

David Picherit

This chapter offers insights into the material assemblage of red sanders smuggling, extending to its recruitment and labour processes and the role of electoral democracy in determining hierarchies and structures of power. By following a number of smugglers/politicians' career trajectories, it explores how electoral politics and the red sanders mafia are entangled in relations of intreccio. It also reveals how the regulation of red sanders smuggling is deeply entrenched in the economic, cultural and political history of Rayala- seema. The latter is further illustrated by the ways the mythical figure of Veerappan is used to negotiate labour, violence and justice in the region.

Background

The 2014 parliamentary elections in the state of Andhra Pradesh (South India) were preceded and followed by a series of reported murders in the Seshachalam forest in the region of Rayalaseema. Six months before the election dates, nine woodcutters were found dead along with two forest officials, whose genitals had been cut off. Seshachalam forest is the only place in the world where a particular species of sandalwood, known as red sanders, grows. This wood was listed as endangered in 1995 and protected by international conventions in 1998.[1] From the early 2000s onward, local and small-scale red sanders smuggling has become glo- balised traffic. Importantly, it has become a major source of political fund- ing in the region. Highly valued on international markets, red sanders are cut, moved by sea, air and roads, and sold to global destinations, China in particular. A year after the 2014 parliamentary election, the Red Sanders Anti-Smuggling Task Force (RSASTF) – implemented by the new Chief Minister, Chandrababu Naidu (from the Telugu Desam Party) – killed 20 woodcutters. According to police sources, 'smugglers linked to Veerappan' – the iconic South Indian sandalwood and ivory smuggler killed by police 10 years ago – were killed in an 'encounter'.[2] A number of investigations led by a Special Investigation Team (SIT) from human rights organisations (such as the National Campaign for De-notified Tribes' Human Rights (NCDNTHR)), however, came up with a different account. Their report describes the labourers as 'poor' and 'passive victims' and shows that the task force killed '20 poor migrant tribal woodcutters brought by middlemen from the neighbouring state of Tamil Nadu'.[3] Other media suggest instances of torture (Janardhanan 2015). The killings were followed by a wave of arrests of the alleged smugglers between 2015 and 2016. More than 7,000 people were arrested but the conviction rate was only 1 per cent in 2017 (Umashanker 2017). Significantly, three days after the mass killing, the Chief Minister argued for lifting the ban on selling red sanders and removing it from the international list of endangered wood (Vadlapatla 2015). His plan was to allow the state to sell red sanders at global auctions in order to finance his populist promises to farmers, and to improve the finances of the new state of Andhra Pradesh after its bifurcation from Telangana.[4] These two subsequent events indicate how political control over state violence and market regulation are central to the structuring and making of the red sanders illegal international trade.

Changing laws and altering regulations, defining and re-defining what is legal and what is illegal in the sandalwood business, is a process dating back to the colonial times (Raj 2014). A major step in such reconfigurations was the 1998 decision to ban the red sanders trade. What was initially designed as a law to control deforestation contributed instead to creating a burgeoning illegal trade fostered by high international demand for red sanders. For Rayalaseema's politicians-cum-business executives this new source of profit quickly became the new El Dorado: a source of criminal capital to be used to finance electoral politics as well as to make personal fortunes. It follows that by the mid-2000s, the struggles to control (and run) the business politically started to become very heated and violent. By then all the logistic operations related to the traffic – from the cutting of the wood to its transportation to major ports in Chennai, Calcutta, Kochi and Mumbai and then shipment abroad – required the pro-active intervention of Rayalaseema politicians and state agents, and a level of impunity that could be achieved only by an electoral victory. The concept of 'mafia', defined as the product of the encounter between profitable violent criminal activities and politics (see the Introduction to this volume), captures the entanglement (*intreccio*) of electoral politics and the criminal economy that I will go on to describe in this chapter,[5] specifically the local red sanders mafia developed by building upon vernacular forms of democracy (Michelutti 2008) and the structure of the informal/illegal economies that are typical of the region. Far from being identical across the world, informal/illegal economies reflect assemblages of local cultural, political and social elements. More specifically the development of the red sanders mafia is the product of the transformation of deeply entrenched cultures of political factionalism and related ideas and practices of leadership, as I will explore below. In addition, the importance of the socio-cultural context in shaping the international traffic in local red sanders is further illustrated by the mobilisation of the Veerappan myth. Veerappan was a sandalwood smuggler who allegedly killed 120 police officers and kidnapped famous cinema megastars. He was murdered by a Special Task Force in 2004. For the police he was a criminal, while parts of the local tribal population viewed him as a 'social bandit'. Veerappan used to control entire forests on the Tamil Nadu and the Karnataka borders, thanks to police and political protection. While his fame flourishes across India and beyond, through cartoons, movies and even global commercial branding, he carries on shaping the representations (and workings) of regional criminal political economies. Throughout this chapter I will pay particular attention to the social and political mobilisation of this mythological figure and the ways it is currently deployed by the police to criminalise labourers and justify their killings. This, together with an exploration of the careers of key violent criminal figures currently involved in the red sanders mafia, will offer insights into the material organisation of the red sanders smuggling organisation, recruitment processes and the role of electoral democracy in determining internal hierarchies and structures of power. This paper relies on ethnographic fieldwork on criminal politics and businesses conducted in the district of Chittoor between 2012 and 2017. It combines methods like participant observation, informal and formal interviews and secondary sources like media and NGO reports.

The emergence of the red sanders mafia

The history of Rayalaseema, and its representations in the media, movies and music, is characterised by a focus on the violent struggles between faction leaders. From the *paregallu* ('the ones who rule') who emerged after the fall of the Vijayanagara Empire in the sixteenth century and maintained their dominance by keeping their own armies, to the con-temporary democratic faction politics, Rayalaseema has been mainly studied through a political lens (Subrahmanyam 1986). The recent polit-ical history of Andhra Pradesh is shaped by the opposition between two landowning castes: the Reddys, portrayed as a caste of politicians, and the Kammas, a caste of business people. Both castes benefitted from the agrarian reforms in the 1960s and used it to reinforce their political and economic dominance in Rayalaseema. They were also able to diversify their activities and branch out into the arms industry, the construction sector, the illegal alcohol trade and the management of petrol pumps, the latter being seen as a cash cow. While the Reddys could rely on their domination over the Congress party to control state resources, the Kam-mas contested their political power by joining the Communist party and then by launching their own caste-based political vehicle, the Telugu Desam party (TDP), in 1982. Success was immediate: they won the state elections in 1983. Since then, the two political parties (Congress and TDP) have alternated in government (Prasad 2015). The regional political landscape changed after the death in 2009 of the Congress Chief Minister, the charismatic leader Y.S. Rajasekhara Reddy (known as YSR). His son, Jagan Mohan Reddy, allegedly one of the most corrupt Indian politicians and a famous figure in the criminalisation of Indian politics (Still 2018; Vaishnav 2017),[6] then launched his own political party, the YSR Congress party. In the 1990s, this criminalisation was also made vis-ible by the emergence of violent politician-businessmen from the Kamma and Reddy communities who partially challenged political dynasties. Murders, kidnapping and rackets were tools used to climb the political ladder and make huge profits in sectors such as mines, quarries and for-ests. Elected as MLAs, they could exercise control over state resources, transfer bureaucrats, command local police forces and use licensed and unlicensed violence against opponents. Political violence was routinised. It is said to have led to 1,800 deaths over the past two decades. But Reddy and Kamma faction leaders are not only a provincial story. It should be noted that nine of the twelve Chief Ministers of the former (and united) state of Andhra Pradesh came from Rayalaseema (Picherit 2018).

Accounts of Rayalaseema political history have often neglected the economic aspects of faction politics. This illustration of the development of the red sanders mafia will highlight the role of the economy in shaping political violence and electoral politics in this part of the world. While small criminals – loosely related to political parties or the Maoist guer-rilla – entered into the red sanders business at the end of the 1990s, the real big business developed after the election of YSR as Chief Minister in

2004. Nevertheless, it is his son Jagan, known for the fortune he made during his father's term, who has often been credited for scaling up the red sanders traffic. After YSR's death, Jagan lost the parliamentary elections with his new political party; his political opponents, Kiran Kumar Reddy (Congress party) and his brother Kishore Reddy, became major actors in the red sanders traffic. Controlling the red sanders business guarantees funding not only for henchmen, party workers and for political campaigns but also for private accumulation. Indeed, as I will detail, many of the conflicts that from the outside may be seen to be moved by 'politics' were actually closely related to the red sanders economy. All the politicians I have mentioned so far have their constituencies in the vicinity of the Seshachalam forest.[7] The forest's spatial and political proximity to these figures could partly explain the silence and fear surrounding the red sanders business in the district of Chittoor, in stark contrast with the ways political violence is usually routinely and openly discussed. Most of my informants attempted to discourage any research: 'The brother of Kiran Kumar Reddy [ex-CM of Congress party] is involved. The brother of the CM! He lives 50 kilometres away. Nobody will dare doing something. This is too dangerous.' Another stated, 'Nobody will talk about red sanders. This is power, everybody fears them.' Another party worker mentioned, 'You should stop asking questions. The son and the brother of the two last Chief Ministers were involved. Now it is the turn of Chandrababu Naidu [leader of the TDP]', one warned me. 'No one can make a direct link between red sanders' criminals and politicians: they use their party workers, their henchmen but they never involve directly.'

Smugglers' careers

I will now start to unravel the linkages between politicians and the red sanders business by exploring a number of smugglers/politicians' career trajectories, beginning with Kollam Gangi Reddy.

Kollam Gangi Reddy, a.k.a the Junior Veerappan

The role of electoral politics in shaping the red sanders mafia became clear a few days after the 2014 election results, when Kollam Gangi Reddy (KGR), a major player in red sanders traffic, had to escape to Dubai, Singapore and then Mauritius. The 2014 elections sanctioned the victory of Chandrababu Naidu – one of KGR's public enemies. The criminal career of KGR dovetails with the history of red sanders smuggling and faction politics, and is similar to the biographical trajectories of many other political figures in the region. He was born in a village in the Kadapa district of Rayalaseema, a few kilometres away from YSR and Jagan Mohan Reddy. KGR began his career as a muscleman. His violent reputation was cemented in 1987 when he led a violent campaign in support of his brother's candidacy in the Mandal *panchayat* elections. Two years later, he attacked some of his rivals using homemade bombs. He allegedly murdered an industrialist in 1992. He escaped a life sentence in 1999 and thereafter dedicated himself to extortion and illegal alcohol production and trade.[8] At the same time he joined the Naxalite guerrilla and entered 'clandestine life' in the forest. According to various sources it was during this period that he became involved in smuggling. At that time he started a partnership with Sahul Hameed, who is allegedly one of the international bosses of the business today, as I will explore below. KGR became famous at the national level when he was accused of taking part in a bomb attack against the then Chief Minister Chandrababu Naidu in Tirupati on 1 October 2003.[9] This attack was allegedly funded by red sanders smugglers. Acquitted, KGR had gained a reputation for being a fearless 'specialist' in violence.

It was around 2004 that KGR moved his line of work from 'political violence' to 'economic crime' by becoming a major actor in the red sanders mafia. Various media reports portray KGR as the master of the transnational transportation of red sanders, crediting him for introducing innovative smuggling methods and opening up new sea and terrestrial routes (*Times of India* 2015a). The red sanders business made him a billionaire (Rangarajan and Venkat Sandeep 2015). He also became the owner of a barite mine in Mangampeta, a region of Kadapa where YSR, Chief Minister between 2004 and 2009, has illegally provided his supporters with mining authorisations. He also owns land and a variety of estates in the Rayalaseema region (Subramanyam 2015). It should be noted that politics has been central to KGR's rise. Close to the Congress party, he greatly benefitted from the protection of YSR and then of Jagan Mohan Reddy, who carried on protecting the business after the death of his father. K. Gangi Reddy managed to secure his position when a former follower of YSR, Kiran Kumar Reddy, became the new Chief Minister in 2012. Despite the competition between Jagan Mohan Reddy (YSR Congress party) and Kiran Kumar Reddy (Congress party), one could suggest that there was an agreement to maintain the red sanders business in the hands of the Reddys, as a caste.

The position of KGR became insecure during the 2014 electoral campaign, when he was nicknamed the 'Junior Veerappan' by the Kamma candidate, Chandradabu Naidu. The first serious threat materialised when police officers arrested him after the seizure of 2,000 red sanders logs (worth INR 5 *crore*) in Rayalaseema on 5 April 2014 – one month before the elections (Umashanker 2015). He was granted bail by the high court on 16 May 2014 and escaped to Mauritius with a fake passport. Just a few days after his election, Chandrababu Naidu wrote a letter to the governor to urge him to arrest KGR. This enmity was probably related to the 2003 bomb attack. On 24 February 2015, KGR was arrested in Mauritius and extradited to India. His arrest brought to light the entangled complicities of state officials and politicians in the red sanders business. According to the Andhra Pradesh police investigations, several Rayalaseema police inspectors and deputy superintendents had been bribed with money, gifts and villas in exchange for impunity. In short, the rise and fall of Kollam Gangi Reddy shows the trajectory of a criminal career that started by offering 'muscle' in the context of violent faction politics and then gradually shifted to the running of an illegal global trade. His biography illustrates how criminals do not necessarily enter directly into politics by contesting elections but rather often rely on the protection of politicians to carry on their illegal activities.

Peddireddy Ramachandra Reddy: from contractor to minister/ smuggler

KGR's career trajectory is not the only path to red sanders smuggling. Unlike KGR, Peddireddy Ramachandra Reddy (PRR) was a small contractor directly involved in politics. For a long time, getting access to public contracts has been a successful route to financial accumulation and entering politics in this part of the world. Many regional politicians started their careers as small contractors in the construction, mines and alcohol sectors. An exploration of PRR's 'contractor' career shows that it is very difficult to distinguish between business and politics – the two activities are fused together. After starting his career by contracting illegal alcohol, in the late 1970s he became a civil contractor for irrigation projects. In 1978, he contested the MLA state elections in Pileru constituency, located close to the Seshachalam forest. He lost the elections but by contesting them he consolidated his name and reputation on the local political/business map.[10] In 1989, he again contested and finally won the elections. His new political position allowed him to further expand his subcontracting activities to road construction, railways and then mining, mostly granite. Despite another defeat in 1994, his company, PLR Projects, continued to grow, and became a major asset for his subsequent electoral victories in 1999 and 2004 in the Pileru constituency. However, this source of funding was not enough to maintain his elected post in the long run. In 2009, following the merging of two constituencies, the ticket for Pileru was given to his local Congress party enemy, Kiran Kumar Reddy. Kiran Kumar Reddy's family is extremely influential locally. His father was a minister in P.V. Narasimha Rao's cabinet between 1971 and 1973. PRR had then to move to Punganur – 50 kilometres away – to be elected again as MLA in 2009. Eventually he managed to become Minister of Forests and Environment in 2010. It is common knowledge that this is the perfect political position to exploit forests resources and 'make money'. As the Minister of Forests and Environment he expanded his red sanders smuggling activities by offering protection. This phase of his career was brief, however. The then Chief Minister resigned, and his enemy Kiran Kumar Reddy was elected in 2012. As a consequence, Kiran Kumar Reddy's brother, N. Kishore Kumar Reddy, emerged as the new leader of the red sanders business. It is at this point that PRR left the Congress party to join Jagan Mohan Reddy and the YSR Congress party. The transition was not peaceful. The struggle between N. Kishore Kumar Reddy and PRR started in 2011 and spilled into a series of non-investigated murders in the Seshachalam forest. The murders were related to red sanders activities. Varaadi, a Tamil close to Kishore Kumar Reddy, was allegedly killed by forest officers who were allegedly controlled by PRR at the time. This murder was followed by the killings of two woodcutters (also Tamil) in December 2012. These murders were allegedly carried out to stop red sanders resources falling into the hands of PRR.[11] The use of legitimate state force to regulate faction politics and criminal economies is not new in Rayalaseema. The CM, Kiran Kumar Reddy, in June 2013 replied to the murders by implementing a task force, which killed another labourer in 29 January 2014.

Exploring the life of PRR unveils the importance of local politics in the organisation of the red sanders mafia. What we witness is the use of licensed and unlicensed violence and related political electoral manoeuvres between the Congress party (Kiran Kumar Reddy) and YSR Congress party (Jagan Mohan Reddy). The situation changed after the 2014 elections with the victory of Chandrababu Naidu and the TDP. PRR, whose assets rose from 4 to 63 *crore* between 2009 and 2014[12], won the YSR Congress party seat in his constituency. He also helped other local MLAs to be elected, like in Madanapalle where I met him, and aided his own son to become a member of parliament (YSR Congress party). However, PRR is now isolated. His second term in the opposition party reduces his influence, and various informants told me that many of his henchmen and followers involved in red sanders traffic have now joined the TDP. This shift is explained by the number of arrests of smugglers who are not affiliated to TDP. As Venkataïah, the henchman of a YSR Congress party leader, explained: 'P. Ramachandra Reddy is in the opposition and has no contracts anymore and no impunity. What to do? Going to jail or moving to TDP and continuing business?'

From small contractor to minister, PRR's career highlights the entanglement of business, politics and violence, as well as the importance of electoral democracy for controlling and governing the red sanders mafia. The two different careers I have so far presented highlight varieties of relations between politics and crime: Kollam Gangi Reddy is a criminal related to politics while Peddireddy Ramachandra Reddy is a criminal politician-businessman. Both depend, however, on electoral politics to survive in the business.

The red sanders mafia organisation

'Veerappan forest': labour force, migration, intermediaries and transport

How can tonnes of illegally cut red sanders be transported by road across India and then by air and/or by ship to China without being stopped? Answering this question will further shed light on the red sanders mafia organisation. So far, we have explored the linkages with politics and the red sanders business. In this section we move on to explore the deep continuities of the red sanders mafia with the Indian informal economy. Smuggling red sanders requires a sophisticated organisation. It involves traders and a variety of agents and labour contractors who are capable of monitoring the collection of wood. Once the wood is cut, it is hidden in safe places and then loaded into vans or trucks with fake registration. Police checkpoints need to be crossed during transportation to the ports, and port customs need also to be passed. Finally, for transportation via sea, ships need to be found and managed. Importantly all these operations require the *active* participation of police and custom officers. Smuggling red sanders requires political support and control, and bureaucrats committed to getting things done for the 'red sanders mafia' (Nemana 2015; NCDNTHR 2014).[13] It requires woodcutters. The business relies heavily on male migrant labour from tribal and Dalit castes originating mostly (but not exclusively) from the Jawadi hills of the neighbouring state of Tamil Nadu.[14] These labourers are widely known to have the special skills needed to work with timber and are experienced working in difficult forest conditions. However, there are also other factors that explain the use of labourers from Tamil Nadu rather than local ones.[15] Firstly local labourers tend not to get involved in the wood cutting business because they are aware of the dangers that working for the red sanders mafia involves. As a local NGO leader I met near the Seshachalam forest explained: 'Local labourers are aware of the consequences, the stakes and the tensions regarding red sanders smuggling. It has become a highly political issue and dangerous. Many local people refuse to work in the forest.' Secondly Dalit and tribal migrant labourers from Tamil Nadu are considered 'special'. They are viewed as fearless due to their alleged history of criminality and linkages with the famous Veerappan. It follows that labour contractors use the brand 'Veerappan forest' to promote the skills of their Tamil labourers and negotiate better wages for them. This branding, while being an advantage when negotiating labour wages, also facilitates criminalising migrants. The Veerappan myth has been used by the police to legitimise the killing of 'smugglers' who originate from 'areas previously controlled by the famous smuggler'. As of today, as I shall further explore in the next section, more than 2,000 Dalit and tribal labour migrant woodcutters from Tamil Nadu have been jailed (Janyala 2018).

Going back to the red sanders mafia organisation, labour contractors are in charge of organising shelter, food and water in the hamlets and villages in the Seshachalam forest, and manage the working schedules. The labourers cut the trees, then carry and hide the logs in the local ravines. Most labourers are paid by weight (between INR 20 to INR 40 per kg). They are paid when they return to Tamil Nadu. In the Seshachalam forest labourers are extremely isolated from the surrounding areas. In Chandragiri, a small town close to the forest, one activist mentioned: 'We never see them, we never meet them. They come at night and stay isolated in the forest.' The invisibility of migrant labourers is common in India; however, in the case of the red sanders mafia it is even more pronounced due to the illegal dimension of their activities.

The red sanders criminal economy is similar in many ways to how the Indian construction sector is organised (Picherit 2009). The isolation of labourers, the existence of multiple middlemen, the inter-state character of the labours, and the ways their payment is delayed until they are back in their villages of origin are not unique features of the red sanders sector. Similar to the case of the construction business, the recruitment of migrant labourers by labour intermediaries has a major advantage:

labourers know who their liaison is and respond only to his authority, but they often have no idea about who their real employer is. This structure is even more critical in the red sanders criminal economy, where there is an extra need to impede the circulation of information and prevent single individuals from having a clear view of the different layers of the mafia organisation. This model is very useful because it prevents anyone from giving information to the police. This is particularly important in the transportation phase of the business. Transportation requires major logistics and the organisation of drivers, 4x4s and lorries, impunity at forest check posts and police check posts. It requires good quality and updated intelligence. Members of the organisation need to be directly connected to the officers who are in charge of monitoring transport to major Indian ports, such as Chennai, Calcutta, Mumbai or Kochi. Sources from human rights organisations and/or the police have documented some of these organisational aspects. For example, once the wood is loaded a first pilot on a motorcycle drives ahead to check that there are no police and forest patrols along the way and keeps the truck driver informed by mobile phone. In case of problems, another car with an agent is always ready to intervene with money and bribe police or forest guards if necessary. 'One fellow spends INR 5 *lakh* to give it to the next fellow, who spends another INR 5 *lakh* until the next stage, and so on so a lot of money trickles down,' declared the Chief Forest Officer in the Seshachalam forest in the local media. 'They're so organised that the drivers don't know the identities of who they're working with. So even if we catch them we can't get to the other links in the chain.' (Nemana 2015).

Transnational smugglers

There is a lack of substantial information about the international dimension of the business and its linkages with local politics in Rayalaseema. Discussions with informants reveal more about the fabric of rumours, fantasy and fictions of power than factual knowledge of the transnational organisation. There is also a huge gap between the very detailed and pervasive analysis of how the red sanders business is embedded in Rayalaseema politics postulated by journalists who are not silenced by the landscape of violent and criminal political economies and the contradictory and spectacular news about the global dimension of the business.[16] It is known from police investigations that before reaching their final destination, red sanders logs are stored in *godowns* or in farmhouses near major ports (M.K. Kumar 2014). The entire operation relies on the complicity of police and customs agents who facilitate the smuggling by affixing government seals to containers, thereby making them 'legal'.[17] Smugglers are then said to register the containers – with fake information about the product to be exported – and have the final seal approved by the Customs and Central Excise Department. The containers are then taken to the *godowns*. In one case near Pune, on the road to Mumbai port, it was reported that once the containers were marked with customs seals, smugglers opened and loaded them with the red sanders. They then sent the wood back to Jawaharlal Nehru Port Trust in Mumbai and got clearance to export their produce on cargo ships as 'agricultural products' (or plywood, rubber mats or other material in other cases).[18] Even should the police manage to seize the smuggled wood, negotiation remains possible. Twenty tonnes of red sandalwood worth INR 3 *crore* were seized by the Local Crime Branch (LCB) Officer of the Pune rural police, but instead of arresting the smugglers, police officers allegedly demanded INR 1 *crore* from the smugglers (Kulkarni 2013).

According to environmental NGOs such as TRAFFIC, the smuggling of red sanders is part of a wider illegal trade in sandalwood within India and also in Africa and Australia (International Animal Rescue Foundation 2013). Those organisations tend to insist less on the everyday working of the trade than on the 'spectacular' elements and believe that red sanders smugglers use techniques deployed in the illegal drug trade, like painstakingly strapping a small container loaded with red sanders to the underside of a ship. These methods involve constant adjusting to ever-changing regulations, routes and new business opportunities, such as the recent implementation of Special Economic Zones (SEZ) in the area. The SEZ in Kochi exemplifies the possibilities offered by later forms of capitalism to the local criminal economy. As mentioned in the official website of the SEZ, 'The Cochin [Kochi] SEZ is a foreign territory in India. Legally, it stands outside the customs territory of India. This positioning permits both fast project approvals in the SEZ as well as a hassle-free environment for running units in the SEZ.'[19] Yet the directorate of revenue intelligence (DRI) complains that the work of the police in this SEZ is seriously hampered by this legislation. In these 'zones' smugglers can practise their illegal operations without being harassed. The rare seizures of containers illegally shipped from the port to various parts of China look like police operations mainly performed for the media. In addition, arrests seem to have a limited deterrent effect. There is no confiscation of the assets of smugglers and smuggling is not a non-bailable offence (see Kollam Gangi Reddy, mentioned previously) (Reddy 2014b).

Police investigations highlight some of the profiles of smugglers at international levels and the ways they play with borders and roads, drawing new maps across and within the interstices of official ones. Shahul Hameed is one of these big traffickers. He is said to have taken the lead in the business after A.T. Maideen, a gang leader who smuggled out red sanders to China and Hong Kong via Dubai, was arrested (Reddy 2014a). But not much is known about Shahul Hameed. A Singaporean citizen, he used to operate from Chennai, where he was arrested in 2004 by customs officials. However, when released on bail, he escaped and started to operate from Dubai. In 2011, the DRI seized his red sanders containers in Kochi port. Hameed is also believed to fund Kollam Gangi Reddy's career. Hameed's name featured in the press in May 2015 when 100 smugglers from Tamil Nadu and AP flew to the UAE to attend his daughter's wedding, even though the Chittoor and Tirupati police tried to stop them at the airport (Reddy 2015).

Despite the limited information, a number of crucial dimensions of the workings of red sanders international trafficking can be extrapolated. The first is the changing scale of the business in Rayalaseema and a shift from faction politics to regional criminal economies to transnational crime. The second point relates to the organisation of the business: the red sanders mafia necessarily builds on a strong state able to guarantee the circulation of trucks, the shipping of the wood logs and the control of the customs. State agents are omnipresent in the trade, implying the need to have politicians in key positions who are able to control and command bureaucrats and ensure the smooth collection and transportation of the red sanders.

The ghost of Veerappan and the criminalisation of labour

A striking point of the red sanders mafia is how a dead smuggler like Veerappan haunts and pervades the representations and practices of this criminal economy, from labour organisation and police investigation to public opinion. As Moffat argues (2018, 180), some dead 'appear as active interlocutors in ongoing political struggles' and have important potential in contemporary politics. Veerappan is a powerful element in the local cultural repertoire of models of authority. A Robin Hood figure (Seal 2009) and protector of forests for some, the figure of Veerappan in South India epitomises the dangerous criminal for the state and the police forces. In doing so it also contributes to legitimising the criminalisation of labourers and the use of state violence against labour in the context of the red sanders criminal economy. Therefore, Veerappan is mobilised by various actors involved in the business in a variety of ways – as an asset, as proof of guilt or innocence.

But the career of Veerappan also mirrors the changing alliance between politics, markets and violence in later forms of capitalism. These dynamics can be seen in two events in April 2015: the massacre of 20 labourers by the Red Sanders Anti-Smuggling Task Force, followed by the decision to remove red sanders from the endangered list to make the business easier (Vadlapatla 2015). As early as July 2014, the Andhra Pradesh government was ready to sell red sanders at auction through global tenders (*Economic Times* 2014). In October and November 2014, the government prepared the first phase of the e-auctions of 4,000 tonnes (seized by police) to be sold at an average of INR 25 *lakh* per tonne. The change of rules in the business cannot be dissociated from the massacre of woodcutters. It is the combination of the private use of state violence with the manipulation of market regulations that unravels how electoral democracy is crucial in determining who is ruling and controlling the business. What we are witnessing from 2014 elections is not the end of smuggling but rather the emergence of a new leadership: the TDP (and the Kammas) have now entered the market. By changing the law, Naidu has stopped a solid source of finance for his own political opponents from the Congress party.

Smugglers vs. labourers

The categorisation of woodcutters as 'smugglers' has serious implications and Veerappan is the point of reference through which a variety of actors (from police to NGOs) seem to interpret, compare and evaluate red sanders labourers. The 'fact-finding report' drafted and released in 2014 by the National Campaign for De-notified Tribes' Human Rights (NCDN-THR) highlights the conditions of workers, the roles of the Kammas and the Reddys in the organisation of the smuggling activities, and the ways labourers have been killed and jailed by the government.[20] The attention paid to labour derives from the fact that woodcutters are the only ones killed and/or jailed in the red sanders economy: 'About two thousand Tamilians are in Andhra jails because of the cases booked against them for red sanders smuggling', according to a lawyer from Kadapa.[21] He traces the history of the recruitment of the labour force and explains that the majority of the Tamilian coolies originate from areas surrounding the Jawadi hills, between Vellore and Tiruvannamalai districts (bordering

Chittoor district of Andhra Pradesh). He links their recruitment to the death of Veerappan: 'These villages were once under the influence of notorious red sanders smuggler Veerappan. After the death of Veerappan, the poor people who used to work for him were rendered jobless. This provided an opportunity for the Andhra smugglers to recruit them easily at cheap wages.'

The NCDNTHR's narrative stresses historical continuities with Veerappan – despite the fact that Veerappan was not active in this part of Tamil Nadu. If the report does not support Veerappan, in other articles, tribal and Dalit Tamil woodcutters are, condescendingly, portrayed as poor, passive and ignorant tribal victims of a traffic organised by upper-caste Andhra politicians (Narasimhan 2014). In this narrative they are exploited because of their tribal identity and they are killed and jailed because they are Tamil:

> Those killed are only coolies engaged by contractors to cut trees at night under the cover of darkness. They are not smugglers. Young tribal men from Jawadi hills in Tiruvannamalai district of Tamil Nadu are lured by brokers with offer of fancy wages and pressed into extracting red sanders from the forests. (Rajappa 2015)

As mentioned above, the mafia can rely on the participation of labourers who do not know who's who in the trade. Such lack of knowledge helps to protect the organisation. Human rights organisations contest the criminalisation and the mass killings of labourers by the state by emphasising this aspect. By contrast police forces argue that labourers are active 'mafia' workers coming from villages historically under the influence of Veerappan: 'Top police officials based in Rayalaseema said that labour gangs employed by Veerappan to chop down sandalwood trees in the Satyamangalam forests are taking part in the red sanders smuggling in Seshachalam forests,' states one source (*Deccan Herald* 2014). Police portray them as active smugglers and rational followers of Veerappan and insist on their deep, historical and undercover engagement with him. As a police officer said: 'These woodcutters are experts and after death of Veerappan in 2004 they were silent for few years. For the past five years they are coming to Andhra Pradesh and cutting the red sanders heavily.' This police perspective turns woodcutters into smugglers. Their geographical origin, their skills in woodcutting and their abilities to remain silent after Veerappan's death are elements 'top' police officials attempt to link to each other: labourers are smugglers and mafia members. This view is reinforced by the alleged structural similarities of the methods of red sanders smugglers to those employed by the late Veerappan. Another top police official said: 'The supply chains, the intermediaries and the other methods used are exactly the same as with Veerappan. Most of the gangs are from Tamil Nadu and are intruding into AP. The issue is of serious concern as the smugglers are turning violent' (Raghavan 2013). Whether as passive victims, followers or active smugglers, labourers are blamed for their alleged links with Veerappan, who continues to haunt red sanders smuggling over activities a decade after his death.

Mass killing of labourers

The Veerappan 'brand' came into force in public media when two forest officials were killed in the forest on 15 December 2013.[22] Local newspapers announced 'Veerappan-style smugglers attack Tirumala rangers, 2 officers stoned to death' (Raghavan 2013). Other newspapers reported that the officials were stoned and hanged to death; others asserted that their genitals were cut off. Ultimately, woodcutters were portrayed as savage and brutal. However, the association between smugglers and Veerappan was popularly viewed with suspicion. 'Will they go unarmed in the forest on their own, without any orders? They are not stupid,' stated an informant. Others declared the necessary involvement of politics: 'This is faction politics, elections are coming. Nothing to do with labour or forest officials.'

The representations of the state, democracy and politics among the local population often converge around a central position: it is impossible to imagine the state and the police forces acting without political intervention. Bosses do give orders and the killings of tree cutters are necessarily related to power relations. As one bureaucrat stressed: 'Forest officials do not go in the forest on their own; they knew electoral campaigning was coming.' These narratives highlight the interpretations of killings in terms of faction politics and echo official reports: 'We suspect these two officials were not killed by the tree cutters and this is a handy work of the corrupt forest and police officials, in connivance with key smugglers and political bosses'(Raghavan 2013).

The visible criminalisation and killings of woodcutters contrast with the limited and less publicised investigations on the relations between smugglers and politicians. As mentioned, most of the top smugglers who have been charged were able to secure bail and escape. Those who are in jail still benefit from political support and receive visits from YSR Congress leaders like Midhun Reddy, member of parliament and son of Peddireddy Ramachandra Reddy. The mass killing of labourers had a huge impact on the media (Nichenametla 2015). Police stated that the RSASTF had spotted a gang of 100 woodcutters from Tamil Nadu on the night of 6/7 April. When challenged, 20 of the woodcutters threw stones at them. The task force responded by shooting the 20 dead (Fact Finding Team 2015). Another report argues ironically about the unreality of the police version: 'Kantha Rao's men deserve President's police medal for the accuracy they have shown in identifying the 20 stone-throwing woodcutters out of 100 in the dead of night without any night vision equipment.' (Rajappa, 2015). RSASTF is also silent on what happened to the other 80 in the gang.

The use of licensed violence and state forces has long been a privilege of bosses and a major way of redefining the business map. What is striking is that this task force has worked as a private army for Naidu. Like paramilitary forces, they have full impunity and attacked only non-TDP smugglers. Whatever the involvement of the leader, this conveyed a strong warning to YSRCP and Congress bosses involved in smuggling activities. Men like Peddireddy Ramchandra Reddy have a reputation that reaches far into villages and towns. They inspire fear and respect. A henchman said: 'If you meet him, you should never turn your back and eat in his house. If something goes wrong, you will get poisoned. Everybody fears him.' With the rise to power of Chandrababu Naidu and his uses of the task force, the fear has changed direction: 'Even Peddireddy Ramchandra Reddy is scared now.' The denial of any rights, the disposal of the labour force and bodies and the complete lack of protection are the crude extension of informal economies (Shah et al. 2017).

Conclusion

This chapter illustrates how current criminal economies, based on alliances between markets, politics, state and violence, have led to a criminalisation of labour and a marked shift from political violence to economic violence in Andhra Pradesh, South India. The history of red sanders traffic highlights the transformation of the local sandalwood economy into a criminal, international mafia-like activity. I showed the crucial role of electoral democracy (and criminalisation of politics and politicisation of crime) in shaping the governance of the red sanders mafia and also stressed how its regulation is deeply entrenched in the economic, cultural and political history of Rayalaseema. The latter is further illustrated by the ways the mythical figure of Veerappan is used to negotiate labour, violence and justice in the region. Local criminal economies are further entrenched in the local socio-political contexts through the logics of intermediation typical of the local informal economy. Such dynamics help to maintain the silence and secrecy necessary to protect the workings of the red sanders mafia. Lastly, I showed how the red sanders business is unstable and always dependent on electoral politics and changes in the laws. However, these uncertainties are also the basis for the making (or losing) of personal fortunes and for making the red sanders business a 'gamble' worth hundreds of *crores*.

Notes

1. Red sanders is protected under the Convention on International Trade in Endangered Species (CITES) of Wild Fauna and Flora (1995) and has been listed as endangered by the International Union for Conservation of Nature (IUCN) since 1998.
2. 'Encounter' reflects the licence delivered to police and army forces to kill unarmed civilians with impunity, notably alleged 'Naxalites' in Andhra Pradesh.
3. For the report see NCDNTHR 2014.
4. The state of Andhra Pradesh separated from the Telangana region in 2014.
5. See also P.S. Jha, quoted in the Introduction.
6. During his father's term, his fortune rose from 10 *lakh* in 2004 to 72 *crore* in 2009, and to 400 *crore* in 2014 (Vaishnav 2017, 28).
7. The constituency of the ex-Chief Minister YSR and his son Jagan is located in Kadapa district, 100 kilometres from the Seshachalam forest; the constituency of the ex-Chief Minister, Kiran Kumar Reddy, and his brother Kishore is adjacent to the forest in Chittoor district. Chandrababu Naidu, the 2014 elected CM, is also based in Chittoor district.
8. To follow the details of the case, see *Indian Kanoon* (1999).
9. Chandrababu Naidu was Chief Minister between 1995 and 2004 and then from 2014 to the time of publication.
10. P. Ramachandra Reddy contested elections for the Janata party in 1978 and for the Congress party in 1985 and lost on both occasions.
11. For a detailed list of woodcutters killed see M.K. Kumar (2014) and NCDNTHR (2014).
12. For official details, see National Election Watch (n.d.).
13. See also Vadlapatla 2015.
14. A detailed report published in 2014 (M.K. Kumar 2014) states that 'woodcutters come from Thrivullaur, Vellore, Krishnagiri, Thiruvannamalai, Kancheepuram, and Villupuram of Tamil Nadu and are supposedly brought by middlemen from Thiruvannamalai and Salem districts'. A detailed news report published in *Frontline* mentions they are mostly 'Vannyars and Malayali Scheduled Tribe hailed from the border districts of Salem, Dharmapuri, Krishnagiri, Tiruvannamalai and Vellore in Tamil Nadu' (Rajasekaran 2015).
15. The characteristics of Indian informal labour markets are well known (Breman 1996; Harriss-White 2003; Basile and Harriss-White 2010), usually presenting strong segmentation by caste, class, gender and geographical origins. Often labour migration is used to reduce manpower costs and to avoid the application of labour laws. Generally economic sectors present multiple layers of intermediation and of subcontracting. Therefore, in this economy it is common to observe migrant labourers, often of a specific caste and/or region, brought by labour intermediaries to work sites.
16. The silence of the population about the red sanders mafia contrasts with the possibility for some journalists to cover and expose the red sanders mafia.
17. It remains unclear if they used duplicate seals or brought customs officials in to affix the seals.
18. According to media coverage, this information came to light during questioning of the customs clearance agent-turned-smuggler. The directorate of revenue intelligence (DRI) had earlier arrested him in 2010 for allegedly smuggling red sanders worth INR 5.03 *crore* to Dubai. He was released from jail in August last year.

19. See the official website at http://www.csez.com/softwares/cedis.htm (accessed 12 February 2018).
20. The committee was made up of advocates, tribal leaders and intellectuals from Andhra Pradesh and Tamil Nadu, convened to 'investigate the death and arrest of thousands of members of de-notified tribes from Tamil Nadu during the anti-smuggling operations by the police in Andhra Pradesh' (NCDNTHR 2014).
21. See also *Times of India* 2015b.
22. A few examples of press headlines: 'Veerappan Gone, But his Group Still Active in Seshachalam Forests' and 'It Bore Veerappan Mark'.

References

Basile, E. and B. Harriss-White. 2010. 'Introduction: India's Informal Capitalism and its Regulation', *International Review of Sociology: Revue Internationale de Sociologie*, 20(3): 457–71.

Breman, J. 1996. *Footloose Labour. Working in India's Informal Economy*. New Delhi: Oxford University Press.

Deccan Herald, 2014. 'Veerappan Gone, But His Group Still Active in Seshachalam Forests', 24 January. http://www.deccanherald.com/content/382539/veerappan-gone-his-group-still.html

Economic Times. 2014. 'AP Gets Centre's Nod to Sell Red Sanders via Global Tenders', 14 July, Hyderabad. https://economictimes.indiatimes.com/news/politics-and-nation/ap-gets-centres-nod-to-sell-red-sanders-via-global-tenders/articleshow/38369463.cms (accessed 18 January 2018).

Fact Finding Team. 2015. 'Fact Finding Report on the Seshachalam "Encounter" Killings of 20 Tamil wage labourers by Andhra Pradesh STF Police'. http://tnlabour.in/wp-content/uploads/2015/08/FFT-Report-Redwoord-Felling-Workers-Encounter.pdf (accessed 12 December 2017).

Harriss-White, B. 2003. *India Working: Essays on Society and Economy*. Cambridge: Cambridge University Press.

Indian Kanoon. 1999. 'Andhra High Court : Kollam Brahmananda Reddy vs State Of A.P on 11 February, 1999', https://indiankanoon.org/doc/1134957/ (accessed 29 April 2019).

International Animal Rescue Foundation. 2013. 'Sandalwood Smuggling. Environmentalism, Chapter 27'. https://speakupforthevoiceless.org/2013/03/04/environmentalism-chapter-27-sandalwood-smuggling/ (accessed 10 February 2018).

Janardhanan, A. 2015. 'Red Sanders Killings: Burn Scars, Bloodless Wounds and Many Question Marks', *Indian Express*, May 20. http://indianexpress.com/article/india/india-others/tirupati-red-sanders-killings-burn-scars-bloodless-wounds-and-many-question-marks (accessed 24 April 2018).

Janyala, S. 2018. 'Bodies of Five Suspected Red Sanders Workers Recovered from Lake in Kadapa', *Indian Express*, 18 February. https://indianexpress.com/article/india/seven-bodies-recovered-from-lake-in-kadapa-red-sanders-smuggling-5068793/ (accessed 24 April 2018).

Kulkarni, S. 2013. 'Red Sandalwood Smuggling: LCB Constables' Role Exposed', *Indian Express*, 23 July, Pune. http://indianexpress.com/article/cities/pune/red-sandalwood-smuggling-lcb-constables-role-exposed/ (accessed 12 February 2018).

Kumar, M.K. 2014. 'Red Sandal Labour Killings', *Kranthisena blog*, September. http://kranthisena.blogspot.fr/2014/09/red-sandal-labour-killings.html#more (accessed 30 March 2019).

Michelutti, L. 2008. *The Vernacularisation of Democracy: Politics, Caste, and Religion in India*. New Delhi: Routledge.

Moffat, C. 2018. 'Politics and the Work of the Dead in Modern India', *Comparative Studies in Society and History*, 60(1): 178–211.

Narasimhan, T.E. 2014. 'The Sad Business of Smuggling Red Sanders Wood', *Business Standard*, 16 August, Chennai. http://www.business-standard.com/article/beyond-business/the-sad-business-of-smuggling-red-sanders-wood-114081400763_1.html (accessed 18 January 2018).

National Election Watch. n.d. 'Asset and declared cases comparison: P. Ramachandra Reddy'. MyNeta. http://www.myneta.info/compare_profile.php?group_id=LTvRnw2ayhEV9via4bwa (accessed 28 April 2018).

NCDNTHR. 2014. 'Fact-Finding Report: Killing of 7 and Detention of 2000 By Branding as Red Sanders Smugglers', CounterCurrents.org. https://www.countercurrents.org/ncdnthr220714.pdf (accessed 18 January 2018).

Nemana, V. 2015. 'Who is Benefiting from South India's Lucrative Red Sandalwood Smuggling Trade?' *Scroll.in*. https://scroll.in/article/724060/who-is-benefiting-from-the-lucrative-south-india-red-sandalwood-smuggling-trade (accessed 14 May 2019).

Nichenametla, P. 2015. 'Red Sanders Smuggling: A Well-oiled Network Behind Andhra's Blood Wood', *Hindustan Times*, 1 June. http://www.hindustantimes.com/india/red-sanders-smuggling-a-well-oiled-network-behind-andhra-s-blood-wood/story-Yd0HN8oGMOxszqa4RB-DIdP.html (accessed 16 December 2018).

Picherit, D. 2009. '"Workers, Trust Us!": Labour Middlemen and the Rise of the Lower Castes in Andhra Pradesh', in *India's Unfree Workforce: Of Bondage Old and New*, edited by J. Breman, I. Guérin and A. Prakash, 259–83. Delhi: Oxford University Press.

Picherit, D. 2018. 'The Henchman', in *Mafia Raj: The Rule of Bosses in South Asia*, by L. Michelutti, A. Hoque, N. Martin, D. Picherit, P. Rollier, A. Ruud and C. Still, 97–127. Stanford, CA: Stanford University Press.

Prasad, P. 2015. 'Agrarian Class and Caste Relations in "United" Andhra Pradesh, 1956–2014', *Economic & Political Weekly* 50(16): 77–83.

Raghavan, S. 2013. 'Veerappan-style Smugglers Attack Tirumala Rangers, 2 Officers Stoned to Death', *Deccan Chronicle*, 16 December, Tirumala. https://www.deccanchronicle.com/131216/news-politics/article/veerappan-style-smugglers-attack-tirumala-rangers (accessed 2 January 2018).

Raj, V. M. 2014. 'Exploitation of Forest Economy under British Rule in Cuddapah District of Andhra', *EPRA International Journal of Economic and Business Review* 2(3): 33–9.

Rajappa, S. 2015. 'AP Encounter Cops Deserve President's Police Medal', *The Weekend Leader. com*, 13 April. http://www.theweekendleader.com/Opinion/4156/ap-encounter-cops-deserve-president-s-police-medal.html (accessed 18 January 2018).

Rajasekaran, I. 2015. 'Law of the Jungle'. *Frontline*, 15 May 2015. https://frontline.thehindu.com/the-nation/law-of-the-jungle/article7146790.ece (accessed 13 April 2019).

Rangarajan, A.D. and B. Venkat Sandeep, 2015. 'The Rise and Fall of Gangi Reddy', *The Hindu*, 7 March, Tirupathi http://www.thehindu.com/news/national/andhra-pradesh/the-rise-and-fall-of-gangi-reddy/article6967812.ece (accessed 28 January 2018).

Reddy, S.U. 2014a. 'Sanders Crooks are from Dubai', *Deccan Chronicle*, 6 January, Hyderabad. http://www.deccanchronicle.com/140106/news-current-affairs/article/sanders-crooks-are-dubai (accessed 12 November 2017).

Reddy, S.U. 2014b. 'Smugglers' Assets go Untouched', *Deccan Chronicle*, 12 January, Hyderabad. http://www.deccanchronicle.com/140112/news-crime/article/smugglers-assets-go-untouched (accessed 18 January 2018).

Reddy, S.U. 2015. 'Red Sanders Smugglers Attend Wedding in Dubai', *Deccan Chronicle*, 10 May, Hyderabad. http://www.deccanchronicle.com/150510/nation-current-affairs/article/red-sanders-smugglers-attend-wedding-dubai (accessed 25 December 2017).

Seal, G. 2009. 'The Robin Hood Principle: History, Myth and the Social Bandit', *Journal of Folklore Research* 46(1): 67–89.

Shah, A., J. Lerche, R. Axelby, D. Benbabaali, B. Donegan, J. Raj and V. Thakur. 2017. *Ground Down by Growth: Tribe, Caste, Class and Inequality in 21st Century India*. London: Pluto Press.

Still, C. 2018. 'The Legend', in *Mafia Raj: The Rule of Bosses in South Asia*, edited by L. Michelutti, A. Hoque, N. Martin, D. Picherit, P. Rollier, A. Ruud and C. Still, 203–28. Stanford, CA: Stanford University Press.

Subrahmanyam, S. 1986. 'Aspects of State Formation in South India and Southeast Asia, 1500-1650', *Indian Economic Social History Review* 23: 357–77.

Subramanyam, M.V., 2015. 'Naidu's Letter Tightened Noose on Gangi Reddy', *The Hindu*, 16 November, Kurnool. http://www.thehindu.com/news/national/andhra-pradesh/naidus-letter-tightened-noose-on-gangi-reddy/article7882002.ece (accessed 23 February 2018).

Times of India. 2015a. 'Gangi Reddy: The "Woodpecker" from Kadapa', Hyderabad, 16 November. https://timesofindia.indiatimes.com/city/hyderabad/Gangi-Reddy-The-Woodpecker-from-Kadapa/articleshow/49795989.cms (accessed 22 January 2018).

Times of India. 2015b. 'Influential Uppercaste Leaders Behind Red Sanders Smuggling', 8 April, Hyderabad. https://timesofindia.indiatimes.com/india/Influential-uppercaste-leaders-behind-red-sanders-smuggling/articleshow/46843212.cms (accessed 19 September 2018).

Umashanker, K. 2015. 'Most Wanted Red Sanders Smuggler Arrested in Mauritius', *The Hindu*, 24 February, Chittoor. https://www.thehindu.com/news/national/tamil-nadu/most-wanted-red-sanders-smuggler-arrested-in-mauritius/article6926968.ece#! (accessed 8 March 2019).

Umashanker, K. 2017. 'Amended Law no Deterrent to Red Sanders Smuggling', *The Hindu*, 22 August, Hyderabad. http://www.thehindu.com/news/national/andhra-pradesh/amended-law-no-deterrent-to-red-sanders-smuggling/article19536408.ece (accessed 23 December 2017).

Vadlapatla, S. 2015. 'Andhra's U-turn: Lift Ban on Red Sander Trees Felling', *Times of India*, 11 April, Chittoor. http://timesofindia.indiatimes.com/india/Andhras-U-turn-Lift-ban-on-red-sander-trees-felling/articleshow/46884097.cms (accessed 18 April 2019).

Vaishnav, M. 2017. *When Crime Pays: Money and Muscle in Indian Politics*. New Haven, CT and London: Yale University Press.

8

The 'land and real estate mafia', West Bengal, East India

Tone K. Sissener

In this chapter, forms of 'small-scale' land grabbing in urban West Bengal shed light on the workings and methods of local 'land mafias' and their entanglement with state officers, the police, judges and politicians. The chapter uses the concept of 'blurred boundaries' to explore local manifestations of intreccio, *particularly* mastan raj *(rule by thugs/enforcers). In the process, the field research reveals how the reach of the state as the provider of justice is limited by at least two factors: first, by an inefficient court system, and second, by corrupt state functionaries and politicians. Ultimately, the chapter shows that the justice system is deeply bound into a nexus of party politics, crime and business, a nexus that is essential to the working of the criminal economy.*[1]

Since the early 2000s India has experienced what has been termed 'a spectacular real estate boom' (Searle 2016: 5). Developers have built new shopping malls, five-star hotels, office and education complexes and high-rise apartment buildings in India's major cities and have bought hundreds of thousands of acres of farmland in order to build more (ibid.: 5). Because of the high demand for and limited supply of land, commonly due to geographic limitations and political restrictions, prices have 'sky-rocketed' (Weinstein 2008: 22) enabling developers to make fortunes, which in turn has encouraged land speculators and pushed land values even higher as they bid for parcels (Chakravorty 2013; Searle 2014; 2016).[2] Kolkata, capital of West Bengal and one of India's major cities, was witness to this building frenzy and to rising real estate prices, while the number of land speculators soared – although perhaps not as much as in cities such as Mumbai and Delhi (Weinstein 2008; Searle 2016).

From the early 1990s, and in the wake of economic liberalisation in India making private and foreign investments in real estate possible, all sorts of enterprising agents and agencies, both public and private, have taken an interest in the real estate market, hoping to make a quick profit.[3]

In this building frenzy and race for profits, land becomes a scarce commodity and researchers have pointed out the costs and consequences of displacing people in the name of development:

> In India, the government has been the primary coercive agent, assisting corporations in accessing cheap land, and so scholars have documented the experiences of people caught up in state projects, particularly those torn violently from their homes and pushed to the urban fringes through flawed slum demolition and resettlement projects, as well as farmers dispossessed of their land for SEZs[4] and other corporate projects. (Searle 2016, 8)[5]

While such large-scale government land acquisition, which in turn gives rise to resistance and political mobilisation, has been extensively researched (Shrivastava and Kothari 2012; Nielsen 2014; Das 2016), small-scale 'land grabbing'[6] in urban areas, which can shed light on the workings and methods of local 'land mafia' and the role of the state, remains to be explored. In Mumbai, Liza Weinstein has followed the rise and transformation of Mumbai's major organised crime groups (OCGs) since the 1950s,[7] arguing that their recent entrance into land and property development is 'a product of the liberalisation and globalisation of the Indian economy' (Weinstein 2008: 23). By following OCGs and seeing their entrance into real estate as a way of sustaining and financing themselves locally and globally, Weinstein finds that, although the majority of Mumbai's major property developers do not have connections to OCGs, their increased participation in and influence on the development industry has led to the criminalisation of land development. While my findings can be seen to support the view that land development is subject to criminalisation, the approach is different. Except for occasional references to state practices of corruption and neglect, Weinstein does not really localise 'the state' and electoral politics. In her discussion she seems to suggest the breaking down or shifting of boundaries between formal and informal governance, between state and mafia; however, she does not provide any illustrations of such shifts. Rather, what she does show is how these OCGs seem to operate in cooperation with, but still separate from, the state: enterprising slumlords taking advantage of the political dilemma of a central government pursuing a strategy of state-supported industrial development that causes migration but includes no accompanying strategy for housing a growing population. In this policy vacuum, OCGs were allowed to operate – undisturbed – 'by registering the new residents to vote for local politicians and paying bribes to police and officials in the Bombay Municipal Corporation' (Weinstein 2008: 26). It is hard not to see the relationship between the state and OCGs, as discussed by Weinstein, as one of binary opposition, with the state on the one side and OCGs on the other,[8] and not, as suggested towards the end, one of shifting or *blurred boundaries* (see Gupta 1995) or *intreccio* (see Introduction to this volume). To avoid presenting the state as a unitary, centralised entity that is separate from society, I find Veena Das and Deborah Poole's *Anthropology in the Margins of the State* (2004) useful. In the introduction to this rich collection of essays, Das and Poole propose that we explore the state *margins*, that is, 'the places where the state law and order continually have to be re-established', because state power is always unstable, 'something best seen when one moves away from the *center*' (Asad 2004: 279). They go on to identify three ways in which the state's margins may be imagined. I, however, am interested mainly in the second, described as 'spaces, forms, and practices through which the state is continually both experienced and undone through the illegibility of its own practices, documents, and words' (Das and Poole 2004: 9). This approach allows us to see what is included and what is excluded in state practices and, as I see it, enables us to understand both what it can and cannot or even will or will not achieve, which is to say its governing limitations as well as potentialities. In the cases discussed in this chapter, the reach of the state as provider of justice is limited by at least two things: first, by an inefficient court system, and second, by corrupt state functionaries, including the police, because the government 'allows' it, or does not control or constrict its functionaries, allowing us to talk about a mafia state – a *mastan* raj.

A short background

Kolkata is the oldest and the third largest metropolis in India, after Mumbai and Delhi. Located in the state of West Bengal, it now extends over 1,854 km^2 on both banks of the Hooghly river and has a population of over 15 million. The Kolkata Metropolitan Area (KMA) comprises three municipal corporations, several small- to medium-sized municipalities, many small and medium-sized cities, and numerous towns and villages. However, the core area of the city, on the eastern bank of the river, also known as the Kolkata Municipal Corporation area, covers about 184 km² and is home to 4.85 million people. The projected population for the KMA in 2025 is 21 million, with most of the increase taking place in the outer districts of the metropolitan area, as growth within the central neighbourhoods has been almost stagnant in the past decade (Chen, Wang and Kundu 2009).

The private real estate business in Kolkata is dominated by the Marwaris. The Marwaris are arguably the wealthiest and most successful business and industrialist community in India. For over three hundred years, migrant merchant traders have travelled from villages scattered over Eastern Rajasthan to towns and cities across Northern and Eastern India, Bangladesh and the wider South East Asian region, as well as to Russia and central Asia. Although these migrant traders belonged to a variety of trading lineages and identified themselves by various sub-castes as well as by religious labels such as Hindu and Jain, by the late nineteenth century these traders had also acquired the multivalent and largely unwanted ethnic tag of 'Marwari'. The Marwaris rose to prominence, mainly in Bengal where they quickly became a formidable economic ruling class under colonial rule; this was even more the case in independent India (Hardgrove 2004). Even today, the Marwaris are behind most large-scale and high-profile development projects in Kolkata, commonly organised as joint enterprises of the government of West Bengal with names such as the Shrachi, Emami, Sureka, MKJ, JB, Merlin and Nahata Groups. As mentioned on the website of one of their latest projects, Urbana, intended to construct Kolkata's tallest towers: 'Over the last couple of decades, these names have been associated with most of the city's landmark buildings and complexes' (including the South City Projects (Kolkata) Ltd.[9]). Besides the mostly Marwari-controlled, large-scale real estate development projects there can be found smaller-scale local developments taking place all over the city: the real estate 'on the margins' that will be the focus of this chapter. The material for this chapter was collected during one year of fieldwork in Kolkata from 2013 to 2014 and during short visits in November 2014 and April 2017. Field-based observations, informal discussions and interviews with key informers (people involved in forced takeovers, lawyers, journalists, industrialists, developers, brokers and promoters) are supplemented by secondary sources such as newspaper and magazine articles, police reports and legal documents.

In the following, I will first explore in some detail the process of buying and developing properties in Kolkata, facilitating an understanding of the present-day real estate market. Through illustrations I will go on to explore what it means in practice to take a property by force in a *mastan* raj, and the risks and multiple layers of violence and corruption involved in the business. Next, the legitimacy of the *mastan* raj will be discussed. At the end, I will discuss the impact of party politics and suggest *blurred boundaries* between the present-day government and its machinery on the one hand and the syndicate raj/land mafia on the other that make it difficult to know the one from the other, furthering acceptance and proliferation of the *mastan* raj.

Understanding the real estate market

A developer that I met through a friend explained (in English) the process of buying and developing properties in Kolkata. As he runs a reputable business, he said, many brokers and landowners approach him offering plots, but he mainly undertakes joint ventures – partnerships where a landowner supplies the land and the developer provides the capital to develop the property. The profit is shared between the landowner and developer, with each making money from the finished product:

> Suppose there are four floors and four car parking, then on a 50/50 sharing basis he gets two floors and two car parking, and we get the balance; two floors and two car parking. The sharing of properties, sharing with the vendor, is a very popular concept in Calcutta and in other parts of the country also. Ratio of the sharing depends on the location, the viability, the market rent, etc. We normally do joint ventures with good landlords. Otherwise, we don't do it. Sharing means, like getting married; potential problems, but when you share with good people things can be sorted out amicably. Otherwise, you may end up fighting.

The other way is to buy out properties, but either way the process is simple, he said. After identifying a plot among the many being offered by both brokers and landowners, a commercial evaluation of that particular plot is made:

> Suppose we are buying this place and the landlord is asking this much of money. So, we buy out this property, at this price, if you buy out at this price, then how much will be the construction, entitlement of that, how much will be the construction cost, what category of building we need to construct, and then, ultimately, what

will be the selling price. So, after doing a proper research on the entire cycle, if it is found positive, we buy out the property. Now, for buying out the properties, first step is locating the property, as per our liking, second is finding out the commercial evaluation, and third is after finding both location and evaluation positive, we say yes to the landlord and then the legal process start.

All the papers are sent to their solicitor, who will discuss the legal matters with the landlord's solicitor. When all papers are found in order, they buy the property and do the registration. When I asked about disputed properties, he laughed and said, 'No, dispute, you know Ma'am, this is a very interesting subject'. In cases of disputed properties, they would first consider the 'depth of the dispute':

> A dispute, which is not solvable by the landlord or the person who is selling, can sometimes be solved by myself. We make a point of good bargain. Suppose he is having a tenant who is going for a legal case with the landlord, maybe a good friend of mine. He is willing to sell the property as it is (with the problem with the tenant). I say that x is your price and if I buy the property, x is the market price and I will pay you x minus y (for the tenant). So, we bargain with the tenant and then we settle with the property and later on I also jungle up with[10] the same guy, the same tenant. The person who sold the property probably sold at a lesser price, but he laughs at his end because he gained some interest part.

The landlord is rid of the problem and has made money on the sale instead of spending his resources on a court case. The developer said that he would consider very carefully before deciding on a property that had potential problems with tenants, but that he sometimes gets it wrong. Here follows an extract from a conversation between me and the developer:

> Developer: So, travelling through this system, the process of evicting a tenant might take as much as 8 to 10 years, or more. As a developer, as a businessman, we always prefer settling across the table by a mutual consent or resolution. But sometimes, just to put the mental pressure on them, we have to file a case. We normally avoid that, but we also have to do that sometimes.
>
> Anthropologist: OK. So, you will tell them that you are taking legal steps?

Developer: I will send them a notice, a legal notice, then I will file a case and they will be served the notice, so they have to run to the court. At times this makes them feel to come to a settlement, but if they are difficult people, then again, they can fight the case. They can also empower a lawyer to do it.

Anthropologist: OK. That means that if you have to wait for the legal system to work, then your investment will be blocked for years. That could be the case.

Developer: That *is* the case. That is the case and at times it happens.

Anthropologist: It happens and that's the part of your business I would think then, that you have to (interrupted by developer).

Developer: You see, we take a view and we buy a property. We consider an adjustment period, but at times it crosses that. Market is regulated by a particular scenario. There is a price and there might be a 10 to 15 per cent escalation in the price or there can be a recession also, but you know that when we do business or when we invest: from that particular day we start calculating the interest factor. Even if it is our own money, not borrowed money, we, as a businessman, should calculate the interest. So now with the passage of time, the investment and the interest is piling up and it is coming close to the profit margin. Cost of construction is also increasing. So if a project after procurement is delayed, then in that case it might so happen that we'll end up entering a loss. It's a risky business and it's a business with a lot of headache. The developers are normally thought of like they're goons, they're anti-socials, not much respect by the government.

Anthropologist: How did this reputation come up, as goons and (interrupted).

Developer: The case is, suppose there are say ten thousand developers in India, so there are also bad people among them. So, these bad people have made this business, a tag, and not a very good thing. But now there are also some very good developers in this city. Like where your kids study, South City, it's a big group and like ourselves we are reputed. So there stands the goodwill of the builder, which ultimately makes them earn more than the other. Suppose I have a buyer and because of my goodwill they come, and blindfolded they buy the property from me. So, they know that I might charge a hundred rupees more, but it is acceptable to them because they want peace of mind. But even after buying the property and starting construction, some person might come up, claiming a right in my property, out of the blue. So, he can file a case. This mainly happens in the suburb properties, which is not in the proper city but in the fringes of the city. So, we have to fight it out.

Anthropologist: And again you have to put the project on hold?

Developer: That depends. If the court finds the filing of a case strong enough, then it might go to the extent of stopping the project. Otherwise, it is called *lis pendens*;[11] one is litigation, the other is *lis pendens*. For example, we are making a ten-storied building somewhere in Gariahat [a retail market and main road in the Ballygunge area in South Kolkata]. We bought a property, our lawyers and our solicitors gave us the go-ahead, and we started the construction for a ten-storied building. After the construction of six stories, we got a notice. We opened the notice and we gave it to our lawyer for inspection. It turned out that there was a tenant 20 years back. All of a sudden, or after seeing the developments there, he filed a suit in the court, probably with the intention in his mind to get money.

Anthropologist: But he moved out 20 years ago?

Developer: 20 years ago, and he doesn't have any case, but he has framed a case against us that has been accepted by the court and we have to fight it. He is not in a position to do anything to our project, our project is moving, but we have to monitor the case. Senior advocates are engaged to deal with it, but we have to go for consultation. What is that tenant's intention? To get money from us. That is one sort of litigation.

Talking about tenants claiming rights to properties and getting cases accepted in the court, he said 'only in West Bengal', due to the former communist regime's policy of offering security to tenants (and thus of securing the vote bank). 'Now there are amendments, there are betterments', he said, 'but the situation is still such that tenants, especially old tenants, follow the property and have to be included in any development plans'.

Now it is controlled by the rental control act and in the rent act there is a limitation. If you are paying less than, let's say, seven or eight thousand rupees, then you are guided by the West Bengal Premises Tenancy Act, which has been amended now so that you can be evicted by proper cause of law, but who wants, Ma'am?

As explained, pending lawsuits and litigations take time and resources, obstruct the completion of a project and put the investment at risk. If, as in some cases, the project is put on hold for too long, the investor loses out on their return. In other words, the stakes are high, margins less and there is no time to waste on disputes. Another approach is to grab and sell or build and keep the case pending indefinitely. In the case presented below, there were several deeds to the same property, some of which had to be false. According to a high court lawyer, the property was registered in Mumbai for a price you would not get for the same plot of land anywhere, 'not even in the Sundarbans':[12]

> Whoever registered that property in Bombay should at least set the price that is available over here. You can't buy a property of 17 *katha*[13] for 10 *lakh* rupees in Calcutta, not now and not then. There would be a queue from here and right up to high court of people waiting to, at that price, to take part in the "lottery" to be allotted that land! (Personal communication in the high court lawyer's Kolkata chambers, April 2017)

His point was that people trying to grab properties do it openly and do not even try to conceal their actions by making it look real. According to him, in the property case to be discussed, which started as a dispute over ownership, there was no sale in the first place. Someone claimed power of attorney, but it was never registered, and the property was 'bought' for a 'throwaway price' that was not even paid to the owner. He said it was a false claim but to establish that in court would take years, even as many as 25 or 30. Rather than trying to take over the property through false court cases, which anyway would take years to prove, it was grabbed by force. It was known that the property was disputed and presided over by a woman and her old and sick uncle; it was considered an easy grab.

Taking a property by force

The setting

Mr Sen owned a property in central Kolkata. When he died in 1946, his two sons inherited the property, which was divided into two equal parts: A and B. The son who inherited portion A was married and had one son, who died. The other son had two sons and portion B was divided into B and C. When the owner of property A died, his wife, who lived in portion B, inherited portion A, which was rented out. What happened to portion A after the widow took over became a matter of dispute. One version was that it was sold to a company with a power of attorney granted by the widow in 1999 and that the sale was legally registered in Mumbai. The other version was that the two daughters of the son who owned property B (after it was divided into B and C) inherited property A from their great-aunt when she died in 2003 and sold it in 2010 to a tenant who had been registered on the property since the early 1970s. He still occupied the property together with his 'niece' who also ran an international play-school there.

Located in the middle of the city and being of some substantial size, the Sen property was considered of high value. In 2010, a Marwari industrialist took an interest in the property. Talking to him about it during an interview in June 2014, he told me that he was looking for a centrally located property to build a new family house. When words got out that he was looking for a property, he was approached by brokers. Among them, one who claimed to have the title deed of a portion of the Sen property. The price was set at INR 8.5 *crore* (INR 80.5 million or US$1.3 million at the 2014 exchange rate) and the money was paid on the condition that the sale be registered, and the property handed over to him within a year. The industrialist said he knew the property was disputed but that the broker had promised to have the dispute settled and the property vacated. After two years he still did not have access to the property, and he bought another property. He told the broker, but the broker claimed the sale had gone through and that the property had already been re-registered. However, it was still occupied.

After March 2013, the industrialist said he was no longer interested in the property because it continued to be disputed and had not been vacated as promised. According to various other sources (the media and interviews with a journalist, lawyers and one of the tenants), the property was caught up in a number of legal tangles. Since 2010, many complaints had been made at the local police station and other police and government offices: against the company claiming to have bought the property from the Sen family; against its directors and others related to or representing the company; and against the Sen family and tenants – but all to no great effect. In 2011, the two Sen daughters challenged the industrialist's claim to the property in the high court, seeking exclusive property rights on behalf of the tenant to whom they said they had sold the property. The lawsuit contested the company's property rights and claimed ownership on the basis of an unprobated will of the widow who owned the property. The industrialist had filed an eviction case against the tenants but realising the legal muddle the property was in and that the tenants remained on the property, he lost interest and wanted out.

The broker handling the deal was known to target litigated properties as a way of making money on real estate. In this case he claimed that he had no interest in the property or the company trying to sell it but had agreed merely to mediate the sale. The industrialist confirmed that he came to him as a broker. The broker's relation to the company selling the property is not clear, but it was registered at the same address as his own real estate company in Kolkata, assumingly established for that particular property deal and expected to be liquidated after the property had been sold with a good profit. And thus, after the property was sold to the industrialist, the company was no longer active. There were three listed directors from September 1997 to October 2010 of whom one also appeared as Director of 17 other companies, mostly Mumbai-based, all between 2010–13. The broker's name was not among the listed, but he was believed to be the one making money on the deal (*The Times of India*, 14 November 2013). When I discussed the case with the broker's wife (who was Joint Managing Director of the broker's real estate company) in November 2014, she said her husband first made a deal with the tenant in 2010 believing he was the owner of the property and paid him INR 85 *lakh* (8.5 million). After having paid the money he discovered that the tenant was not the owner of the property, but the money was never returned, and the tenant remained on the property. He then bought the property from the company and sold it to the industrialist in 2010. After that she said they had nothing to do with either the property or anybody connected to it.

The media reported on a link between the broker and the tenant, questioning also the latter's integrity, claiming that he had taken money from the broker to vacate but then stayed on the property. According to the niece, there were no such connections or deals, and they never had any plans to vacate the property. On the contrary, she said, they were preparing a lawsuit against the broker, but then everything changed. The broker decided to take the property by force.

The case

When I came to Kolkata for a year of fieldwork in August 2013 my children aged 3 and 6 were admitted to the international school on the disputed property. The dispute was not known at the time and the school was recommended as the best international playschool.

On a Sunday afternoon in September, when the school was closed and the principal (the aforementioned niece) was away for the weekend, there was an incident on the school property. One newspaper reported it as vandalism by a gang forcing their way into the compound, trashing the school, beating up the uncle, his aide and the school caretaker, and tearing down the school signboard replacing it with a company signboard (*The Telegraph*, 16 September 2013). Another newspaper, under the headline 'Goons ransack school at gunpoint', reported that after holding the caretakers at gunpoint, one of the intruders was said to have shouted '*Yeh jagah tum logon ko khali karna parega* (You have to vacate this place),' and before leaving, '*Aj sirf chaunakaya hai, agla din fod denge* (We have only threatened you today. We will beat you up tomorrow)' (*Times News Network*, 16 September 2013).

At a school meeting with the parents after the incident, the principal confirmed that there was a property dispute and that the attack had been a warning, but that they and the school were not going anywhere. School security was strengthened, and the school continued as usual until there was another attack in November 2014. Later we heard that in the period between the two attacks the principal had received daily telephone threats; somebody calling her to say that unless they left, they would be removed by force. She repeatedly informed the police and asked for protection but got no response. They stayed on and the threats were put into practice. In the dark of night, a group of 21 men and women, mostly fit young men sent by a private, unregistered security agency, made a forced entry. On advice from police, lawyers and others she had talked to about the threats, the principal kept her uncle's old firearms available. Surrounded by intruders, she and one of the caretakers started firing in the air, hoping to scare them away and attract the attention of the police stationed at the police commissioner's house next door. She had tried calling the local police station, but they refused to respond. When no police came, she ran to the police commissioner's house desperate for help. By the time the police finally arrived several rounds of ammunition had been fired. In addition to some less serious injuries, two bouncers were found dead in one of the playhouses. The police arrested everyone, including the principal and her helpers. Three days later the police also arrested the broker at the airport on his way to Mumbai. The media speculated that he was trying to escape on a one-way ticket.

The broker was singled out as the one behind the attack, but lawyers and named company directors were also arrested and charged with trespassing, unlawful assembly and criminal conspiracy. Two months later, the police arrested another bouncer said to have 'dabbled in the world of crime' and whose arrest led the detectives to 'unearthing a gang that helped various builders to illegally occupy land belonging to others' (*Times News Network*, 8 January 2014). The bouncer was believed to have been instrumental in convening at least eight of the several other bouncers who had entered the premises in September, vandalised the property and attacked the uncle, his helper and the school employees. A senior officer from the local police station was also arrested and charged with neglect of duty. The principal had lodged several complaints against the broker, but no action had been taken. She said the police had been paid not to interfere and she had also made complaints against the local police station. She tried to lodge her complaints higher up the hierarchy but was constantly referred back to the local police station and to the same senior police officer. She believed he was just 'small fry' and that he must have had support 'from above', from superior police officers and politicians. The name of a Trinamool Congress leader from the ruling party was mentioned, also in the press, as the broker's political ally, but his alleged involvement was not disclosed.

The mastan *raj*

Upon the arrest of the senior police officer, he told the press that he had acted on 'instructions from his superior' and the press speculated that 'more heads are likely to roll' in the police (Ghosh 2013c) – but the case never really developed into one concerning police corruption either. Evidently, the broker had initially asked two of his aides to 'get the local cops on their side' and later paid out between INR 30 to 65 *lakh* to officers at the local police station to 'hush up the role of the real culprits of the shooting' (Ghosh 2013b).[14] The newspaper claimed that the senior police officer knew what was going on as he had been seen in a restaurant a few days before the November attack talking to those later accused of 'conspiracy to crime'. It was also reported that call records showed that the police officer had called them several times between 2am and 6am on the night of the attack, and that not only were the police aware of the takeover bid that day, they had actually tipped off the goons that there would be no police patrol at the time. Allegedly, the duty officer had been told to 'divert force' on that November night (Ghosh 2013c). According to media reports, other complaints against the same police officer had been filed within the same year and had been supressed. Apparently, officers from the local police station had been 'under the scanner for inaction on the series of complaints and counter complaints filed since 2010 and their delayed reaction' (Ghosh 2013c) but nothing had been done about it.

Obviously, many were involved and there was much uncertainty about who played what part. Court cases are pending but the broker was believed to have planned and orchestrated the attack so as not to lose out on his investment. When the industrialist was asked if the broker was unwilling to pay him back the rest of the money, he said he was not unwilling, that he would return the money as soon as possible. The money he had taken had gone to other 'investments' but the sale would bring in more than enough to repay in full. However, the property was occupied and he was not able to get the tenants out.

According to various sources, the broker had made a lot of money on litigated properties. When he was taken into police custody after his arrest, the principal said she overheard him saying, when the police were trying to handcuff him, 'You are putting handcuffs on me? You know that I am a guy of 500 *crores*!' The press also estimated his fortune at several hundred *crores*, but this could not be confirmed. What was confirmed to me by business people who knew him was that he was considered to be a man of considerable assets, that he had close connections with a local political leader and the local police, and that he was regularly seen socialising with a section of Kolkata's business elite. When he appeared in court after his arrest, *The Times of India* wrote 'In blue shirt, black trousers and boots, he looked very much a corporate honcho. He was seen exchanging greetings with family, friends and even other accused' (Ghosh 2013a). According to his wife, he was not at all as the press was portraying him and he had nothing to fear because he had done nothing wrong. On the contrary, she said, he was a hardworking, honest and generous man regarded highly by business associates and colleagues, as well as by everyone who knew him.

However, his name came up in relation to several upmarket, litigated properties in Kolkata. Appearing as the Director of 23 unlisted companies and the Managing Director of a listed export-import company, the broker's 'penchant of acquiring litigated properties seems unsurpassed,' claimed a reporter (Sen 2013). Even his own company's headquarters were said to be co-owned by three persons against whom banks had initiated legal proceedings for an estimated INR 36 *lakh* default. The property in question appeared as only one among several litigated properties that he had gone after for a quick profit. As expressed by the principal's lawyer dealing with the property case, legal tangles may put off an average buyer, but not this one, asserting that, 'his modus operandi is to acquire litigated properties in rich neighbourhoods in Kolkata at throwaway prices and make a killing by selling it later' (interviewed on 8 June 2014). A female real estate developer (interviewed on 26 June 2014) told me that she was fighting the broker in high court for a 16 *katha* property valued at around INR 20 *crore* that she claimed ownership to and that the broker claimed to have bought for INR 36 *lakh*. She said she also used to develop properties (build apartment buildings and sell flats) in Kolkata but that she had moved her business to another, up-and-coming city in West Bengal. She said she had bought the property in question in central Kolkata in 2002 and registered it to one of the three real estate companies that she owned. In her case, the broker took an interest in the same property and paid government people for new documents (a title deed in his name) and the Calcutta Electric Supply Corporation (CESC) for proof of residency (electricity bill issued in his name). When she received the bill, her name was no longer there, and she understood that he had paid off the electricity company for the service. She went to the local police station, but he had paid them off too and they were not interested in listening to her, never mind doing anything for her. She filed a court case and in 2012 he was arrested for false registration of property but was granted bail by the court after 45 days in custody. She said that this is his business: litigating properties and making money on them. In five years, she claimed, he made INR 300 *crore* on similar business deals, falsifying title deeds and other official documents claiming ownership and making money on illegal sales. She mentioned one case where he had sold apartments in a building he claimed to be constructing. He even persuaded a journalist from Kolkata TV to buy an apartment, taking money for an apartment in a building that never materialised. For that project alone he was paid between a few hundred *lakhs* to 1 *crore* in rupees for each apartment sold. 'A lot of people lost their savings and he is a big-time swindler,' she said. 'There are many operating like him, selling properties they don't even own, but he is the worst,' she claimed. She said he had threatened her on a number of occasions and even sent goons with guns to her apartment building. Security guards were present but when they saw the weapons they ran away. One time he even had her picked up by the police and arrested in public on false grounds. She came out of a meeting and was walking towards her car when the police arrested her: 'He pays off anybody willing to take his money and help him get away with his scams', she said, 'including the police'. Instead of arguing with the police she had taken him to court, which is the only way – provided you have the best lawyers, she told me (with a little laugh). For the past 12 years, she had been coming to Kolkata every month to fight the case in court, which consumed a lot of resources. She even bought an apartment to have a place to stay whenever she had to appear in the high court and spend days at a time in the city.

Legitimacy of the *mastan* raj

A journalist interviewed about recent urban developments said that land is scarce, particularly in Calcutta,[15] because the city has not spread out like Bombay and Delhi. 'We've not expanded and therefore what's happened is that the value of even small plots has kept soaring because ultimately everybody is eying that property,' he explained. Even for large developments, the associated infrastructure is not in place. Rajarhat, for instance, located on the North Eastern fringes of the city and part of the fast-growing planned satellite city of New Town, is considered by city people to be outside Calcutta. New Town mainly consisted of huge acres of cultivable lands and water bodies that has been developed into a new information technology and residential hub. However, while this area could be developed in a planned manner because of government land acquisition policies under the leadership of the then Chief Minister of West Bengal Buddhadeb Bhattacharya (Communist Party of India-Marxist, CPIM) in the late 1990s, the present Trinamool government (from 2011) has practised a hands-off policy regarding land, preventing forced acquisition and adhering to the Urban Land Ceiling Act. Without large holdings, developments are small and, without government involvement, negotiating for land is left to the private market, which is presently pushing prices up – astronomically. Meanwhile, the present government is doing nothing to stop these developments, the journalist told me. What he was saying was that without government intervention and political ambitions to control development, it all comes down to money and power. In the city, he said, 'land is scarce and possibilities for making big money on land are limited. As you step out of the city, however, land values are increasing as the city is expanding. There you find the mafia, profiting from the booming real estate market by taking possession of land by force and making money on illegal land deals'.

Although largely undocumented except for some media coverage, Rajarhat New Town is seen as 'an area notorious for its syndicate goons' (*Frontline*, 3 August 2016). Less visible are the struggles over properties going on in the city, where land is scarce and development possibilities are limited, restricted also by the governments 'hands-off' policy enforced through the Urban Land Ceiling Act (ULCA). The ULCA was introduced in 1976 with the intention of preventing the concentration of urban land in the hands of a few, preventing profiteering and seeking to ensure the equitable distribution of land for the benefit of the entire population (The Urban Land (Ceiling and Regulation) Act, 1976). The Act prescribes the limit on vacant land in urban areas as 7.5 *katha* (one-eighth of an acre or

500 m²). Industry players claimed that this limit stood in the way of implementing projects in the urban area and the government was put under pressure to repeal the Act. In 1999, the central government repealed the ULCA, prompting other states to rescind the Act. Gujarat, for example, followed the central government and abolished the Act, but West Bengal did not. In 2006–7, the CPIM-led state government made similar efforts but failed to convince its allies. Since Trinamool Congress came to power in the summer of 2011, it has been under pressure to repeal the Act but has made it clear that it will not reconsider its refusal to do so (*Business Standard*, 30 December 2013). In practice, the restrictions are seen to promote abuses of power, as expressed by the interviewed journalist:

> In our city, a large section of plots around the EM Bypass, as you go towards the south, which is towards Gariahat, as you go towards that area, a large section is owned by somebody who is now a minister in the government. Now, we have something called the Land Ceiling Act, which allows you to own, I think it would be not more than 7 *kothas*, but he has acres through *benami* properties, that means not in my name, but in my son's name, in my niece's name, my wife's name or some other, even my employees, I raised the plots in their names. Some plots I don't register at all. So when you have somebody like him, who holds a ministerial position and owns such tracts of land, what do you call him, a minister or a mafia? (Interview in Kolkata, 13 November 2014)

As this journalist says, even ministers are believed to hold land illegally and beyond government control. Even when cases are brought to the courts for mediation, there is no certainty when, or even if, a case will come to an end and be decided, due to the endless appeal system. A lawyer friend told me that once in 1988 he had been in court to defend a case for a client. While waiting for his case to come up, he suddenly heard the judge shout, 'Enough is enough!' The judge, who was hearing a dispute case between a tenant and a landlord, told the tenant he was giving him six months to vacate the property. From 1952 he had been filing one petition after another. 'Mind you', he told me, 'the landlord in 1952 had won his case in the supreme court, but to evict the tenant?' They had fought the matter for 35 years and avoided the process of eviction. 'So, for 35 years he had remained on the property after the Supreme Court said to give it up, but that is the law', he mused. According to him, the principal and her uncle could simply have used their position as tenants to stay on the property indefinitely. In that sense, the claimed ownership was not important: under the Tenancy Act, if you sell a property, the tenants become your tenants. You cannot buy a property and say, '"Sorry, but that man sold the property and you have to get out." You cannot do that,' he explained. 'You buy the property with the tenants. Should the uncle's sale not be held valid, the property reverts back to the original owners, but both he and his niece would remain tenants.' He continued:

> Now, her rights flow from the fact that her mother had got this tenancy 40 years ago. She had rent receipts from one family for this and from another family from this, the one room over here (illustrating on a piece of paper). [The uncle] had another room over here and he was also a tenant. Now, very often tenants buy out the property. That is what [the uncle] did, but as far as [the niece] is concerned, after her mother's death, Mrs Sen transferred the property to her and made her the tenant. She has rights. You cannot throw a tenant out except by process of law.

But this is what is happening in Kolkata. The West Bengal Tenancy Act of 1997 provides strong protection for tenants from eviction, and owners seeking to evict a tenant legally to repossess their property may end up in an apparently never-ending appeal process, as described above and seen in numerous other cases.[16] In 2011, *The Telegraph* reported on a civil servant 'locked in a seemingly endless legal combat with his tenant'. Ten years earlier, he had filed an eviction suit at the city civil court but 'thanks to appeals and countersuits filed by the tenant, the issue is now entangled in complex legal procedures' (*The Telegraph*, 15 June 2011). As explained by the developer cited before, when they consider buying a property for development, they also have to consider the situation with tenants and the likelihood of reaching agreements and settlements with them, as well as with the owners. Also the lawyer in the school case said that if they wanted to develop the property they should have offered as much space in a new building as they were occupying in the old – but the buyer wanted the property to himself and they had to be evicted; otherwise, the buyer was not interested. Even if the sale had been legal it would take years to establish that claim.

In some cases, even just the threat of litigation when occupying a property can be enough to force a settlement. The lawyer told of a case where a man had taken a flat by way of *salaami* (a type of long-term lease),[17] an agreement where he paid 8 *lakh* in advance to take the flat. He had just retired; the payment was made in cash and the amount was documented. They also signed a written agreement stating the conditions and that he and his family were entitled to keep the flat for as long as he lived. Usually, if you are a *salaami* tenant you can transfer the agreement to someone else if you move out, in which case 33 per cent of the new *salaami* goes to the landlord and the tenant keeps the rest. In this case, when the tenant died, the owner of the property asked his family to move out and hand over the flat. By then, the *salaami* for the flat was believed to be between 60 and 80 *lakh* and the tenants asked the owner to pay them 50 *lakh* to move out. The owner refused, and the family told him that if he wanted the property back, he should settle or spend the next 25 to 30 years trying to get possession from the courts: appeal court, high court, supreme court, and after 30 years he may still not have succeeded. In the meantime, tenants will be present, occupying the property (original tenant and/or his descendants). 'Wouldn't it be better to settle outside court than hanging on for 20 or 30 years like that?' the lawyer reasoned – and he is not alone in his way of thinking.

In suburban Kolkata, walled-in vacant plots of land bearing name signs and with just a guard or two watching are a common sight. Owners may be biding their time waiting for an acceptable offer to sell, dealing with potential builders to develop the property, or busy disputing property rights. On every undeveloped land there is a risk of land grabbing or forceful takeover. In the story of *The Godfather of Bangalore* (Carney 2008), it took a gang of marauders only a minute to overpower the guards, overrun the premises and paint over the name sign stating ownership. By the time the police arrived, the sign was just a memory and the attackers had achieved their goal. Thanks to the convoluted rules surrounding land ownership, the removal of the name sign throws the owner's claim into question and the dispute is 'no longer just a criminal matter of a gang of outlaws taking over a piece of ground; now it's a civil issue that will have to be mediated in the courts. This kind of legal battle, with its near-endless appeal process, could easily last 15 years' (Carney 2008). If the owner wants to develop or sell the plot during that time, 'he'd be better off just letting his assailants have the property in exchange for a fraction of its value' (Carney 2008). According to my journalist friend, giving similar examples of land grabbing and forced takeovers in Kolkata, the land mafia clears the way and the legal system keeps it open. Even Kolkata's wetlands, protected by multiple domestic laws and an international convention, are openly sold off in parcels to make space for high-rise housing, malls and offices.

> What is happening, a very deadly thing, is that we have to the east, just beyond the Bypass, we have what is known as the East-Kolkata wetlands. It's a Ramsar site. Ramsar is the international convention

for protection of wetlands, internationally recognised wetlands; it's a UN convention. These wetlands are used for fish farms. You have these large water bodies, but they are not very deep, they are about 4 to 4.5 feet deep, and they are being filled up. You have fifty fishermen working over there. All you need to do is to offer these fishermen, who would earn maybe 50,000 rupees or one *lakh* in a year, you give them a 10 *lakh* rupees check. It's a windfall. So, 50 of them and 10 *lakh* each; 5 *crore* in total.[18] Then you develop a huge building, containing 300 flats sold for 1.5 *crore* each. So it's like that. That is what's happening to the east of the city, but not only there… Behind Ruby Hospital, you also have this huge school called Heritage. That school is built entirely on wetland and that school's owners have already acquired several water bodies in that locality. So they purchase the wetlands, drain out the entire water and build walls around in broad daylight. They do not seem fearful of anything and why should they?

If litigated at all, by the time cases are even brought to the courts (less still by the time the courts have reached a final decision) the land has been sold, developed and changed forever. Had the forced takeover of the school property gone as planned, the occupants would have been evicted and the property sold and developed into a luxurious villa or a modern housing complex. Sending in a group of goons, the *mastan* raj, can be an effective way of taking possession of a property when the police are either directly or indirectly involved, making sure nothing is done to stop the takeover in light of a court system taking as much as 20 to 30 years to settle disputes. People seeking justice are left waiting by the open but guarded door for the rest of their lives, like the protagonist in Kafka's *The Trial* (Ferme 2013: 958).

Conclusion

As mentioned earlier, there have been and still are many building activities in Kolkata itself: large-scale complexes (housing, malls and offices), mostly on the peripheries of the city (Rajarhat New Town and lately around E.M. Bypass) but also centrally (South City), mainly built by well-known Marwari business families[19] although not exclusively. The focus of this chapter has been on real estate 'on the margins' where, on a daily basis, properties are illegally and sometimes also violently captured and sold without anybody necessarily taking notice or doing anything to prevent it from taking place. As has been seen in this chapter, the government is heavily involved through its functionaries, who regulate, document, sanction, etc., as well as through neglect.

In 2016, under the headline 'Shock to the syndicate mafia', *Frontline* (3 August 2016) reported that Bangladeshi Prime Minister Sheikh Hasina had called West Bengal Chief Minister Mamata Banerjee on behalf of a friend in Kolkata 'who was being harassed by Anindyo Chatterjee' (senior Trinamool leader and Municipal Corporation councillor) over building issues. According to the magazine, 'At long last Mamata Banerjee's Trinamool Congress government in West Bengal has woken up to the increasing menace of the "syndicate raj", a euphemism for extortionists and other criminal elements operating in the private housing and infrastructure industries in the State. It has begun to crack down on the groups by arresting (as of July 26) 49 persons' – including Mr Chatterjee. Concurring with what I was told by political commentators in the field (both former political activists and social scientists), the magazine also claims that the 'syndicate raj' took root during the previous regime under the Left Front, but while the Communist Party of India (Marxist), 'with its structured and disciplined network of cadres had kept the syndicates in check and they were confined to certain areas', syndicates have proliferated all over the state since the Trinamool government came to power in 2011. The assumed growth of syndicates, the ruling party's perceived links with criminal organisations and the way they have been allowed to carry out their operations have 'made the Trinamool Congress practically synonymous with "syndicate raj"'.

When I was back in Kolkata in April 2017, this was a much-debated theme. It was generally acknowledged that the reasons for the growth and strengthening of syndicates are that they have funded and secured votes for the Trinamool and that they have provided a source of income to unemployed youth. According to the magazine, the decision to take on the syndicates came as 'a bit of shock to the thousands of young people and syndicate workers who have been the loyal foot soldiers of the Trinamool army and a pleasant surprise to urban middle-class voters who had all but lost hope of ever being delivered from the clutches of the syndicate goons' (*Frontline*, 3 August 2016). The magazine also made a number of suggestions as to why the Chief Minister could afford to make such a decision at that particular time (including the party's huge win in the 2016 assembly election and the weakness of the opposition parties, the desire to clean up the party's image and win back the confidence of middle-class voters tired of being harassed by syndicate goons, and the ambition to be a key player in national politics) but also indicated that the trend might not be forever, or even totally sincere, as there is much at stake, such as money and power. *Frontline* concluded that 'It remains to be seen whether Mamata Banerjee, after consolidating her political supremacy in the State, will focus on good administration and continue to clamp down on the syndicates or stop with a token gesture of good governance by arresting some small fry' (and by removing the small fry consolidating the bigger ones in a long-term plan to streamline this illegal industry). And what are a few arrests anyway? All the people arrested in the school shooting case were out on bail within the first year after the incident where two young men were shot dead and, years later, the trial is still pending. In the meantime, they all go about their lives as usual, including the principal, who runs several educational centres in and outside Kolkata, teaching full time, and the broker, who continues running his real estate business much as before.

When discussing Chief Minister Banerjee's position during my last visit, the general feeling was that she has little or no control over party cadre and administration. She may be able to call for a few arrests to be made, but do away with the syndicates? Besides, if syndicate bosses and members (or at least their political allies) are now in government, as widely believed,[20] and courts can be managed, who or what is to be done away with, and how? Are we talking mafia and syndicates on the margin of the state or a state on the margin of law and order, of legal/illegal? Following Gupta (1995), seeing the state 'as an inherently translocal entity, which localizes itself in particular sites, and at particular times' (Ferme 2013), enables it at the same time to be seen as legal/illegal, law and order/corruption and disorder, just/unjust, all at once instead of one or the other; boundary *unmaking* instead of boundary making, because it – the state – is not a coherent unity of 'practices, documents, and words' (Das and Poole 2004: 9). In this case, where the government ends and the syndicate raj/land mafia begins is difficult, if not impossible, to determine, and the terms mafia state or *mastan* raj appear as a suitable way of describing the practices explored in this chapter.

Notes

1. I am greatly obliged to friends and interlocutors in India for making fieldwork possible and for sharing their lives and stories with me. I would also like to thank Lucia Michelutti and Barbara Harriss-White for careful reading and thoughtful comments.
2. According to Liza Weinstein, property prices in Mumbai's business districts reached record levels in the mid-1990s, with the districts 'becoming, for a brief period in 1996, the most expensive real estate in the world'.

3. For more on the social and relational aspects of recent urban property developments, see De Neve and Donner (2015).
4. Special Economic Zones. For a critical view of SEZs in India, see Sampat (2008).
5. For more on how capital accumulation has been made possible through the state's role as land broker see Harvey (2003) and Levien (2012, 2015) on 'accumulation by dispossession'; Batra and Mehra (2008), Dasgupta (2003) and Doshi (2013) on slum demolition and resettlement projects in Delhi, Kolkata and Mumbai; and Levien (2012, 2015), Majumder (2010, 2012), and Shrivastava and Kothari (2012) on farmers dispossessed of their land for SEZs and other corporate projects.
6. Following Gardner and Gerharz, I am using 'land grabbing' according to its temporal association; as imagery depicting land that is *apparently* 'suddenly and violently seized' (Gardner and Gerharz 2016: 6).
7. For studies of mafia and OCGs in Italy and Russia, see Diego Gambetta (1993) on the Sicilian mafia and Federico Varese (2001, 2011) on the Russian mafia and mafia on the move (see also the Introduction to this volume).
8. Like the distinction between state and civil society or, as in Partha Chatterjee's case, state and political society (Chatterjee 2008), which is hardly observable in practice.
9. South City is a 31.14-acre (126,000 m²) complex of buildings in Kolkata, India, constructed between 2004 and 2012. It is situated in Prince Anwar Shah Road close to the Jodhpur Park and Tollygunge areas of the city. Most of the recent real estate developments in Kolkata have taken place in the E.M. Bypass area, New Town and Greater Kolkata, but the South City complex is located in the heart of the city. It features a residential complex, which includes a number of recreational facilities, as well as a school, hospital, shopping mall and social club. Filmmaker Ranu Ghosh made a documentary featuring the sacrifices made to build South City, *Quarter Number 4/11*, which is 'a ground zero perspective of urban real estate development, as witnessed by director/cinematographer Ranu Ghosh and narrated through the plight of an ex-factory worker Shambhu Prasad Singh, a victim of this development in Calcutta's South City, a residential complex-cum-shopping mall-cum-school for the wealthy. It is about one man's lone, long, losing fight to hold on to his ground where he was born, grew up and earned his living. It is the narrative of a man who is being forced to evacuate his ground to make space for "development"' (film synopsis).
10. By 'jungle up with' he means trouble with later.
11. *Lis pendens* is Latin for 'suit pending' and is a written notice that a lawsuit has been filed concerning real estate, involving either the title to the property or a claimed ownership interest in it. Recording a *lis pendens* against a piece of property alerts a potential purchaser or lender, as well as the general public, that the property title is in question, which makes the property less attractive to a buyer or lender. Once the notice is filed, anyone who purchases the land or property described in the notice and takes possession of it is subject to the ultimate decision of the lawsuit.
12. The Sundarbans are a mangrove forest area in the southern part of West Bengal in the river delta on the Bay of Bengal.
13. A *katha* (also spelled *kattha* or *cottah*) is a measure of land used in Bangladesh, India and Nepal. It is still in use in much of Bangladesh and India, though the size connoted varies. In West Bengal 1 *katha* is equal to 720 ft².
14. Estimates of the pay-outs varied, but one suggested that 65 *lakh* was paid in three installments, 'one of which was of INR 30 *lakh* on September 27, 12 days after the first failed attack on the property'. The senior officer claimed he only made INR 5 *lakh* and that the rest was 'distributed among others' (*Times of India*, 15 December 2015).
15. Calcutta was the official name of the capital of the Indian state of West Bengal until 2001, when it changed to Kolkata; the old name is nonetheless still in use.
16. Particularly to tenants paying less than INR 6,500 as monthly rent for residential premises in Kolkata (usually tenants who have stayed for a long time, even through generations).
17. *Salaami* or *bhada salaami* is a rental agreement where rent is paid in advance, usually in cash, and the lease is inheritable from father to son and does not have an expiry date. The rent is low because of the advance arrangement. Another word for similar practices elsewhere in India is *pagdi* (literally 'turban').
18. To get them out of the way and not to cause any trouble.

19. There is something to be said about business and communities, and the fact that the big industrialist who bought the school property in the case discussed earlier was a Marwari and the broker wanting to sue him was a Gujarati, but that is another story.
20. During fieldwork, I often heard statements similar to *Frontline*'s claim that 'syndicate operators got the party ticket to contest civic elections and also got to hold key party and administrative posts'.

References

Asad, T. 2004. 'Where are the Margins of the State?', in *Anthropology in the Margins of the State*, edited by V. Das and D. Poole. New Mexico: School of American Research Press: 279–89.
Batra, L. and D. Mehra. 2008. 'Slum Demolitions and Production of Neo-liberal Space, Delhi', in *Inside the Transforming Urban Asia: Processes, Policies, and Public Actions*, edited by D. Mahadevia. New Delhi: Concept Publishing Company: 391–413.
Carney, S. 2008. 'The Godfather of Bangalore', *Wired Magazine*, 16 November.
Chakravorty, S. 2013. *The Price of Land. Acquisition, Conflict, Consequence*. New Delhi: Oxford University Press.
Chatterjee, P. 2008. 'Democracy and Economic Transformation in India', *Economic and Political Weekly*, special feature, 19 April: 53–62.
Chen, X., L. Wang and R. Kundu. 2009. 'Localizing the Production of Global Cities: A Comparison of New Town Developments Around Shanghai and Kolkata', *City and Community* 8(4): 433–65.
Das, R. 2016. 'The Politics of Land, Consent, and Negotiation: Revisiting the Development-Displacement Narratives from Singur in West Bengal', in *Land, Development and Security in South Asia* by K. Gardner and E. Gerhartz. *South Asia Multidisciplinary Academic Journal* [Online].
Das, V. and D. Poole 2004. 'State and Its Margins: Comparative Ethnographies', in *Anthropology in the Margins of the State*, edited by V. Das and D. Poole. New Mexico: School of American Research Press: 3–35.
Dasgupta, K. 2003. 'Evictions in Calcutta: Creating the Spaces of "Modernity"', *City: A Quarterly on Urban Society* 4: 31–43.
De Neve, G. and H. Donner. 2015. 'Introduction. Revisiting Urban Property in India', *Journal of South Asian Development* 10(3): 255–66.
Doshi, S. 2013. 'The Politics of the Evicted: Redevelopment, Subjectivity, and Difference in Mumbai's Slum Frontier', *Antipode* 45(3): 1–22.
Ferme, M. 2013. 'Introduction: Localizing the State', *Anthropological Quarterly* 86(4): 957–63.
Frontline. 2016. 'Shock to the Syndicate Mafia', *Frontline*, 3 August.
Gardner, K. and E. Gerharz. 2016. 'Land, "Development" and "Security" in Bangladesh and India: An Introduction', *South Asia Multidisciplinary Academic Journal* [Online] 13: 1–19.
Gambetta, D. 1993. *The Sicilian Mafia. The Business of Private Protection*. Cambridge, MA and London: Harvard University Press.
Ghosh, D. 2013a. 'Cops may question Sureka, another realtor held', *The Times of India*, 15 November, p. 3, Kolkata.
Ghosh, D. 2013b. 'Short Street shooting: Prime accused Parag offered cops Rs 35L, co-accused said', *The Times of India*, 12 December. https://timesofindia.indiatimes.com/city/kolkata/Short-Street-shooting-Prime-accused-Parag-offered-cops-Rs-35L-co-accused-says/articleshow/27233568.cms (accessed 17 April 2019).
Ghosh, D. 2013c. 'Arrested cop blames seniors in Short Street case', *The Times of India*, 15 December. https://timesofindia.indiatimes.com/city/kolkata/Arrested-cop-blames-seniors-in-Short-Street-case/articleshow/27390125.cms (accessed 17 April 2019).
Gupta, A. 1995. 'Blurred Boundaries: The Discourse of Corruption, the Culture of Politics, and the Imagined State', *American Ethnologist* 22(2): 375–402.
Hardgrove, A. 2004. *Community and Public Culture: The Marwaris in Calcutta*. New Delhi: Oxford University Press.
Harvey, D. 2003. *The New Imperialism*. Oxford: Oxford University Press.
Levien, M. 2012. 'The Land Question: Special Economic Zones and the Political Economy of Dispossession in India', *Journal of Peasant Studies* 39(3–4): 933–69.
Levien, M. 2015. 'Social Capital as Obstacle to Development: Brokering Land, Norms, and Trust in Rural India', *World Development* 74: 77–92.

Majumder, S. 2010. 'The Nano Controversy: Peasant Identities, the Land Question and Neoliberal Industrialization in Marxist West Bengal, India', *Journal of Emerging Knowledge on Emerging Markets* 2: 1–27.

Majumder, S. 2012. 'Who Wants to Marry a Farmer? Neoliberal Industrialization and the Politics of Land and Work in Rural West Bengal', *Focaal* 64: 85–98.

Nielsen, K.B. 2014. 'Saving the Farmland: The Making of Popular Anti-Land Acquisition Politics in Singur, West Bengal'. Akademika forlag 2014 364 s. Series of Dissertations submitted to the Faculty of Social Sciences, University of Oslo (481) UiO.

Sampat, P. 2008. 'Special Economic Zones in India', *Economic and Political Weekly* 43(28): 25–9.

Searle, L. G. 2014. 'Conflict and Commensuration: Contested Market Making in India's Private Real Estate Development Sector', *International Journal of Urban and Regional Research* 38(1): 60–78.

Searle, L.G. 2016. *Landscapes of Accumulation. Real Estate and the Neoliberal Imagination in Contemporary India*. Chicago, IL: University of Chicago Press.

Sen, S. 2013. 'Realtor who chased litigated property', *The Times of India*, 15 November.

Shrivastava, A. and A. Kothari. 2012. *Churning the Earth: The Making of Global India*. New Delhi: Penguin Viking.

The Telegraph. 2011. 'Ranting over rent', *The Telegraph*, 15 June. https://www.telegraphindia.com/opinion/ranting-over-rent/cid/386326 (accessed 17 April 2019).

The Telegraph. 2013. 'Vandalism at Montessori, gang blamed', by A Staff Reporter, *The Telegraph*, 16 September, p. 18. https://www.telegraphindia.com/states/west-bengal/vandalism-at-montessori-gang-blamed/cid/1288068 (accessed 17 April 2019).

The Times of India. 2013. 'Broker behind Short Street plot takeover bid held at airport', *The Times of India*, 14 November, Kolkata. https://timesofindia.indiatimes.com/city/kolkata/Broker-behind-Short-Street-plot-takeover-bid-held-at-airport/articleshow/25720241.cms (accessed 17 April 2019).

Times News Network. 2013. 'Goons ransack school at gunpoint', *The Times of India, Kolkata*, 16 September. https://timesofindia.indiatimes.com/city/kolkata/Goons-ransack-school-at-gunpoint/articleshow/22613338.cms (accessed 17 April 2019).

Times News Network. 2014. 'Bouncer held in Short Street case', *The Times of India, Kolkata*, 8 January. https://timesofindia.indiatimes.com/city/kolkata/Bouncer-held-in-Short-Street-case/articleshow/28531155.cms (accessed 17 April 2019).

Varese, F. 2001. *The Russian Mafia: Private Protection in a New Market Economy*. Oxford: Oxford University Press.

Varese, F. 2011. *Mafias on the Move. How Organized Crime Conquers New Territories*. Princeton, NJ: Princeton University Press.

Weinstein, L. 2008. 'Mumbai's Development Mafias: Globalization, Organized Crime and Land Development', *International Journal of Urban and Regional Research* 32(1): 22–39.

9
Politics, capital and land grabs in Punjab, India

Nicolas Martin

Engaging critically with the concept of 'political society', this chapter examines the issue of land grabbing in Punjab, and focusses in particular upon the systematic small-scale encroachment on village communal land in a rural Punjab district. It shows how politicians often help farmers to continue occupying village common lands illegally, doing so for electoral gains not necessarily consistent with the logic of 'the market' or of capital. In these cases, politicians seem to be driven by political motives related to electoral calculations rather than solely by financial ones. However, the chapter illustrates how these clientelistic bargains ultimately serve politicians and local elites more than they do those facing the prospect of dispossession.

This chapter offers an ethnographic perspective on land grabs in Punjab, focussing in particular on processes of appropriation of village common lands in rural Punjab: land that should in theory be available for rent to the highest bidder and of which a third is reserved for members of the Scheduled Castes (SCs). I argue that the processes at stake are somewhat different to those emphasised in the growing literature on land grabbing, which focusses on how capitalist accumulation by elite interest groups dispossesses the poor (Whitehead 2008; Adnan 2013; Springer 2013). This literature tends to draw on David Harvey's (2004) notion of accumulation by dispossession and sees land grabs as the result of over-accumulated capital seeking new opportunities for profit. As such, it tends to focus on 'land grabbing' projects that displace thousands of villagers or urban dwellers in order to make space for Special Economic Zones or real estate developments (Adnan 2013; Levien 2011; Sampat 2010; Cross 2014). In this chapter, however, I focus principally on more routinised and small-scale processes around encroachment on village common lands in a rural Punjabi district. As Geert De Neve (2015) has argued, 'large scale state-led land grabs and mass displacements do not form the only – and perhaps not even the main – form that [primary] accumulation takes in post-reform India'.

Partha Chatterjee (2008) has argued that in post-liberalisation India, politicians are more than ever subject to the hegemony of corporate capital; corporate capital flows rather than electoral mobilisation are increasingly dominating politics, he argues. This is because state-level leaders are competing with each other in order to attract the capital that is necessary to generate economic growth. Corporate capital is gradually pauperising small farmers, small shopkeepers and indigenous communities. Corporate land grabs are one of the many ways this is happening. The concentration of capital also means that large retail and agribusiness companies can put small shopkeepers and small farmers out of business through the use of economies of scale and/or loss-leaders which undercut their prices. Civil society and the judiciary, he argues, are complicit in these processes. The middle classes, as Baviskar (2011) also shows, are tired of the messy reality of electoral politics. For example: the world of politics is the reason why, in their view, urban landscapes are blemished with illegal slums. It is politicians who allow people illegally to occupy land because they obtain votes in exchange for favours. The middle classes want the law to be implemented and the slums to be cleared.

The ad hoc illegal arrangements that prevent squatters from being evicted are the defining characteristic of what Chatterjee calls political society. The sphere of political society is one that operates on the margins of or even outside the law; it is a sphere in which politicians circumvent or break the law in order to appease popular pressures. For Chatterjee, political society has the merit of, for example, providing slum dwellers with a place to live, even though it might not give them the secure legal rights to settle permanently. Were politicians to stick to the letter of the law, slum dwellers would find themselves on the street. As such, he has argued that what he calls the sphere of political society is in fact the principal sphere of activity where resistance to capital and to primitive accumulation takes place. Its main achievement is to prevent the dispossessed from turning into 'dangerous classes' who have nothing to lose and are therefore potentially revolutionary.

In this chapter however, I show how so-called 'political society' can also be complicit in processes of dispossession. The dynamics around land grabbing that I describe here – particularly in the case of village common lands in rural Punjab – bear the imprint of political meddling that is informed by the prerogatives of electoral politics rather than, strictly speaking, those of corporate capital. But what this chapter shows – echoing previous work (Martin 2014) – is that the ad hoc clientelistic bargains characteristic of political society can overwhelmingly benefit local elites at the expense of subordinate social groups (Dalits in particular). Moreover it illustrates how the frequently partisan nature of clientelistic interventions means that they further benefit some people at the expense of others. This makes these interventions a cause for conflict and social division, and therefore prevents people from getting together in order to find genuine political solutions to protecting their livelihoods.

The material presented is based on 15 months of ethnographic fieldwork starting in 2013 in villages around a *tehsil* (sub-district) headquarters within Patiala district, together with some research in the urban *tehsil* headquarters itself. Much of the material presented is based on interviews with interested parties in a number of land disputes. Given the hotly contested nature of these disputes, and that everyone has their own version of events, I attempt to triangulate people's different versions and points of view. I begin with the broader picture of land grabbing at the state and *tehsil* level and its relationship with politics, and then move on to examine three case studies of village-common land grabs. In these case studies, politicians often intervene in order to allow supporters to continue possessing village common lands illegally against the logic of the market – much like Chatterjee's politicians who help slum dwellers to continue encroaching upon land that does not belong to them. Were 'the logic of the market' to prevail, this land would go to the highest bidder, and prices for the lease of village common lands would rise significantly. Based on these case studies I try to determine whether it is in fact, as Chatterjee seems to suggest, the poor and lower caste who most benefit from these interventions. Moreover, I examine whether and how these political interventions succeed in preventing the popular unrest that arises out of the dispossession that accompanies the expansion of capital in agriculture.

Shiromani Akali Dal: 'Goonda Raj' and property grabs in Punjab

During the Shiromani Akali Dal (SAD) party's two terms in power in Punjab, people frequently claimed that it had instituted a reign of *goonda raj* (thugs) that was just as bad as the one in Bihar under Laloo Yadav Prasad. People – even lifelong Akalis – frequently claimed that corruption and criminality in the Punjab was at its worst. Everywhere people told me that *tehsildars* (revenue collector at the *tehsil* level), Block Development Officers and police Superintendent House Officers (SHOs) were forced to provide tens of *lakh*[1] every month to their local MLA. While this was nothing new – as Robert Wade's (1985) work on the market for public office in India illustrates – people claimed that the extent of these exactions was unprecedented. In the *tehsil* headquarters, I mostly heard about police exactions. Transporters complained about incessant harassment. People also complained about an SHO nicknamed 'Dabang' because he acted and behaved like a gangster. One local transporter told me that Dabang had asked him to gift him a new motorcycle.

Many informants alleged that in the past corruption in the state happened only at the highest levels. Congress leaders in the state, they claimed, only took money from big business, whereas the Akali government – then in its second term – took money from everyone. The party leadership allegedly had shares in every business in the state, from media outlets to *dhabas* (roadside restaurants) and bus services to commercial property and industry. Businessmen who refused to pay tribute to the party leadership faced bureaucratic hurdles that caused their businesses to shut down. Police officers harassed transporters by asking them to produce documents that they were unlikely to possess. In the *tehsil* headquarters, the leader of the Tempu (light transport vehicles) Union described a protection racket whereby the Ministry of Transport issued SAD party membership cards that essentially gave Tempu drivers immunity from police harassment. Cardholders paid INR 150 per month, which was allegedly distributed among local police officers who consequently let them go without checking their documents, and who even let them get away with transporting illegal liquor and drugs. Likewise, a lucrative *dhaba* might find that if it did not pay tribute, its licence might be withdrawn, or that the police might discourage customers from patronising it by not allowing them to park near it. On a more sinister note, people claimed that the ruling coalition controlled organised crime in the state. The Congress-leaning English-language press in the state often reported on the misdemeanours of Youth Akali Dal (YAD) leaders. The YAD was essentially the strong arm of the SAD and was used to harass opponents, rig elections and, it appears, distribute drugs – principally *bhukki* (poppy husk) – to purchase votes during elections. A close relative of the Chief Minister controlled the outfit and there were widespread rumours about how he used them as a *sena* (private army) in his home constituency. Throughout the state YAD youths used their police immunity to settle personal vendettas and to make money through drug trafficking and the capture of disputed properties. In 2013–4 one of the main stories dominating the press related to allegations that the head of the YAD was also the lynchpin of the drug trade in Punjab. These allegations came to light after a notorious drug smuggler was captured and interrogated by the police (Sehgal 2014).

Moreover, the SAD politicians stood widely accused of involvement in a variety of land grabbing schemes. One of the SAD's manifesto pledges was to build motorways linking all major cities in Punjab. The process of acquiring land from farmers to build these motorways was murky, and well-connected Akali politicians were widely believed to have amassed significant amounts of money through it. The farmers who had to sell their land to make way for these projects felt cheated. There were stories, for example, about Akali middlemen buying land from farmers at low prices and then reselling it to the government at much higher prices (Vasudeva 2016). Farmers in one village alleged that influential people had spread false rumours to the effect that the middleman in question was going to pay them more than the government would be willing to pay. The rumours even suggested that the government might not give farmers any compensation whatsoever so that it was best to accept the middleman's offer. There were also plenty of stories about land grabs around expanding urban centres. Land prices around cities such as Chandigarh, Ludhiana, Patiala and Bathinda have skyrocketed in recent years. There were stories about moderately prosperous Jat farmers becoming multi-millionaires because their farmland happened to be located in urban peripheries that were being incorporated into the cities. High land values led to a scramble for land located on these peripheries. I also read and heard about a number of cases in which politically influential people were alleged to have somehow managed – using both their influence and bribes – to register portions of village common land in their names and then sell it on to urban developers.

Land values in the *tehsil* headquarters where I carried out my fieldwork may not have shot up to the same level as in Punjab's major cities, but they also rocketed and were subject to speculation and disputes. The most notorious land grabber here was the president of the Youth Akali Dal, and a village *Sarpanch* (elected village headman). The young man, whom I will call Gurbachan Singh, started his political career during his college days when he was a *kabaddi* (a muscular Punjabi contact sport) player. During those days he proved his worth in several fights against rival student groups and eventually defeated rival contenders to the student union leadership. People who knew him from college days told me that he was always getting into fights and that he had already had a number of cases filed against him back then. However, the feat that established his notoriety was his capture and subsequent sale of a widow's valuable urban property. The wealthy widow, from the Bania urban trading community, was being harassed by relatives who wanted to gain control over numerous assets, which included a bottling plant, several shops and a couple of urban residential properties. She asked Gurbachan to help her intimidate her relatives and he eventually moved into a wing of her house as her permanent bodyguard. The story goes that it was only after he had gained her full confidence that he turned on her. People claim that he managed to get her to put her large residence in the centre of town in his name; some claim that he did so through persuasion and cunning and others that he did so through threats. Gurbachan eventually took control of the property, kicked the widow out and then used it to host drinking parties before transforming it into a commercial property and selling it off for 3 *crore*. One of his relatives said that Gurbachan constantly had college girls visiting him there, and even that he started 'providing' girls to politicians and wealthy businessmen.

Speaking with lawyers I learned that while property and land grabs had always happened, the incidence had increased as a result of soaring land prices in the last 10 years. Everywhere people told me that up to 10 years ago property speculation had been a comparatively muted affair; people mostly bought property to farm or to live on, not as a speculative investment. Many farmers told me that they regretted selling land back in the day when an acre of farmland was worth only 2 *lakh*, and others regretted not buying land when it was still affordable. Now an acre in rural areas is worth up to 40 *lakh*.

First the rise in land values brought in speculators from as far as Chandigarh. Being outsiders, some such speculators were allegedly duped by locals, in collusion with local government officers, into buying plots without the consent of the actual owners. Government officers in charge of verifying people's identity would fraudulently attest that a person was the owner of a plot and wanted to sell it when the person was in fact just a dummy. The dummy would sell a plot that was not theirs to sell and then share the proceeds with the officers, while the actual owner and the buyer were left to fight protracted legal battles. A young man who had been involved in such a transaction told me that duped buyers rarely got all of their money back, particularly if the *kabza* group (property grabbing group) was well connected politically.

Today it is more difficult to pull this sort of scam off because the government has introduced more stringent identity checks including the use of *Aadhaar* (ID) cards and photographs of the parties involved in land transactions. While more difficult to carry out, fraud is nevertheless still possible, but according to people in the know it is now increasingly limited to large transactions involving huge sums of money, and for which a *tehsildar* near retirement might be willing to risk suspension and a protracted legal battle. The way it is now done is that people obtain other people's land records, scan them onto their computers and then, using image manipulation software, replace the owner's name with theirs. They then come to some sort of an agreement with the *tehsildar*, who will somehow enter the amended title into the system. The person who told me about this, a young man who earned his livelihood from disputed properties, told me that a *tehsildar* would do this sort of thing only for sums of money above at least 10 *crore* and that they would also generally only get involved in such a venture if they were close to retirement and thus in any case about to lose their job. He said that if a *tehsildar* managed to pull this off, his earnings from the fraudulent transaction would far outweigh the potential loss of income due to being suspended as well as the costs of having to fight a protracted legal battle.

In urban areas today the most common type of property scam involves speculators with some political clout – such as Gurbachan from the YAD – investing in disputed properties. Here fraud is not as obvious, but muscle power and political connections are indispensable. Speculators buy disputed properties for a third of their value, sort out the dispute with the help of money and/or force, and then sell them off for their full value. Disputes most commonly arise when a tenant who has proof of long-term residence at a property refuses to pay rent and/ or vacate it. Because of laws protecting tenants it is difficult and in some cases even impossible to evict them. For this reason many owners try to prevent their tenants from accumulating proof of long-term residence, and many owners even try to keep their tenants' electricity and water bills in their own names. In Chandigarh, the state capital, as throughout much of Punjab, many property owners would rather leave their properties vacant than lease them out. Moreover, the issue has gained political salience because many wealthy non-resident Indians (NRIs) who live abroad in the UK, Canada and Australia are unable to regain possession of properties captured by locals – often relatives – in their absence.

The reason why investors in disputed property need some political clout is to be able to evict the people occupying the disputed properties they purchase. While some may accept money to vacate, many others do not. In these cases disputed property speculators need to use force, and for this it appears that some degree of complicity from the police, and the administration more generally, is required. Gurbachan of the YAD appears to have this necessary support. Lawyers in the sub-divisional court complex tell me that while Gurbachan has a couple of cases against him dating from his student days, he had no cases registered against him during the Akali Dal's tenure in government; he had the full protection of senior politicians in the party. In his lounge I saw pictures of him with very high-ranking leaders – who his relatives tell me call him on a regular basis – and with the local MLA and Minister, whom he regularly meets. Among the reasons why Gurbachan had political support were that he helped mobilise crowds for SAD rallies, he intimidated and harassed regime opponents and he captured ballot booths during local elections.

Rural land grabs

In many of the above cases, politicians and their intermediaries and cronies were principally involved in land grabs for financial gain. The logic of these land grabs was that of capital. However in the case of village common lands, politicians facilitated small-scale land grabbing principally for electoral gain. The logic of these land grabs was therefore closer to that of political society: the sphere in which, according to Chatterjee, resistance to capital and to primitive accumulation takes place.

The issue of control over village common lands needs to be understood within a rural context where politically-connected farmers, often associated with the state government, controlled village politics and were able to appropriate the greater bulk of government resources—including common lands—in their villages (see Martin 2015). They often did so at the expense of their village rivals aligned with opposition parties but also at the expense of the Dalits (or Scheduled Castes – SCs). As a result, control over village common lands was a highly divisive issue. And if political society and patronage benefitted anyone in this context it wasn't the Dalits, those who formed the most disadvantaged sector of Punjab society.

Despite their rising independence and assertiveness, members of the SCs still do not wield significant power at state or village level in Punjab. SCs may have become less submissive and they may be flocking away from Jat-dominated Sikh institutions and to *deras*;[1] they may be pressing for a greater share of government resources (Jodhka and Prakash 2003) and they may be avoiding agricultural work under the command of exacting, dominant-caste Jat farmers (Gupta 2005). Yet my observations suggest that because they remain politically dependent on the dominant-caste Jats who control *panchayats* (village councils) they continue to be deprived of a wide variety of government entitlements.

Most notably, politically connected Jats continue to control village common lands and also land that should technically be managed by Dalit cooperatives. The latter is known as *Nazool* land: land that once belonged predominantly to Muslim evacuees who left for Pakistan at partition and which was meant to be handed over to Dalit cooperatives. Jat-caste farmers often illegally occupy Nazool land. Farmers with political connections – usually in the ruling party – have likewise captured the larger share of *shamlaat zameen* (village common land), including the share of it reserved for Dalits. Village common land belongs to villages as a whole, and village *panchayats* are meant to lease it out to the highest bidder in open auctions and on a rotational yearly basis. Decades ago, this land used to be used for grazing livestock. However, the growing demand for agricultural land has meant that it has gradually been turned over to growing Punjab's staple crops: wheat and rice. The landless have, in the process, been deprived of land to graze their livestock, and fewer now own livestock (see Jodhka 2014).

Some villages have almost no common land, but others can have hundreds of acres of it. The money generated from the lease of this land is meant to go to *panchayats* to be used for village development projects. Villages with lots of common land should in theory generate significant income from it. A village with 200 acres should, for example, be able to generate up to INR 8 million per year. Furthermore, one-third of village common land is reserved for Dalits. This should in theory allow them to grow some cash crops or fodder for cattle. It should also provide them with opportunities to gather firewood, and also – if farmers deny them access to their fields – with a place to go to the toilet.

In practice however village common lands have tended to generate little income for villages, and both ordinary farmers and Dalits are routinely deprived of their rightful share in it. In some villages that I visited, village common land tended to generate little income because much of it was under the *kabza* (capture) of both rich and poor Jat farmers. In some cases the land had been under the *kabza* of a single family for decades and generated no income for villages at all. Such families felt entitled to the land because they had worked hard to improve it: levelling sand dunes, clearing scrub forest, and investing in tube wells for irrigation. In other cases it generated little village income because politically influential farmers were paying far below market prices to lease the land. I found that in a number of villages people were paying no more than INR 8,000 per acre annually while prices for the lease of irrigated agricultural land in Malwa had reached an unprecedented INR 40,000. Moreover I found out that a black market in village common land had developed in at least one village. Village common land was being traded but at rates far below the market rate for private agricultural land since it was not possible to obtain legal ownership over it.

It was often the case that *panchayats*, in collusion with *panchayat* secretaries and senior politicians, failed to hold the stipulated *kulli boli* (open auctions) for the lease of village common lands. *Sarpanches* and their allies were able to encroach upon village common lands by holding these 'auctions' in the privacy of their homes without publicly notifying villagers. In practice this meant that only *Sarpanches* and their supporters were given the chance to make a bid. Dalits, but also farmers from rival political factions often found that they were denied the opportunity to lease village land. Senior politicians were often complicit to the extent that they failed to take administrative measures to redress the situation, particularly when it benefitted loyal party workers and supporters. As will be illustrated below, they also sometimes actively tried to prevent encroachers from being evicted.

In order to get around the provision that a third of the land was reserved for Dalits, *Sarpanches* used dummy candidates to make their bids. The dummies were often their own farm servants. Thus, on paper the land was allotted to a Dalit, but in practice it was that Dalit's master who actually cultivated the land.[2] Dalits did not always protest because they did not have the tools to farm with and because *panchayats* had failed to equip village lands with tube wells. This meant that only farmers who owned tube wells on land adjacent to particular plots of village common land could actually cultivate it. During my fieldwork, Dalits in some villages that I visited blamed the government for failing to provide them with the equipment necessary to farm, and for failing to invest in tube wells that would allow them to irrigate plots of village land.

During fieldwork in 2013–4 many *Sarpanches* were involved in lengthy court cases aiming to clear village common lands of encroachers. The ostensible aim of this legal procedure was to boost village revenues. The government had an interest in the process too, because roughly a third of the income generated was to go into state coffers. These cases were highly contested. The left-leaning Dakonda farmers' union, for example, strongly opposed this clearance because it risked depriving farmers of land that they had improved and cultivated for decades – some since Independence. It also opposed clearing village common lands of encroachers on the grounds that the rule of the market would dramatically raise the price for leasing village common land and would put it beyond the reach of ordinary small farmers who could barely make a living. Village-level Dakonda Union leaders also alleged that the government was making way for corporate agriculture, although the extent to which this was the case was unclear. Pointing to a perhaps more immediate threat, they asserted that the policy did not necessarily do away with the malpractices associated with village common land and that it was frequently implemented in ways that harmed the interests of those in the political opposition. The following three cases illustrate some of these dynamics, and also how politicians often protected some encroachers at the expense of others and thus ultimately hampered the emergence of a workable joint solution to the issue of control over village common lands.

Case I: Daroli

The case of Daroli illustrates how the issue of control over village common lands was a source of conflict and acrimony, and also demonstrates the role of politicians in exacerbating these conflicts and acrimonies. It illustrates how politicians, with their ad hoc interventions, could fail to effectively protect people from dispossession.

In this village, Kuldip Singh Kombhoz initiated the process of clearing village common land of encroachers when he was *Sarpanch* from 2008–13. He claimed to want to improve the 60 acres of common land in order to increase village revenues for development. However, his detractors claimed that he merely wanted to evict his political rivals from the land and redistribute it to his supporters. A local newspaper even reported that Kuldip had cleared village common lands of encroachers merely to replace them with his friends, relatives and supporters. He denied this, claiming that the newspaper in question had fabricated the story. They had purportedly blackmailed him by telling them that unless he paid them some money they would fabricate a negative story about him. Whatever the case may be, he was able to evict the encroachers who had taken hold of 36 acres of village common land in 2012. He was proud of his achievement, and claimed that thanks to his efforts the village had earned INR 1.2 million from its lands.

His policy had, however, proven to be highly divisive and in 2014 villagers were reluctant to place any bids on village common land, because doing so risked antagonising those who had traditionally cultivated particular plots of land but who had been evicted. The Dakonda Kisan Union had become involved on behalf of the farmers and its members had clashed with the police when the latter had come to remove the farmers from the land they were occupying.

Kuldip Singh claimed that the Minister for *Panchayats* and Rural Development had initially supported his initiative, but when the minister had seen that it might cost him party votes he had not only backtracked but also turned against him. He claimed that the minister had first started supporting the farmers by helping them obtain court stays that allowed some of them to remain in possession of the land for an extra year. He also claimed that the minister was in all likelihood responsible for the fact that the construction of an electrical line through the village common lands had been halted. Without electricity he would not be able to install tube wells on the land and village revenues from village common lands would not rise. This, he explained, served the interests of the farmers because they would be able to continue renting village common lands at the lower rate for unirrigated land. He also claimed that the minister had once told the farmers that if he – Kuldip – continued to insist on the issue that they would give him a good beating. The minister had apparently said this during one of his meetings with his constituents at his mansion outside Patiala. Kuldip even claimed that the minister had encouraged the farmers to fabricate a case against him and supported them in the endeavour. So he was taken to court for allegedly building a part of his house on village common land. The case was spurious, and it failed, but it worsened village level animosities.

Balvinder Singh, the owner of four acres of land, confirmed that the minister had supported the 'encroaching' farmers, and helped some of them obtain temporary stay orders from the court. He and his parents and grandparents before him had cultivated five acres of village common. His grandfather had cleared the land of *tibbas* (sandy hillocks) and made the land cultivable. The land was irrigated with water from a polluted river that ran past the village, but he claimed that the dirt in the water meant that he did not have to use much fertiliser to obtain good crops. He rejected Kuldip's claim to the effect that he was an encroacher. He said that he had always paid to cultivate the land but that he could not provide full proof of this because Kuldip, while he was *Sarpanch*, had never provided him with receipts for his payments. He had relatives who were close to the minister; they had got the minster somehow to intervene in the court case on his behalf, and he had obtained a stay order. However the minister's intervention was merely ad hoc and temporary and he was eventually forced to vacate the land and forgo half of his income.

The issue of village common land polarised the village, and those who didn't want to get embroiled in the conflict were reluctant to place their bids on land that others had improved and cultivated all their lives. The current *Sarpanch* was an SC who had obtained the post because it was reserved. He told me that he did not want to get involved in this contentious issue, and that as a Chamar he could not afford to antagonise anyone. It was a highly contentious issue because people's incomes – and some people's very subsistence – depended upon the village common land that they had encroached upon. One Jat whom we interviewed told me that the politicking of village leaders had ruined him. He had cultivated some 10 acres of village common land his entire life and now because of Kuldip he had almost nothing left. However, he also blamed the ruling Akali Dal for letting it happen and claimed that the minister's efforts to help them obtain a stay order were not particularly helpful: that he had made a token gesture out of political expediency. The Jat owned only one and a half acres, which was not enough to live from. On top of that he was unable to work due to back problems and did not know how he would make a living.

Case II: Tullewal

The case of Tullewal likewise illustrates how the most senior local Akali politician ended up supporting encroachers because he feared the political fallout that would result from evicting those illegally encroaching upon village common lands. Again, however, he ended up supporting one faction at the expense of another and thus contributed to further dividing the village into two irreconcilable camps. As in Daroli, he exacerbated village factional rivalries and thereby contributed to preventing villagers from finding a joint solution regarding the control and use of village common lands.

Harpal, the village *Sarpanch* until 2013, had initiated a judicial process against encroachers and had managed to clear some 56 (of roughly 90 total) acres of village common land. He had also managed to obtain six tube wells from the government to irrigate some of it. The process had, Harpal claimed, been expedited by the Minister of Agriculture and Rural Development. Harpal's chief village rivals, Malvinder and his supporters, had allegedly placed spurious corruption cases against him in response, because his actions threatened them. Malvinder had captured four acres of village common land and Sukhvinder – an ally and farmer union leader – had allegedly captured 13 acres. Despite his efforts however, Harpal was not able to have either evicted because the minister had prevented the police from doing so despite court orders. He claimed that the minister was 'playing politics' because he feared that by evicting them he would lose votes. He had become 'frightened' when he had seen that the farmers' union had gathered a large number of people in protest; he worried that it would cost him not only the support of the Tullewal villagers but also that of the broader public, because news of the protests had come out in the newspapers.

Partly as a result of all the unrest caused by the clearing of the village common lands, Harpal lost the 2013 *panchayat* elections to Malvinder, his chief rival. Harpal had been very close to the minister, and he had many pictures to prove it, but the relationship had somewhat soured after the minister had started supporting the encroachers. Later, after Harpal had lost the 2013 elections, the minister started collaborating with Malvinder – and was doing so even though Malvinder was not a loyal Akali. He did so, according to Harpal, because that was allegedly the way of politicians: they knew no loyalties, and all they cared about were votes. Harpal, and five others who were there on one of the occasions when I interviewed him, told me that Malvinder had held the latest auction for village common land in the secrecy of his home. He said that Malvinder had bribed the Block Development Officer in order to do so, and that he had the support of the local Akali Minister. As a result, none of those present had been given the chance to place their bids and obtain some land. On the other hand, Malvinder and his friends had all obtained land and had secretly agreed to ensure that the leasing price for any plot should not rise above INR 20,000. Harpal complained that the *panchayat* should in reality be obtaining over INR 35,000 per acre for that land because almost all of it was now irrigated with the tube wells he had obtained from the government. Sukhvinder, one of Malvinder's allies, seemed to give this latter claim some credence when he told me that he was paying INR 22,000 per acre. Moreover, Harpal claimed that Malvinder was technically banned from renting village common land because he was a defaulter: he had, over several years, failed to pay a single cent for the four acres of village common land that he had cultivated. In order to circumvent this hurdle, Malvinder had entered the name of his Dalit farm servant as the new tenant for that land.

Sukhvinder and Malvinder obviously had an entirely different perspective on the issue. Both accused Harpal of initiating the clearance of village common lands through the courts – not because he was interested in augmenting village revenues but rather because he bore a grudge against them as a result of their longstanding political rivalry at village level. They also suggested that if he was interested in increasing village revenues it was merely in order to be able to steal more from the *panchayat*. Malvinder accused Harpal of gross corruption, and had placed a case against him for embezzling over INR 400,000 during the construction of a stretch of road and some associated drains. Malvinder said that Harpal had stolen far more than that during his tenure but that he did not have the evidence necessary to take him to court for all of the corruption cases. The case against Harpal was successful at the *tehsil* level, and he was ordered to pay a INR 355,000 fine. But Harpal subsequently placed an appeal and was eventually exonerated.

Case III: Fatehpur

The case of Fatehpur likewise illustrates the socially divisive nature of political interventions in the issue of village common lands, and most clearly illustrates the extent to which the complicity of politicians could benefit the few at the expense of the rest. The case is different to those of Daroli and Tullewal to the extent that in Fatehpur the clearance of village common lands was complete by the time I finished fieldwork in 2014. As a result of the implementation of public auctions, village common lands had become subject to market values and leasing them had become more expensive. This, as the Dakonda farmers' union leaders had feared, meant that poorer farmers ceased to be able to lease village common land.

Legal disputes for control over village common land in Fatehpur started in 1986 when Nirmal Singh took Khem Singh to court for capturing 86 of a total of 180 acres of village common land. Both Khem Singh's rivals and his supporters told me that Khem Singh's family had controlled that land for several decades thanks to their political connections, and had worked to improve it. Khem Singh and his two brothers only owned four acres of land, and it was widely agreed that they had been able to build a large house with all the modern domestic appliances and to purchase two new four-wheel drive cars and also a new tractor thanks to their control over those 86 acres of village common land.

Khem Singh had been involved in court cases against Nirmal Singh and other rivals over this land for over three decades. Nirmal Singh, and a friend of his, eventually landed in jail for the murder of a woman who he had purchased some land from. His successor as faction leader, Naib Singh, alleged that Nirmal Singh was innocent and that it was Khem Singh who had set him up with the help of his police and political contacts. Despite the court cases against him, Khem Singh's family had been able to continue cultivating at least some of the village common land and in 2013 he and others told me that he was renting 30 acres at INR 20,000 per acre.

Aligned with the ruling SAD, Khem Singh won the 2013 local elections. The previous *Sarpanch* had been a Dalit Mazhbi Sikh – aligned with the Congress party and with the Nirmal Singh faction in the village – who had not been able to complete his term because Khem Singh who had close relations with the local Akali leader had had him suspended. The Dalit *Sarpanch* had apparently performed the auction for the village common land in the privacy of an allied Jat farmer's home without advising anyone but his own allies, and on a Sunday when none of the concerned block-level officials could attend. This blatant and blundering act – in the words of his own allies – got him suspended, and Khem Singh finished his term for him before going on to win the 2013 local elections. While not entirely denying that there had been irregularities in that auction, one member of Nirmal Singh's faction said that the only reason why the *Sarpanch* was suspended was that he and his supporters were affiliated with the Congress party at the time of an Akali government. He claimed that there was always some 'little irregularity' in village common land auctions, but that the Akalis only turned it into an issue when it was members of the opposition who were responsible for these irregularities.

Once in power, Khem Singh was said to have performed village common land auctions according to the rules, and everyone who wanted to had managed to place their bids, but the cost of renting village common land shot up dramatically. One of Khem Singh's supporters, an impoverished Jat who collected and sold milk, told me that he used to rent three acres of village common land but that he could no longer afford to do so. He had rented the land at INR 10,000 per acre, but the price had shot up to INR 45,000. Naib Singh cited the same numbers and told me that although he still cultivated village common land it had become too risky for him to continue to do so. If crops failed for some reason, he would make a loss. Various people told me that the rental price had risen so much that only the richest farmers could now cultivate village common land. One person told me that roughly since 2012, only 20 people cultivated village common land: all of them wealthy farmers. Prior to 2012, however, over 40 people had cultivated it. Nevertheless, Khem Singh paid only INR 20,000 per acre while everyone else was paying INR 40–45,000 per acre. One of his supporters said that the reason for this was that the land in question did not have any tube wells on it. However, Naib Singh told me that the land did not have any tube wells because Khem Singh had intentionally avoided placing any on that particular area of land in order to be able to lease it at half the rate. But in fact, the land was irrigated because Khem Singh possessed two tube wells on his own four adjacent acres, and used them to irrigate those 30 acres. One person even alleged that Khem Singh was, in fact, not paying any rent at all for 10 of those 30 acres, but there was – as with many of these allegations – no way for me to confirm this.

Some people also had mixed views about what Khem Singh had done with the money that was flowing into the *panchayat's* coffers. The village was earning roughly INR 4.5 million from its village common lands, and Khem Singh had used this money to fix all the village gutters and pave its alleyways with cement bricks. However, many of his Congress party opponents alleged that he was appropriating a share of the new revenue stream. They believed that even more works could have been carried out in that village with those revenues and that Khem Singh was undoubtedly taking a share. They claimed, however, that it was difficult for them to confirm their suspicions because Khem Singh kept the village *panchayat* records in his home. Local government regulations stipulate that these records should be freely available for public scrutiny; in practice *Sarpanches* tend to keep them in the secrecy of their homes. Moreover, they claimed that no one was willing to place a Right to Information (RTI) request because people believed it would be futile and potentially dangerous. Futile because the Akali government would botch any investigation against a party loyalist; dangerous because the Akali government might help Khem Singh place fabricated and spurious police charges against those seeking to investigate him (see Martin 2015, 2018).

Last but not least, there was further cause for acrimony because Khem Singh had allotted some village common land for subsidised government housing plots. This had given rise to yet another legal dispute because the land granted was almost entirely cultivated by Khem Singh's opponents. These opponents alleged that Khem Singh had purposefully sought to harm their interests. They told me that they had proposed an alternative, 'better place' for those plots, but that Khem had insisted on putting them on land that they cultivated. In 2014, the plots were already demarcated and 11 persons had moved in and built houses. However, many people – mostly landless Dalits – were hesitant to move in and build their houses, saying that the legal dispute about the placement of those plots meant that their legal status was unclear. Those who had already moved in told me that they had not yet been granted land titles, and that without land titles they could not hook up to the electricity supply. Moreover, they complained that they could not defecate in adjacent fields because those fields belonged to the very Jats who had issued the legal challenge against those five *marla* plots.[3] One Chamar woman told me that the Jats had hurled abuse at her and threatened to beat her and her husband up if they ever dared make use of their fields again.

Conclusions

The first thing to emerge from these case studies is that political society may protect some people from the expansion of capital, but not all. The context described is one in which politicians bend and break the law, often – but not always – for members of an already comparatively privileged class. Many of those for whom they bend, break or simply fail to ensure the application of the law are even very privileged. In this process, the most disadvantaged – namely the Dalits – have been and continue to be deprived of their lawful share of village common land. The argument could nevertheless be made that these case studies illustrate how the operations of political society do, nevertheless, put the brakes on processes of accumulation by dispossession. Besides large-scale farmers, a number of smaller farmers were seemingly able to sustain their livelihoods thanks to the fact that politicians didn't press the administration to apply the law and evict encroachers.

As members of the Dakonda farmer's union warned, and as villagers in Khanpur confirmed, allowing open and market-based auctions for village common lands placed village common lands beyond the reach of all except the richest farmers. In other words, allowing the market to rule would contribute to the gradual expansion of capital and to the dispossession of petty capitalists.

The above case studies certainly suggest that there is some truth to the idea that the ad hoc arrangements of political society put a break on dispossession. However because of the frequently partisan nature of how this is done, it is a divisive practice that prevents farmers from getting together to find a solution to the issue of village common lands. In all of the three cases above, political interventions had benefitted one faction at the expense of another, and had contributed to exacerbating existing rivalries.

As I have argued elsewhere (Martin 2018), the Akali Dal governed in a highly partisan manner. It protected supporters, regardless of whether or not they were corrupt, and it harassed political opponents on the basis of both real and fabricated corruption charges and allegations. Thus in the case of Tullewal described above, the minister allegedly intervened on Harpal's behalf to help him escape corruption charges. As already noted in the first section, accusations to the effect that the government supported its corrupt intermediaries were common. Gurbachan – the YAD thug and *Sarpanch* discussed above – was, for example, widely believed to have full police cover for his activities. This became crystal clear to me when I saw him capture a polling booth in full view of the police during the 2013 local elections. The police did nothing as he and his comrades barred Congress supporters' entry into the polling station and then attacked them with sticks, swords and stones.

Other cases were perhaps less clear but accusations at the very least point to the fact that people believed that Akalis had impunity. In Fatehpur, for example, people believed that it would be futile to investigate Khem Singh for corruption because the administration would not be responsive. Some even feared physical harassment at the hands of either thugs or the police. When on the other hand people were opposed to the minister or to his party, they were harassed. In Gurbachan's village, Congress party opponents who tried to resist Gurbachan's capture of the polling booth ended up facing attempted murder charges. In Daroli, when Kuldip obstinately pursued the clearing of village common lands, the minister allegedly helped manufacture a spurious case against him.

As I have argued elsewhere (Martin 2018) such partisan political interventions in village affairs exacerbated village-level disputes and animosities. These interventions had the effect of fuelling and escalating disputes that may not have otherwise flared up. Everywhere, people told me that it was politicians and political parties that caused people to fight, and that made village life unbearable. An opposition Congress party worker put it this way:

> Politicians don't resolve disputes; they aggravate them. If someone asks me to help resolve some dispute, I'll approach the opposing party and try to engineer a *samjhota* (compromise). An Akali party worker will, on the other hand, use his power to get the police to bring charges against the opposing party and, as a consequence, the parties will never speak to each other again.

What consequence did political meddling have for farmers' prospects of finding a workable solution to the issue of control over village common lands? In this context, the effect of the ad hoc political meddling – characteristic of political society – was to keep farmers fighting each other and trying to kick each other off village common lands, not to ensure that all of their livelihoods were shielded from the expansion of capital. Lack of unity meant that – in the end – farmers were sometimes unable to resist the clearing of village common lands. The process had been completed in Khanpur and the Akali minister's attempts to obtain a stay order and to stop the police from evicting encroachers in Daroli was merely a stopgap measure.

Finally, I would like to suggest that there is a sense in which these ad hoc measures to facilitate illegal encroachment were in fact ultimately exploitative. Both politicians and *Sarpanches* could exploit the legal uncertainty of these arrangements for electoral gain. The case of the five *marla* housing plots in Fatehpur clearly illustrates how this worked, and how the precariousness of extra-legal arrangements could serve to create semi-captive vote-banks. Khem Singh had granted people land over which there was a legal dispute, meaning that the possibility of putting those plots in their name was uncertain. Members of the opposition Congress party faction had mounted a legal challenge to keep control of that particular area of village common land because they had been cultivating it for decades. A number of villagers asserted that Khem Singh – in collusion with the MLA – had purposely put the prospective plot owners in this precarious position, claiming that if he had given them secure land titles he would have had no guarantee that they would vote for him the next time round. As it was, however, Khem Singh could claim that it was his opponents who were preventing the SCs from getting the housing plots, and that their only chance to secure their property titles was by rallying behind him.

A similar dynamic seemed to underwrite the capture of village common lands. People aligned with the local Akali minister and his local allies were more likely to be able to continue illegally controlling and cultivating village common lands than were members of the political opposition. The latter were the ones most frequently evicted from village common lands while those with government support seemed able to maintain their grip on village common lands even when they paid little or nothing to cultivate them.

However, their hold over that land was contingent upon the continued good will of Akali politicians and upon the latter's willingness to prevent the Ministry of Panchayats from taking action against them, and even upon Akali politicians' willingness to hold the police back when courts had ordered their eviction. Were they to suddenly start opposing the SAD by joining – for example – the Congress party, their semi-legal hold over village common lands would likely be subject to sudden legal scrutiny. In other words, the legal precariousness that is an intrinsic part of informal arrangements in political society allowed politicians to hold citizens to account for their political loyalties and even arguably for their electoral choices.

So even if politicians did sometimes help to put a temporary brake on accumulation by dispossession through ad hoc and clientelistic favours, they were at least partly responsible for the lack of an adequate solution to the problem of village common lands. Ultimately however it is important to keep in mind that they were crucial parties to processes of accumulation by dispossession. The literature on land grabs cited above shows that in Punjab – as in other states in India – it is politicians who are brokering land deals for local and international corporations. This is particularly true in the context of post-liberalisation India, where – as Kanchan Chandra (2015) has argued – state-level political corruption revolves around brokering land deals for big money. As indicated at the outset, it is also often politicians themselves who are involved in acquiring land – through occasionally dubious means – for their own purposes.

Notes

1. Frequently non-denominational religious institutions centred around holy men.
2. This, and the capture of *Nazool* land, led to the emergence in 2013 of a movement called 'Zameen Prapti Sangarsh Committee' in the district of Sangrur. The movement seeks to ensure that Dalits obtain their rightful share of village common land and that *Nazool* land is handed back to them. More ambitiously, the movement also hopes to reduce the ceiling on landownership to 10 acres.
3. One *marla* is roughly the equivalent of 25 square metres, but *marlas* have been defined differently in different periods and regions of the subcontinent.

References

Adnan, S. 2013. 'Land Grabs and Primitive Accumulation in Deltaic Bangladesh: Interactions between Neoliberal Globalization, State Interventions, Power Relations and Peasant Resistance', *The Journal of Peasant Studies* 40(1): 87–128.

Baviskar, A. 2011. 'Cows, Cars and Cycle-rickshaws: Bourgeois Environmentalists and the Battle for Delhi's Streets'. In *Elite and Everyman: The Cultural Politics of the Indian Middle Classes*, edited by A. Baviskar and R. Ray, 391–418. London and New Delhi: Routledge.

Chandra, K. 2015. 'The New Indian State: The Relocation of Patronage in the Post-Liberalisation Economy', *Economic and Political Weekly* 50(41): 46–58.

Chatterjee, P. 2008. 'Democracy and Economic Transformation in India', *Economic and Political Weekly* 43(16): 53–62.

Cross, J. 2014. *Dream Zones: Anticipating Capitalism and Development in India*. London: Pluto Press.

De Neve, G. 2015. 'Predatory Property: Urban Land Acquisition, Housing and Class Formation in Tiruppur, South India', *Journal of South Asian Development* 10(3): 345–68.

Gupta, D. 2005. 'Whither the Indian Village: Culture and Agriculture in "Rural" India', *Economic and Political Weekly* 40(8): 751–8.

Harvey, D. 2004. 'The "New Imperialism": Accumulation by Dispossession', *Actuel Marx* 1: 71–90.

Jodhka, S.S. 2014. 'Emergent Ruralities: Revisiting Village Life and Agrarian Change in Haryana', *Economic and Political Weekly* 49(26–7): 5–17.

Jodhka, S.S. and L. Prakash. 2003. 'Caste Tensions in Punjab: Talhan and Beyond', *Economic and Political Weekly* 38(28): 2923–6.

Levien, M. 2011. 'Special Economic Zones and Accumulation by Dispossession in India', *Journal of Agrarian Change* 11(4): 454–83.

Martin, N. 2014. 'The Dark Side of Political Society: Patronage and the Reproduction of Social Inequality', *Journal of Agrarian Change* 14(3): 419–34.

Martin, N. 2015. 'Rural Elites and the Limits of Scheduled Caste Assertiveness in Rural Malwa, Punjab', *Economic and Political Weekly* 50(52): 37–44.

Martin, N. 2018. 'Corruption and Factionalism in Contemporary Punjab: An Ethnographic Account from Rural Malwa', *Modern Asian Studies* 52(3): 942–70.

Sampat, P. 2010. 'Special Economic Zones in India: Reconfiguring Displacement in a Neoliberal Order?' *City and Society* 22(2): 166–82.

Sehgal, M. 2014. 'Den of Drugs: How Punjab Politicos are Linked to Rs 700-crore Drug Racket', *India Today*, January 12. https://www.indiatoday.in/india/north/story/punjab-politicians-in-dock-for-alleged-connections-to-drug-lords-176476-2014-01-12 (accessed 14 May 2019).

Springer, S. 2013. 'Violent Accumulation: A Postanarchist Critique of Property, Dispossession, and the State of Exception in Neoliberalizing Cambodia', *Annals of the Association of American Geographers* 103(3): 608–26.

Vasudeva, R. 2016. 'Hoshiarpur land scam: Politically connected dealers bought land at throwaway prices', *Hindustan Times*, 18 June. https://www.hindustantimes.com/punjab/hoshiarpur-land-scam-politically-connected-dealers-bought-land-at-throwaway-prices/story-Dww0uUe4UeUIC0y8lP8tFI.html.

Wade, R. 1985. 'The Market for Public Office: Why the Indian State Is Not Better at Development', *World Development* 13(4): 467–97.

Whitehead, J. 2008. 'Rent Gaps, Revanchism and Regimes of Accumulation in Mumbai', *Anthropologica* 50(2): 269–82.

10

The politics of contracting in provincial Bangladesh

Arild Engelsen Ruud

This chapter explores Wild East forms of criminal economies by investigating tender and contracting processes and the roles of the media in contemporary provincial Bangladesh. Here, the 'mafia' is described as a syndicate of mas-tans (enforcers) that work in collaboration with local politicians and police. This mafia syndicate controls certain local resources: milk, sand, shrimp farming, real estate, bus routes, infrastructural contracting and a host of other business opportunities. In Barisal an extractive system that feeds off government budgets is revealed. The chapter confirms the complexity of legal and formal procedures that surrounds local criminal political economies. Without law, crime does not pay. The complex contract and tender system that is uncovered is marked by rules and counter-rules whose manipulation helps to cover, hide and camouflage illegal activity.

Introduction

This chapter explores the elaborate system of mutuality, services and networking that helps to extract funds from the local state in provincial Bangladesh. While factories and industry are the main vehicles for money generation and rent-seeking in the capital and in the textile hubs of the country, in the provinces it is the local state and its financing of local infrastructure that performs this role. In this system contractors and contracting play a vital role in the networks and operations that centre on the major politicians in the region.

One of the main drivers behind this system is the cost of everyday politics and election campaigns. There is no legitimate source of funding, and yet the demand is huge. As a university professor who was running for parliament in a district just north of Dhaka explained in some detail:

> In this constituency the population is four *lakhs*. We have more than 200 villages, hamlets and markets that need to be covered, and then the town. In each village or neighbourhood I need a group of activists. They need material, a stall, tea and food, money for their mobiles, money for petrol, then the mikes and the platforms, and the activists need rented offices. I need to travel to each campaign stall, and to Dhaka, I travel with my advisors and my protection. And buses for big meetings [to transport the audience].

He then went on to explain that if his rival has *mastans* (goons) he would need some too. A little later in the conversation he hinted that he was prepared and had an armed group of some 20 to 25 *mastans*. In addition to the various running costs he mentioned, there was the election campaign itself. A campaign will consist of speeches in front of as large an audience as possible: as large as the local activists have managed to mobilise. Then there are the walkabouts, shaking hands with as many people as can be reached. But behind the stage, and just as important, is the reputation that you as a candidate create through lending your assistance to anyone requesting it. Individuals or representatives will ask for your intervention: the owner of a small private school needs an official certificate; the local shop-owner association has a problem with a band of criminals; a group of villages has been asking for a better road for years – and on it goes. As a prospective MP seeking votes and support, you need to convince everyone that you have the contacts and the means to solve such problems. To be successful in politics, you need not only money but connections too. My interlocutor continued:

> I don't have money. I am a university professor. So how will I get money? I get money because people help me. Business people. They give me a car to use, money for petrol, they organise buses, someone gives me one lakh, someone else two lakhs. And someone ten lakhs. And if I am threatened, my toughs will show my power. With all of this, I show off how efficient and useful I will be. (Interview, Narsingdi town, September 2006)

Money is necessary in politics, both to run a campaign and to operate in a way that will satisfy your extensive network of allies, the goons and so on that you must hire for intimidation and protection – and to ensure you are re-elected. As Jha has pointed out (see the Introduction to this volume), the absence of public funding for political parties in India has created a situation whereby illegal money is procured through backroom deals. The situation is no different in Bangladesh (Jahan and Amundsen 2012; Amundsen 2012; Chowdhury 2013). The university professor running for office had been involved with his party for many years and knew what he was getting into. He hinted at the web of debts that he was accruing and that would need to be repaid later: 'They are businessmen. They invest', he said. In addition, goons are required in local politics, to fight off your opponents' goons but also to intimidate the recalcitrant business owner who will not pay, and to protect those who will.

This web of debts is a straightforward intermeshing of politics and business. Another way that business and politics join hands is in the convenience of business for people in politics. A business operation helps finance their political engagement. 'As a politician', a former student leader turned businessman explained, 'you depend on people who perform tasks for you – your henchmen, your *mastans*, your associates, the corruptible police officer who has arrested one of your men'. To feed the constant need for more money, the easiest and most legitimate way to obtain funds is to have a business operation. A business operation may generate money, but even if it does not it allows you to hide a variety of incomes or mask illicit transactions as business deals. Moreover, the relationship between politics and business also works the other way around. A student leader-turned-businessman explained that 'As a businessman, you will need to be involved in politics because you will need protection, you will need contacts in the right offices, and you will need influence over government decisions – such as permits. So, you need to be involved in politics.' This need to be involved indicates a deeper engagement, an entanglement (*intreccio*; see the Introduction to this volume). We will return to this a little later. For now we note that this close collusion of business and politics is not a marginal phenomenon in Bangladesh. Four of every five MPs in the 2014 parliament described themselves as 'businessmen' (Liton 2015). The number rose from 63 per cent in the preceding parliament and 51 per cent in the 2001 parliament.

This chapter is about the nexus of money and politics in Bangladesh and draws material from Barisal, a provincial city in the south.[1] In this nexus more or less stable yet competing networks encompassing criminal gangs, local political elites, the local police, legitimate enterprises and businessmen (mostly contractors) and government officers have formed to usurp the flow of government funding. These are all 'men in the middle' in Nikita Sud's terminology, intermediaries performing different and necessary tasks for the whole (Sud 2014). In the specific business of contracting in provincial Bangladesh, the central character is the local politician and his network of intermediaries of various kinds. The system revolves around contracting for local government works, mainly construction works, but also involves 'items' such as permits and licences, and every so often a request to the police or government office to turn 'a blind eye' to certain aspects of a business operation. Increasingly, the system has also come to include the local media, which is more a political tool than a political watchdog. This chapter investigates these networks and how they enable this distribution of money and influence.

The collusion of muscle, money, activist politics and political party hold over the state machinery has combined to create a perpetual self-serving regime that benefits the local political and economic elites. In some ways the nexus of politics, criminals, bureaucrats and business forms a *pax mafiosa*. It is generally accepted that political power over the state apparatus, including the police, is solid in Bangladesh. The term 'partyar-chy' has been used to characterise the near monopoly of power that the ruling party enjoys (BRAC 2006). The collusion with business and criminals is less explored in the literature but hinted at in the proportion of MPs who identify themselves as businesspeople and, for instance, in the use of crime and violence as tools in student politics (see, for example, Andersen 2013; Ruud 2014; Klem and Suykens 2018). The nexus of politicians and businesspeople has clear similarities with what Varese (Varese 2011) calls 'mafia' – that particular situation in which a criminal and violent group enters into tacit agreements with members of the state. The killing of criminals and undesirables by the police would be typical of a *pax mafiosa* state and in Bangladesh the number of deaths caused by so-called 'crossfire' by police or RAB forces is high and heavily criticised (Human Rights Watch 2011). As the editors of this volume point out, criminal bands seeking profit in collusion with elected officials, the police or other members of the state can be found in much of 'middle' South Asia. Moreover, in South Asia, including Bangladesh, the term 'mafia' has come to denote business enterprises with political protection that monopolise certain trades through extra-legal means. In this sense a mafia is different from a pure criminal band. A South Asian mafia is a syndicate of *mastans* who work in collaboration with local politicians and police, and this syndicate controls certain local resources: milk, sand, shrimp farming, real estate, bus routes and a host of other business opportunities.

The term 'consociational mafia-owned democracy' (Armao 2015 coined for Latin America, Italy and other places is used to denote a regime based on cooperation between politicians, entrepreneurs and muscle. However, much of the literature on armed criminal enterprise has been developed using material from Latin America and largely portrays criminal gangs as autonomous actors who enter into deals with political actors. But in provincial Bangladesh muscle is not an independent force. Even a generation or so ago, in the violent and chaotic decades following the bloody and disruptive war of liberation in 1971, armed groups were only rarely autonomous. Most of these groups functioned as the armed wings of political parties or as extensions of the reach of individual local bosses (see, for example Jahan 2005; Ahmed 1984). Even in the democratic if conflictual 1990s and early 2000s, violent groups functioned as an appendix to politics – seeking protection as payment for performing services, all the while being allowed within limits to manage their own turf and income sources. Their patron-bosses (for the concept of bosses, see Michelutti et al. 2018) were almost invariably active players in the political field, and using armed gangs was subject to political calculation and manoeuvring (even if the hired gun often proved to be a loose cannon).

Thus, in many ways the situation in provincial Bangladesh is the reverse of Armao's 'mafia': instead of the criminals controlling part of the state for profit, it is the politicians controlling the *mastans* and the police – for profit and, above all, to continue in power. Other 'members' of these provincial politico-business syndicates are activists, contractors, bureaucrats and others. In short, the regional political economy is a clientelist state, where power is exercised through congeries of relations between businesspeople, politicians, criminals and the police. At the centre, the politician-bosses act as CEOs of multi-pronged business enterprises (Ruud and Islam 2016). In the clientelist state formation of provincial Bangladesh, a number of smaller and larger syndicates operate in competition with one another, each 'managed' by local leaders. In the local political landscape it is these political leaders who are the strongmen, the predatorial big fish, the bosses – referred to mostly as *neta* (leader), sometimes as 'godfather'.

In their struggle to build and maintain power, these bosses rely on associates, including contractors, criminals, bureaucrats, police officers and political activists. Each needs to be kept happy and prevented from jumping ship and joining a rival syndicate. In addition, the local political landscape is such that among the many rival syndicates are potential allies. These, too, need to be kept happy; in local political parlance, this is referred to as 'balancing'. This balancing resembles the informal governance system in Russia that Ledeneva calls *sistema* and that, in her words, is about personalised power networks that ensure the distribution of government largesse, privileges and kickbacks. *Sistema* is 'linked to patrimonial rule and traditional forms of governance' (Ledeneva 2013, 1136). Whereas Ledeneva's Russian *sistema* is a national system that centres on a crucial figure in the middle, the system in provincial Bangladesh is decentralised and elaborate. The party leader and Prime Minister may be powerful at the national level but in provincial cities the power radiating from Dhaka is not felt acutely. The local landscape does not feature any particular dominant figure that represents Dhaka, or one single dominant network. As noted above, the local political landscape consists of a range of political leaders, contractors, newspaper editors and bureaucrats who together form crisscrossing networks of mutual benefit and antagonism – balancing. Fissures within the 'PGP'[2] constitute central elements in this environment and create the conditions that make balancing possible and necessary.

The term 'balancing' is used in local political vocabulary to denote the intricate play of actors in these large, shifting networks. The English term is used to describe the efforts local leaders engage in to maintain or enhance their position through alliance building. This may entail allying with someone from a rival political wing or party, or compromising one's ideology orientation, reputation or even moral standing. The informal and behind-the-curtain negotiations take place in private, in the backroom, at one another's homes, on the phone or, in the case of Barisal, at the exclusive Barisal Club (see, for example, Piliavsky 2013). Balancing is a complex and continuous game at several levels. When in power, you can be inclusive and welcome rivals and potential allies, or exclusive to the extent that you rely much more on the local administration. But the local bureaucrats may be playing their own game and seek to influence your decisions with a view to life after you have fallen from power. Being involved is also risky, as any blemish on your reputation can be exploited later on by others – *netas* – in search of a favour or a media reporter in search of a story. Having a tarnished reputation is a mechanism central to the system, where a service received constitutes a debt. The exposure to legal vulnerability that involvement in deal-making entails is recreated into suspended punishment (Favarel-Garrigues 2011) by leaders who act as benevolent patrons. Legal vulnerability is essential to becoming an insider, while the suspended punishment ensures continued loyalty to the patron.

These large, elaborate and informal enterprises, these syndicates, have operations that are often illicit or straight-out illegal. Even close collaborators do not know all the different activities of the network or even who the other members of these informal networks may be. But they do not need to. What they need to know is that the CEO-*neta* can get the job done: ensure the contracts, the deals, the permits and the acquiescence.

This chapter is an investigation into politicians and contractors in provincial Bangladesh making deals to extract funds from the local state. Whereas the struggle over government resources 20 to 30 years back tended to be violent, it has increasingly turned into 'soft' crime, with violence as a lingering threat that has receded into the shadowy background where it is used sparingly and is largely managed by the police forces. This chapter suggests a shifting focus from violent crimes to soft crimes, i.e. the criminal life of legal commodities – here, the allocation of government contracting works. This was made possible by the country's significant economic growth as well as the official and World Bank-supported decentralisation policy over the last three decades. More and more money was available locally from the central government's allocations and from international development agencies, and implementation relied on local administrative processes and local contractors. These new tools and opportunities changed the game. Politics became about money and positions from which to influence its flow.

Provincial Bangladesh: Barisal

The politicians and contractors portrayed in this chapter are all born and bred in Barisal and are part of the city's elite. In a city of some 400,000 inhabitants, these are the rich and powerful, including the city's mayor, MPs, major party leaders and business leaders, and often all of these rolled into one and the same person. These are the publicly known bosses. For example, when Kamal was mayor the municipal building displayed on its wall a huge poster of him, several metres tall, as a younger man. Now that the Awami League is in power, since 2014, posters featuring local strongman Hasnat pictured alongside the Prime Minister and the father of the nation, Mujibur Rahman, are ubiquitous.[3] Over the last few years photos of Sadek, Hasnat's son and possible heir, have also begun to appear, mainly in the streets around the central party office. When Hiron was mayor, his photo was everywhere, while BNP strongman leader Mojibur Rahman Sarwar's photo is on all BNP posters. Lesser figures do not appear on posters so often, with the exception of election posters. These main bosses are very public figures, even if they do not appear in person in public. Hasnat, in particular, is known to be reticent (and is the MP of a neighbouring constituency).

Less publicly known figures also belong to the elite and form part of the syndicates that feature below. They amass money through intimate contacts with decision-makers in government positions. Some of them are contractors, others business leaders; some are political activists and others are relatives. Provincial Bangladesh is the country's equivalent of 'Middle India' (see Harriss-White 2015). These are the provincial outskirts of the country's growing and increasingly globalised economy. Bangladesh has 16 to 18 provincial towns, each with a population of 2–700,000, and around which much of the countryside's economic life revolves. These provincial towns service a rural hinterland with their retail shops and bazaars, in addition to housing the district administration, sometimes a local university and usually the district hospital. Industrial output in these towns is generally very limited. They are also crucial to the country's political system as most members of parliament and the powerful district secretaries of the ruling party belong to the provincial rather than metropolitan parts of the country. Barisal, in the south of the country, is a good example of this kind of provincial town.[4] Its industrial sector is confined to a few textile mills and some metal production for local consumption, and, although the retail business is vast because the city services a large rural hinterland and coastal communities, this sector consists mostly of small businesses and shops. The turnover in this sector is limited, according to informants, as is profit. Beyond this the city has a moderate-sized port and also houses the administrative apparatus of the district and the division.[5]

It is the local government that constitutes the largest source of money for local entrepreneurs. Barisal City Corporation has a limited budget, and most of the money is tied in salaries and other fixed expenses. Tax revenue is also limited, so almost all of its budget comes from fixed state allocations. After salaries and other regular expenses are deducted there is practically no money left. Funds for any development work and most maintenance work have to be found outside the tax income and fixed state allocations. The most common sources for such funding are project funding from government ministries and departments, and some international development organisations (UN organisations, the Asian Development Bank, the Japan International Cooperation Agency (JICA), and others). These sources allocate funds mostly for individual projects such as sports stadiums, feeder roads, hostels and school buildings, street lighting, drainage, water supply pipes, municipal buildings, etc. In order to obtain funding, city corporations and municipalities apply to ministries or approach foreign donors with their plans. This application process involves outlining one's needs and an estimated budget, but it is very much a process that involves negotiations, networking and lobbying. The city mayors are involved, along with the councillors, the local MPs and other officials and political leaders. To be successful a city needs to exploit whatever contacts it has in the relevant ministries or departments. This lobbying is a significant part of the job for elected representatives at the various local levels and demands considerable skill. Local elected representatives spend much of their time in the capital. As a consequence, elected leaders are central to the money flow into provincial towns; securing funds is how local politicians show their worth. The next step is to find a contractor willing to take the job and help the politician finance his or her politics.

Tender politics and licences

A good entry point into the role of political leaders is the practice of allocating projects using tenders. There are aspects of the tender system for bidding for government jobs that have been designed to prevent cheating and ensure a fair process. There are two main kinds of tender calls: the open tender system and the direct tender system. The direct tender is for smaller jobs, often local jobs or for urgent works. 'When we learn that the Prime Minister will come in two weeks to some function, we must repair that road or paint this building', an official said. In such cases, there is no time for extensive tender calls and bids. The officer in charge will find a contractor or company they trust to be capable of doing the job satisfactorily and within the time available. To cite a typical example, a friend of mine was approached by a Medical Officer to obtain a particular kind of machinery for blood analysis for a government hospital. My friend, Manik-bhai,[6] had in his wide network an acquaintance who imported medical equipment and who could expedite the job. Manik-bhai himself also had a reputation for efficacy: 'It helps to know someone, to have a good reputation'. Typically, a Chief Medical Officer or a Chief Engineer can allocate jobs or purchases worth up to BDT 5 *lakh* and the contractor will be entitled to a certain percentage.[7]

The other type of tender, open tender, is used for larger works. There are rules for which jobs can be given directly and which jobs need to be advertised. Very large projects advertised as open tenders are increasingly announced online, as a result of Bangladesh's emphasis on e-governance. However, this is mostly the case in Dhaka or for very large projects on a national scale which would not be directed out of such a small place like Barisal. In provincial towns tenders are still on paper.

They are advertised in the local newspapers, the specifications are available on paper from government offices, and the submission of the tender must be put in a particular, physical box in a government office (or in some cases in one of several boxes).

There are many problems with these boxes, which is why donor agencies have insisted on e-governance. 'Tender politics' is a favourite source of income among party activists of the youth or student wings of the PGP. It consists of ensuring that only bids that are of interest can be submitted. The common practice is to place one's *mastans* in front of the office where the tender box is placed to prevent unwanted bidders from placing their bid. This is very common (Ruud 2010). In February 2015 a national newspaper reported the following incident that took place in Barisal:

> The activists of Bangladesh Chhatra League and Jubo League clashed in Barisal city yesterday, each group trying to drive out the other during the submission of bids for a BDT 10 crore infrastructure development work in three *upazilas* [subdistrict].
>
> Eight people were injured, including local photojournalist Suhad of the daily Kaler Kantha, when police and Rapid Action Battalion used batons to stop the hour-long fight.
>
> Executive Engineer of Local Government Engineering Department (LGED), Barisal Md Ruhul Amin Khan, said submissions were invited on December 31, 2014 for the BDT 10 core project, involving construction of roads and culverts, and yesterday was the deadline.
>
> They were engaged in fist fights and pelting each other with projectiles. BCL city President Md Jasim Uddin, and General Secretary Ashim Dewan took part in the clash, the witnesses said. (*Daily Star*, 5 February 2015)

Interestingly the two organisations involved, the Chhatra League and the Jubo League, are both organisational wings of the same ruling Awami League party. Typically all those involved deny that anything untoward happened. The Sub-Inspector of the police station said that 'no such unpleasant incident occurred'; the party leader allegedly involved did not answer his phone, a student union leader said no one from his party was involved and the executive engineer said he knew nothing about the incident.

In order to ensure such incidents do not happen and to avoid the process being manipulated in this fashion, police officers can be posted next to the drop-box. The decision on whether to post the police officers lies with local officials who, in many cases, will find themselves under pressure from local politicians. Few officials will be able or willing to withstand pressure from local politicians. Another requirement in the process is that the bidder hold a licence. These licences can be obtained by applying to a government office. But few in Barisal seem to know exactly what the requirements are or which office to approach, and the obvious reason is that these details do not matter. Licences can simply be 'borrowed'. People who have licences but are not using them might lend them or be coerced into lending them to someone else. A former contractor in Barisal explained the business of the licences. When I spoke with him he had retired after several decades as a relatively successful entrepreneur in the construction business, and was running a small medical store in the centre of the city in addition to devoting much of his time to his religious life.

> Once I had 14 licences. But when I left the business, the political leaders of the ruling party began to ask me to give them the licences so that they could get the work order or contract in my name. This created so many problems for me that I have cancelled all my licences except one. That one I have to keep because of tax authorities. But to keep it I have to pay some taxes because I lend it to political leaders [when a licence is used a tax is automatically due]. MPs borrow the licence saying that their brother will take the job.

The journalist through whom I had made contact with this somewhat reticent retired contractor told the same story rather differently: 'They force him to let them use his licence. For many years they have been forcing him.' The people who make use of his licence are former associates. They are well connected politically. He knows that they can create much trouble for his medical store if he does not comply. In general, he does not lose money from this and they cover his taxes. But he is asked to sign papers and every now and then he is required to appear at meetings and on occasion even in court.

The politics of bidding and of subcontracting

There are of course dozens of tenders every year for municipalities and several dozens for larger city corporations such as Barisal. In order to prevent the undue influence of force or intimidation, a number of measures are regularly implemented to ensure that the bidding process is done in a transparent and accountable manner. For instance, the selection committee will have a large number of members, representing both the administrative and the elected wings of the local government, including technical staff. Boxes where the paper bids are to be deposited are placed in more than one office and, if needs be, police officers are posted to guard against activists. Moreover, as a general rule, the job should be awarded to the lowest bidder. And, as another general rule, in order to ensure real competition, there must be at least three bids for each job. If three bids are not received, a higher authority may decide to award the work discretionally but normally the job will be re-advertised to a wider audience. One important condition of the general rules has to do with quality. It is important that the bidder can ensure quality and this requirement puts extra emphasis on paperwork. References, bank statements and audit reports need to be enclosed with the bid. The licence too needs to be enclosed. A senior officer in the district administration said that the system is foolproof, but does not work:

> We put the boxes [for the bids] in different places, we place police to watch over the boxes, we appoint a committee of many people, we grant the job to the lowest bidder, all to ensure that no irregularity occurs. But it does not help: the contractors negotiate among themselves before dropping the bid.

It is a very simple move. When work is advertised, a senior contractor explained, the contractors will sit down together and negotiate among themselves.

> The man who will do the work will give the other participants of the bidding an amount of money. As the tender has been negotiated [beforehand], there is no competition. The contractor can place a bid for a higher sum of money than he otherwise would have been able to. Through negotiations the contractors reach a sum that is then shown to the government [the work is allocated, and eventually] money is released. The political leader who negotiates the tender takes a chunk of money for that. The political leader, such as the mayor, needs the money, although he may also be thinking of the quality of the works.

Sometimes the officials are also involved: 'The officials who make the estimates and issue the work order in favour of some contractor, they too will take a portion of the allocated money'.

The actors engaged in negotiations beforehand are aware of the need to adhere as closely as possible to the formal requirements of the tender process. There are two elements to this process. The first is identifying the players involved. Someone will take an initiative, a contractor for instance, and he will invite others to talk. Some will be his old allies, and others people he will need. A *neta* is also invited or may hear of the initiative and will want to weigh in: 'I will send my man to help you' – as if the friendly gesture was without ulterior motive. But as one of the contractors said, 'If you do not have political power you cannot drop the bid'. In the negotiations the *neta*'s agent will lay out the conditions on which the bid – any bid – will be successful. The second element is for the others to agree on a deal. The need to adhere to the formal requirements is clear, and hence at least three bids will be submitted. It is cumbersome to have to re-advertise and go through the entire process again. Besides, it delays the distribution and the work by months and possibly a year. Because there must be three bids, there will be three bids. As one minor contractor with good political connections said, 'If there had to be a hundred bids, there would be a hundred bids'. But above all, at that early meeting they will agree on who should submit the lowest and hence winning bid. The two other bids will be higher, and not serious: The contractor concluded that '… if we agree that you should get the bid, then you will get the bid. To cheat the system is very simple.' As an official in the city corporation explained:

> Say there is a job, and it is worth one *crore*. The three of us are contractors [indicating himself and two friends]. We agree that I will get the job. So my bid will be BDT 1.1 *crore*. And his and his will be 1.3 *crore*, 1.4 *crore*, like that. No one else will be allowed to bid. Naturally I will get the job. And some of the profit I will give to them.

This is the bottom line: the profit is shared. A contractor who had taken part in many such negotiations and deals explained that the sharing is decided on before the bids are submitted, and that occasionally political leaders and chief engineers are part of the deal.

> Say there is this 1 *crore* job. The chief engineer will say it is a 1.1 *crore* job and that is how it will be advertised. The contractors will get together, you and you and me [pointing to the three of us in the room], and we decide that I will do the job. So I hand in a bid of 1.3 *crore*. You hand in a bid of 1.4 *crore*, you 1.5 *crore*. 1.3 is the lowest I can go, but because it is the lowest I will get it. You get 10 *lakhs* [0.1

crore], you get 10 *lakhs*, and the chief engineer gets 10 *lakhs*. Then the political leader gets 20 *lakhs*. And I do the job so I will have 30 *lakhs*. So how much remains? Fifty *lakhs*. That is how much [the] job will be done [for]. Even less!'

I asked him how money is handed over from one person to the next. He said smaller sums of 10 or 20 *lakh* may be handed over in cash or in an envelope – 'Openly!'

In some cases the *neta* or his right-hand man is directly involved in the negotiations, and in other cases the *neta* is himself a contractor and negotiates with the others. But whoever submits the lowest and winning bid will depend on the assistance of other contractors and entrepreneurs. Much of the job and sometimes the whole job is passed on to others, as subcontracting. The winning contractors are often not real contractors and even if they are they are not entrepreneurs. They rely on good contacts both with real contractors, who will be able to write the bids and do the actual job, and with politicians to be selected for the job. Submitting a tender entails complicated and technical paper work which requires specialised knowledge. Tender invitations are often quite detailed and the contractor submitting a bid for the contract needs to be quite specific when meeting both technical and financial requirements.

These hurdles are easily circumvented, however. I was a little surprised that Manik-bhai, whom I met sporadically over the years, could submit bids for complicated construction works, including feeder roads. In 2014 this had become his main source of income as a contractor – and he claimed to have a turnover approaching 1 *crore* per year. When I first met Manik-bhai some years earlier he had been a student leader not particularly interested in his studies (international relations). He had no education in engineering or management studies or anything else that might have been remotely relevant to a later career as a contractor. What he did have was many years of experience as a student leader. 'What about the technical details?' I asked, 'and the certificate and auditing?' But he never bothered about these matters: 'No, no, I have someone who does that for me, someone I work with'. Contractors do not necessarily own the machinery required for mixing cement or laying the tarmac on a road, and very often they do not even have any experience with the particular work. In order to construct a building or a road, they hire in expertise or machinery in different fields. Subcontracting is a common feature of contract work all over the world. The speciality in Bangladeshi Subcontracting is to let the entire job be done by someone else. 'Sub-contracting in the Bangladeshi sense', said a medium-scale contractor in Barisal, 'means that you buy the work order from the contractor who got the work'. Subcontracting is particularly interesting when it comes to building alliances and maintaining networks and ties. Projects are invariably distributed among contractors who are politically connected. Some of the contractors are political leaders themselves. If a contractor gets a major job, he is expected to share with his colleagues. An elderly contractor explained that when a tender is awarded to someone, 'then the contractors who did not get the work … will come to you and tell you to give them a share'. The obligation to share is generally accepted. It is a matter of mutual benefit and understanding, and constitutes a tradition that has evolved over time: 'Next time it is you who will need to ask me for a small sub-contract'. The elderly contractor continued

> The contractors also have associates in the [government] offices. And the offices take care of contractors who have not received any commission for a long while. We contractors maintain good relations among ourselves to maintain our position. Some contractors may be solvent and have good personal relations to important leaders, but not all. Normally contractors do have relations with politicians. And some contractors are party men … . But for the others it is not difficult to get work because you can purchase work from other contractors who do get jobs.

Often the subcontracting is negotiated and agreed before the bid is handed in. There is the practical side to subcontracting, which has to do with expertise, equipment, etc. But there is also the mutual support. The senior contractor claimed there are *samaj* (associations of contractors) – and that there is an element of solidarity among contractors (for the role of identity, family and dynasties in shaping these il/legal economies see Singh and Harriss-White on coal (Chapter 1) and Michelutti and Martin on caste/clans (Chapter 6 and Chapter 9)). If a contractor is down on his luck, others may help him by giving him subcontracts, it was claimed. However active these loose associations for mutual benefit among contractors may be, they constitute webs of relationships that stretch to include members of the administration as well, from clerks to high-ranking officials and medical officers or engineers. At the centre is the indispensable political leader who can influence the awarding of the contract. He will have his ear to the ground and will know that other contractors are getting together to bid for a particular job. He will smooth the process for a certain percentage but he will also ensure that his allies are awarded subcontracts. Maintaining that web of relations is the *neta*'s main job; it keeps him in in a position of power and enables him to exercise that power.

Veiled violence

There are many stories about violence marking a distinction between politicians on the one hand and criminals on the other.

> I gave up the business about 20 years ago. In those days politicians did not control the tender business in the same way as they do today. In those days terrors [using the English word, in the sense of people who instil fear, violent extortionists and criminals] extorted money after we got government jobs. We feared violence and so we paid them.

The extortionists did kill people, but most narratives of murder in Barisal tell of associates being killed or the extortionists killing one another rather than the contractors or political leaders being killed. 'The *netas* often used muscle power to control the tenders and contracts' informants say. Both business people and political leaders maintained a number of armed retainers in order to further their interests, to extort, or to protect themselves and their investments, in particular machinery at building sites. So to some extent it seems to have been a matter of hired goons being killed by other hired goons.

There are several stories of people being killed, including one that revolves around the large Barisal contractor Gulzar and his brother Mehedi. Mehedi was known as a bit of a rogue, a 'terror', and was close to Kamal, the city BNP president at the time. At some point in 2006 Mehedi was killed 'in crossfire' by RAB, the elite police force. This was the first 'crossfire' incident in Barisal. The term crossfire refers allegedly to a shootout between the armed forces and criminals, but more often than not it is the extra-judicial killing of known criminals or other undesirables (see Human Rights Watch 2011). It is alleged that Sarwar ordered the killing, to get rid of a troublesome *mastan* and send a strong signal to his political and business rivals.

A significant change over the years is that violence has become less visible. In the old days individuals could be hunted down and killed at night. Sometimes there would even be a dramatic hunt through the backstreets with shots fired from illegal firearms and the next morning a bloody body would be found in the gutter. Or perhaps individual businessmen and their families received threats, as the elderly contractor we met above put it:

> For example one day your daughter comes from school and says someone on a motorcycle has followed her. And you look out the window and see them. They are just standing there. Two, three men, smoking. After a while they go away. Then you pay.

As murder and bodies in the gutter have become rarer, 'disappearance has become more common'. When a goon disappears, no one really knows whether he has been paid off and gone into hiding or if he has been killed and dumped somewhere at sea. The general consensus seems to be that when the body is missing it is probably a disappearance. Stories of someone encountering 'the disappeared' later on confirm the notion that not as many people are murdered now as in the past. One such story is that of Rafik. He was the right-hand man of a BNP-affiliated contractor, but after a few months of tension between this contractor and a rival, also in the BNP, Rafik suddenly disappeared. This weakened his employer and the employer and his rival put their differences aside. My interlocutor told me, however, that he had met Rafik in Chittagong many years later: 'Is it you, Rafik? Yes, it is I. And we talked for a while'. When dealt with properly, disappearances can be as effective as murder in terms of establishing a reputation or weakening a rival. To avoid the sullying effect of a police investigation, bothersome *mastans* can be got rid of using the law enforcers themselves. One such case is the story of the disappearance of Sarwar's right-hand man.

Santu was a *mastan* and a youth leader. He was known to be violent and very efficient. He was an important part in Sarwar's set-up because of his efficiency and because he helped maintain Sarwar's reputation as someone not to be crossed. However, during the 2007–8 caretaker government, Sarwar was put in prison and Santu lost his protection. One evening he was picked up by RAB, the elite police unit. The same evening and over the following days, his friends and fellow party activists went to the RAB offices looking for him. RAB denied any knowledge of his whereabouts. He was never seen again. The inside story, which is common knowledge, is that it was Sarwar's rivals in the party that took advantage of Sarwar being in prison to get rid of his right-hand man. They allegedly paid BDT 25 *lakh* to a RAB officer who organised the arrest and killing. Allegedly three intra-party rivals of Sarwar were behind the plot.

There are violent pockets in Bangladesh still today, such as the city of Narayanganj or the port of Chittagong. But Barisal and most other places are comparatively peaceful because violence no longer serves a purpose. Local politicians have figured out that negotiations and deals are a better mode of operation than *mastans* and violence.

> Nowadays none of the main party leaders wants to be involved in clashes. To be associated with clashes is bad for their reputation. Today the media is very important. If they are in clashes, the media will report this and the voters don't like it. So, all leaders nowadays try to avoid clashes. Nowadays, vandalism is no more than breaking some windows of some buildings. Previously clashes could be deadly.

This development is linked to the new media landscape in Barisal and the country. Even newspapers with political leanings find it impossible not to report on violent clashes. The emergence of a new and privately owned mediascape after the 1990s changed the game of politics. It shifted to a new arena, with new rules, and now violence has become less interesting to the ambitious. In the more mature and media-saturated era of contemporary Bangladeshi democracy, a clean reputation untainted by disruptive activities plays a larger role. And thus ownership of newspapers becomes interesting. But while the new media landscape has helped bring down violence as a political weapon, it has expanded the field of deal-making by bringing in more actors and opening new opportunities for the adventurous entrepreneur.

The provincial mediascape

The provincial mediascape has changed tremendously over the last few decades and has influenced the practice of politics considerably. In the 1980s there was only one local newspaper, and although the national dailies had local stringers, and still do, national reporting on provincial matters is sparse at best. However, from the 1990s onwards the number of local dailies rose and in 2014 it stood at 15. The majority were relatively simple, comprising a four-page-long single sheet of folded paper, such as *Barisaler Katha*, *Satya Sangbad*, *Bhorer Alo*, *Ajker Barta*, *Dakshinanchal*, *Matabad* and *Paribartan*. The quality of print was not particularly good, with only one of the local papers, *Ajker Barta*, printed in colour ('The only colour newspaper in Barisal' was in fact its slogan).

This large number of dailies could easily be mistaken for an active mediascape, but an old-school journalist and former reporters' association activist dismissed them all as *dhaincha* (weeds). He also pointed out that in spite of the lack of industry and big businesses able to fund papers through advertisements, etc., provincial Barisal still featured this large number of newspapers – each with 10 to 15 or more reporters, photographers, subeditors, office staff and offices.

But it is as an extension of politics rather than as an independent news source working outside politics that this mediascape has grown. Two decades ago there were incidents of political leaders threatening reporters with imprisonment and violence. This has changed and the local media has become an extension of political deal-making. Newspapers are often owned by political leaders or contractors. One of the main political figures of Barisal, Hiron, was behind the four-page *Dakshinanchal*. Hiron earned money as a contractor and was an active political leader who became the mayor of Barisal and then went on to become an MP. He had plans to establish another newspaper when he died prematurely in 2014. Another interesting illustration of the business–politics divide is the city's 'only colour newspaper', *Ajker Barta*, owned by Kazi Babul. In the 2000s this was the largest local paper. Its editor was a contractor formerly aligned with the BNP when it was in power and then with the Awami League as power shifted. His son and wife had also been involved in the BNP, the wife as a councillor, the son in the youth wing, but both later shifted to the Awami League. Both son and wife ran their own newspapers, and the son dabbled as a contractor and was known as a terror. He ran a brothel and had had bombs thrown at his house. He regularly carried a gun, which he showed me with some pride. Both father and son used their newspapers as a 'shield', according to a local journalist, to protect their unorthodox business careers, political alliance building and private lives.[8]

Newspapers were versatile tools in the hands of contractor-editors, used to protect themselves and forward the interests of their allies. The curious thing pointed out by this local journalist was that the majority of the local papers did not pay their reporters. Instead, reporters were given ID cards identifying them as reporters and the opportunity to have their material printed in the newspaper if approved by the editor. Apart from this potential income, most reporters were left to fend for themselves. They earned their money, a retired reporter said with a smile, 'in their own ways'. Mostly they received payment from whomever they chose to write about in the paper. This Bangladeshi version of 'paid news' is so common that all government offices have funds set aside for 'media money'.

The organiser or the office or the organisation behind an event has an allocation for the journalists who cover it. After the event the journalists are paid a certain amount of money. It could be 5000 taka [in total], and it is distributed among those present. TV journalists get a greater share and local journalists a little less. The money is only given at the end of the function. In the meantime the journalists gather in a corner and wait. You may wonder why they are not leaving after the speeches but they will wait until they have received the money. One hundred taka, two hundred, three hundred, or a larger sum for them to distribute among themselves. The money is mostly given in envelopes, but quite openly. No shame.

When the money has been handed over and the amount is deemed good, the journalist will publish the report, with a photograph; the report will be phrased in a neutral tone or given a positive spin. But if the sum was insufficient, the news story might be published with a different twist. It may be a smaller report, on one of the inside pages, possibly without a photo, possibly with a quote from rivals.

Another significant source of income is 'blackmailing'.

They find some problem or irregularity, and then they talk to the person who is to be blamed with whatever error or fault they have unearthed. This person will then pay the reporter and the editor money in order to save his social standing or respect.

Such information is potentially rewarding. Reporter and editor will often choose to sit on it until the person accused is informed (allegedly so as to offer a 'right to respond'). To have allegations of serious misconduct published even in a small local newspaper can be detrimental to a political career because such stories are quickly picked up by larger newspapers or even national dailies. In 2014 a case was filed by the national Anti-Corruption Commission (ACC) against a minor contractor for substandard quality work done at the Barisal docks. I read the news in the national press and asked a local reporter why this was not in the local press. 'That contractor is not the main villain', he said.

The main villain is Shamsul [a contractor], who got the job and subcontracted. But Shamsul is a friend of all, including my editor. We will not run the story. No one here will. And where will be the proof? The man accused by ACC will pay a fine, that's it.

Only on rare occasions are allegations against major political leaders published. Mostly the *neta* and the editor will reach an agreement, or the editor may decide that the story is not worth the risk. 'You do not publish such stories. Not against people in power', said one editor. Smaller leaders or low-ranking officials may be targeted, but again they mostly come to an understanding rather than having their names brought into the limelight. The volume of corruption cases and deal-making in provincial towns such as Barisal may be very high, but the number of reports in the numerous local news media is correspondingly low. Occasions for black-mailing individual leaders are hard to come by, of course, because the proof of malfeasance is not something people will talk about. Nonetheless, there are numerous occasions for allegations and suggestions, and these might be sufficient to prompt the media personnel and the officials in question to work out a relationship sufficiently generous to maintain the number of newspapers and reporters.

Balancing

Although the number of incidents of violence has reduced considerably in Barisal politics and contracting business, the threat still lingers. And there are many other forms of use of force, mostly hidden. A political leader may demand money directly from contractors, irrespective of any bidding. A contractor who needs to stay in the good books of a party leader will pay up (the term often used is 'donate') or at least try to. A contractor who had had years of dealings with city politics, including with the strongman, former MP and former mayor Sarwar, put it like this:

> So Sarwar will call you one evening. He will say, "I need four *lakhs*". With more words, better words. Sarwar is very persuasive. He will not demand money from you, he explains his needs. Then you offer to help and he is grateful. "I will send my man over tomorrow." So you manage to get hold of three *lakhs* and you give it in an envelope to Sarwar's man. Then you call Sarwar's brother [*bhai*], not Sarwar himself. "I am so sorry. I could only manage this little. I have had so many expenses."

It is a complicated game. Sarwar was well-known as courteous, exceedingly well connected and dangerous. He was a former bodybuilding champion, former trade union leader famed for muscular politics, and is alleged to have been involved in a few murders. If the contractor contacted by him had not done his bidding, the contractor would be out of favour the next time around. He might find that his suppliers are not as forthcoming as they once were or that certain trade union leaders are making a fuss. He might even find that machinery on one of his construction sites is damaged. Some years earlier, when Sarwar was MP and his party was in power (2001–6), he had been the most powerful man in the division.

Sarwar then fell from power but continued to operate as a contractor and as someone powerful. 'But Sarwar is still powerful!' The contractor almost leapt out of his chair in order to emphasise his point. His party has been out of power since 2006 and he himself has spent time in prison (during the caretaker government 2007–8). And even if he was still MP, because his party was out of power nationally, he was marginalised and powerless. He did not appear in government offices, was not asked to sit on committees or boards, and people did not know him. Nonetheless, he continued to operate as a contractor. After years out of power, he was still known as 'the biggest contractor in Barisal', or one of the biggest. The contracts were not in his name – they may have been in his brother's name or the name of an associate – but no one doubted that it was Sarwar who was the real man. The contractor who insisted that Sarwar was still powerful had been in the business for several decades and had had many dealings with the city's *netas*. He explained that Sarwar's loss of formal positions of influence had not severely affected his work as a contractor.

Sarwar could continue as such because of several features of how business and politics are conducted in Barisal and in Bangladesh. A crucial reason for Sarwar's continued prominence as a contractor was cross-party alliances – his ability to 'balance', as it were. A main ally was Hiron, for years mayor of the city and an Awami League leader. 'They are like old friends', a BNP leader said, laughing: 'when they meet, they embrace warmly'. This may have been exaggerated, but they did accommodate each other's needs. Hiron, as mayor, shared some contracts with Sarwar and his men, even though they belonged to rival political parties. A local leader belonging to Hiron's party was very upset by this arrangement.

> Hiron … has basically embezzled a lot of money. That is the reason we started in the Awami League! [To fight corruption.] Hiron was first with Jatiyo Party and then he came to us. But he shows no *shomman* [respect]. He is not a good leader. He shows no respect to people who have been in the party long, who have sacrificed for the party. Instead he is a friend of Sarwar.

He complained that Hiron gave government work to Sarwar's people instead of to people who had spent a lifetime in the Awami League. For this he deemed Hiron disrespectful. A respectful leader gives government contracts to his own party's people, not to others. In reality this was not always the case. A journalist and correspondent for one of the large national dailies explained the situation in simple terms. Public works jobs are mostly distributed among contractors somehow close to the ruling party.

> But the ruling party doesn't entirely deprive the contractors who have a close tie with the opposition. Contractors who are with the opposition have to pay more.

Another journalist, also a senior correspondent, said that the ruling party (PGP) will reach 'a balance' with the opposition. They will keep most works for themselves but will share a portion with the opposition, because it is prudent to have allies on the other side: 'Next time, you will be out of power, and I will give you some contracts.' Such political connections across party lines are not confined to government works contracts. In the endless political game, your enemy's enemy is your friend and someone to be treated with care. This was seen as the main reason for Barisal being relatively quiet during the troublesome months leading up to the 2014 elections – when the capital and some provincial cities saw bus-burning, bombs and mayhem.[9] The opposition leader insistently called on her party leaders and activists to take to the streets, and yet the traditionally BNP-supporting Barisal was quiet. The ritualised early-morning demonstrations under the leadership of Sarwar, sitting MP, were not going to scare anyone. It was held that Sarwar was going quietly because of his relationship with Hiron. Sarwar was hedging his bets, and so was Hiron. The outcome of the unrest was uncertain and it would pay to have an ally on the winning side.

Conclusion

In contrast with Latin America, inter alia, provincial Bangladesh does not exhibit autonomous violent groups that conquer or enter into alliances with representatives of the state. Nor is provincial Bangladesh quite the South Asian mafia-owned democracy in which armed and violent groups dominate certain trades in collusion with members of the state. What we have encountered in Barisal in this chapter is an extractive system that feeds off government budgets. It has politicised crime along with all interesting parts of the state apparatus. Representatives of the clientelist state – *netas*, bosses, patrons – have entered into collusion with non-state representatives such as businesspeople, criminals and representatives of the media, as well as non-elected state representatives such as bureaucrats, police officers and judges. These elaborate and delicately intertwined networks of illicit deal-making centre on political leaders and draw their sustenance from their important alliances with contractors. Combined with the other actors, who may be willing or otherwise, they weave networks that allow government money to be siphoned off to sustain themselves in politics – which is a costly business.

The small pond that is provincial Bangladesh is easily stirred up by larger, national forces such as elections, and no matter how locally entrenched they may be these provincial networks are never immune from the waves created at higher levels. Nevertheless, largely semi-autonomous as they are, these networks operate in partial isolation from the national centre of power. A national election victory creates new opportunities while a defeat wreaks havoc – but not entirely; not for the clever boss. The never-ending internal rivalry coupled with the constant outside threat to one's position makes 'balancing' a necessary element in a sound survival strategy. The deal-making involves criminals performing certain irregular tasks, but as contractors, business executives, entrepreneurs and bureaucrats have adapted to the realities of a violent climate, actual violence has to some extent been replaced by make-believe violence, such as disappearances, and by threats.

For the individual contractor, activist or bureaucrat, participating in the network involves becoming entangled in a mutually supportive system that keeps you safe while in power but augments the risks of a backlash after falling out of power. It is primarily connections via a *neta* in power, or closely aligned with someone in power, that will ensure suspension of the punishment. The development of a mediascape in which papers are numerous and yet for sale has increasingly helped solidify this extractive system by making defection dangerous, because it means exposure to potential blackmailing and no protection.

Notes

1. Interviews were carried out in Barisal during annual visits between 2012 and 2017. Most interviewees have preferred to remain anonymous. I talked with journalists, activists, present and former politicians from all major political parties except the Islamist Jamaat, members of the civil service, NGO staff, and contractors and other businessmen. I am greatly indebted to Md AbuBakar Siddique for his vast experience and assistance during my fieldwork.
2. 'PGP' connotes 'Present Government Party' – a cynical, inside joke among journalists, officials and other observers of Bangladeshi politics.

3. This is also a family portrait, since Hasnat is Sheikh Hasina's cousin (Prime Minister 1996–2001 and 2008 to present). Hasina is the daughter of Bangabandhu Sheikh Mujibur Rahman, whose photo is found everywhere, and Hasnat is Mujibur's nephew. On these photos others too will appear with some regularity, such as Hasnat's father, who was Mujibur's brother-in-law, and various other family figures. Many of them feature in the national history of the liberation (1971) and the bloody coup (1975) that killed then President Mujibur and most of his family – including Hasnat's father.

4. Barisal used to be a municipality, but due to its strategic importance and status as the largest town in this part of the country it was elevated to a city corporation in 2000, and granted city status in 2003. It has a population of about 300,000 and houses a university, a large divisional hospital, municipal, district and divisional administrations and other state services, besides having a modest industrial sector and a large retail sector.

5. Bangladesh is administratively divided into eight divisions, each comprising several districts (*zilla* or *jela*). The district is again divided into *upazilas*, which are the administratively more significant unit. Although there is an approximation, *upazilas* and national parliament constituencies do not necessarily overlap.

6. Names have been changed.

7. BDT 5 *lakh* equals INR 3.8 *lakh* or USD 5,400.

8. Kazi Babul is alleged to have been a *razakar*, providing the Pakistani army with prostitutes during the 1971 war of liberation. *Razakar*, used in the sense of collaborator, is probably the worst label one can have in contemporary Bangladeshi politics.

9. The opposition BNP, supported by the Jamaat Islami, demanded the reintroduction of the caretaker government system. This had been introduced in 1996 and entails a politically neutral cabinet taking power three months before a general election. It was introduced to ensure a fair election. It was abolished in 2012 on the grounds that it was undemocratic. The opposition wanted it reintroduced because it did not trust the sitting government. The boycott failed and the election went ahead without the opposition participating.

References

Ahmed, M. 1984. *Bangladesh: The Era of Sheikh Mujibur Rahman*. Wiesbaden: Franz Steiner Verlag GMBH.

Amundsen, I. 2012. 'Democratic Dynasties? Internal Party Democracy in Bangladesh', *Party Politics* 22(1): https://doi.org/10.1177%2F1354068813511378.

Andersen, M.K. 2013. 'The Politics of Politics: Youth Mobilization, Aspirations and the Threat of Violence at Dhaka University'. PhD diss., University of Copenhagen.

Armao, F. 2015. 'Mafia-owned democracies: Italy and Mexico as Patterns of Criminal Neoliberalism', *Estado, Criminalidad y Cambio Político, Entre Italia y Latinoamérica* 1(April), 4–21.

BRAC. 2006. *The State of Governance in Bangladesh 2006: Knowledge, Perception, Reality*. Dhaka: Centre for Governance Studies, BRAC University, and BRAC Research and Evaluation Division.

Chowdhury, F.A. 2013. 'Funding of Political Parties', *Daily Star*, 13 October.

Daily Star. 2015. 'BCL, Jubo League Clash in Barisal', 5 February. https://www.thedailystar.net/bcl-jubo-league-clash-in-barisal-63325 (accessed 7 April 2019).

Favarel-Garrigues, G. 2011. *Policing Economic Crime in Russia: From Soviet Planned Economy to Privatisation*. London: Hurst.

Harriss-White, B., ed. 2015. *Middle India and Urban-Rural Development: Four Decades of Change*. New Delhi: Springer.

Human Rights Watch. 2011. '*Crossfire*': Continued Human Rights Abuses by Bangladesh's Rapid Action Battalion. Human Rights Watch Report.

Jahan, R. 2005. *Bangladesh Politics: Problems and Issues*. Dhaka: University Presses Limited.

Jahan, R. and I. Amundsen. 2012. 'The Parliament in Bangladesh: Representation and Accountability', *CPD/CMI Working Paper* 2.

Klem, B. and B. Suykens. 2018. 'The Politics of Order and Disturbance: Public Authority, Sovereignty and Violent Contestation in South Asia', *Modern Asian Studies* 52(3): 753–83.

Ledeneva, A. 2013. *Can Russia Modernise? Sistema, Power Networks and Informal Governance*. Cambridge: Cambridge University Press.

Liton, S. 2015. 'News Analysis. Business Factor in our Politics', *Daily Star*, 14 October.

Martin, N. and L. Michelutti, 2017. 'Protection Rackets and Party Machines: Comparative Ethnographies of "Mafia Raj" in North India', *Asian Journal of Social Science* 45(6): 693–723.

Michelutti, L., A. Hoque, N. Martin, D. Picherit, P. Rollier, A.E. Ruud and C. Still. 2018. *Mafia Raj: The Rule of Bosses in South Asia*. Stanford, CA: Stanford University Press.

Piliavsky, A. 2013. 'Where is the Public Sphere? Political Communications and the Morality of Disclosure in Rural Rajasthan', *Cambridge Journal of Anthropology* 31(2): 104–22.

Ruud, A.E. 2010. 'To Create a Crowd: Student Leaders in Dhaka', in *Power and Influence in India: Bosses, Lords and Captains*, edited by P.G. Price and A.E. Ruud, 70–95. London: Routledge.

Ruud, A.E. 2014. 'The Political Bully in Bangladesh', in *Patronage as Politics in South Asia*, edited by A. Piliavsky, 303–25. Cambridge: Cambridge University Press.

Ruud, A.E. and M.M. Islam. 2016. 'Political Dynasty Formation in Bangladesh', *South Asia: Journal of South Asian Studies* 39(2): 401–14.

Sud, N. 2014. 'The Men in the Middle: A Missing Dimension in Global Land Deals', *Journal of Peasant Studies* 41(4): 593–612.

Varese, F. 2011. *Mafias on the Move: How Organized Crime Conquers New Territories*. Princeton, NJ: Princeton University Press.

11

Putting out the Baldia factory fire: how the trial of Karachi's industrial capitalism did not happen

Laurent Gayer

In this chapter the network of connivance between the provincial bureaucracy and local industrialists is traced. It describes the symbiotic relations between the criminal economies of local 'industrial capitalism', Karachi's turbulent urban environment and a state torn between the strength of the law and the 'justice' of the powerful. This intreccio *is explored through a detailed documentation of trials following the Baldia textile factory fire. They reveal the routinised coercive exploitation of the workforce and the systematic bypassing of labour laws and safety regulations, non-compliance with which had evidently become widespread in the industrial zones of the economic capital of Pakistan. It also shows how immunity develops and operates, and the role of crime-friendly law in facilitating it.*

On 11 September 2012, 259 people were killed and more than 100 injured in a textile factory fire in the Baldia area of Karachi (see Fig. 11.1). This was the deadliest industrial fire in world history and the worst industrial disaster in the history of Pakistan. The judicial proceedings that began in the following months had a considerable impact on the country and, as the testimonies of survivors and various investigative reports started piling up, Karachi's unbridled capitalism was put in the dock. These investigations revealed practices of coercive exploitation of the workforce and a systematic bypassing of labour laws and safety regulations, which had evidently become widespread in the industrial zones of the economic capital of Pakistan. And because the company in

Figure 11.1 The remains of Ali Enterprises, Baldia Town
(August 2017 – Photograph by Laurent Gayer)

question was working mainly for a German group (KiK) and had received
an SA8000 certificate of 'social accountability' from the Italian inspection
company RINA, the trial threatened to involve international companies
and monitoring authorities. The law suddenly seemed to have caught up
with global supply chains and their regulatory regime.

Soon enough, however, the judicial machinery went awry. Instead
of singling out the illegalities of Karachi's industrial capitalism, it threatened to put the city at large on trial. Because of the sheer scale of the
disaster, as well as how poorly it had been managed, the Baldia factory
fire case brought the city's 'ordered disorder' (Gayer 2014) under the
microscope. And while doubts persisted about the exact origin of the
fire – largely because of the lack of resources of the investigators, as they
themselves admitted – what is commonly referred to in Pakistan as the
bari sarkar ('deep state' – namely the army and its intelligence agencies)
invited itself to the bar and gave a new political twist to the case. On the
basis of the alleged confessions of a suspected hit man, the paramilitary
Rangers succeeded in reorienting the trial against the party dominating
Karachi's political life, the Muttahida Qaumi Movement (MQM), which
was accused of having set the factory on fire as part of a racket deal.
What had started out as a judicial probe to find those responsible for the

tragedy became an instrument of political repression and repositioning of the Rangers on the local scene, one that targetted criminal practices and in particular the economy of *bhatta* (protection), set up by local political parties in the 1980s (see Box 1).

Through a detailed study of these judicial proceedings and their successive bifurcations, this chapter aims to grasp the relations of interdependence between a distinctly unbridled blend of capitalism, a turbulent urban environment and a state torn between the strength of the law

Box 11.1 Karachi's violent entrepreneurs

The first illicit enterprises to have emerged in post-colonial Karachi were related to smuggling, and primarily involved ethnic groups with transnational connections, such as the Baloch and, later on, the Pashtuns. Baloch smugglers operating from the inner-city neighbourhood of Lyari provided the wholesale markets of the Old City with the bulk of illegally imported goods. Following the ban on alcohol and gambling in 1977, Lyari's burgeoning criminal economy received a shot in the arm. However, it was only with the development of the heroin trade during the 1980s that a large-scale criminal economy developed in Karachi.

The main operators of this new criminal economy were Pashtun tribes (Afridis, in particular) controlling transport routes and fleets between Afghanistan and Karachi. The profits of the emerging drug trade were reinvested by criminal entrepreneurs into the unofficial land market, and the city's new slumlords imposed a reign of terror that disrupted patterns of occupation and inter-ethnic relations in the city's unofficial settlements. In 1985–6 a series of riots and massacres centred on this new slum economy contributed to making ethnicity the dominant framework for socio-economic conflicts and political mobilisations in the city at large.

The new political forces that emerged from these ethnic conflicts promptly developed their own criminal enterprises. The Mohajir Qaumi Movement (MQM, later renamed the Muttahida Qaumi Movement), in particular, which became the predominant political force in Karachi during the second half of the 1980s, became notorious for its institutionalisation of *bhatta*, or protection rackets. This market of protection was inspired by the so-called 'goonda tax' levied by petty criminals in the city's bazars. The MQM took these practices to a whole new level, however, by extending them to virtually every economic actor (from industrialists to traders, and from shopkeepers to hawkers) and by systematising the collection of *bhatta* (through regular contributions as well as through more exceptional donations, such as at the time of Eid, when the retainers of the party were expected to contribute in cash or kind – with animal hides, in particular – to the party's finances).

During the years 2011–13, the MQM's gradual loss of authority over the city translated into a deregulation of the market of protection. The gangs of Lyari (which, under the patronage of the Pakistan People's Party grew to be a force to be reckoned with, with considerable firepower), as well as the Pakistani Taliban, were new entrants into these protection rackets. While the extortion activities of the Taliban were limited to the sectors of the economy controlled by Pashtuns (such as the transport sector or the marble industry), the gangs of Lyari competed with the MQM for the role of 'protectors' of the city's traders, builders and industrialists.

Even as they disrupted the activities of entrepreneurial classes, the Lyari-based gangsters of the People's Aman Committee (PAC) or the petty criminals associated with political parties also helped industrialists maintain discipline in their factories. Some were appointed as labour officers and entrusted with the surveillance of the workforce, in order to prevent any attempt at organisation on its part. This practice of recruiting *goondas* for union-busting activities dates back to the early years of Karachi's industrialisation process (which began in the late 1950s). However, after the launching of a new paramilitary operation in the city in 2013 this task was entrusted to the Rangers, who now play a prominent role in the policing of industrial areas.

and the 'justice' of the powerful. From its inception, during the so-called 'decade of development' of 1958–68,[1] Karachi's industrial capitalism was characterised by a propensity for various types of illegalities. Tax fraud, unfair labour practices, violations of health, safety, building and environmental regulations, illicit procurement of water, as well as the use of *goondas* (thugs) to crush attempts at unionisation have all been key to the operations – and the profits – of the manufacturing sector, especially in the textile industry. At the same time, these industries never operated entirely beyond the reach of the law. Industrialists also encouraged the development of legal conventions that both strengthened their domination and regulated it.[2] Karachi's industrial capitalism can thus be characterised as an *irregular* production system – a type of organisation of the manufacturing economy resorting heavily to various illegalities without completely evading legal norms and the regulatory action of the courts. Rather than by its outwardly criminal nature, this mode of organisation of the economy is thus characterised by its uneven relationship with the law.

Besides their documentary value, the judicial proceedings considered here provide an opportunity to think through the irregular nature of this production system, and more particularly to reflect upon the force of the law in a society where it is constantly undermined by the illegalities of 'delinquent elites' (Lascoumes 2014), extrajudicial forms of coercion, and the ubiquity of informality. Taking as a starting point the reflection of E.P. Thompson on the law as a double-edged sword (Thompson 1975), before engaging with a series of works discussing the social and political uses of the law (namely, the literature on legal mobilisation theory and cause lawyering[3]), this case study also aims to assess the extent to which the most vulnerable sections of Pakistan's society can expect justice in such a context. In the face of a society and economy where the display of might is generally deemed to prevail over the assertion of rights, Thompson's work is a useful reminder that the effectiveness of the law as an instrument of domination in the service of the powerful rests on its apparent universality and impartiality – and 'it cannot seem to be so without upholding its own logic and criteria of equality; indeed, on occasion, by actually *being* just' (Thompson 1975, 263).

This contribution is part of a larger, ongoing investigation of Karachi's irregular capitalism, for which I have already spent four months in Karachi (March 2015; July–August 2016; July–August 2017). The data collected during these fieldtrips mainly include legal documents (labour courts awards and judicial proceedings of several civil and criminal cases), as well as interviews with approximately 80 industrialists, workers, labour activists, lawyers and members of law enforcement agencies. Considering the sensitive nature of the topic – which covers various forms of illegalities on the part of industrialists, practices of collusion between public enforcers and private entrepreneurs, as well as resistance tactics under scrutiny from the state and corporate security departments – I guaranteed anonymity to most of my interlocutors. As a result, the names of interviewees quoted in the text have generally been withheld. The only exception to this rule concerns Faisal Siddiqui, the legal counsel of civil society organisations representing the families of the victims of the Baldia factory fire. He agreed to his name appearing here and, given the prominence of the case, it would have been impossible to hide his identity anyway.

Trial by fire: the revelatory effect of the Baldia factory disaster

At the instigation of the provincial authorities of Sindh, the owners and managers of Ali Enterprises were initially charged with murder under section 302 of the Pakistan penal code, while government officials were charged with criminal negligence. Parallel to this criminal case, which was registered with the additional district and sessions judge of West Karachi, a civil case for compensation was filed by a collective of labour and civil society organisations (including the National Trade Union Federation and the Pakistan Institute of Labour Education and Research). Through a constitutional petition,[4] these organisations sought directions for judicial enquiry, compensation for the victims' families, and enforcement of labour laws in the industrial sector.[5] The fact that labour organisations and their legal counsel could not convince a single victim's family to file a case for compensation reflected the intimidation exerted by industrialists over their workers.[6] This benefitted the owners of Ali Enterprises, as under Pakistani criminal law only victims and their families can assist the prosecution.

On paper, these various cases were independent of one another. However, especially after the accident was re-qualified as an act of terrorism, the civil case became increasingly dependent upon the criminal case, with those judges hearing constitutional petitions asking directions from the trial court while examining criminal evidence on their own. Moreover, both criminal and civil cases relied upon the investigation conducted, on the one hand, by a group of high-level police officials headed by a superintendent of police (SP),[7] and on the other hand by two teams of investigators acting independently of the local police – a tribunal of enquiry constituted at the request of the Sindh Home Department and a Federal Investigation Agency (FIA) team.[8] The findings of these investigators were largely convergent. All of them came to the conclusion that a short-circuit was the most probable cause of the fire, especially as the factory was working on overload at the time of the incident, consuming 318 kW electricity, as against the 210 kW for which it had been given permission.[9] But even as they ruled out any foul play, investigators could not establish the cause of the fire with any degree of certainty; the margin of doubt that remained in their conclusions led to much speculation and contributed to the politicisation of the trial, as we shall see later.

Ali Enterprises was the property of Abdul Aziz Bhaila and his two sons, Rashid Aziz and Shahid Aziz. Like many other industrialists in Karachi, especially in the textile industry, the Bhailas belong to the Memon community, a mercantile ethno-linguistic group tracing its roots to the current Indian province of Gujarat, which played a prominent role in the industrialisation of Karachi during the 1950s and 60s.[10] The Memons of Karachi are a tight-knit community, structured around professional and philanthropic organisations, as well as around centres of worship doubling as educational and welfare centres (known as *jama'at khanas*). The prominence of Memons among Karachi's industrialists translates into their over-representation within the city's professional bodies. Thus, at the time of the Baldia fire, A.A. Bhaila was a member of both the Karachi Chamber of Commerce and Industries (KCCI) and the Pakistan Readymade Garments Manufacturers and Exporters Association (PRGMEA). In other words, the Bhailas were not black sheep resorting to exceptionally ruthless practices: on the contrary, they were prominent and rather typical members of the local business community. Similarly, their malpractices were not exceptional, and the various legal cases opened against them revealed the banality of these illegalities and the collusion between local industrialists and public officials that made these systematic violations of labour laws and safety regulations tenable in the long run.

As the investigation of these cases began, various public institutions were summoned before the courts. What they revealed was a vast network of connivance between the provincial bureaucracy and local industrialists. The provincial Labour Department commenced by informing the judges that Ali Enterprises was not even registered with its department, and that in any case, any kind of violation of law under the Factories Act (1934) was punishable with a maximum penalty of PKR 500 (5 euros). The Sindh Employees' Social Security Institution (SESSI) and the Employees' Old-Age Benefits Institution (EOBI) followed suit and informed the courts that most employees of Ali Enterprises had not been registered over the years (only 200 workers at Ali Enterprises, of a total of 3,000, were registered with EOBI, and 268 with SESSI). Like most textile and garment companies,[11] the Bhailas resorted to the so-called 'third party' system of labour recruitment, through which recruiting agents (known locally as contractors, or *thekedars* in Urdu) provide industries with cheap, casual workers who are not entitled to any form of social protection.

The contracts of these temporary workers are renewed every three months, contravening the existing labour laws, which require employers to provide permanent contracts to those workers they aim to keep on after a three-month probationary period. This system of outsourcing allows employers to lower their production costs significantly by avoiding monthly contributions towards their employees' social security and pensions. Outsourcing also allows employers to avoid any legal responsibility in case of accidents and deters workers from organising, as it is even more difficult for contract workers than for permanent ones to unionise. Meanwhile, using various contractors within the same factory further divides the workforce and discourages workers from uniting on a single platform. It is also easy for employers to dismiss those workers trying to unionise; they simply refuse to renew their contracts. In fact, such flexibility in recruiting/terminating workers is one of the primary incentives of the third-party system for employers, besides its economic benefits. Significantly, there was no union at Ali Enterprises, although a handful of workers were members of the Sindh Hosiery, Garment and General Workers Union, a general union of textile workers.

Meanwhile, the regulatory body overseeing the patterns of land occupation and factory construction plans in the Sindh Industrial Trading Estate (SITE, the factory district where the Bhailas' factory was located), known as SITE Ltd, claimed that it was not its responsibility to ensure that individual factories complied in practice with health and safety regulations. The director and chief engineer of SITE also acknowledged that any violation of the construction plan of a given factory (such as the construction of an additional floor or the absence of fire escape provisions) could be regularised after the payment of a minimal fee. The officials of the civil defence, who are theoretically responsible for monitoring the safety of the country's factories, claimed that they had not visited that particular factory because it was not registered with the Labour Department. Taking advantage of this situation, the Bhailas had not even installed the most basic emergency facilities. The statements of workers who survived the blaze suggested that emergency exits were often locked from outside and that fire extinguishers were not in working order, even though a fire had already broken out in the warehouse of the same factory a few months earlier.[12] For the owners of Ali Enterprises, regulating the workers – whether to prevent theft or coerce them into working longer hours than they were supposed to – took precedence over their safety. Both the police Investigation Officer (IO) and the FIA emphasised that three of the four gates of the ill-fated building were closed permanently, mainly to prevent pilfering, while the few CCTV cameras installed in the building that were in operating order were oriented towards the surveillance of the workers rather than towards the mitigation of safety hazards.[13] Sub-Inspector Jehanzaib Khan, the second IO assigned to the (criminal) case, went as far as comparing this intensely coercive factory environment to a jail.[14]

The investigation also revealed the dismal state of the inspection regime in Sindh (which is no exception in this regard: while there are more than 100,000 factories in the country, there are only 541 labour inspectors, of whom 17 are female (Mansoor 2016)). EOBI officials claimed that they repeatedly tried to inspect the factory but were denied entry by the management (Kamal 2012). Labour inspections have been suspended in Sindh since 2003. This decision followed a similar move by the provincial authorities of the Punjab, the country's other major industrial hub, and was encouraged by a prominent textile industrialist operating from SITE, Zubair Motiwala, who at the time served as an economic adviser to the Chief Minister of Sindh.[15] Even when inspections did take place, they were utterly ineffectual. The limited human and financial resources of these services made it highly improbable for a given factory to ever be inspected, and this risk was further neutralised through bribes. As a last resort, workers would be instructed to lie about their wages and working conditions to inspectors – a practice which has become systematic when facing local or foreign auditors, as explained by a supervisor in his 30s who oversaw 20 workers at a garments factory located in the industrial area of Korangi:

> When some auditors visit from *bahar* (outside/abroad), they just come and go. They tell the workers, "Come on, tell us the truth, is the food OK here?" The workers always lie. If they told the truth, they would be fired immediately. (…) A few days in advance, the administrative officer hands over a paper to everyone, with instructions about what to say. (…) It says that the workers are entitled to bonuses, that the food is excellent, that they are allowed to take vacations, etc. As a result, everything they tell the auditors is a pack of lies. (Hasan, garments factory supervisor, interviewed in Karachi, July 2016)

All in all, what early investigative reports revealed was a production process relying upon systematic breaches of the law. This is made explicit in the Alavi tribunal report, which does not mince its words to denounce these practices:

> We would indeed hold that collectively the entire system of Karachi is responsible for the cause of death as at each and every stage; from the setting up of the factory and drawing up of a drawing plan, for meeting the high standards of safety and precautions, to the architects who do not create fire escapes and who compromise on these safety factors for reasons best known to the approvers of the drawing plan and their nonchalant attitude towards basic details, to the owners of the factory who try to fit in the maximum number of machinery into the minimum space without bothering about the provisions of law which require at least breathing space, to the law itself relating to the factories and the labour working therein

which is totally defective and needs to be updated on a war foot-
ing, to the several departments who are existing purely and simply
for serving the cause of the factories and the labour who pay lip
service to the law on several grounds including non-availability of
staff, to the system which does not provide for adequate staff for
sustaining and servicing a running industry, to the helplessness of
the Civil Defence System who show that total lack of facility as the
main cause of failures to provide relief and rescue in times of emer-
gencies, to the inspectors of all departments who for a petty amount
compromise on quality, to those who have fatalistic approach and
feel that nothing is going to happen, to the entire system and the
laws relating thereto which hampers progress and effective working
of a factory or a business concern. (...) To the powers of discretion
that enshrines each and every act that is promulgated which retards
effective implementation of law.[16]

Karachi on trial: urban disorder as an amplifying factor of the disaster

The Alavi tribunal report extrapolates that, besides a particularly exploitative system of production, it is the entire political and economic system
of Karachi that is to blame for this disaster. The city, here, is much more
than a context for the catastrophe. It is party to the crime and, as such, is
directly indicted by investigators and prosecutors. As always in Karachi – a
megalopolis that still lacks a mass transit system and where the regulation of road circulation is at the heart of the struggles for the city (Gayer
2016) – traffic and its disruptions were held responsible for the scale of the
disaster. Thus, according to the FIA report, the dispatch of backup vehicles
by the fire brigade was delayed by the dismal state of the road network in
SITE: 'The dilapidated condition of roads in SITE might be a contributing
factor. Due to the road condition it takes a long time for vehicles to reach
from one point to another.'[17] The Alavi tribunal report also suggests that
the 'pathetic traffic conditions' in the city contributed to the fire brigade's
relatively late arrival on the scene of the fire. This provides an opportunity
for the author of the report to indict political and economic elites, whose
convoys regularly disrupt traffic in the city: 'It would not be out of place
to mention here that traffic jams created due to VIP movements on the
main arteries of Karachi have repeatedly resulted in precious loss of lives.'
At this point (as in several other parts of the report), Justice Alavi makes
himself the spokesperson of the denizens of Karachi, allegedly brutalised

by corrupt and insensitive elites. This posturing was consonant with the particular brand of judicial activism that had emerged in the preceding years around Chief Justice Iftikhar Muhammad Chaudhry (Gayer 2009). This mobilisation had reached its acme the preceding year during the so-called Karachi law and order case, which saw a special bench of the supreme court indict politicians, public servants and even security officers for the dismal state of affairs in the country's largest city. The overall tone of the Alavi tribunal report and its lament for a city betrayed by its elites is revealing of this particular moment in the history of the Pakistani judiciary and its relations with civilian authorities.

The controversy around the role of the fire-fighters during the accident is exemplary of this extension of the trial to the city at large. During the fire itself, 'there was a tremendous altercation between the public and fire engine personnel as there was not enough water in the fire engines'.[18] Critiques of the Fire Brigade Department only increased after the catastrophe. The Bhailas claimed that they had informed the department right after the fire broke out, but that the fire brigade had taken an hour to reach the site; that it had not sent enough fire tenders and that it had taken excessive time to refill once the water was exhausted. The Chief Fire Officer of Karachi, who appeared in front of the Alavi tribunal, defended his services, claiming that his personnel arrived at the site within 10 to 15 minutes after first receiving information about the incident. TV footage suggested that the first fire tenders reached the site less than half an hour after Lyari fire station was first informed of the incident, thus invalidating the claim of the owners.[19] However, it is clear that the fire-fighters were completely unprepared for a catastrophe of this magnitude. At first, only two fire tenders were sent to the scene and they soon ran out of water. In the next few hours, nearly all the fire vehicles available in the city (45)[20] were brought on site, with reinforcements including fire tenders from the navy, Karachi Port Trust, Defence Housing Authority (DHA – an elite residential area), the cantonment board, etc. Meanwhile, the Edhi Foundation, Pakistan's most respected philanthropic organisation, which manages the largest fleet of ambulances in Karachi, had difficulties reaching the site. According to a prominent member of the organisation, who was part of the rescue team, Edhi's ambulances were initially denied access to the site by gun-toting MQM activists, who tried to monopolise rescue operations through their own welfare branch, the Khidmat-e-Khalq Foundation (KKF).[21]

The forensic division of the Karachi police also came in for criticism during the investigation. Justice Alavi complained that the division had failed to deliver any useful information and suggested that 'in the absence of and lack of any competent facility and persons available to carry out complete modern forensic investigation which is available throughout the world perhaps this Division might as well close down as no tangible purpose is being served'.[22] Even the Edhi Foundation was accused of adding to the confusion. As usual in Karachi, the bodies of the victims were taken over by the foundation and stored in the Edhi morgue pending their identification – a process delayed and complicated by the condition of some of the corpses. As a report by the police surgeon deplored three months after the incident, Edhi staff were not qualified for such an arduous task, which according to the surgeon considerably disrupted the work of forensic experts. In its conclusion, the report notes that:

i. Dead bodies identified after DNA test with same Tags/PM numbers are found in Edhi Cold Storage.
ii. On one stretcher two or more than two dead bodies were lying leading to mixing of papers & body fragments due to large number of dead bodies and the short space of the cold storage.
iii. As information obtained that some Dead bodies taken away by relatives without legal formalities and buried by them. But after DNA test identification another dead bodies [sic] were received by claimants.
iv. As staff working at Edhi Cold Storage is not educated that's why mixing of Tags and PM numbers incorrect disposal of bodies had happened.[23]

The lack of coordination between these various actors – a characteristic of Karachi's governance often decried by the political class as well as by urban planners – also complicated relief efforts and subsequent investigations. This is made explicit in the Alavi tribunal report, which suggests that 'too many agencies have jumped in to investigate the cause of fire and the loss of lives. To our mind there has been a great tampering of evidence'.[24] Finally, the lack of technical expertise within the Fire Brigade Department and the Sindh police forensic division seriously hampered the work of investigators and prevented them from reaching a definitive conclusion about the cause of the fire. According to the FIA report:

It must also be mentioned here that no expert opinion in this regard was available from the fire department or the Sindh Police Forensic division. It appears that there is lack of expertise on fire and arson investigation. (…) Absence of expert opinion in the relevant fields made reaching a definite conclusion extremely difficult.[25]

This indictment of the city at large in the tragedy had important legal consequences and, especially in the case of the Alavi tribunal, was not devoid of ulterior motives. However critical it may seem of the powers that be, the Alavi tribunal report did not come as a threat to political or economic elites. Within the legal fraternity, Justice Alavi was reputed for his docility, particularly when adjudicating cases involving members of the business community. The elitist background of this retired judge from the Sindh high court may explain this leniency. Alavi, who was born in 1941, belongs to the old elite of Karachi (he hails from the Bohra family that gave Karachi its first Muslim mayor, Hatim Alvi). Over the years, he headed numerous government-appointed commissions, which earned him the reputation of being pro-establishment. Within the legal fraternity, his reputation has also been tainted by his chairmanship of a regulatory body reputed to be one of the most corrupt in Sindh province, the Sindh Land Committee, which oversaw the process of regularisation of illegally-occupied lands. According to Faisal Siddiqui, legal counsel for civil society organisations acting on behalf of the victims, the Alavi tribunal report was consistent with the past record of its chairman. By 'dividing the anger all over the place' and introducing contradictory evidence regarding the responsibilities of the owners – in particular by questioning the assumption that most of the exits of the factory had been closed at the behest of the management – he helped them obtain bail and paved the way for their gradual exoneration of all charges.[26]

Enter the security state: the politicisation of the Baldia factory fire case

Whatever their ulterior motives may have been, the reluctance of investigative agencies to pronounce a clear verdict on the cause of the fire provided an opportunity for the military to divert the judicial process and turn the whole exercise into a political trial. This diversion occurred during the spring of 2015, after the paramilitary Rangers used the confession of an alleged 'target killer' of the MQM to requalify the Baldia fire as an act of terrorism. This whole enterprise relied upon the testimony of Muhammad Rizwan Qureshi, alias 'Pringle', a 55-year-old Mohajir who was suspected of leading a double life: a sanitary sub-inspector at the Saddar Town branch of the Karachi Municipal Corporation (KMC), Qureshi allegedly confessed to his involvement in dozens of murders and kidnappings dating from the mid-1990s onwards, as the head of an MQM 'death squad'.[27] Qureshi was arrested by the police of Karachi's South District in 2013 and, in view of the high profile of the case, was investigated by a Joint Investigation Team (JIT) comprised of representatives from the Karachi police, the Inter Services Intelligence (ISI), the Intelligence Bureau (IB), the Rangers and the FIA. The JIT was conducted on 22 June 2013 under the supervision of the Senior Superintendent of Police (SSP) for District South. However, the JIT report was only presented in court on 6 February 2015. By then, the configuration of Karachi's political scene had drastically changed. In late September 2013, Prime Minister Nawaz Sharif announced a massive crackdown on militant and criminal groups in the city. The paramilitary Rangers were entrusted with operations on the ground, which paved the way for a re-engagement of the army in Karachi's politics.

Like their counterparts in the Punjab, the Sindh Rangers are a paramilitary force placed under the authority of the Federal Home Ministry; however, because they are commanded by top officers of the Pakistan army (their Director General is systematically a serving major general), they tend to evade civilian control and serve the designs of the military. While the mandate of the Rangers was initially focussed on protecting Pakistan's eastern border with India, they were called in to support the police in Karachi at the end of the 1980s. They never left the city and now, with 13,000 officers (against 26,000 police), they currently play a prominent role in law enforcement and regulating the city's political economy. Over the course of time, the Rangers have developed their own economic activities, both licit (shooting clubs, petrol stations, printing presses, canteens, public model schools, cement factories, etc.) and otherwise (in collusion with the so-called 'water mafia', they have taken control of the water hydrants and the tanker service supplying water-starved localities).[28] These economic activities have brought the Rangers closer to the city's business community, which relies heavily upon the paramilitaries for its security – while the Rangers have been deployed in every industrial area, they sometimes provide an additional layer of security for a fee, through the private security company that they set up in 2012, the Rangers Security Guards (RSG). Besides patrolling these areas and monitoring video-surveillance installations, the Rangers frequently intimidate labour activists and workers trying to organise themselves. Industrialists openly acknowledge their contribution to the maintenance of corporate order. As a former chair of the KCCI told me during a focus group discussion at the Pakistan Employers Federation in July 2017:

> We give less importance to the ministers [than to the Rangers] ... Because they are deterrents ... So that we go to our industries in such an atmosphere that, you know, there will not be a labour ...

[he takes it back and only continues after some hesitation] ... a law and order issue. Because a violent mob, or any kind of morons, they can attack the factories. Now they are afraid to do that openly. So they are a deterrent for us, like the nuclear bomb that we have, otherwise Indians and others would come and attack us.[29]

It is in this context of strengthening ties between the holders of capital and the wielders of coercion that the Sindh Rangers and the army started intensifying their operations in Karachi, with a focus on the so-called 'militant wing' of the MQM. The JIT report was a key part in this political offensive, which aimed to downsize the MQM at large and deprive it of its prominence in Karachi's politics. While previous investigations had ruled out the possibility of foul play, the JIT report laid the blame for the fire squarely at the door of the MQM and its extortionists. During his interrogation by the JIT team, Qureshi allegedly revealed that a 'well-known party high official' from the MQM had tried to extort PKR 200 million, 'through his front man', from the owners of Ali Enterprises. Following their refusal, the sector-in-charge of the MQM in Baldia, Rehman Bhola, with the support of 'unknown accomplices', allegedly 'threw chemical substances which creates fire in factory' (sic).[30] On the basis of these 'revelations' (which were merely based on what a suspected criminal had allegedly heard from fellow party workers), the provincial Home Ministry constituted a new JIT under the supervision of the deputy inspector general (DIG) of the central investigation agency (CIA), with representatives from the Karachi police, the ISI, military intelligence (MI), the IB and the FIA. On 29 March, the SITE superintendent of police (SP), Sajid Ameer Sadozai, was tasked by the JIT to reinvestigate the case. During the course of this investigation, this police officer – who acted under tremendous pressure not only from his own hierarchy but also from the army and its intelligence agencies – concluded that 'this kind of fire cannot be caused by an electric short circuit'. The progress report of the JIT presented in the court of the additional district and sessions judge of West Karachi, Maqbool Memon, in 2016, thus concluded that Rehman Bhola and his accomplices had set the factory on fire after the Bhailas refused to hand over PKR 250 million (the inflation of this sum from the 200 million mentioned in the previous JIT report was never explained). Allegedly, the owners of the factory were ready to settle for PKR 10 million, but this arrangement would have been refused by Bhola and the 'party high official' on whose behalf he acted. The report claimed that Bhola and his men set fire 'to the *godown* [warehouse] and several other places' – a claim which contradicted all previous investigations as no evidence suggested that the fire could have broken out from different points. The report added that the pressure by MQM top officials on the owners of the factory did not stop there, and that these officials continued to 'terrorise' the owners and tried to extort money from them after the fire. Under pressure from the MQM as well as from the courts, the Bhailas would finally have agreed to transfer PKR 50 million to an MQM account in Hyderabad, where the money would have been used to acquire a plot of land.[31]

The evidence put forward was circumstantial at best and mainly relied upon testimonies from an accountant at Ali Enterprises who claimed that the fire had engulfed the whole building within minutes, despite the efforts of the workers and the owners to extinguish it. The value of this testimony was itself questionable, especially as earlier investigations had revealed that the owners had in fact fled the site after the fire broke out. This would remain a controversial claim, especially since the workers who attested it later on retracted their statements, most probably under pressure from the police. Meanwhile, if the experts of the Punjab forensic science agency (PFSA)[32] recruited by the JIT concluded without hesitation that the fire was 'a clear case of arson', their report was not made public.[33] The members of the JIT did not really care about the weakness of their case, however. They knew that their version of the story coincided with the dominant interpretation of the events in public opinion. This is not to say that they cynically tried to manipulate the public: most of the members of the JIT were firmly convinced of this interpretation of events, which sometimes pitted them against their more sceptical colleagues. By an ironic quirk of fate, a senior police officer who had taken part in the JIT was subsequently posted to the same department as some of the participants in the FIA investigation team who had suggested in their report that the fire was probably accidental. It did not take long for this police officer to confront his colleagues, asking them if they did not feel any shame for having exonerated mass murderers. 'I was really angry. How can you condone the murder of 260 people? How can you be a police officer and be so shameless?' this officer asked me rhetorically during an interview, with a voice shaking with anger.[34]

However weak the new 'evidence' brought to the fore by the JIT might have been, it concluded that 'the factory fire was a planned terrorist activity and not an accidental fire'. The response of the media, the judiciary and political authorities was largely sympathetic to this conclusion and did not question its veracity. Similarly, for the general public, it confirmed what everyone already thought: that the MQM was the main culprit. This is precisely what the owners of Ali Enterprises had suggested all along, and this revised version of the facts worked in their favour. Here, the interests of the owners (and of their supporters among Karachi's business community) clearly converged with those of the state security apparatus. The new political ambitions for Karachi of the Rangers and the army merged with the interests of a group of industrialists on the defensive, and this convergence led the Baldia factory fire case to take a new course. However, in this context convergence did not imply similar interests, as while the Rangers and the army were determined to discredit and cut the MQM down to size, industrialists aimed to ward off the threat of labour reforms.

On the basis of what was presented as new evidence to the judiciary and in the court of public opinion, the members of the JIT requested of the Sindh government that the original first information report (FIR) – on the basis of which the Bhailas had been charged with murder – be cancelled, and that a new FIR be registered against Rehman Bhola and his accomplices under the Anti Terrorism Act (ATA). Despite the protests of the petitioners' legal counsel, a new investigation team was appointed and placed under the direction of the Sindh Inspector General of Police, A.D. Khawaja, an officer reputed to be close to the army. This investigative team started preparing a new charge sheet, which was finally submitted in August 2016. While the owners (who had left the country) as well as some factory employees had initially been charged with murder and criminal negligence, this time they were exonerated of all charges and were made to appear as prosecution witnesses. Two MQM cadres, Rehman Bhola and Hammad Siddiqui, as well as '3/4 other unknown accused persons', were charged under the anti-terrorism law.[35] On 27 August 2016, the additional district and sessions judge of West Karachi, who was hearing the criminal case against the Bhailas and others, decided to transfer the case to the administrative judge of the Anti Terrorism Courts (ATCs), after observing that it was a case appropriate for an ATC and not a regular court because the charges were framed under the Anti Terrorism Act, 1997. On 5 September, the administrative judge of the ATCs transferred the case to the ATC-II for a regular hearing. But then something unexpected happened, which – momentarily – disrupted the new course of the trial. Despite pressure from security agencies and civilian political authorities, the sitting judge of the ATC-II refused to accept the charges brought by the police. More specifically, the judge argued against the exemption of the Bhailas from any form of prosecution, by recalling that 'serious allegations are levelled against the owners that they had locked emergency gates which resulted in 259 deaths of workers'.[36] Three months later, however, the same judge had to back down after presumed arsonist Rehman Bhola was arrested by Interpol in Bangkok and extradited to Pakistan, where he allegedly confessed to having set the factory on fire – yet another 'revelation' paving the way for the indictment of the MQM and the exoneration of the Bhailas.

As of May 2018, the trial of Bhola and his alleged associates is yet to begin. It may well never happen. According to a close observer of the case, the main reason for this delay would be dissension within the security apparatus. While the Rangers would press for a quick trial to further weaken the MQM, the ISI would delay it, seeking to exonerate Hammad Siddiqui. After being indicted by the police in the third and fourth charge sheets presented in August 2016 and January 2017, and after Bhola allegedly confessed to having set the factory on fire on Siddiqui's order, everything was set for their prosecution. But in March 2016, Siddiqui, the former head of the MQM's *tanzeemi* (organisational) committee, was instrumental in the creation of the Pak Sarzameen Party (PSP), a rival group set up by MQM dissidents and allegedly supported by the ISI. The fact that Siddiqui has not been arrested yet, even after the ATC-II issued a non-bailable arrest warrant against him, tends to validate the assumption that the security state itself has become divided over the possible political repercussions of these judicial proceedings.[37]

The law of the strongest? Capital and coercion in the Baldia factory fire case

The various investigations and litigations that followed the fire generated their own coercive forces, which added to the suffering of the survivors. As the owners of the factory strove to obtain bail, their former workers suddenly started changing their statements in favour of their former employers.[38] On 14 September 2012, Muhammad Omer, a former machine operator at Ali Enterprises, had told the police of SITE-B that, while trying to escape from the building under fire, he had found three exit doors locked from outside.[39] Two months later, he retracted this statement and claimed that it was made under duress, after he was detained in the SITE police station for four days (from 14 to 18 September):

> During this period (…) some other officer [than Zafar Iqbal, the IO] came and directed me that I have to give statement to the effect that doors were locked from outside. I informed them that due to intense heat and smoke I was not able to reach to the door, therefore I cannot say the doors were locked from outside. The police

officials informed me that I will be released only when my statement is recorded before Magistrate as such during this period I remained at the police station SITE-A. (...) I say that on 18.09.2012 I was taken to the court of Magistrate and police informed me that I have to state before the Magistrate along with other details that the exit doors were locked from outside. I was made to believe that unless I give statement as directed by the police I shall not be released. I was under tremendous mental pressure due to the incident and remaining at police station and for that reason gave statement before Magistrate as desired by police.[40]

Other witnesses who had testified that the doors of the factory were locked from outside later on retracted this testimony and claimed that they were coerced into making such statements so as to strengthen the case of the police against the owners. Nazeer Ahmed, a clerk in the Accounts Department of the factory, registered an affidavit in November 2012, where he claimed that:

on 14.09.2012 around 7 a.m. police party headed by Choudhry Zafar Iqbal came at my residence and started shouting at me and my family members, they even extended no courtesy towards women and used abusive language extended threats and demanded Cell phones of every person in the house such demand was also made to the ladies. (...) Thereafter police party took me to (...) police station, there also I was inhumanly treated and was not even allow to answer nature's calls which was very painful and torturous in my age which is 67. (...) I was kept in wrongful confinement for about one week.[41]

Several elements in these accounts suggest that these witnesses were pressured to change their earlier statements in favour of the owners. Contrary to earlier investigative reports, which suggested that the owners had fled the scene and abandoned entrapped workers to their fate, all these affidavits were given in favour of the Bhailas and claimed that the latter did everything they could to quell the fire, that fire extinguishers were both present in large numbers and in working order, and that it was essentially the delay in the intervention of the fire brigade and its lack of professionalism that resulted in a disaster. This coincided with changes in the version of the story given by the police. Whereas the original FIR and the preliminary charge sheet accused the owners of murder and criminal negligence, subsequent charge sheets prepared by the Investigation Officer (IO), Sub-Inspector Jehanzaib, withdrew the murder charge (*qatl-i-amd*, which comes under section 302 of the Pakistan penal code) and replaced it with involuntary homicide (*qatl-bis-sabab*, an offence which comes under section 321 of the penal code and which does not provide for jail sentences). The alteration of the charge sheet made it easier for judges to succumb to the pressures inciting them to grant bail to the Bhailas, even before the Rangers started shifting the blame onto the MQM.

What is unclear in the statements of these former employees of Ali Enterprises is not so much whether they were coerced into giving statements coinciding with the version of the police, but rather at which stage of the investigation they were coerced. It is probable that the owners' representatives and the police themselves – who, under a new IO, insisted on exonerating the Bhailas of the charge of murder – pushed these witnesses to testify in favour of the owners' bail application. Faisal Siddiqui, the legal counsel of petitioners demanding compensation on behalf of the victims' families, claims that the owners used two tactics to deter their former workers from testifying against them: through middlemen, they distributed food to their families while simultaneously threatening them using the infamous 'gang war people' (gangsters) of Lyari.[42] Gang members would have visited these families and openly threatened them to dissuade them from going to court.[43] The support extended to the Bhailas by the 'industrialists' lobby', or what is identified as such by Faisal Siddiqui, also explains why the owners of Ali Enterprises managed to go free despite all investigations pointing unequivocally at their having been involved in the worst industrial accident in Pakistan's history. On 29 December 2012, the KCCI requested that Prime Minister Raja Pervez Ashraf intervene in favour of the 'wrongly accused' owners of Ali Enterprises. These industrialists claimed that the implication of the Bhailas in a murder case was a clear example of 'misuse of state power', which carried the risk of 'scaring away new investment'. Thus, it was now the 'duty' of the state to revoke the FIR and to absolve these entrepreneurs of the charge of murder so that they could soon resume their activities while sending a positive message to the whole business community of Karachi (Chambers of Commerce 2012). To this the Prime Minister replied, during his speech, that 'Authorities should reinvestigate the case and provide justice to the employers of Ali Enterprises if a wrong case has been registered against the factory owners under section 302'. Shortly thereafter, the Finance Minister announced on behalf of the Prime Minister that the murder charge against the owners of Ali Enterprises had been withdrawn – a public announcement that provoked moral outrage across the country, leading the Prime Minister to backtrack and announce that the case was only being reinvestigated (as we saw earlier, this was merely a damage control operation, and the charge of murder would indeed be withdrawn by IO Jehanzaib in the next charge sheet). Commenting upon this PR fiasco, a group of advocates at the supreme court and the high court later on suggested that the matter should have been handled more cautiously, and informally, by the Prime Minister:

> A more careful and balanced approach would have been that Prime Minister should have been taken into confidence and through whisper in the ears asked if Railway accident takes place and large number of passengers are killed, have the Chairman or Chief Executive Officer of those Airlines been charged for murder. It goes without saying, that if the industrialists are charged for murder only because there has been a fire in the factory resulting in death of large number of workers, this does not necessarily mean that the intentions of the employers was to kill or murder his workers. (Ghani, Ghani and Faisal 2014, 86–7)

While the legal professions were divided on the issue, the so-called 'business community' of Karachi gave a remarkable display of unity. This solidarity was reinforced by the ethnic ties that bound the Bhailas with the powerful Memon community, as well as by their membership in various professional organisations. As mentioned earlier, A.A. Bhaila was a member of the KCCI and the PRGMEA. Even if he never occupied any position of leadership in these organisations, it was enough to make him a respected member of Karachi's business community – membership in professional associations and in multi-sectorial trade associations or chambers of commerce is an important marker of status among Karachi's entrepreneurs. Besides its symbolic value, membership in these organisations ensures privileged access to state regulators, as these organisations – especially the KCCI and the trade associations linked with each of the city's industrial estates – are the main interlocutors of provincial and federal authorities, both civilian and military, in their dealings with Karachi's business community.

The show of unity around the Bhailas largely transcended their individual case, however. Local entrepreneurs, especially in the textile and garments sector – which is the most prone to violations of labour laws and safety regulations[44] – were aware that, beyond the fate of the Bhailas, what was at stake was their own autonomy from the law and from state regulators. By expressing their solidarity with the Bhailas and mobilising all their resources to put pressure on the government and the judiciary, they simultaneously voiced a collective sense of belonging and defended their private interests against potential government interference in their affairs (through a resumption of inspections, for instance). Bailing out the Bhailas was therefore essential for these industrialists, and the day the court finally succumbed to pressure they celebrated their victory, as advocate Faisal Siddiqui recalls:

> On the day they were granted bail in court, the entire … I mean, what was amazing was that … 255 people have been burnt alive so you would imagine that the court would be full with victims and their families. But the entire court room … There were about 50, 60 people in the courtroom, and they were all industrialists and supporters of these people. And they were clapping … (Faisal Siddiqui, interviewed in Karachi, July 2016)

Later on, when the blame started shifting from the owners of the factory to the MQM, many industrialists rejoiced – so much so that F. Siddiqui suspects that it was these industrialists who 'pushed this story forward', so that the owners would become complainants in the FIR.[45]

The legal and political developments sketched out above suggest three things. First, coercion, here, is an integral component of the legal process. Law enforcement agencies resort to coercion in order to reduce the uncertainty of legal proceedings. Second, the power relations mediated by the law unfold on the margins of court procedure. They involve unofficial practices – whether coercive or collusive in nature – that contribute to the informalisation of judicial processes and largely untie the latter from the formal institution of the tribunal. Members of the legal professions themselves participate in this informalisation through various kinds of background deals. Third, while the law, as an apparatus of domination, can be the terrain of an apparent convergence of capital (here, law-breaking industrialists) with coercion (here, law enforcement agencies with a political agenda), this convergence is not a given and is prone to contestations and adjustments. As a result, despite all the elements pointing in this direction, the law cannot be said to be simply a symbolic and strategic weapon in the hands of dominant elites. Whether this instability opens the way for the law to provide some sort of comfort to the most vulnerable sections of society is another issue, to which I turn now.

The 'anarchy of the law' and the quest for justice on behalf of the victims

In July and August 2016, I spent some time at MCAS & W Law Associates, a prominent law firm based in Karachi, which was founded by some of the most renowned lawyers of the country, including Munir Malik, a key leader of the Lawyer's Movement of 2007–8 and a former attorney general of Pakistan.[46] A staunch critic of military regimes, Malik has been joined by other advocates with a penchant for cause lawyering – that is, for political uses of the law from a perspective of activism (Sarat and Scheingold 2001; Gaïti and Israël 2003). This was the case, in particular, of Faisal Siddiqui, currently one of the most prominent human rights lawyers in the country, who made a name for himself by specialising in pro bono human rights litigation. After we first met at the office of the Pakistan Institute of Labour Education and Research (PILER – Pakistan's most prominent think tank and advocacy group for labour rights, of which he is a board member), I spent several days (and nights) at Siddiqui's firm, going through the files of the so-called Baldia factory fire case. Every now and then we met to discuss the case and more generally the status of the law in the regulation of Pakistan's politics and society. In August 2017, we pursued this discussion in light of the recent developments; by then, Siddiqui was no longer involved in the case and he could reflect on its larger implications with more serenity.

Siddiqui received a BSc in sociology from the London School of Economics (LSE) and has retained a keen interest in the social sciences from his student days, as well as an institutional affiliation with the LSE (he is a former Visiting Fellow at its Centre for the Study of Human Rights). After I discussed my project with him, he made several suggestions that significantly oriented the course of my research, especially by encouraging me to revisit E.P. Thompson's argument on the 'double-edged sword of the law', which he found particularly relevant when assessing the role of the law in contemporary Pakistan. My research on the Baldia factory fire case was therefore coproduced with a legal practitioner, and it reflects his own hopes and occasional disillusionment regarding the potentials of legal activism in Pakistan.

Throughout the summer of 2016, one of the recurrent themes in our discussions was what Siddiqui referred to as 'the anarchy of the law'. According to him, the state of disorder prevailing in Pakistan was, at large, reflected in its legal system. And while this often complicated his work, it also played in his favour. Thus, the way Siddiqui and the petitioners he represented approached the issue of compensation was legally dubious:

Nobody files compensation cases through constitutional jurisdictions. According to [Pakistani] law, every victim has to come to court and prove his claim. There's a very elaborate structure of private law which guarantees that no victim [ever] gets compensation. Nobody can really check whether [petitioners] have received their pensions, whether government compensation has been dispersed ... Very early on, we realised that we could not mobilise 255 people, filing their individual claims. So we took the gambling route. It was really a gamble: you get a good judge, [then] you get good orders ... It's really the Wild Wild West form of public litigation ... So we have been able to achieve about 18,000 dollars per victim, within a period of two years, whereas a normal civil claim would have lasted between fifteen to twenty years. (Interview with Faisal Siddiqui, Karachi, July 2016)

Later in our discussions, Siddiqui elaborated upon this theme of the 'anarchy of the law'. For him, Pakistan faces a huge disjunction between 'the law in books' and 'the law in practice' – a disjunction which, in his view, 'creates anarchy about interpretation and application of the law'. In the Pakistani context, the law would not be a rational architecture of legal norms bringing about certainty in matters of government and in the dispensation of justice, but a source of unpredictability benefitting the shrewd and the mighty. This vision of the 'anarchy of the law', as opposed to the rule of law, finds an echo in some works on organised crime, particularly on the mafia in Italy, where according to this literature 'the uncontrolled proliferation of laws and regulations' would only be matched by 'the arbitrary way in which they are applied' (Lyttelton 1994). These writings pertain to what J.-L. Briquet refers to as a 'paradigm of degeneration' (Briquet 2007, 20), which laments the political and moral decay of democratic institutions in order to call for their reform and renovation[47] – a position which raises a number of issues, if only for its normative claims (what is the benchmark of an 'authentic' rule of law?). Within the legal field, Siddiqui's denunciation of the 'anarchy of the law' may also seem to resonate with those indictments of legal formalism that end up perpetuating a positivist reading of legal norms as coherent and univocal (Israël, Sacriste, Vauchez and Willemez 2005, 5). Once we shift our attention from Siddiqui's representation of the legal system to his actual engagement with the law, however, a different image starts to appear: one where, far from being constrained by their juridical culture and normative presumptions, jurists engage creatively with the legal arsenal at their disposal, for personal or political sakes. These tactical uses of the law on the part of lawyers and judges generally imply a strict literalism, such as that displayed by judges resisting authoritarian regimes (Osiel 1995). Siddiqui's legal activism is of a different kind, however, and instead of being constrained by the existing legal framework, aims to exploit its alleged 'disorder':

When you have this disjunction between "the law in books" and "the law in practice", that creates a space for anarchy and the rich take advantage of it. Not because of their money but because they are organised. So the strategy we adopted was to organise ourselves to get the same advantages. If you [judges] had taken a strict view of the law, some compensation should not have been granted. But since there was legal confusion, we took advantage of it, without resolving that confusion. In a civil court, most of them [victims' heirs] would have ended abandoning their claims and I don't think even a generous judge would have granted them more than 5 or 6,000 dollars. (...) So, this anarchy of the law, it's wrong to say that only the powerful take advantage of it. It is people who are organised that take advantage of it. I've gone against very powerful people, and I think the key element has been how organised and 'strategised' you are. It's something we used in this case. It worked very well. (Interview with Faisal Siddiqui, Karachi, July 2016)

As Siddiqui himself highlighted, the main reasons for this success were twofold. First of all, as we already briefly saw earlier, the Baldia factory fire case unfolded at a peculiar historical moment, as far as the politics of Pakistan's judiciary were concerned. This catastrophe happened in the wake of the so-called Lawyers' Movement, and Siddiqui – who was himself an active member of this movement – engaged with judges who 'had realised that they had to change the basis of their legitimacy, from constitutional legitimacy to public legitimacy'. If high court judges took up this case so 'aggressively', it was essentially to redeem themselves of their past compromises with military regimes, in order to consolidate their position as an autonomous institution whose power would rest with its public legitimacy.

Besides these unique historical circumstances, Siddiqui emphasised the contribution of one particular judge, who exemplifies in his eyes the role of individual agents in collective struggles, judicial and otherwise. Maqbool Baqar was a widely respected member of the legal fraternity who was confirmed as judge of the Sindh high court in 2003 and then appointed chief justice of the province in 2013. Baqar was among the few judges who had refused to take oath under the Provisional Constitutional Order (PCO) enforced by General Pervez Musharraf in 2007; he maintained his stand against military rule by refusing to be reinstated after Musharraf restored the deposed judiciary in March 2009. Besides his commitment to democracy and the rule of law, his liberal stance was acknowledged by all, including by the Pakistani Taliban, who attacked his convoy in June 2013 – an attack which he survived but which left eight security personnel dead. According to Siddiqui, Justice Baqar was determined to provide justice to the victims of the Baldia fire and their families and it was he who passed most of the orders in favour of the petitioners.

The conditions in which the protective bail of the Bhailas was revoked, in October 2012, also suggest that economic and political elites are not alone in exploiting legal loopholes or circumventing the law altogether.[48] Indeed, the decision of the judges to allow petitioners to interfere with the criminal case was legally dubious because NGOs are normally not allowed to interfere with such cases. This is because the expectation is that the initiative should come from the victims' families – who, for obvious reasons in this case, were reluctant to do so. As a result, the owners of Ali Enterprises were arrested and briefly sent to jail. According to Siddiqui, the judge in the trial court at that time was 'a relatively independent person' and there was 'a lot of pressure from the Sindh government to do something, to deflect their own criminal negligence'; these two factors momentarily converged against the owners. However, as we saw earlier, the mobilisation of Karachi's industrialists soon disrupted this configuration, to the benefit of the owners of Ali Enterprises, who were all freed by early 2013. This led the petitioners and their legal counsel to change their approach. As F. Siddiqui told me,

> Very early on, I realised that you had to use the same tactic that the owners used with the victims to get the victims to come forward. It had to be both carrot and protection – I wouldn't say "stick" ... What we did is that we tried to make this case high profile, then we got them [victims' families] compensation. Then they realised that they could benefit from these people, from these NGOs, and they got out of their fear, also. They understood that these people could protect them. Then, for the last couple of years, we were able to mobilise these victims. (Interview with Faisal Siddiqui, Karachi, July 2016)

But as Siddiqui himself acknowledges, this tactic came at a cost:

> We made a strategic mistake. We got bogged down in money matters. By trying to get this compensation, we really didn't concentrate on other things [e.g. the passing of a new safety law or on the resumption of inspections in factories]. The monetisation of the

entire struggle was a big mistake. It had a very bad effect on the victims, also. It really limited their consciousness to the sole issue of money. Really, we played on the wicket of the enemy. They were willing to give us money if we gave up all other rights – the right to accountability, the right to labour rights enforcement … That was the deal. I think we fell into that trap. (Interview with Faisal Siddiqui, Karachi, July 2016)

This self-criticism echoes the frustrations of other legal activists fighting similar cases in the region and beyond. In Bangladesh, for instance, the activist group called Activist Anthropologists has filed a public interest litigation (PIL) in the country's high court to demand justice for the victims of the November 2012 Tazreen Fashions factory fire. And as the court and industrialists colluded to promote compensation as the sole response to the tragedy, these activists came to realise that 'public recognition of suffering and the rights of compensation that it entails remains a largely *ad hoc* affair and generates a political program for compensation that keeps particular demands for structural change at bay' (Sumon, Shifa and Gulrukh 2017).

Overall, Siddiqui is not a fetishist of the law. His legal activism – that is, his inclination to 'talk law to power' (Abel 2001) – cannot be isolated from his larger commitment to social reform, a project in which the law certainly has a role to play but where it should not take precedence over political mobilisation:

> The legalisation of social struggles is another dangerous road to take. The law should always be seen, at best, as a tactical weapon, and sometimes, in the right circumstances, as a strategic weapon. It should never be the main weapon. The major reason why this case ended up as a complete failure – because that's how I see it – is because we have this obsession with the law. We think we can legalise these … I wouldn't say these are political struggles … These are social struggles … We had an opportunity to a certain extent to mobilise people in the textile sector, and we lost that opportunity … (…) We thought we would enforce all rights and change the entire structure through the legal system. (Interview with Faisal Siddiqui, Karachi, July 2016)

Siddiqui's account of the Baldia factory fire case and of his own role in this legal battle was often puzzling for me. Part of this confusion had to do with his tactics of 'ethnographic seduction' (Robben 1996), and in particular with the way he punctuated his account with sociological references that seemed somewhat uncanny in the mouth of an informant, who obviously enjoyed confusing me by appropriating 'my' analytical language to reflect upon his own practice. What further confused me – and this unease grew even stronger after I started transcribing our taped conversations months later – were his apparent hesitations about the outcomes of his struggle, and about the role of the law in it. If Siddiqui was a truly unusual legal activist, it was less for his influence and affluence than for his lack of faith in the capacity of the law to order the social world, convey its iniquities and propose solutions for its reform.[49] Indeed, here was a cause lawyer who presented his legal successes as political defeats, who expressed scepticism about the politics of rights[50] and who, instead of mobilising for an extension of the domain of the law (and its professionals), claimed that the 'fetishism of the law' (Comaroff and Comaroff 2006) had done a disservice to his cause.

Conclusion

The successive changes of course of the Baldia factory fire case kept returning me to the tensile equilibrium that has been the trademark of Karachi's politics since the mid-1980s at least. All around, disorder reigned supreme: in the systematic violations of labour laws and safety regulations by local industrialists; in the traffic jams that delayed the response of emergency services; in the blatant amateurism of philanthropic organisations and law enforcement agencies in the face of a catastrophe of unprecedented magnitude; in the bungling by political authorities of an 'accident' that could not even be qualified as such with certainty; in the about-turns of victims and police officers called on in court; in the shift of the accused to the status of prosecutors; in the jubilant engagement of a legal practitioner with the 'anarchy of the law'. But disorder was not all there was to this case. Behind the apparent chaos, several forces capitalised on the disorder and to some degree contained it at the same time. The forces of capital, in the shape of the business community, reorganised themselves and succeeded in securing their economic interests by containing the threat of a resurgent state regulator. In the process, the Bhailas were gradually rehabilitated through 'restorative rituals' that compensated the stigmatising impact of judicial proceedings, minimised their responsibility and ruled out any intentional wrongdoing – a process of restoration that generally protects delinquent elites against the forms of degradation reserved for less privileged offenders (Lascoumes 2013).

This restoration process, which beyond the individual case of the Bhailas exonerated Karachi's industrialists at large, operated through a requalification of the incident and a redistribution of responsibilities. However deadly they had proven to be, the illegalities upon which Karachi's manufacturing industries thrived were gradually overshadowed by the wrongdoings of the so-called 'extortion mafia' associated with the MQM and its racketeers-turned-arsonists. In the process, the army, the paramilitary Rangers and the 'agencies' succeeded in sidelining the party that had ruled over Karachi as a personal fiefdom for almost three decades. The MQM was not eradicated but it was reduced to a shadow of its former, terrifying self. Decades of militancy and political strife were replaced by a new agenda of 'security' that promised to be no less coercive and that, at least momentarily, seemed to overlap with the irregular capitalism that brought both wealth and death to the city. And finally, between and betwixt these forces of capital and coercion, mediating their tensile relations, was the law. That blunt, rusty, double-edged sword of the law, which as E.P. Thompson famously – and at the time, at least for orthodox Marxist historians and social scientists, controversially – argued, is never entirely subsumed in the institutions of the ruling class (Thompson 1975, 260). Of course, the status and creative appropriations of the law in contemporary Pakistan have little to do with those of eighteenth-century England. But it is precisely because of its apparent weaknesses and internal disorders that the role of the law in the adjudication of political and economic disputes in contemporary Pakistan is so intriguing. For all its circumventions, abuses and informalisation, it remains a common ground and a common language – Thompson would say a common 'ideology' – for various social forces struggling for power, wealth and dignity. This is particularly true for the issue of labour rights – a cause which has largely disappeared from the public scene since the trade union movement and larger social struggles were brutally crushed by successive democratic and military regimes from the early 1970s onwards. As the perspective of collective mobilisations and the visibility of workers in the media receded, the courts became the last site to publicise labour issues and adjudicate workplace conflicts.

As Thompson underlines, this common ground of the law is essentially a terrain of *conflict*, for it is in the nature of this medium to frustrate the ambitions of the ruling classes who had turned to it 'for their own self-defence' (Thompson 1975, 264). What the Baldia factory fire case also exemplifies is that the outcome of these battles can never be taken for granted. Even as they serve the strategies of domination of the powerful and generate their own forms of coercion, as well as their own illegalities, legal proceedings always retain a contingent part – the historical and individual 'circumstances' evoked by F. Siddiqui – which introduces some indeterminacy in the game and, as such, contributes to its reproduction. This was exemplified in the Baldia factory fire case by a handful of lawyers and judges who, in the name of social justice, did not hesitate to bend the rules. The limited and contested successes of these jurists with a cause were therefore obtained less by applying the law by the book – thus entrapping the dominants into their own rhetoric of self-preservation, as Thompson would suggest – than by twisting the law in order to deliver justice. While legal mobilisation theory, for its part, generally insists on the creative appropriation of legal norms by social movements and the jurists helping them 'talk law to power' (McCann 2004), the present case study led us to uncover a less literalist use of the law by a group of activist lawyers and judges, whose complicity was itself the outcome of a political mobilisation of the legal fraternity.

Even as it underlines the resilience of the rule of law as a shared language and terrain of conflict in contemporary Pakistan, this case study speaks volumes about the ability of local economic elites to neutralise it, whether in their day-to-day operations or in more dramatic situations, when their illegalities suddenly come under public scrutiny. While questioning the power of the law, these illegalities and the relative impunity guaranteed to white collar criminals raise the question of the dissolution of state authority in a situation of industrial dis/order based on the selective application of the law. The judicial proceedings analysed here undoubtedly reveal the limited capacity for intervention of state regulators in the day-to-day operations of Karachi's industries. At the same time, the very existence of these judicial proceedings, as well as the various turns of the investigation, attest to the persistent role of state actors in delimiting the horizon of possibilities for these economic actors. Even if the state in question is a deeply fragmented one, torn between divergent logics of action, its capacities of influence and regulation – which largely operate through informal networks, upon which court orders themselves are dependent – are far from being negligible. As such, this case study is also an invitation to move beyond the dichotomy between strong and weak states while observing the penetration of polycentric societies by state forces, in particular by security establishments feeding upon various forms of disturbances to impose their own conception of public order.

Notes

1. This period of industrialisation corresponds to the rule of Pakistan's first military ruler, Ayub Khan, which saw the emergence of a developmentalist state that set the basis for the country's manufacturing sector; see Amjad 2007; Naseemullah 2017.
2. Legal technicalities and the use of English during court proceedings liken labour courts to quicksand where workers' or unions' claims tend to sink. For a recent appraisal of Pakistani labour courts, see PILER 2009.
3. See McCann 2004; Sarat and Scheingold 2001.
4. CP No. 3318 of 2012, PILER and Others vs Federation of Pakistan and Others.
5. Another constitutional petition was filed by PILER and others (CP No. 295 of 2013), focussing on the accountability of international inspection firms like RINA; this particular legal initiative is beyond the scope of the present paper.
6. Interview with Faisal Siddiqui, advocate for the petitioners, Karachi, July 2016.
7. Zafar Iqbal was the first Investigation Officer (IO) of this group; he was suspended on 20 September 2012 and replaced by Sub-Inspector Jehanzaib.
8. The FIA was created in 1974, with the objective of providing the federal government with investigative resources extending across the country. It comes under the federal Home Ministry and is headed by a director general who enjoys the powers of an inspector general of police (IGP).
9. Charge Sheet No. 238 - A / 2012, 12 Nov. 2012.
10. With the encouragement of the military regime of Ayub Khan (1958–69), a significant number of Memons shifted from their traditional specialisation in the *kirana* (spices/food grains) trade to the textile industry, the only industry to offer return rates as high as those merchants were accustomed to. On the Memons of Karachi and their contribution to the city's industrialisation, see Papanek 1973.
11. This casualisation of labour, which became widespread from the late 1980s onwards, is not limited to the textile/garment industry; according to EOBI officials, only 6 million Pakistani workers (of an estimated employed labour force of 54 million) were registered with them at the time of the Baldia factory fire (see Kamal 2012).
12. Statement U/s. 161 Cr. P.C., 14 September 2012, PS SITE-B (statement made by Muhammad Umer, machine operator at Ali Enterprises).
13. Charge Sheet No. 238 – A /2012, 12 Nov. 2012; FIA Report, pp. 8–9.
14. Charge Sheet No. 238 – A /2012, 12 Nov. 2012; FIA Report, pp. 8–9.
15. Interview with a prominent economic journalist at the daily *Dawn*, Karachi, July 2016.
16. Tribunal's Report For Ascertaining the Circumstances and Cause Leading to the Fire and Subsequent Deaths and Injuries in the Incident That Took Place on 11.09.2012 in the Factory of M/S Ali Enterprises Located at Plot No. F-67 SITE Karachi, pp. 30–31.
17. Federal Investigation Agency, Sindh Zone Karachi, *Enquiry Report. Fire Incident At Ali Enterprises S.I.T.E. Karachi On 11th September 2012*, 3 October 2012, p. 10.
18. *Ibid.*, p. 22.
19. Federal Investigation Agency, Sindh Zone Karachi, *Enquiry Report. Fire Incident At Ali Enterprises S.I.T.E. Karachi On 11th September 2012*, 3 October 2012, p. 10.
20. Karachi's fire brigade has only 22 fire engines in working order; most of them are 30 years old; interview with Faisal Edhi, head of Edhi Foundation, Karachi, July 2017.
21. Interview with a prominent member of Edhi Foundation, Karachi, July 2017.
22. Tribunal's Report For Ascertaining the Circumstances and Cause Leading to the Fire and Subsequent Deaths and Injuries in the Incident That Took Place on 11.09.2012 in the Factory of M/S Ali Enterprises Located at Plot No. F-67 SITE Karachi, p. 16.
23. Office of the Police Surgeon Karachi, N°PSK/4305/6, 8 December 2012, p. 3.
24. Tribunal's Report For Ascertaining the Circumstances and Cause Leading to the Fire and Subsequent Deaths and Injuries in the Incident That Took Place on 11.09.2012 in the Factory of M/S Ali Enterprises Located at Plot No. F-67 SITE Karachi, p. 17.
25. Federal Investigation Agency, Sindh Zone Karachi, *Enquiry Report. Fire Incident At Ali Enterprises S.I.T.E. Karachi On 11th September 2012*, 3 October 2012, p. 20.
26. Interview with Faisal Siddiqui, Karachi, August 2017.

27. In the high court of Sindh at Karachi, C.P. No D-3318/2012, Report of Pakistan Rangers (Sindh), 20 January 2015.
28. On the political history and economic activities of this force, see Gayer 2010.
29. Interview with a former chair of the KCCI and SITE Association of Industry, Karachi, July 2017.
30. In the high court of Sindh at Karachi, C.P. No D-3318/2012, Report of Pakistan Rangers (Sindh), 20 January 2015, p. 6.
31. B'adaalat Janaab Joint Additional District & Sessions Judge Sahab vs Karachi West, Progress Report (in Urdu), 2016.
32. The PFSA is a newcomer on the (burgeoning) forensic science scene in Pakistan. It was established in 2007 under the Home Department of the province of Punjab and claims to have solved 280,000 cases in less than 10 years. See Sharif 2017.
33. I was never able to see a copy of this report despite repeated requests to police officers who had access to it.
34. Interview with a senior officer of the Sindh police and former member of the JIT, Karachi, August 2017.
35. Charge Sheet No. 238-C/2012, SITE-B Police Station, Karachi West, 19 August 2016.
36. In the Court of Judge, Anti Terrorism Court No. II, Karachi Division, Order 16.09.2016.
37. Interview with a close observer of the Baldia factory fire case, Karachi, August 2017.
38. The testimonies of most witnesses were not presented in court because successive alterations in the charge sheet delayed the formal opening of the trial. According to the legal counsel of the petitioners acting on behalf of the victims, most of this evidence (to which he did not have access) might have been destroyed by Investigation Officer Jehanzaib.
39. Statement U/s. 161 Cr. P.C., 14 September 2012, PS SITE-B.
40. Criminal Bail Application No. 1208 of 2012 (Arshad Abdul Aziz & Another vs The State) in the high court of Sindh, affidavit of Muhammad Omer, 8 November 2012.
41. Criminal Bail Application No. 1208 of 2012 (Arshad Abdul Aziz & Another vs The State) in the high court of Sindh, affidavit of Nazeer Ahmed, 8 November 2012.
42. Lyari is Karachi's oldest working-class area. This decaying inner city area gave birth to a specific criminal scene in the course of the 1990s, leading to a series of deadly 'gang wars' in the following decade. Until recently, these gangs were rumoured to be patronised by the Pakistan People's Party (PPP); on the connivance of these gangs with the economic and political elites of Karachi, see Gayer 2014, chap. 5.
43. Interview with Faisal Siddiqui, Karachi, July 2016.
44. In Pakistan as elsewhere, the creation of value in the textile industry implies a policy of cost reduction which, in this labour-intensive sector, relies heavily on the compression of wages. This has led textile industrialists to circumvent labour laws in various ways, either by subcontracting parts of their production to unregistered sweatshops or by resorting to 'third parties' to provide them with 'contract workers'. In Karachi, the textile industry also colludes with the so-called 'water mafia' to procure water unofficially, at a reduced cost. The illegalities of the local textile industry also have to do with their mode of insertion into the global economy and with the still-limited constraints exerted by their foreign clients, as far as labour laws and safety regulations are concerned. The situation is markedly different in the pharmaceutical sector, where the creation of value is less dependent upon the exploitation of labour, where there is more emphasis on the development of human resources through the training of workers and where there is much greater impetus to conform to international production norms and health regulations.
45. Interview with Faisal Siddiqui, Karachi, July 2016.
46. On the political and professional trajectory of Munir Malik, see Gayer 2009.
47. In this perspective, 'The Mafia can be seen as the logical extension and the ultimate degeneration of a climate of clientelism, favoritism and the appropriation of public resources for private gains' (Chubb 1996, 289).
48. The Bhailas escaped from the site on the night of 11 September 2012. The police never made any serious attempt to arrest them. They then obtained protective bail from the Lahore high court, which allowed them to travel to Sindh without risking arrest. They later on received protective bail from the Sukkur bench of the Sindh high court so that they could appear in front of local courts prior to the trial. They were subsequently arrested in October 2012 but were granted bail a few months later.

49. On this profession of faith of cause lawyers, see Gaïti and Israël 2003, 30.
50. During an interview in August 2017, Siddiqui emphasised how the language of rights, with its moderating effect on political claims, had done a disservice to social reform in Pakistan. This was another departure from typical legal activists, who have made 'rights consciousness raising' a central aspect of their action; see Scheingold 1974.

References

Abel, R. 2001. 'Speaking Law to Power: Occasions for Cause Lawyering', in *Cause Lawyering. Political Commitments and Professional Responsibilities*, edited by A. Sarat and S. Scheingold, 69–117. New York: Oxford University Press.

Amjad, R. 2007. *Private Industrial Investment in Pakistan, 1960-1970*. Cambridge: Cambridge University Press.

Briquet, J.-L. 2007. *Mafia, justice et politique en Italie. L'affaire Andreotti dans la crise de la République (1992-2004)*. Paris: Karthala.

Chambers of Commerce. 2012. 'Prime Minister Visits Karachi Chamber of Commerce and Industry', 29 December. http://pakistanpressreleases.com/prime-minister-visits-karachi-chamber-of-commerce-industry/ (accessed 8 April 2019).

Chubb, J. 1996. 'The Mafia, the Market and the State in Italy and Russia', *Journal of Italian Studies* 1 (2): 273–91.

Comaroff, J. and J. L. Comaroff, eds. 2006. *Law and Disorder in the Postcolony*. Chicago, IL: University of Chicago Press.

Gaïti, B. and L. Israël. 2003. 'Sur l'engagement du droit dans la construction des causes', *Politix* 62: 17–30.

Gayer, L. 2009. 'Le général face à ses juges: la fronde de la magistrature pakistanaise', *Critique internationale* 42: 95–118.

Gayer, L. 2010. 'The Rangers of Pakistan: From Border Defense to Internal "Protection"', in *Organized Crime and States. The Hidden Face of Politics*, edited by J.-L. Briquet and G. Favarel-Garrigues. London: Palgrave.

Gayer, L. 2014. *Karachi. Ordered Disorder and the Struggle for the City*. London: Hurst.

Gayer, L. 2016. 'The Need for Speed: Traffic Regulation and the Violent Fabric of Karachi', *Theory, Culture & Society* 33 (7–8): 137–58.

Ghani, M.A., F.M. Ghani and N. Faisal. 2014. *No Light at the End of the Tunnel. Labour Laws to Nowhere*. Lahore: Pakistan Law House.

Israël, L., G. Sacriste, A. Vauchez and L. Willemez. 2005. 'Introduction', in *Sur la portée sociale du droit*, edited by L. Israël, G. Sacriste, A. Vauchez and L. Willemez. Paris: Presses Universitaires de France.

Kamal, N. 2012. 'Burning Questions: The Karachi Factory Fire', *Newsline* (Karachi), October.

Lascoumes, P. 2013. 'Elites délinquantes et résistance au stigmate: Jacques Chirac et le syndrome Teflon', *Champ pénal*, Vol. X. https://journals.openedition.org/champpenal/8388

Lascoumes, P. 2014. *Sociologie des élites délinquantes. De la criminalité en col blanc à la corruption politique*. Paris: Armand Collin.

Lyttelton, A. 1994. 'Italy: The Triumph of TV', *New York Review of Books*, 11 August.

Mansoor, H. 2016. 'Laws of the Devil', *Dawn*, 1 May.

McCann, M. 2004. 'Law and Social Movements', in *The Blackwell Companion to Law and Society*, edited by A. Sarat. Oxford: Blackwell.

Naseemullah, A. 2017. *Development After Statism. Industrial Firms and the Political Economy of South Asia*. Cambridge: Cambridge University Press.

Osiel, M.J. 1995. 'Dialogue with Dictators: Judicial Resistance in Argentina and Brazil', *Law and Social Enquiry* 20(2): 481–560.

Papanek, H. 1973. 'Pakistan's New Industrialists and Businessmen: Focus on the Memons', in *Entrepreneurship and Modernization of Occupational Cultures in South Asia*, edited by M. Singer. Durham, NC: Duke University Press.

PILER. 2009. *Pakistan mein labour courts ki surat-e-hal. Survey report* (in Urdu) (The situation of labour courts in Pakistan. Survey report). Karachi: PILER.

Robben, A. 1996. 'Ethnographic Seduction, Transference, and Resistance in Dialogues about Terror and Violence in Argentina', *Ethos* 24(1): 71–106.

Sarat, A. and S. Scheingold, eds. 2001. *Cause Lawyering and the State in a Global Era*. New York: Oxford University Press.

Scheingold, S. 1974. *The Politics of Rights. Lawyers, Public Policy, and Political Change*. New Haven: Yale University Press.

Sharif, S. 2017. 'Assessing Forensic Science Landscape in Pakistan', *MIT Technology Review* (Pakistan), 4 May. http://www.technologyreview.pk/assessing-forensic-science-land-scape-pakistan/ (accessed 8 April 2019).

Sumon, M.H., N. Shifa and S. Gulrukh. 2017. 'Discourses of Compensation and the Normalization of Negligence: The Experience of the Tazreen Factory Fire', in *Unmaking the Global Sweatshop. Health and Safety of the World's Garment Workers*, edited by R. Prentice and G. De Neve. Philadelphia: University of Pennsylvania Press.

Thompson, E.P. 1975. *Whigs and Hunters. The Origin of the Black Act*. London: Penguin Books.

Epilogue
South Asian criminal economies

Barbara Harriss-White

By way of conclusion this chapter reviews the findings of the book along four dimensions: first, the project's contribution to scholarship on the crime-business-politics nexus; second, the meaning of 'wildness'; third, contributions of micro-economic and anthropological studies to macro-level models of the criminalisation of politics and the politicisation of crime; and last, the thorniest question: of what is to be done.

Part one: the crime–business–politics nexus

This book is an exploration in political economy and field economics, and in anthropology and ethnography, focussing on the day-to-day social realities of the criminal economy. While it has been years in the making, formally since 2012, with most of the 12 contributors spending months in the field, its actual genesis covers a much longer period, since researchers returned to familiar places which they had often studied over many years in the past. The case studies all find local economies that are dominated by forms of capital that ignore state regulative law or selectively manipulate it to their advantage. These formations control party politics, simultaneously depriving the state of resources while plundering it of the resources it receives from others; they control the sectors they invest in, using violence wherever necessary. Accumulation then runs through political parties and individual criminal organisations and families. Bound to these criminal organisations are extensive networks involving both bonded and/or migrant wage labour and small-scale self-employed workers in the sector concerned, as well as the police, officials in revenue administration and other state agencies, and party politicians. A multitude of other activities is also required to co-ordinate these economic and political transactions: fixers, protectors, middlemen, contractors and subcontractors, clientelist funders and money managers for political parties, lawyers, forgers and vigilantes. And these in turn are embedded in collective institutions, from political parties, chambers of commerce, business associations and trades unions to criminal syndicates and lobbies, illegal cartels, 'rackets' and gangs, clans and families.

Studies on the accumulation of billionaire wealth and the politics of apex public-private partnerships often ignore the systemic nature of the criminal economy (Gandhi and Walton 2012; Bernie 2012; Crabtree 2018). To reduce its social relationships to 'corruption' or 'rent seeking' is to neglect the abundance of behaviours implicated in the system as a whole. Calling them 'supply chains' (as this project's political economists initially did) does not convey their complexity or their manifold activities, objectives and uncertainties. Even the concept of a 'sector' fails to convey the close interlinkages between a series of commodities and areas of criminal endeavour. Ruud finds the concept of 'syndicate' useful (Chapter 10) while Gayer refers to a 'network of connivance' (Chapter 11). Michelutti and Harriss-White call the messy bundle of social relations and variously structured components 'assemblages'.[1] Portfolios can be extensive in a criminal assemblage, mixing the criminal with the 'up-front legal' and sometimes with accumulation from illegal commodities (as happens in these three examples: i) fuel-oil, kerosene, oil adulterants, sand, real estate, hotels and transport in Chapter 6; ii) coal, iron, media, tourism and hotels, liquor, real estate, education and transport in Chapter 1; iii) illegal arms, illegal timber, illegal alcohol, quarries, construction and control over petrol pumps in Chapter 7).

Our case studies of the supply of timber, oil, coal, procurement and real estate show how criminal organisations form a continuum both with the informal economy – activity under the threshold for regulation (or above it and covered by regulation which is not enforced) – and with the formally registered, state-regulated economy. Non-final demand for criminally supplied commodities and services also forms a continuum – ranging from workshop firms not eligible for state-regulated provisions (e.g. coal) to telecom's corporate oligopolists, building contractors, dam builders and international timber businesses. Mafia houses – criminal families accumulating profit by using violence and politics in business – may be legally registered and may even declare and pay tax on some of their turnover.

Assemblages in which the mafia are the leading but not the sole protagonists are entwined with politics. Sectors such as coal and real estate are organised through a system of interlocking transactions – legal and illegal, political and economic – all backed by licensed and unlicensed violence and threats, which bind the state and its agencies to the market and its agencies. For this, Michelutti et al. (2018) have invoked the Italian concept of *intreccio,* signifying that the criminal economy and the actually existing state and politics are not separate worlds, but are fused. Under conditions of *intreccio,* the state as designed in law is unable to control the regulation or taxation of the market.

While it is widely accepted that qualitative research can generate higher-order generalisations about processes (Becker 2017; Flyvbjerg 2006), our findings do not say anything definitive about the extent of the criminal economy in India, Bangladesh and Pakistan, nor its relation to democratic politics. Yet the authoritative intimacy with reality that had to be developed in all the fieldwork has made it hard not to see the findings as part of wider patterns. Building arguments through analogies and examples, they include (following the order of the preceding chapters): a mafia state; mafia criminality; predatory, violent commodification and a pork-barrel state; a policy no-man's-land, ethno-accumulation, and a politics of accumulation by corruption; a criminal caucus, business fused with politics in systemic plunder; *goonda* raj, competitive to monopolistic mafia raj; syndicate raj and *mastan* raj; internationalised criminal capitalism; a mafia state; and finally party-politicised legality and politicised predation.

Is it unwarranted to see these as general phenomena? Is the criminal economy confined to Gandhi and Walton's 'rent-thick' sectors – which we happen to have researched – outside which the economy is legally compliant? In fact, Gandhi and Walton found that less than half of the Forbes list of Indian billionaires had actually accumulated their wealth in rent-thick sectors (2012, 13). The NCAER's State Investment Potential Index Report for 2017 found that corruption was still the single biggest problem for 'entrepreneurs'. Yet while for 56 per cent of Indian business executives corruption was more or less of a problem, 44 per cent of those surveyed in 2017 had 'no problem with corruption' (which of course does not mean they were not involved in corrupt practices) (NCAER 2017, 9–10). How useful are the concepts of 'rent-thick sectors' or summary indicators like 'corruption', when we see here that the criminal economy is so much more complex and dispersed?

Are there 'clean' – or much cleaner – sectors that our research design has missed? Not the rapidly growing sector of waste, where the supreme court banned manual scavenging in 1993 and again in 2014. Yet, among the litany of waste-crimes, every year hundreds of 'scavengers' continue to be suffocated to death by methane in sewers that municipal authorities have demanded they unclog (Harriss-White 2019). Food and agriculture are still the largest single employers and repositories of poverty. In an argument for reconfiguring welfare subsidies, Bhalla (2014) identified fraud and incompetence in the food economy, reporting that half the grain purchased for the public distribution system was 'misplaced' between the warehouse and ration shop and that a further 30 per cent was 'left to rot in government storage facilities'. Meanwhile research on the regulation of land, agricultural markets and real estate confirms a 'political space' in which tenancies are regulated by caste relations and not by law; agricultural wages are also stratified by caste, maintained below the legal minimum with Dalits worst paid. Crop sales face illegally collusive agents. Meanwhile regulators are bribed to grant multiple licences for agri-processing and to enable pollution controls and quality standards to be ignored. Agricultural transport is 'taxed' using prepaid cards in return for illegal overloading. Every office peon is well versed in extortion. The law is ignored, is at the mercy of conflicts within the local capitalist class, or is flouted without sanction and buttressed by illegal private markets. Prakash (2017) has extrapolated from his field research to conceptualise the state as 'hybrid' – where multiple formal and informal institutions are intertwined in collusion, rent-seeking and rent-giving, simultaneous patronage and clientelage, in which control over this sector is distributed outside the formal state (2017, 182–4). So agriculture and food can certainly not be assumed a priori to be 'clean'.

Is there less crime in welfare? Rajshekhar's (2015–2017) three-year pan-Indian 'Ear to the Ground' project reports widespread inadequacies in redistributive and welfare projects in which crime is one of many processes of democratic failure.[2] Fernandez's meticulous study (2012) of the technologies of bureaucratic power at play in implementing a welfare policy for poor tribal women shows a system replete with arbitrary manipulation, irregular procedural reinterpretations, retrospective legitimations, unauthorised improvements, abuse and fraud, delays, lack of coordination, underperformance and non-compliant targetting and selection of participants, such that apparently intended beneficiaries become victims and vice versa (Fernandez 2012). To judge from Rajshekhar's and Fernandez's research, the field of welfare is consistent with *intreccio*, not separate from it.

Furthermore, many aspects of the criminal economy also have direct effects on welfare. Chapter 2, on fire, also shows the dangers to the welfare of contracted mineworkers through the blatant disregard for health and safety regulations at work, while the more or less forced resettlement of Scheduled Tribal people at risk from subsidence and surface fire in ready-made slums without social infrastructure, social entitlements or work is an affront to their welfare. Meanwhile the failure to regulate quality standards, as for fuel (Chapter 6), or the permitting of fuel to be self-regulated in criminally adulterated forms, together with the failure to prevent extortion on tenancies for private childcare (Chapter 8) and the failure to allocate property to entitled SCs (Chapter 9) – all reduce welfare.

So, is the criminal economy confined to certain regions? After all, epicentres of 'severe' corruption in India are said by the NCAER to be confined to West Bengal, Tamil Nadu, Rajasthan, Punjab and Assam (NCAER 2017). Three of these states – West Bengal, Tamil Nadu and Punjab – figure in our project, but so do other states: Arunachal, Andhra, Jharkhand, Uttar Pradesh and the metropolitan megacities. And, while the criminal economy is far from being confined to remote places and border areas, it most certainly crosses state borders, exploiting the impunities conferred by state boundaries. It uses SEZs in this way too. Other research on the informalisation of food policy and on labour regulation has shown that state boundaries can mean significant changes in the scope, practices and economic outcomes of government policies (Mooij 1999; Mahmood 2017). Yet significant regionalised differences in a range of economic activities have been shown to have negligible relation to the frontiers of states (Fouillet 2011; Harriss-White et al. 2014; Basile, Harriss-White and Lutringer 2016). States are often arbitrary data-containers, and it is hard to believe that the criminal economies we have studied do not spill over into other places. It is also unlikely that our examples are not replicated elsewhere.

Our conclusions can thus be treated as hypotheses to be refuted. They are as follows: that the criminal economy is now normal. Where we have investigated it, it is pervasive and systemic. Popular fantasies about its tight organisation notwithstanding, it is also fluid, opportunist and fragmented, but it is nonetheless durable; its heights are socially, economically and politically exclusive. While individuals may be scapegoated and even fall, the system itself survives and thrives through shifts among ruling parties after elections (as shown in detail here for coal, sand, timber and public procurements). The criminalised state is not a failed state.

In addition, while macro-political conditions differ in Bangladesh and Pakistan, their criminal economies are similar to Indian cases. They invoke characterisations as Pax Mafiosa and 'partyarchy', a consociational mafia-owned democracy (for Bangladesh); and a paradigm of degeneration, ordered disorder, the anarchy of the law, of struggle and convergence between civil and criminal law, unbridled capitalism and the 'Wild Wild West' (for Pakistan).

So, in the process of expanding and refining knowledge, immediate priorities for further research include answering these questions:

1. The extent to which, and conditions under which, criminal economy assemblages are alternatives to the state or are entwined with it;
2. The related question of whether *intreccio* and the mafia raj are to be understood as 'normal' capitalism and the 'normal' form of the state in South Asia;
3. Relations between the registered, formal economy and what are known to be larger informal and criminal components, and between legal and criminal behaviour inside capitalist firms and state corporates;
4. The extent to which our case studies are peculiar, state-specific, regional or at times perhaps sectoral variations in the forms taken by criminal economies. Are there less criminalised fields of economic life and how do they, and their regulators, engage with the criminal economy?

These questions have implications for field methods. Clipboards/laptops and pre-designed and coded multiple-choice questions will not yield answers to these questions. Ethnographic approaches are more appropriate.

Part two: the Wild East justified

While 'Wild West' capitalism is a term frequently used pejoratively to refer to Russia – and rule by oligarchs – and even China, connoting unfettered accumulation – how useful did the framework considered in the Introduction, supplied by its two accounts of Wild West anarcho-capitalism and primitive accumulation, prove to be? Both narratives emphasise the establishment of the rule of law, either in the collective law-making of settlers or in the pro-capitalist, property-protective American state after Independence. Our case material by contrast explores the realities of long-established regulative law and its breaking.

In the Wild East, states clearly matter, and these differ in their capacities to regulate and enforce the law – and in the extent of their reach and of their capture. Laws to protect labour are partially or completely unenforced because most people do not see the labour laws as being broken, since they do not know these laws exist. Our case studies also show that the practice of law can be distorted in ways that are not criminal – for example policies may be retrospectively altered to make ad hoc exemptions to benefit political cronies (as in telecom, Chapter 5; see also Bernie 2012; Thakurta et al. 2017). The case studies also reveal a vast repertoire of pathways to criminal accumulation, including resource seizure (for example land, energy, etc.); labour displacement and eviction; the elimination of competition (between market and state, between sectors, scales, regions and castes); monopoly rents; preferential allocations of resources (such as subsidies, physical infrastructure, learning rents/privileged information); the under-pricing of resources (including labour); tax evasion; capital flight; the sabotage, capture and destruction of policy; the evasion of regulations (especially respecting environment, labour and licences); the formation of markets in physical protection (including the protection of non-criminals); and control over the means of social redistribution. Any attempt to bring order to this list would do injustice to the variety of ways in which they are mixed in the criminal economy.

Wildness in the rule of law

Evidently the rule of law is broken. How does this happen? The appendix summarises laws alleged or established to have been broken in our 11 case studies. Despite the variation in detail, a number of features stand out.

The state: Law-breaking is not confined to criminal organisations with the complicity of the police and politicians. Many state agencies are extensively involved, at different levels, in failing to raise tax and non-tax revenue, diverting state resources to private uses, and failing to regulate the economy through law. These range from central government corporations and vigilance services, such as customs and excise, through state-level corporations and most departments of government responsible for regulating the sectors we studied, down to local *panchayat* government. Some crimes, such as bribery, fraud and tax evasion, are pervasive; but some are specific (as in the case of the derecognition of eligibility for rehabilitation and resettlement for people threatened by underground fire).

Assemblages: Attempts in the appendix to identify and summarise single types of offender (as in 'mafia' or 'state') gloss over the clustered but differentiated social relations that characterise a criminal assemblage. Criminal dealings in legal commodities may be interlocked with dealings in illegal commodities (drugs, arms, types of liquor, sports betting, trafficking), in which case the antagonistic individual and party politicisation appear to be a more prominent part of the assemblage – as do privatised protection and extreme violence.

Legal complexity: In South Asian societies where knowledge of legal processes is likely to be better developed than that of the law itself,[3] each sector we researched is festooned in a legal complex likely to have been publicly debated only by legislators at its inception, if then. Many criminal assemblages cut through and ignore great swathes of legal complexes that lawyers themselves have difficulty mastering.

Corruption: Bribery is widespread and is a precondition for fraud, waiving regulations and sharing illegal profit, purchasing votes and party allegiance from workers, and purchasing silence. Cash is not the only form it takes; exchanges in kind are also common, sometimes codified at publicly known rates/prices. Despite its central role in corruption theory, however, bribery seems less important than other kinds of law-breaking unrelated to bribery, particularly defrauding the state – to which bribery has often been linked (Roy 1996; Bernie 2012).

Existence conditions: Finally, in the appendix we have also noted activity that is not criminal but does form part of the existence conditions of the criminal economy. These are not confined to, but include: violation of customary 'norms of violation' (as in access to watercourses and forests, Chapter 4); clashes and power asymmetries between custom and law; preferential prioritising and practice of regulative policy (airwaves for example, Chapter 5); unregulated commodification (as in speculation in MoUs or disputed titles, Chapters 4 and 8); politicised media ownership enabling stage-managed reports, forced silence and blackmail (Chapters 9 and 10; see also Thakurta 2010); threats generating fear that leads in turn to self-censorship and silent complicity; and the deliberate casualisation and disenfranchising of the unskilled labour force, which deprives those workers – who are not necessarily toiling in ignorance – of any alternative to complicity (see the red sanders timber case, Chapter 7).

Why is economic law found here to be so difficult to enforce? Why is punishment so rare? The case studies suggest several reasons:

Resources: Resources (transport, computers, legal resources) may be scarce and personnel inadequately skilled or incompetent.

Complexity: Legal regulation can be technically complex (as the Kolkata real estate and Barisal procurement cases show in Chapters 8 and 10). Complexity intensifies the difficulty of enforcement and the ease of criminal evasion.

Crime-friendly law: Our field material suggests that certain kinds of law are crime-facilitating. By this we mean laws that are either deliberately or through incompetence drafted to leave loopholes and incentives for crime (as is the case of MoUs in Arunachal, the environmental law concerning construction over water bodies and water courses in Chapters 4 and 8, and police investigation procedure in Karachi in Chapter 11). Second, crime-friendly law features punishment for infringement so disproportionate to the 'crime' that it incentivises criminal evasion (the Antiquities and Art Treasures Act of 1972 being a famous example; Vaish and Marwahah 2015). Third, any law where the evidence needed for court cases is stipulated in forms and with a degree of detail that is exceedingly difficult to provide also incentivises criminal evasion (as we saw to be the case in compensation valuations in Chapter 4, tenant protection in Chapter 8 and victim compensation in Chapter 11). Manifestly socially unjust law or law unable to prevent injustice is also crime-friendly (see the case of negligent resettlement and rehabilitation provision in the face of the threat from fire; Chapter 2). Finally, any law whose text shifts faster than the arrangements for its enforcement may also facilitate its own breaking (for example the 59 amendments to the Essential Commodities Act[4]). There may be many more kinds of crime-friendly law.

Complicity: Under conditions where the costs of delivering services efficiently do not threaten criminal bureaucratic accumulation, the latter can co-exist with the former. But state employees – in the bureaucracy, the police and the courts – often benefit privately from failing to uphold or enforce the law, in contexts where their incentive to enforce is overbalanced by their incentive to fail to enforce. The latter incentive takes many forms – in kind (vehicles, even land) as well as cash, sourced from the state as well as provided by criminal organisations, and maintained through greed or fear. Fractions of the state behave as criminal businesses – sometimes alongside compliant public corporations, public service and administration. As shown in earlier research on the sociology of tax law and practice of commercial taxation in Tamil Nadu, cultures of non-compliance mean that, as a Tamil proverb has it, 'an honest man is he who does not know how to live' (Jairaj and Harriss-White 2006).

Order without law

Without any regulation at all, as in mining in Jharkhand (Chapters 1 and 2), extractive activity is dangerous to the workforce underground, to people's homes and lives at the surface, to public infrastructure, and – as the chapters on fire, sand and timber illustrate so well – to what is left of the natural world including the atmosphere it poisons. In the neoliberal era if the only case for the state involved reducing such dangers, it would be a convincing case.

Substitutes for the law

Much of the criminal economy is ordered through forms of authority grounded in pre-existing customary and collective action. Chapter 4 shows how the current criminal turn in Arunachal Pradesh represents a flouting of both customary norms – even the norms for responses to the violation of custom – and state law. The extensive informal economy is regulated through authoritative practices grounded in culture: patriarchy constrains the assets and occupational choices of (inferior) men as well as women; caste and ethnicity supply a corporatist ideology, structure access and define insiders and outsiders with whom transactions may vary; religions meanwhile supply collective identity and institutions to regulate accumulation and distributive activity. Business associations consolidate socially corporatist economies (Basile and Harriss-White 2010). In the so-called neoliberal era, while law-making institutions and the protection of property and people are being privatised, sites of economic authority multiply. However, the case studies indicate that, wherever they operate, the mafia have paramount regulatory authority.

Intreccio

Illegal markets based on plundering state resources and illegal markets run by local mafias are not without order but are idiosyncratically meshed with legally compliant activity. The informal is meshed with the formal, and interlocked transactions form structures of control involving systems of taxation and tribute interwoven with those of the Revenue Department, policed by privatised and politicised forces.

It is remarkable that in an era of rampant and tightly defined nationalism, the unit of moral accountability in the criminal economy – clan, caste, dynasty, family – is so far removed from the banner of the nation.

Wildness as violence

As Marx wrote, force itself 'is an economic power' (1887, Chapter 31). Not all law-breaking is violent, but, in this book, the only case where the use of physical violence was not mentioned was crime in spectrum allocations, at the apex of the national economy. The Bangladesh case

(Chapter 10) tracks a move away from violent predations on the local state and on people to economic crime or soft crime – 'the criminal life of legal commodities' – and from the use of weapons to negotiations and deals. In most of this book however economic crime is not reported as being 'soft'. On the contrary, in every case except spectrum allocation, criminal activity is policed by threats and intimidation; in many cases by extortion, by violent and abusive enforcement (often with private militias, goons, armies, in family vendettas) and by 'structural violence' (Galtung 1969) permeating work conditions (with special oppression meted out to trade unionists). Order is enforced through physical assault and injury, mutilation and torture, kidnap, abduction and disappearances. Over half the case studies report murder as a weapon of regulation. While most of this violence reflects the power of patronage of criminals over the state and over economic and political rivals, in certain cases (as in the timber economy) the state's own task forces kill suspected smugglers in 'encounters'. The brutal treatment of labour as 'smugglers' also leads to questions about the political interests behind the marginalisation, oppression, mass imprisonment and slaughter of tribal labour (Chapter 7).

While the era of American primitive accumulation is said to have pieced together the wage labour force in a 'discontinuous process' (Baker 1990), in South Asia, its 'making' remains violent and coercive as well as discontinuous. Labour has been co-opted into complicity in crime by money or force and by the absence of alternative livelihoods. Violence takes yet other forms in our research: the seizure of resources and property using armed robbery; the vandalism of pipelines and infrastructure; the trafficking in, and destruction of, endangered species, riverbeds, water-bodies and beaches, geological/mineral resources, soil and slopes; and wanton air pollution. The natural world, victim of the criminal economy, can defend itself only in a Latourian way, when extreme events wreak havoc on society,[5] without regard for virtue or criminality.

Victims

Those that lose from criminal economies are not always assetless workers and dependent people. The exchequer is a major loser. Estimates of its losses from the fraudulent 2009 coal auction varied between the official US$30 billion and an earlier (leaked) US$210 billion, and the eventual re-auction raised US$33 billion (Crabtree 2015, citing a former comptroller and auditor general).[6] Foregone resources of this magnitude might have been invested in hard or soft infrastructure in support of public and/or private accumulation, or in implemented policy for redistribution. The degradation and pollution of the environment also hits the middle and bourgeois classes even if the damage to health they cause is thought to be inversely related to class (PHFI 2017).

At the micro scale too, the losers through real estate swindles are not necessarily poor (Chapters 8 and 9); nor are the scions of mafia dynasties who fall victim to violent vendettas (Chapters 1, 2, 6 and 7). The zealous administrator, punished by re-posting – and occasionally by assassination – for seeking to root out mafia criminality is not poor. Workshop producers and consumers, sometimes unentitled to state provisions, who purchase products on black markets are also not necessarily poor.

In the hierarchies of patronage and clientelage and the fluid arrangements of criminal assemblages, the most numerous victims of the criminal economy are those who make it possible through their labour and those whose livelihoods are destroyed by its environmental impact. It is the victimised workforce that drives criminal growth and accumulation. Evoked in detail in Chapters 2 (fire) and 7 (timber), they are typically lowest-caste and tribal people, petty producers and traders, precarious and unfree wage labour, or migrants bonded to contractors, ignorant of other stages of the system in which they are embedded, ignorant of local languages. They do dangerous work in exacting conditions for poor and delayed pay, suffer poor health and early drop-out, are controlled under intense physical discipline, are victims of threats or violence and are targetted for punishment by the state. Described in detail in Chapters 3 on sand, 4 on water, 6 on fuel, 7 on biomass and 8 and 9 on land, the victims of criminal economic activity are those denied their legitimate access to common property resources, to formerly clean and available water and soil; people whose air, water, soil and biodiversity are compromised and polluted. In the tense relationships between identity, citizenship and welfare entitlements, they are also those most frequently excluded from eligibility for state welfare and most dependent on informal parodies.

Resistance

Practically every case study bore witness to resistance to, or in, criminal economies. It is not that there is little resistance, or that it lacks access to the state, but rather that it is poor resistance, lacking effective countervailing power over states riddled with political-criminal complicity. Resistance to the local mafia is part of the discourse of competing parties ahead of elections. Winners may use moments of political change to prosecute formerly immune criminal politicians or criminals formerly protected by rival parties (Chapters 1, 6, 7 and 10). But this is comparatively rare, and the minute proportion who are sentenced find ways to secure bail or are reported as freed early (as in Chapter 5).[7] Mafias are resisted by other elements in the criminal assemblage – in black coal these are syndicates and cycle wallahs (Chapter 1), as well as by labour organisers (Chapter 2), civil society organisations, movements of victims (Chapters 8 and 9), social and political activists, students and exceptional journalists and public interest lawyers (Chapters 3, 4 and 5). Expert commissions of enquiry have exposed crimes (Chapter 3). The judiciary has played an important role in identifying economic crimes and ordering the state to proceed against criminals – but it lacks enforcement powers (Chapters 3 and 11). Of course much resistance – and to judge from the case studies, the most effective resistance – comes from criminal organisations and assemblages to challenges not from the institutions listed above but from labour, to the threat posed by reprisals due to political competition, and to hostile competition from rivals.

In the Braudellian terms of our Introduction here, has the notion of wildness helped the 'interpretation of events'? To sum up our concept of wildness: the process of creating capital reported here is a highly conflictual and wasteful process. The case studies more resemble primitive accumulation than the Wild West's anarcho-capitalism. Criminal accumulation involves the coexistence and mutual dependence of capitalist accumulation (profit from wage labour invested in expanded reproduction) with primitive accumulation (seizure of resources for productive investment and separation of labour from their means of production) and with common or garden theft for non-productive ends. Our evidence allows for various interpretations of the concept of the primitive: capture of the state, plunder from the state (Harvey's accumulation by dispossession (ABD)), under-priced/under-invoiced transactions, market transactions with varying degrees of violence, pillage, together with the creation and preservation of coercively controlled, unfree labour under conditions akin to slavery. A further distinctively South Asian characteristic of criminal accumulation is the perpetuation of small-scale activity alongside vast criminal empires.

Evidently more research needs developing on several topics:

1. The balance between the roles of culture, political power and the logic of profit-making in criminal accumulation;
2. The politics and economics of law-breaking within the state apparatus and public corporations, their internal victims and beneficiaries, the roles of vigilance and punishment in public agencies and agencies regulating private markets;

3. Sectoral and regional variations, pursuing the intense specificity of much of this behaviour inside South Asia;
4. The status and roles of compliant behaviour in cultures of non-compliance;
5. Explorations of crime-friendly law;
6. The varied social and political responses to crimes against the environment, property and persons of differing status;
7. The impact of fear and terror on economic behaviour in large and in small businesses;
8. Granular policy studies (after the method of Fernandez 2012) in sectors affecting, and affected by, the criminal economy, e.g. finance, the police and other regulators and vigilance agencies;
9. The politics of complicity.

Part three: macro and micro – contributions from field economics and anthropology

As it goes to press, this book joins other new contributions to a scholarly understanding of the neoliberal economy and its threat to democratic politics. We have space to sample three here.

Kapur and Vaishnav (2018) see the neoliberal democratic threat as a worldwide phenomenon in which India, the world's largest democracy, is embedded. India's considerable election costs, many legitimate,[8] must be met either by candidates' self-financing (Sircar 2018) or by business funding to parties (a telling example being the cement industry) in return for favours. Alternatively, in the case of cash-strapped subaltern parties, symbiotic relations with larger parties in alliances involve cross-party subsidies in return for sacrifices and compromises in the allocation of party candidates (Collins 2018). All three mechanisms constrain the entry and success of candidates. The complex business of political money sometimes flows multi-directionally; elsewhere the three ways of meeting election costs characterise different levels of electoral business politics (Bussell 2018). In the institution of the election commission, the state has acted with integrity but presides over poor quality election legislation which political parties have no interest to reform. In Kapur and Vaishnav's project, where flows of campaign money from politicians to voters are understood as gifts signalling exchanges rather than outright purchase of votes, where the black economy is argued 'counterintuitively' as capable of 'generating positive consequences' (growth, employment and social networks) (Bussell 2018, 27), the criminal economy itself is not characterised as among the driving threats to democracy.[9] Crime is a matter of 'background' or quantifiable 'cases', and mafias are hardly mentioned. Our book contributes to the 'more research' Kapur and Vaishnav call for, with accumulation at its heart.

Second, James Crabtree, a former economic correspondent for the *Financial Times* in India, has pieced together five years of access to the new billionaire class and the regulative and banking elite serving it, not only chronicling the unprecedented inequality it creates, its ballooning numbers, wealth (rising from US$176 billion in 2011 to US$500 billion by 2018) and its vast and globally conspicuous consumption, but also unearthing its politics (Crabtree 2018). At odds with a ruling party-political discourse extolling equality and anti-fraud, elections are found by Crabtree to be working through faction and patronage, funded by crony capital that is enriched in feedback relations of nepotism, undetected political funding and corrupt state agencies. Decentralised to constituent states, the pork barrel as described by Jeyaranjan (Chapter 3) is reinterpreted as 'entrepreneurial municipal corruption'. Under the BJP, Crabtree sees a rebalancing of relations between politics and business (using digital technology, public auctions, tougher loan conditions, etc.) and no reason why India should not move into a progressive era. Set beside Crabtree's 'journey through a gilded age', our project is almost entirely underneath his navigation system, often in Ruud's 'provincial ponds' (Chapter 10). Only two of our cases involve US dollar-denominated billionaires (in airwaves and in a portfolio built on timber, the latter not appearing among the 140 Indians on the Forbes lists). Our local case studies of the practice of crime may explain how the ruling party could appear in his eyes relatively distanced from the mafia (Crabtree 2015, 2018), how the criminality of the neoliberal economy is not confined to its apex but is systemic and how the move towards a progressive era is strewn with vast obstacles.

Third, Rajshekhar's project for *Scroll.in*, 'Ear to the Ground' (Rajshekhar 2015–17), involved three years of field research from early 2015 in six states, examining the biggest changes in a 'nation in flux' – flushing out the principal conundrum of widespread malfeasance against poor people, amid the Forbes Rich List's egregious wealth. In 77 reports, this malfeasance ranges from failure to protect people from arsenic contamination in Bihar through opaque party-political meddling and declining profitability in Gujarat's milk cooperatives; informalising local ruling party political power over the police and revenue administration, thereby marginalising the elected representatives in Punjab; preferential contracts for local ruling party workers, etc. Finding no single explanation for such behaviour on the part of the state, he invokes poor revenues, fiscal conservativism and defective and withering competences in state bureaucracies, the understaffing of state services, and the overriding need to attract business. He finds 'drift' – path dependence and lack of manoeuvrability – and cannot avoid recording the damaging effects of the centralising and extractive tendencies of political parties. He sees the criminal economy, tax evasion and parallel politicised taxation systems as underlying the political and bureaucratic abandonment of the concept of public interest. He also finds no single convincing explanation for feeble resistance to this behaviour. In our project, the centrality of crime acts as a complement to the centrality of the state in Rajshekhar's.

What can be contributed by our cases' two distinctive features:

1. Adding micro-level evidence on the nuts and bolts of the criminal economy and local democracy;
2. Applying insights from an ethnographic lens to the macro-level scenarios?

The mature clientelist state: criminals and politicians

Jha's (2013) account, laid out in this book's Introduction, of the evolution of what he calls the 'mature clientelist state' as a congeries of relations between business, politicians, mafiosi and the police has been broadly corroborated here. Our case studies show, however, that the justice system, the central focus of two chapters (Chapter 8 on tenancy and Chapter 11 on the perpetrators of a factory fire), is also bound into this nexus. Its roles are context-specific. For every instance of the courts' marshalling expert evidence, nailing crime and meting out punishment (Chapters 2, 3, 4, 5, 9 and 11), there is other evidence of the court being avoided entirely (so quasi-legal settlements are made elsewhere or illegal ones are forced) or ignored (Chapters 3 and 9). Irregular investments are made to delay or suspend hearings and to determine judgments and their outcomes (Chapters 8, 9 and 11). Money power may yield to that of organised interests. Party political pressure can force legally unjustified interpretations of procedure and evidence, the non-appearance of witnesses, threats to witnesses in court, etc. (Chapters 3 and 11).

Our material also shows that Jha's 'congeries' involves much more extensive co-option and participation of non-corporate fractions of capital than he had space to describe – or Crabtree chose to investigate. Under the radar of census authorities, significant numbers of part- or full-time livelihoods are engaged in the criminal economy. Criminal assemblages survive post-election changes in government and maintain profitable relations with politicians out of office as well as with election winners from whom paybacks are demanded. Mafiosi rarely form a 100 per cent criminal organisation and their reach varies. Meanwhile, the police are an important component of a large range of other institutions formally responsible for regulating society, economy and state. The informal economy, which limits the scope of the powers of these regulating agencies without breaking any law, is as necessary to their functioning as the criminal economy is necessary to privatised trajectories of wealth within these vigilance agencies. Immature new states (Jharkhand, Arunachal and Andhra in this project) are far from immune to colonisation by Jha's 'congeries' and bear signs of precocious maturity.

Criminals

Our cases show that criminal capitalists are lured into politics by the possibility of combining these prospects with immunity from prosecution for crime once elected.[10] Professional managers of criminal protection and organisers of labour for criminal organisations have also entered politics themselves directly (see Chapter 1 on coal). Others control politics by funding parties and shaping their pre-election mixes of pork-barrel and private vote-buying activity, and their post-election allocation of preferential policies, subsidies, state resources and other favours (as in Chapter 3 on sand). A criminal business executive may not need to enter politics directly but will profit from being a client of a politician and a patron of bureaucrats. Mafia control over labour and petty enterprises also supplements direct plunder from the state and/or illegal production and distribution as sources of criminal accumulation. Legislators are increasingly wealthy and facing criminal charges. Of the winning candidates in the 2014 All-India elections, 34 per cent had outstanding charges for crimes, 21 per cent for serious crimes (a 50 per cent increase on the previous election).[11] From UPA-1 to UPA-2, the proportion of wealthy *crorepati* MPs doubled to 48 per cent. By 2014, 82 per cent of MPs were *crorepatis* with average assets of INR15 *crore*.[12] For such politicians it is most unlikely that politics is not a business.

Politicisation of crime, criminalisation of politics

In processes of double regulatory capture, independent regulators are captured by the criminalised state while the state bureaucracy, the management of public corporations supplying essential commodities and infrastructure (whether hard like railways or soft like education) and the hierarchies of the judiciary are objects of capture by politicians seeking to serve their private interests. Flows of criminal tribute inside the state, not only from bribery but also from criminal systems of tax, subject the bureaucracy to intensely politicised pressure. Yet while in corruption theory the category of politician is frequently fused with that of the official, our case studies (of sand, of timber, of rental markets) often show them as having discrete interests, so that threat or coercion will be deployed by politicians to secure the necessary concessions.

Impact on the economy

For Jha, the criminalisation of politics and the politicisation of crime have serious negative economic outcomes. These involve path-dependent inefficiencies due to maximising profit from suboptimal technological choices, dysfunctional delays, the perpetuation of subsidies and the fragmentation of state investments into capturable components, not to mention the spending of plundered resources on private interests and capital flight (so such spending may be abroad). Our case studies supply suggestive evidence of nepotism and cronyism in resource allocation unrelated to merit, efficiency, price or competence (see Chapter 4 on hydro-electricity, Chapter 5 on spectrum, Chapter 10 on procurement). They also document vast and extensive operational inefficiencies in state enterprises (e.g. coal in Chapter 1, in the (intermittent) regulation of sand in Chapter 3 and in the management of land and water use in Chapters 4 and 9), in which technocratic discretion in the efficient running of state enterprises is subordinated to the profits of criminal organisations.[13] As Rajshekhar stresses, and as our case material testifies by its absence, distributive policy is a very low priority in the arrangements we have studied, except when the distributions flow downwards for political advantage and upwards for protection and profit.

    Several distinctive features of the economic impact of the criminal economy stand out. One, we repeat, is the fusion of legal activity with crime. In the telecom case, the neoliberal ideology of 'markets' is kidnapped for ransom by big business cronies: wild behaviour is masked by layers of incentivist policy, discretionary support and bailouts.[14] Neoliberalism for the credulous.[15] Does the criminal economy perhaps contribute to growth through its labour intensity? Not necessarily. For all its penumbra of petty scavenging, pilfering, small-scale criminal trade and services, criminal business can and does mobilise heavy machinery, large-scale transport (multiple 'rakes' for coal, for instance, or containers for timber), and makes full use of access to the global banking system. While India's growth is part-produced by such assemblages, they are invisible in the official record and in macro-scale political economy.

Some implications of *intreccio* for democracy

Scholars of current electoral politics have given it a profusion of critical labels: 'weak democracy', 'immature democracy', 'democratic decay' or 'decline', 'democratic deficit', 'erosion', and so on.[16] Our case studies of *intreccio* provide rich detail of the undemocratic practices flowing from tangled criminal-political transactions. When the electoral cycle is criminalised, entry costs exclude poorer people and small parties and limit opposition to the process of domination of elites and dynasties. Electoral democracy survives alongside the privatisation, decentralisation and multiplication of relations of coercive control and with battles for centralised authority (Chapters 4 and 7). At one end of the scale, commodified relations with voters become normalised, while at another, capital flight compromises the capacity of political elites to counter theft from the state – supposing they are inclined to. In rural regions where revolutionary parties have mobilised support, operating at war with the state, the 'terrorist' cadres are routinely incorporated through cesses/levies and protection from attack into criminal economic assemblages, which at the same time assimilate the police and private militias (Chapter 1). All this is in sharp contrast to orthodox political analyses, in which the criminal economy is ignored or marginalised (Chapters 1 to 5). When the criminal economy drives politics, uncertainties result from the contradiction in which the mafia's penetration of all local parties provides them with stability, which in turn facilitates accumulation, while mafia houses also favour party-political instability because it protects them from prosecution.

The contributions of anthropology and ethnography

Anthropological reporting compensates for the complicity and silence of media (showing how it works; see Chapter 10) and reveals categories of behaviour neglected in official statistics. Our case studies show conclusively that ethnography is not to be parked in a pigeon-hole labelled 'non-economy'. Given that our ethnographies have covered multiple scales, they are also not to be regarded as excessively small-scaled and irrelevant to political economy. It is not simply a matter of the detail of criminal transactions, contracts and deals; the rich anthropological chapters also show how the criminal economy requires, and is permeated by, non-market exchanges – the reciprocities involved in the defence of class privileges, clientelist favours and the redistribution of criminal tribute (Chapters 6, 9 and 11). They reveal the criminalisation of politics through dimensions of politics not confined to those of class or of political party. Culture, in particular, is embedded in economic crime, debunking the idea that, despite the compulsions of accumulation, crime has a simple economic logic or organising principle (see also Michelutti et al. 2018). And while the criminal economy is overwhelmingly male, gender nonetheless matters. Women (and children) are visible not simply as particularly oppressed labour, scavengers and oustees (Chapters 2 and 7), trafficked commodities, victims of vendettas and battles over honour (Chapters 6, 9 and 11), but also as political agents: as consumers (Chapter 5), as a major player in the scams and violence over the protection of tenancies (Chapter 8), as key political forces in the dynastic reproduction of mafia families (Chapter 1) and as activist lawyers (Chapter 3). Faction, kinship (real or symbolic) and patronage also structure criminal economies. Over and above the mobilisation of criminal political upper-caste caucuses to oppose and crush the emancipatory aspirations of OBCs, SCs and STs,[17] intermediate/dominant caste rivalries – Thakurs versus Jats (Chapter 6), Kammas against Reddys (Chapter 7), Rajput Singhs among themselves (Chapters 1 and 2) – use the criminal economy for status and not merely for profit. Caste and ethnicity stratify the bureaucracy – 'vernacular *netas*' (Kumar 2015, 5) – and permeates the politics of parties not overtly set up to further specific caste interests.

Jha uses the transaction costs of untraceable fundraising to explain dynastic politics in terms of efficiency. However, our ethnographies find other reasons for the dynastic politics that structure criminal assemblages. Mafia dynasties are units of trust, in which leadership, honour and displays of masculinity are valued. These qualities have other uses in the criminal economy. In Chapter 7 on timber, for example, we see the heroic and honourable status of the masculine, semi-mythical social bandit, which informs popular imagery of the timber smuggler, influencing and justifying police brutality against vulnerable migrant timber labour.

In Bangladesh (Chapter 10) – where the macro-scale political economy is one of confrontational party political competition, and the 'black' or 'shadow' economy accounts for anywhere between 45 and 80 per cent of GDP – the regulation of violence, the criminalisation of state procurement procedure and of plunder from the state proceeds regardless of the party in power and is structured through neighbourhood, friendship and threat, which override the rules of tendering. Pakistan (Chapter 11) is ruled by (para)military factionalism in an economy suffused with military investment in natural resource extraction, agri-industry, the built environment, finance and insurance – and illegal commodities. Nevertheless, our case study of a lethal factory fire shows how criminal prosecution was delayed, politicised and diffused through the lobbying of the elite capitalist class – tensely separate from the military but ultimately manipulated by them – and by conflicts rooted not just in aggressive relations between the military and paramilitary 'security' forces but also in ethnicity and neighbourhood. Ethnography reveals the social relational content of high growth, not only in India but also in Pakistan and Bangladesh – even if this content also prevents growth from being higher.

Possibilities for developing multi- and inter-disciplinary research into the feedback relations between macro and micro include the following:

1. Economic biographies of *crorepati* legislators in state and central governments charged with serious crimes (a statistical base already exists, ready for ethnographic enquiry);
2. Power relations between politicians, bureaucrats and the police;
3. The judicial politics of politicised crime, of charges, of prosecution and sentencing and the roles of lawyers in these processes;
4. The political economy of law-breaking by law-abiding firms compared with that of criminal organisations;
5. Crime and efficiency: the relation between, on the one hand, criminal assemblages, crony appointments and the allocation of privileges, transactions bidding, etc., on grounds other than either law or efficiency and, on the other hand, the co-existence of multiple technologies in sectors of the economy, their relative economic efficiency, safety and labour intensities, and the competence of their management;
6. Domestic politics and international relations of tax evasion.

Part four: what is to be done?

What is to be done if the agents of reform are agents in the criminal economy? How to expand inclusive development when the criminal economy is doing the same, busily irrigating the nutrient base of party coffers and political redistribution systems that gamble on buying allegiance – if not directly benefitting holders of high office? *Quis custodiet ipsos custodes* – who watches the watchmen and regulates the regulators? In setting the context for this final set of reflections there is no lack of suggestions from others based on a range of approaches to South Asia's political economies, business–state linkages and more or less expected neoliberal corruption. PricewaterhouseCoopers' (2016) global economic crime survey examined in the Introduction exemplifies the corporate discursive approach to policy. Laws exist, therefore their enforcement failures need to be addressed. These failures are manifestations of weak institutions, incompetence, unskilled personnel inside businesses, the police and the judiciary. To restore the reputation of business and the legitimacy of states, poor recruitment standards need reform, non-performing assets have to be corrected and capital flight must be prevented. Questions of agency and politics, so central to this book, do not arise. Kapur and Vaishnav (2018) argue for transparent funding, a realistic lifting of caps on election spending by individuals, greater disclosure and more powers for the election commission as *sine qua nons* to increase the accountability of Indian democracy. Elsewhere Vaishnav sees the regulation of political finance and the abolition of black money in politics as urgent supply-side reforms to the political market place (2017, Chapter 8). Crabtree roots his suggestion that a combination of corruption crackdowns and basic improvements in public services will eventually 'reassert' good governance in analogies from America in the 1930s. Gandhi and Walton (2012) also see an analogy with the anti-trust movement (the popular movement against the robber barons in early twentieth-century America, backed by some of the executive and judiciary), although they fear that the Indian state lacks the capacity to manage the 'rising corporate sector'. The political preconditions to this list of measures and mobilisations are not developed. But then there is 'more privatisation' (Shah 2018). Given the failure to reach an 'optimal mix of incentives and sanctions' and given the levels of plunder and criminal activity inside the state, further privatisation is a proposal grounded in the neoliberal logic of reducing inefficiencies – except that our evidence shows how dangerous it is to privatise the state's regulative agencies. Other technocratic suggestions involve tighter, un-corrupt audit, exemplary punishment for offences and digitisation, to enable the same data trail for politics as for the economy. Ghosh, Chandrasekhar and Patnaik (2017) see a need for reforms first to the tax administration, second to economic monitoring (for example, for real estate transactions, over- and under-invoicing, movement of funds and defaulters abroad) and third to transparency in party-political funding. Kumar (2015) emphasises reforms to improve the professionalisation of the bureaucracy, the police and courts to strengthen their independence from political domination. In Kumar's account greater technical competence is another necessary condition to break the nexus of criminality and politics.

These suggestions, flowing from a range of theoretical approaches, all miss an analysis of the forces and institutions that need to be in place first to identify and then to counter opposition to such policies. Political will is the most notorious of several escape hatches. Jha (2013, 22), reasoning through the technical case for a state funding system for financing elections, admits that 'no single reform of the political system has been proposed more often; and no proposal has been more consistently rejected'. His contribution explains why.

How is the (current) BJP government in India responding to this deluge of advice? The elimination of 'corruption' and the 'black economy' was a popular theme in the 2014 election. 'I have come to cleanse politics', said Narendra Modi (quoted in Vaishnav 2017, 282). Four years into his governing term, Prime Minister Modi used the Independence Day 2018 speech to promise a better quality of life for all citizens. But citizenship is a process (in a state like Assam, citizenship is threatened by the very mechanisms to deliver this promise: evidence of identity, which is required in the form of a crime-friendly inappropriate detail; see Hazarika 2018).[18] Quality of life connotes not a dematerialised state but a development process requiring resources evaded on a grand scale by the criminal economy described here. And the turn to welfare distracts attention from the failure of the BJP's attempt to crush the criminal economy.

What has failed? While apex accumulation strategies are resilient to changes in government,[19] the final reflection in this epilogue focusses on the BJP's important intervention in the criminal economy. It shows two things: how many of the dimensions of criminality covered in this book were involved in the state's own attack on it; and why, despite the trigger of surprise and the weighty lever of state power, the existing political economic structure cannot be expected to reduce crime.

Demonetisation and the criminal economy[20]

On 8 November 2016, a sudden announcement made illegal most of the common paper tender in which 86 per cent of India's cash currency transactions took place. 'Notebandi' was officially declared to be aimed at destroying corruption, counterfeiting, terrorism and black money. On 27 December 2016, the Prime Minister declared that this mission had been accomplished. But on 29 August 2018, when the Reserve Bank had finished counting banknotes, over 99 per cent had been returned. Only an outstanding 11,000 *crore* was written off, punishing its criminal owners – or those holding it in neighbouring countries (Anand 2018).

Taking the stated objectives of demonetisation in turn, while corruption is the common man's normal expectation in his encounter with the state, it has long been understood that tax evasion is far more quantitatively significant (Roy 1996; Bernie 2012). In fact, while only 3 per cent pay income tax, tax revenue rose by 12 per cent in the year following demonetisation.

The circulation of counterfeit money has been greatly overrated, however and does not justify the considerable economic disruption involved in demonetisation. Unless counterfeit notes are detected when deposited in a bank, demonetisation cannot eradicate them. The production of forged notes depends on access to (illicit) technology and (imported) paper. The new currency is easier to forge. While the RBI reports a drop of some 30 per cent in the total seizure of counterfeit currency in 2017–18 (Reserve Bank of India 2018), the number of forged INR500 and INR2000 notes detected increased from 837 in 2016–17 to 27,821 in 2017–18 (*Scroll.in* Editorial 2018).

As for terrorism, two facts speak eloquently about the practical success of the note-ban in combatting terror: first, the fact that money denominated in new INR2000 notes was recovered within six weeks of demonetisation from the corpses of terrorists in Kashmir and other places, and second that a rise in violence attributed to terrorism was documented subsequent to (but not necessarily related to) demonetisation (Tripathi 2017). Hence, the criminal black economy was the most significant declared objective for an unprecedentedly disruptive reform (Ghosh, Chandrasekhar and Patnaik 2017).[21]

Black political funding: Our case studies have confirmed the need for election costs to be met by untraceable funds. Indeed over 75 per cent of funds officially recorded as received by Indian political parties in 2004–11 were from 'unknown sources'. While the Indian government admits the need to reform political funding, the bill to do this has languished before parliament for two decades thanks to permanent cross-party reluctance to discuss it, let alone make party funding transparent. At this rate, until a government feels secure in its funding India will have to wait for reform. Yet the sudden announcement of demonetisation does not seem to have surprised the ruling party. The media reported unexpected large-scale land purchases outside future Smart Cities in advance of 8 November 2016 by ruling party members, and the use of cooperatives – at least in Gujarat – to receive unusually huge deposits. Parties depositing demonetised currency notes in their accounts were exempt from income tax provided individual donations were below INR 20,000. Reports suggest that deposits of less than INR 2.5 *lakh* in political party accounts will 'not necessarily be chased by the Income Tax' (*Livemint* Editorial 2016).

Black money: As for the black economy, expert estimates of its size vary massively, from between 17 per cent (PTI 2017) to 52 per cent of GDP (Kar 2010; Sharma 2016). But the proportion of the black economy held in money form is thought to lie between 1 and 6 per cent. On demonetisation, this money was returned to banks using a range of mechanisms.[22] The rest of the black economy is in kind – about half in real estate (not widely expected to have changed after demonetisation), less in gold and jewellery and the rest exported or laundered overseas through well-established *hawala* and 'layering channels' that operate through Nepal, Singapore, Dubai and Mauritius (Kar 2010). From there it may return in whitened forms, and may even be eligible for investment subsidies. Black money also escapes through untaxed donations to temples – and certain colleges and hospitals – that may benevolently return some fraction of the receipts to their donors.

Currency notes are neither black nor white but move in and out of this black cash sub-sector. In the first six weeks after demonetisation, of the INR 500 *crore* seized by the Income Tax Department, nearly 20 per cent was already denominated in INR 2,000 notes.

Criminal business: On 29 December 2016 the PM was quoted as concluding that demonetisation had had a 'crippling impact on damaging illegal activities' (*India Today* 2016). Yet there has been far less research into the impact of demonetisation on the apex of the criminal economy than on the policy's monetary and fiscal effects, and what analysis there is mostly takes the form of low-quality evidence and press reports.

Demonetisation seems to have had mixed effects on the criminal economy, and these effects are changing over time. We need to know much more about each mafianised sector. For instance, there are fragments of evidence that the trade in stolen coal from tailings and abandoned mines in Jharkhand and West Bengal, and the hub in Assam dealing in illegal 'rat-hole' Meghalayan coal, all initially paused due to the cash shortage and the need to invest time in depositing illegal tender. However, in 2018 they restarted. Others gamed the system: a coal mafioso was seized in West Bengal one month after demonetisation holding INR 33 *lakh* in the new notes, plus arms and ammunition, in the company of a local BJP leader, while a Tamil Nadu sand baron was arrested in late December after an IT raid. Other crackdowns, however, – as in August 2016, on boats and engines of the Gujarat sand mafia, and in the September destruction of psychoactive plants in Himachal Pradesh – had preceded the 8 November decision, proving that demonetisation was not needed to punish criminal activity – enforcement agencies simply needed to enforce the law. With respect to illegal commodities, it appears from reports by 10 rescue groups and the testimony of Nobel peace prize winner Kailash Satyathi that the massive cash-based supply chain through which girls and women are trafficked for prostitution rapidly dried up after demonetisation. Contradictory reports find that cash demand for prostitutes atrophied, that the new bank notes create demand for 'higher quality' (young and new) sex workers and that prostitutes quickly turned to work on credit, for digital payment and even temporarily for pay to cover board and lodging. Law Ministry claims of a permanent drop in the flesh trade are denied by prostitutes (Bhattacharya 2017). Meanwhile, local narcotics control bureaus reported drugs seizures as dropping in Himachal Pradesh, Mumbai and on the Bangladesh border. Yet the significant international trade in hard drugs uses hardly any cash and was said to have been unaffected. There is little subsequent evidence to suggest that the objective of destroying the criminal economy was successful.

Demonetisation dealt a far keener blow to incomes, investments and livelihoods in the informal economy (Guerin et al. 2017) than to black wealth or the criminal economy. Cleaning up the criminal economy needs two kinds of political preconditions: first, triggers and second, levers of economic power. In India, the extreme event of demonetisation was one such trigger but it failed. The state is also a lever of power that has largely been co-opted. It is not able to prosecute individual company officials. Its progressive legal decrees are often ignored.

Our book develops an alternative position. Mafia assemblages and *intreccio* will only be threatened under three kinds of circumstances: first, when sufficient assets have been accumulated to reduce the need for criminal rents; second, when viable state apparatuses and publicly funded political parties are needed by capital to control criminal rents and regulate the economy. The case material shows, however, that there is no guarantee that processes of predatory rent and the undermining of legal-ethical obligations and organisational capacity will yield to those from legitimate profit-seeking capitalism. The third condition is when the workforce can no longer be deceived, captured and bought off. At present trade unions do not have sufficient countervailing power; some are viciously crushed by criminal organisations while others are in thrall to local mafias. Until such a time when these conditions develop, scholars will have to develop and debate South Asia's mafia raj and openly mainstream its many and serious implications for the economy, politics and policy analysis, in teaching and in public deliberation.

Notes

1. This is to invigorate political economy by borrowing insights from assemblage theory about multiple functionalities and fluidity in the elements/components of a social territory, while not accepting that field's ahistoricity and abandonment of structure (see Karaman 2008 on LaLanda).
2. See 'Ear to the Ground' at *Scroll.in*: https://scroll.in/topic/24308/ear-to-the-ground.
3. Legal illiteracy is a worldwide phenomenon.
4. The UK visa system has had 5,700 amendments between 2010–18; it is now 375,000 words long and 'a disgrace', according to a senior judge (Bozic et al. 2018).
5. At the time of writing flooding in Kerala has devastated the land, due not only to extreme weather (following extreme storms in Northern India earlier in 2018 and extreme floods in Chennai in 2015–16) but to neglect and poor management of the fragile tropical biosphere, including criminal quarrying, illegal deforestation and illegal construction (see Gadgil 2011).
6. Using World Bank modelling, Dev Kar's estimate for the losses to the Indian economy of capital flight from Independence to 2008, in 2008 prices, was IS$500 billion. While 10 per cent of black income is exported (Kumar 2017) over 70 per cent of assets in India's criminal economy are held abroad (Kar 2010).
7. See Kumar 2015 (pp. 190 and 199) for case material on the politics of non-prosecution and non-punishment in contemporary Bihar.
8. Rising from US$2 billion in 2009 to US$5 billion in 2014 (Kapur and Vaishnav 2018, citing Centre for Media Studies data).
9. Communalism is another driver; the multifarious cultural seeds of fascism (Banaji 2013) a third.
10. They can also secure immunity by crossing state borders (see Michelutti in Chapter 6 of this volume).
11. See http://adrindia.org/content/lok-sabha-elections-2014. Of course it is countered that accusations are part of the regular political to and fro and so such crimes are fabricated, but with immunity extending during and often 'informally' after the period of office (a minute proportion have been successfully pursued) it is hard to judge this argument.
12. Approximately US$2.1m, in a society where 70 per cent own less than US$70,000 (INR 50 *lakh*) in wealth. See also Kumar 2015, 44–6.
13. This does not imply the absence of other sources of inefficiency, or that state enterprise cannot be efficient.
14. See Dasgupta 2014 and Crabtree 2018.
15. The relation between the predictions of neoliberal theory that pruning the state would reduce corruption and the apparent rise in corruption under neoliberal reforms was researched in general terms in White and Harriss-White 1996. The resilience of corruption in a neoliberal era has led to critiques of the intentionality of neoliberalism (Joseph 2018).
16. Respectively Khan 2000; Sundaresan 2013; Van Dijk 2017; Kulova and Varghese 2017, 126 and 132; Kumar 2015.
17. See Chapter 5 of Kumar 2015 for the gang-mediated, state-supported caste war over land between Rajputs and Yadavs in Bihar.
18. The Assam government, compiling a new National Register of Citizens, threatens with statelessness and deportation an estimated 5 million people (of a state population of 32 million) who are unable to supply 'legacy documentation' of settled status prior to 1971.
19. From a number of sources, under the NDA from 2014, these include the alleged criminal history of the party high command, cronyism in the allocation of land, natural resources and customs refunds, enabled absconding of individuals with allegedly massive unpaid loans, and fugitive money-launderers.
20. Unless referenced otherwise, this summary is based on evidence and sources in Ghosh, Chandrasekhar and Patnaik 2017; Harriss-White 2017; Kumar 2017.
21. The annual growth rate dropped by between 1.5 and 1.9 per cent. According to CMIE data the labour force fell from 440 million in 2016–17 to 426 million in 2017–18 and 402 million in the first quarter of 2018–19. In the first two years, the participation rate fell from 46 per cent to 44 per cent as a result of demonetisation and General Sales Tax reforms (Vyas 2018).
22. Ghosh, Chandrasekhar and Patnaik (2017) report multiple ID cards and bank accounts, use of accounts belonging to friends, relatives and employees, use of middlemen converting at discount rates of 18–40 per cent, conversion to gold and jewellery, backdated receipts, advance payments for travel and fuel, receipts for agricultural transactions and the payment of taxes!

References

Anand, N. 2018. 'India's Central Bank Just Proved Demonetisation Was for Nothing', *Quartz*, 29 August. https://qz.com/india/1373030/modis-demonetisation-did-nothing-for-india-shows-rbi-report/ (accessed 30 April 2019).

Baker, E. 1990. 'The Primitive Accumulation of Capital in the United States', *Iskra* 1(1): 1–14.

Banaji, J., ed. 2013. *Fascism: Essays on Europe and India*. New Delhi: Three Essays Press.

Basile, E. and B. Harriss-White. 2010. 'India's Informal Capitalism and its Regulation', *International Review of Sociology* (special issue) 20(3): 457–71.

Basile, E., B. Harriss-White and C. Lutringer, eds. 2015. *Mapping India's Capitalism: Old and New Regions* (EADI Series). London: Palgrave.

Becker, H. 2017. *Evidence*. Chicago, IL: University of Chicago Press.

Bernie. 2012. 'All Sorts of Roguery? The "Financial Aristocracy" and Government à Bon Marché in India', *Monthly Review MROnline*, 19 August. https://mronline.org/2012/08/19/bernie190812-html/ (accessed 30 April 2019).

Bhalla, S. 2014. *Dismantling the Welfare State*. Carnegie Endowment for International Peace, 20 June. http://carnegieendowment.org/2014/06/10/dismantling-welfare-state-pub-55885 (accessed 30 April 2019).

Bhattacharya, R. 2017. 'Trafficking Never Stops: Don't Live in a Fool's Paradise', *Indian Express*, 12 November. https://indianexpress.com/article/india/trafficking-never-stops-dont-live-in-a-fools-paradise-demonetisation-sex-worker-4933286/ (accessed 30 April 2019).

Bozic, M., C. Barr, N. McIntyre and P. Noor. 2018. 'Revealed: Immigration Rules in UK More than Double in Length', *The Guardian*, 27 August. https://www.theguardian.com/uk-news/2018/aug/27/revealed-immigration-rules-have-more-than-doubled-in-length-since-2010 (accessed 8 April 2019).

Bussell, J. 2018. 'Whose Money, Whose Influence? Multilevel Politics and Campaign Finance in India', in *Costs of Democracy: Political Finance in India*, edited by D. Kapur and M. Vaishnav, 232–73. New Delhi: Oxford University Press.

Collins, M. 2018. 'Navigating Fiscal Constraints: Dalit Parties and Electoral Politics in Tamil Nadu', in *Costs of Democracy: Political Finance in India*, edited by D. Kapur and M. Vaishnav, 119–52. New Delhi: Oxford University Press.

Crabtree, J. 2015. 'Has Narendra Modi Cleaned Up India?' *Prospect*, 23 April. https://www.prospectmagazine.co.uk/magazine/cleaning-up-india (accessed 30 April 2019).

Crabtree, J. 2018. *The Billionaire Raj: A Journey Through India's New Gilded Age*. London: Oneworld.

Dasgupta, R. 2014. *Capital: A Portrait of 21ˢᵗ Century Delhi*. Edinburgh and London: Canongate.

Editorial 2016. 'Deposits of Old Notes in Accounts of Political Parties Exempt from Income Tax, with Riders', *Livemint*, 16 December. https://www.livemint.com/Politics/83hSnXRdZmz3K7RAfxPx-VK/Deposits-of-old-notes-in-accounts-of-political-parties-exemp.html (accessed 30 April 2019).

Editorial 2018. 'Number of Fake Rs 2,000 Notes Increased Significantly in 2017–18 Financial Year, Reveals RBI report', *Scroll.in*, 29 August. https://scroll.in/latest/892426/number-of-fake-rs-2000-notes-increased-significantly-in-2017–18-financial-year-reveals-rbi-report (accessed 30 April 2019).

Fernandez, B. 2012. *Transformative policy: a new feminist framework for policy analysis in developing countries*. Abingdon: Routledge.

Flyvbjerg, B. 2006. 'Five Misunderstandings about Case-Study Research', *Qualitative Inquiry* 12(2): 219–45.

Fouillet, C. 2011. 'Spatial Inequalities and Financial Inclusion Dynamics in India', paper presented at the 13th EADI-DSA Conference, *Rethinking Development in an Age of Scarcity and Uncertainty*, York, UK.

Gadgil, M. (Chair). 2011. *Report of the Western Ghats Ecology Expert Panel*, Ministry of Environment and Forests, New Delhi, Government of India. http://www.moef.nic.in/downloads/public-information/wg-23052012.pdf (accessed 30 April 2019).

Galtung, J. 1969. 'Violence, Peace and Peace Research', *Journal of Peace Research* 6(3): 167–91.

Gandhi, A. and M. Walton. 2012. 'Where Do India's Billionaires Get their Wealth?' *Economic and Political Weekly* XLVII(40): 10–14.

Ghosh, J., C.P. Chandrasekhar and P. Patnaik. 2017. *Demonetisation Decoded: A Critique of India's Currency Experiment*. New Delhi: Routledge.

Guerin, I., Y. Lanos, S. Michiels, C. Nordman and G. Venkatasubramanian. 2017. 'The Use of Social Networks in a Self-Inflicted Macro-Economic Shock Context: The Case of Demonetisation in India', *NOPOOR Policy Brief No 36*, Paris.

Harriss-White, B. 2017. 'On Demonetisation (Parts 1 and 2)', *Madras Courier*, 13 January. https://madrascourier.com/policy/barbara-harriss-white-on-demonetisation-part-1/ (accessed 30 April 2019).

Harriss-White, B. 2019. 'Waste, Order and Disorder in Small-town India', *Journal of Development Studies* 55. https://doi.org/10.1080/00220388.2019.1577386.

Harriss-White B., E. Basile, A. Dixit, P. Joddar, A. Prakash and K. Vidyarthee. 2014. *Dalits and Adivasis in India's Business Economy: Three Essays and an Atlas*. New Delhi: Three Essays Press.

Hazarika, S. 2018. 'Defining Citizenship: Assam on the Edge', *Economic and Political Weekly* 53(30): 12–13.

India Today. 2016. 'Demonetisation Forced Black Money into the Open, Claims PM Modi', 29 December. https://www.hindustantimes.com/india-news/demonetisation-forced-black-money-into-the-open-claims-pm-modi/story-nCHgAcBY6fMjEWADZwzGkI.html (accessed 30 April 2019).

Jairaj, A. and B. Harriss-White. 2006. 'Social Structure, Tax Culture and the State: Tamil Nadu, India', *Economic and Political Weekly* XLI(51): 5247–57.

Jha, P.S. 2013. *How did India Become a Predatory State?* Unpublished manuscript available via authors.

Joseph, N. 2018. *The Socio-politics of Producing Silk and Accumulating Gold in a South Indian Town through the Liberalisation Reform Period*. PhD diss., EHESS, Paris-1.

Kapur, D. and M. Vaishnav. 2018. *Costs of Democracy: Political Finance in India*. New Delhi: Oxford University Press.

Kar, D. 2010. *The Drivers and Dynamics of Illicit Financial Flows from India 1948–2008*. Washington, DC: Global Financial Integrity.

Karaman, O. 2008. 'A New Philosophy of Society: Assemblage Theory and Social Complexity by Manuel DeLanda', *Antipode* 40(5): 935–7.

Khan, M. 2000. 'Rent Seeking as a Process', in *Rents, Rent-seeking and Economic Development in Asia*, edited by M. Khan and K Jomo, 74–144. Cambridge: Cambridge University Press.

Kulova, T. and M. Varghese, eds. 2017. *Urban Utopias: Excess and Expulsion in Neoliberal South Asia*. London: Palgrave.

Kumar, A. 2015. *Criminalisation of Politics: Caste, Land and the State*. Jaipur: Rawat.

Kumar, A. 2017. *Demonetization and the Black Economy*. New Delhi: Penguin.

Mahmood, Z. 2017. *Globalisation and Labour Reforms: The Politics of Interest Groups and Partisan Governments*. New Delhi: Oxford University Press.

Marx, K. 1887. *Capital, A Critique of Political Economy. Volume one. The process of production of capital*. https://www.marxists.org/archive/marx/works/download/pdf/Capital-Volume-I.pdf (accessed 28 May 2012).

Michelutti, L., A. Hoque, N. Martin, D. Picherit, P. Rollier, A. E. Ruud and C. Still. 2018. *Mafia Raj: The Rule of Bosses in South Asia*. Stanford, CA: Stanford University Press.

Mooij, J. 1999. *Food Policy and the Indian State*. New Delhi: Oxford University Press.

National Council for Applied Economic Research (NCAER). 2017. *The NCAER State Investment Potential Index, 2017*. New Delhi, NCAER. http://www.ncaer.org/uploads/photo-gallery/files/1500629311N-SIPI_2017.pdf (accessed 30 April 2019).

PHFI (Public Health Foundation of India). 2017. *Air Pollution and Health in India: A Review of the Current Evidence and Opportunities for the Future*. New Delhi: PHFI.

Prakash, A. 2017. 'The Hybrid State and the Regulation of Land and Real Estate', *Review of Development and Change* XXIII(1): 173–97.

PricewaterhouseCoopers. 2016. *Global Economic Crime Survey*. https://www.pwc.com/gx/en/economic-crime-survey/pdf/GlobalEconomicCrimeSurvey2016.pdf (accessed 30 April 2019).

PTI. 2017. 'Indian "Shadow Economy" to Shrink to 13.6 per cent of GDP by 2025: ACCA', *Indian Express*, 2 July. https://indianexpress.com/article/business/economy/indian-shadow-economy-to-shrink-to-13–6-per-cent-of-gdp-by-2025-acca-4731993/ (accessed 8 April 2019).

Rajshekhar, M. 2015–17. *Ear to the Ground*. https://scroll.in/topic/24308/ear-to-the-ground (accessed 30 April 2019).

Reserve Bank of India. 2018. *Reserve Bank of India Annual Report 2017–18*. https://rbidocs.rbi.org.in/rdocs/AnnualReport/PDFs/8VIIICURRENCYEBA72A2F77784806B26D8F22FAD05C35.PDF (accessed 8 April 2019).

Roy, R. 1996. 'State Failure in India: Political-Fiscal Implications of the Black Economy', *Bulletin, Institute of Development Studies* 27(2): 22–30.

Shah, R. 2018. 'Editorial: Rationalise then Privatise', *Times of India*, 6 March. https://blogs.time-sofindia.indiatimes.com/toi-edit-page/rationalise-then-privatise-else-public-sector-banks-will-continue-to-be-a-bottomless-hole-for-taxpayers-money (accessed 30 April 2019).

Sharma, C. 2016. 'Estimating the Size of the Black Economy in India', *Munich Personal RePEc Archive, Paper No. 75211*. https://mpra.ub.uni-muenchen.de/75211/1/MPRA_paper_75198.pdf (accessed 30 April 2019).

Sircar, N. 2018. 'Money in Elections: The Role of Personal Wealth in Election Outcomes', in *Costs of Democracy: Political Finance in India*, edited by D. Kapur and M. Vaishnav, 36–73. New Delhi: Oxford University Press.

Sundaresan, J. 2013. *Urban Planning and Vernacular Governance: Land Use Planning and Violations in Bangalore*, PhD diss., London School of Economics.

Thakurta, P.G. (Chair). 2010. *Report on Paid News*, Press Council of India. http://presscouncil.nic.in/oldwebsite/councilreport.pdf (accessed 30 April 2019).

Thakurta, P.G., A. Palepu, S. Jain and A. Dasgupta. 2017. 'Modi Government's Rs 500-Crore Bonanza to the Adani Group', *The Wire*, 29 June (withdrawn from *Economic and Political Weekly*). https://thewire.in/business/modi-government-adani-group (accessed 30 April 2019).

Tripathi, R. 2017. 'Tackling Terrorism and Fake Currency: More civilian Deaths in J&K, Fewer Naxal Attacks', *Indian Express*, 8 November. https://indianexpress.com/article/explained/demonetisation-narendra-modi-kashmir-terror-funding-stone-pelting-naxal-attacks-burhan-wani-black-money-4927207/ (accessed 30 April 2019).

Vaish, V. and S. Marwahah. 2015. 'Law Relating To "Antiquities" In India', *Mondaq*. http://www.mondaq.com/india/x/407126/music+arts/Law+Relating+To+Antiquities+In+India+Be+Aware+Of+Your+Obligations (accessed 30 April 2019).

Vaishnav, M. 2017. *When Crime Pays: Money and Muscle in Indian Politics*. New Delhi: HarperCollins.

Van Dijk, T. 2017. 'The Impossibility of World-class, Slum-free Cities and the Fantasy of Two Indias', in *Urban Utopias: Excess and Expulsion in Neoliberal South Asia*, edited by T. Kulova and M. Varghese, 19–36. London: Palgrave.

Vyas, M. 2018. 'Employment Stagnates in 2017-18', Centre for Monitoring the Indian Economy. https://www.cmie.com/kommon/bin/sr.php?kall=warticle&dt=2018-07-17%2009:45:21&msec=123 (accessed 30 April 2019).

White, G. and B. Harriss-White. 1996. 'Liberalisation and the New Corruption', *IDS Bulletin* 27(2): 1–5.

Appendix
Laws alleged or established to have been broken – with main offenders

Chapter 1: coal

- Scavenging coal from abandoned mines and tailings
- Illegal transport of coal – syndicates and coal traders
- Illegal sales to legal businesses
- Extortion, forgery, manipulation of auctions, control of railways, violent enforcement (paramount regulatory authority), murders, paper companies, paper transactions, widespread bribery to private managers and state officials – mafia
- Tax evasion – coal traders and mafia
- Simultaneous leadership of several labour unions – mafia

Chapter 2: fire

- Neglect of laws for fire-fighting and prevention – central and state corporations
- Neglect of stabilisation of abandoned mines – central and state corporations
- Restrictive re-interpretation of eligibility for resettlement and rehabilitation, evasion of liability for resettlement and rehabilitation, forced eviction of 'trespassers' – state corporations and departments, police
- Unregulated subterranean mining – central and state corporations, private companies
- Illegal opencast mining – coal mafia
- Violation of fire regulations – general

- Violation of mining regulations in proximity of infrastructure – central and state agencies
- Total neglect of health and safety regulations (e.g. electricity cables) – central and state agencies
- Neglect of treatment/compensation for preventable accidents and explosions – central and state agencies
- Complete lack of implementation of environmental law – central and state agencies
- Diversion of sand for stowage, false invoicing – state agencies, coal mafia
- Illegal private subcontracting of fire control – central and state agencies
- Negligent planning – state agencies
- Theft from mines and tailings – at all levels of coal-mining operations and criminal organisations
- Theft from rail wagons – organised for larger criminal coal-mining operations by unions
- Threat of violence against trade unionists (murder) – mafia
- Extortion of scavengers – state agencies and criminals
- Appointments in state enterprise based on mafia allegiances throughout the system – all India

Chapter 3: sand

- Violation of dozens of riverbed sand-mining regulations (unmarked mines, unrecorded extraction, depth exceeded, shift length exceeded, lorry loading limits exceeded, unauthorised roads constructed, unauthorised diversion of water courses) – sand miners on an increasing scale and party members
- Misuse of permit allocation procedure – politicians
- Negligent failure to monitor and enforce – state agencies
- Sabotage of court cases; failure to implement judgments; failure to act on state-ordered enquiry commissions – mafia, state (and judiciary)
- Extensive complicity with criminal mining, criminal sharing of illegal profits – mafia, bureaucracy and politicians
- Physical assault and murder
- Massive tax evasion – mafia
- Purchase of votes – political party cadres funded from apex
- Threats and fear leading to press self-censorship

Chapter 4: water

- Opaque memoranda of understanding leading to the emergence of criminal markets in MoUs – state and speculative capital
- Violations of laws for environmental clearance, compensation – state
- Discretionary and nepotistic awards of contracts and permits – political elite
- Theft of and black market in materials – business
- Threat and abuse of illegitimate force – politicians
- Widespread violations of state and tribal customary norms – engineering and procurement companies
- Diversion of resources and unauthorised privatisation of common property – business, local headmen
- Bribes to voters – local politicians

Chapter 5: spectrum

- Criminal abuse of insider information – state and business
- Undeclared conflicts of interest between business and politics – state and business with pressure on regulators
- Unpunished violations of policy/ad hoc (retrospective) policy changes – state
- Discretionary queue-jumping in allocations – state and business
- Negligent enforcement – state
- Bribery, favours in kind and nepotism – business
- Undermining of regulations

Chapter 6: fuel oil and sand

6.1. Fuel oil

- Vandalism of pipelines – mafia and engineers
- Unauthorised tunnelling – mafia and engineers with labour
- Theft from pipelines – mafia and engineers
- Illegal mini refineries – mafia
- Unlicensed tankers, trucks and retailers – mafia
- Forgery – mafia
- Adulteration of fuel oil and kerosene – mafia with skilled labour

- Illegal trade in adulterants – mafia
- Distribution of petrol station licences through political patronage not merit – politicians and mafia
- Pollution from violations of air quality legislation – state and business
- Manipulation and evasion of state regulations to avoid prosecution – mafia
- Tax evasion – mafia
- Structuring of operations through cross-state impunity – mafia
- Illegal protection by mafia as brokers for political protection – mafia
- Violence, murder – mafia
- Bribes to Police, Civil Supplies Department bureaucracies and village-level politicians and officials – mafia

6.2. Sand

- Widespread violation of environmental and mining laws and regulations as per Chapter 3 – mafia
- Illegal rental markets for trucks – mafia
- Bribery of police – mafia
- Bribes to Regional Transport Office and to check-post goons – illegal transporters/mafia
- Extortion of taxes from small miners and transporters – mining mafia
- Murder, violent injury and abduction

Chapter 7: red sanders timber

- Violation (and manipulation) of legislation protecting endangered species – state and mafia
- International trafficking
- Bribery and criminal protection by politicians and officials at every stage of inter-State trade and international export, diversion through SEZs, concealed storage in forests, port *godowns*, SEZs, containers, fake registration of trucks, forged government seals on containers, fake customs information – mafia with complicity and direct involvement of politicians
- Mafia control over – and profits from – markets for postings in bureaucracy, police, customs and excise and port authorities.

Bribes and in-kind payments to officials in Forest Department, check-posts, regional transport authorities, extortion from mafia by officials in police – mafia and state agencies

- Torture, mutilation, encounters and murder on massive scales – mafia, politicians and state agencies
- Private party-politicised use of machinery of state violence – politicians
- Politically justified brutality on the part of the state's task forces – politicians and private militias
- Coercive control of labour; criminalisation of labour – mafia with state and police
- Arrests disproportionate to convictions – police and state

Chapter 8: real estate

- Breaches of Urban Land Acts (Regulation and Ceilings) and Rent/ Tenancy Acts – landlords and brokers
- Manipulation of contracts (unfulfillable conditions) and procedure – lawyers and brokers
- Speculative litigation and brokerage as businesses; intimidation, threats by hired thugs and killings – brokers and criminal gangs
- Bribery of police and courts – litigants
- Clashes of custom and law for tenant protection – power asymmetries in out-of-court settlements

Chapter 9: land

- Breaches of rights to rural tenancies of SCs
- Fraudulent re-registration of common land – local politicians and mafia
- Illegal privatisation (and politicisation) of encroachments on urban land – local politicians and mafia
- Extortion by hired thugs – politicians and police; private armies – criminal businesses in illegal commodities
- False charges – bribed police
- Forced land sales – landlords, speculators and brokers
- Forgery of documents – landlords, speculators and brokers
- Bribery in return for protection from charges – landlords, speculators and brokers

- Arbitrary fines and delays raising costs of non-compliance with non-compliance – land speculators
- Emerging speculative business in disputed titles

Chapter 10: procurement (Bangladesh)

- Criminal businesses in legal goods, in goods plundered from the state, and in protection services
- Police corruption in return for non-prosecution – contractors
- Bribery of officials in return for political favours and speed – contractors
- Illegal contracting from state – state and politicians
- Intimidation and threats, violent enforcement (murders and disappearances) (in decline) – politicians and contractors
- Collusion and politicisation of bids – contractors
- Illegal commodification of licences – state
- [Politicised ownership of media and use to blackmail and silence]

Chapter 11: factory fire (Pakistan)

- Violation of building regulations – delinquent architects
- Illegal water supply – state and construction firms
- Abuse of energy supply – factory owner
- Lack of emergency procedure – factory owner
- Banal criminality against factory labour; brutal violations of health and safety; inadequate labour inspection force; factory labour controlled by extortion squads; compliance on paper with international labour standards although disregarded in practice – factory owner
- Egregious neglect of compensation claims – factory owner, with the state
- Party political interference at all levels with investigations and charges; forensic investigation neglected by police; owners exonerated without investigation by police – politicians
- Criminal incompetence in handling and preservation of corpses – police
- Pressure on judiciary – (para)military and intelligence
- Coercive pressure on witnesses – police and politicians
- Illegal taxes – politicians, factory owner

- Violent vendettas between groups of thugs for control of factory labour – contractors
- Intimidation of labour – contractors
- Tax evasion – factory owner and others
- Deliberate casualisation and evasion of social protection obligations – factory owner

Glossary

Aadhaar	unique identity number
Adivasi	indigenous tribal person
Anganwadi	nursery
Badmash/dabang/mastan	goons
Baloo	regular sand
Baraa	big
Bari sarkar	deep state
Bayalishi	gathering of 42 villages
Benami	contracts disguising the identities of transacting parties
Bhai	brother (not necessarily biological; can refer to someone close to you)
Bhatta	protection
Bhukki	poppy husk
Bhumihar	a high caste
Chamcha	lit. spoon; fig. sycophant
Chandabaazi, hafta, goonda tax	protection money
Chungi	check point
Crore	10 million
Crorepati	millionaire
Dalit	member of lowest, oppressed castes, untouchable
Darbar	court
Deras	usually non-denominational religious institutions centred on holy men
Dhaba	roadside restaurant
Dhaincha	weed
Dharna	non-violent sit-in protest
Gaon burha	village headman, generally considered as the chief of the 'traditional'/ customary village institutions of the tribes, recognised by the government as running in parallel to the system of *panchayats*.
Gherao	a form of protest in which employees prevent employers from leaving their workplace until their demands are agreed or met.
Godown	warehouse or storage space
Goonda	thug
Hawala	a method of transferring money without any money actually moving
Hydel	hydroelectric power
Jama'at khanas	centres of worship doubling as educational and welfare centres
Jat	traditionally agricultural community in Northern India and Pakistan
Kabaddi	a muscular Punjabi contact sport
Kabza	property grabbing
Kebang	village council
Khap	unit of 84 villages
Khap panchayats	assembly of *Khap* elders or extra-legal caste/community courts

Katha (also spelled kattha or cottah)	a measure of land used (to connote varying areas) in Bangladesh, India and Nepal; in West Bengal 1 katha is equal to 720 ft^2
Kirana	spices, grains
Kulli boli	open auctions
Ladai/yudh	war
Lakh	one hundred thousand
Lok Sabha	lower house of India's bicameral parliament
Marla	Measure of land connoting roughly 25 square metres, though variable in different periods and regions of the subcontinent.
Meena	tribe
Nazool land	land which once belonged predominantly to Muslim evacuees who left for Pakistan at partition, and which was meant to be handed over to *Dalit* cooperatives
Neta	leader
Octroi	municipality entry tax
Panchayat	system of local government
Paregallu	those who rule
Parivar	family
Patta	the legal ownership document for land
Qabza	land-grabbing operations
Rajput	a caste claiming Kshatriya ancestry and military occupations
Randari	informal
Razakar	collaborator
Salaami/bhada salaami	a rental agreement for heritable, non-expiring leases where rent is paid in advance, usually in cash. The rent is low because of the advance arrangement. Similar practices elsewhere in India are termed *pagdi* (literally turban)
Samaj	association, group
Sarpanch	village *panchayat* head; elected village headman
Sena	private army
Sepahi	soldiers
Shamlaat zameen	village common land
Shomman	respect
Tal	local shops that sell construction materials
Taluk	subdivision of a district
Tehsil	sub-district
Tehsildar	revenue collector at the *tehsil* level
Tekhedar	contractor
Tel	oil
Tempu	light transport vehicles
Thana	police station
Tibbas	sandy hillocks
Vidhan Sabha	legislative assembly
Wallah	a suffix to denote a person practising a particular activity (e.g. coal cycle wallah)
Yadav	a low to mid-ranking caste of pastoral agriculturalists
Zila parishad	district council

Index

Lightning Source UK Ltd.
Milton Keynes UK
UKHW020250110919
349531UK00005B/19/P